# 101 WAYS TO PROMOTE YOUR WEB SITE

Second Edition

W9-DIL-482

# Other Titles of Interest From Maximum Press

*Marketing on the Internet, Fourth Edition:* Zimmerman, 1-885068-36-0

*Business-to-Business Internet Marketing, Second Edition:* Silverstein, 1-885068-37-8

*Marketing With E-Mail:* Kinnard, 1-885068-40-9

*Internet Marketing Success for Your Tourism Business:* Sweeney, 1-885068-47-6

*Internet Marketing for Information Technology Companies:* Silverstein, 1-885068-46-8

*Exploring IBM Technology , Products, & Services, Third Edition:* edited by Hoskins, 1-885068-44-1

*Building Intranets With Lotus Notes and Domino 5.0:* Krantz, 1-885068-41-7

*Exploring IBM Personal Computers, Tenth Edition: Hoskins, Wilson, 1-885068-25-5*

*Exploring IBM RS/6000 Computers, Ninth Edition:* Hoskins, Davies, 1-885068-27-1

*Exploring IBM AS/400 Computers, Ninth Edition:* Hoskins, Dimmick, 1-885068-34-4

*Exploring IBM S/390 Computers, Sixth Edition:* Hoskins, Coleman, 1-885068-30-1

For more information, visit our Web site at
*www.maxpress.com*
or e-mail us at *moreinfo@maxpress.com*

# 101 WAYS TO PROMOTE YOUR WEB SITE

## Second Edition

*Filled with Proven Internet Marketing Tips, Tools, Techniques, and Resources to Increase Your Web Site Traffic*

## Susan Sweeney

MAXIMUM PRESS
605 Silverthorn Road
Gulf Breeze, FL 32561
(850) 934-0819
www.maxpress.com

Publisher: Jim Hoskins

Manager of Finance/Administration: Donna Tryon

Production Manager: ReNae Grant

Cover Design: Lauren Smith Designs

Compositor: PageCrafters Inc.

Copyeditor: Andrew Potter

Proofreader: Kim Stefansson

Indexer: Susan Olason

Printer: P.A. Hutchison

This publication is designed to provide accurate and authoritative information in regard to the subject matter covered. It is sold with the understanding that the publisher is not engaged in rendering professional services. If legal, accounting, medical, psychological, or any other expert assistance is required, the services of a competent professional person should be sought. ADAPTED FROM A DECLARATION OF PRINCIPLES OF A JOINT COMMITTEE OF THE AMERICAN BAR ASSOCIATION AND PUBLISHERS.

Copyright 2000 by Maximum Press.

All rights reserved. Published simultaneously in Canada.

Reproduction or translation of any part of this work beyond that permitted by Section 107 or 108 of the 1976 United States Copyright Act without the permission of the copyright owner is unlawful. Requests for permission or further information should be addressed to the Permissions Department, Maximum Press.

Recognizing the importance of preserving what has been written, it is a policy of Maximum Press to have books of enduring value published in the United States printed on acid-free paper, and we exert our best efforts to that end.

*Library of Congress Cataloging-in-Publication Data*

Sweeney, Susan, 1956-
101 ways to promote your web site / Susan Sweeney.— 2nd ed.
p. cm.
Includes bibliographical references and index.
ISBN 1-885068-45-X (pb)
1. Internet marketing. 2. Web sites—Marketing. I. Title: One
hundred one ways to promote your web site. II. Title: One hundred and
one ways to promote your web site. III. Title.
HF5415.1265 .S93 2000
005.2'76—dc21
00-008349

00-008349
CIP

## Acknowledgements

The Internet is a vast, publicly accessible resource from which we can learn a great deal. Any individuals with a little bit of initiative can educate themselves on any topic simply by researching the many online resources. I'd like to thank all those people who share their information so freely on the Net with sites like WilsonWeb *(www.wilsonweb.com)* by Dr. Ralph Wilson and newsletters like The Internet Home Business Marketing Newsletter by Robert Smith, Jayde Search Smart, Chronicles, Internet Gazette, and I-Sales by John Audette.

This second edition was written during a very busy season for my company. Although, as an Internet marketing company, we live and breathe this stuff every day, the research, compilation, writing, editing, and rewriting needed to compile this concise resource is a huge undertaking. It was very much a collaborative effort which consumed hundreds of hours. I'd like to thank my dynamite team for their many hours of dedication, writing, and research assistance—Ed Dorey, Lynn Wilson, Andy MacLellan (I'm stressin'), and Raland Kinley.

I would also like to extend gratitude and appreciation to Stefan Gashus, CA for his valuable contribution to the e-commerce section of this book.

Thanks to Maximum Press—it's been a pleasure to work with Donna Tryon and Jim Hoskins. Many thanks to ReNae Grant at PageCrafters for her guidance and patience. Sorry for overflowing your mailbox so often!

Special thanks to my husband Miles and our three wonderful children—Kaitlyn, Kara, and Andrew—for their love, encouragement, and support. All those "You can do it Mom!" comments were really appreciated.

Special thanks to my mom and dad, Olga and Leonard Dooley, for always being there and for instilling in me the confidence to know that I can do anything I set my mind to. It's amazing what can be done when you "know you can."

## Disclaimer

The purchase of computer software or hardware is an important and costly business decision. While the author and publisher of this book have made reasonable efforts to ensure the accuracy and timeliness of the information contained herein, the author and publisher assume no liability with respect to loss or damage caused or alleged to be caused by reliance on any information contained herein and disclaim any and all warranties, expressed or implied, as to the accuracy or reliability of said information.

This book is not intended to replace the manufacturer's product documentation or personnel in determining the specifications and capabilities of the products mentioned in this book. The manufacturer's product documentation should always be consulted, as the specifications and capabilities of computer hardware and software products are subject to frequent modification. The reader is solely responsible for the choice of computer hardware and software. All configurations and applications of computer hardware and software should be reviewed with the manufacturer's representatives prior to choosing or using any computer hardware and software.

## Trademarks

The words contained in this text which are believed to be trademarked, service marked, or otherwise to hold proprietary rights have been designated as such by use of initial capitalization. No attempt has been made to designate as trademarked or service marked any personal computer words or terms in which proprietary rights might exist. Inclusion, exclusion, or definition of a word or term is not intended to affect, or to express judgment upon, the validity of legal status of any proprietary right which may be claimed for a specific word or term.

# Table of Contents

## Chapter 3:
## Be Kind to the Search Engines                    39

## Chapter 4:
## Search Engine and Directory Submissions                65

## Chapter 5:
## Effective Promotional Use of Newsgroups              113

## Chapter 6:
## Utilizing Signature Files to
## Increase Web Site Traffic      130

## Chapter 7:
## The E-mail Advantage      140

# Chapter 8:
# Effective Mailing List Promotion 160

# Chapter 9:
# Establishing Your Private Mailing List 175

## Chapter 10:
## Develop a Dynamite Links Strategy      193

## Chapter 11:
## Winning Awards/Cool Sites and More      209

## Chapter 12:
## Maximizing Promotion with Meta-Indexes      221

## Chapter 13:
## Productive Online Advertising      233

# Chapter 14:
# Affiliate Programs

**263**

## Chapter 15:
## The Cybermall Advantage                                 281

## Chapter 16:
## E-commerce                                                    298

## Chapter 17:
## Keep 'Em Coming Back                                          321

## Chapter 18:
## Maximizing Media Relations                              347

## Chapter 19:
## Online Publications                                                 370

## Chapter 20:
## Web Rings As a Promotion Tool                                      381

## Chapter 24:
## Grand Opening Tips for Your
## Web Site Virtual Launch       437

# Introduction

*We are crossing a technology threshold that will forever change the way we learn, work, socialize and shop. It will affect all of us, and businesses of every type, in ways far more pervasive than most people realize.*

*Bill Gates, Comdex 1994*

Over the last few years a tidal wave of companies have been building Web sites. This phenomenal boom in Web site creation and online traffic has intensified the battle for the consumer's time and attention. The secondary component or required follow-on to Web site design involves developing comprehensive online marketing strategies to capture online market share. The need for information and advice on developing Internet marketing strategies is tremendous.

Building a Web site, however, is just the first step. Driving business to your site takes knowledge, planning, time and effort. If you are intent on maintaining a competitive advantage, then you need to build the traffic to your site by implementing an effective Internet marketing strategy.

Whether you are an experienced marketing professional or just dreaming of starting your own Internet business you will benefit from the information contained in this timely book. *101 Ways to Promote Your Web Site* offers comprehensive, hands-on, step-by-step advice for building Web site traffic using hundreds of proven tips, tools and techniques to achieve optimal results. You will find out how to:

- Make your site unique, attract new visitors, and keep them coming back

- Prepare and submit to hundreds of search engines and directories to be listed in the top search results

- Maximize your Web site promotion using meta-indexes

- Pull traffic to your site by implementing a personalized, targeted e-mail campaign

- Develop an effective banner ad campaign to draw the right customer to your site

- Use newsgroups and mailing lists to communicate with your target market and build your reputation

- Hype your company in the media for increased exposure through interactive press releases

- Increase company and brand awareness with Webcasting (rich media)

- Use one of the most effective Internet marketing tools—*Links*

- Find and use free promotion tools available on the Internet

- Keep visitors coming back to your site

- Develop your own affiliate or associate program.

You will be provided with a wealth of information on how to use specific promotion, marketing, and advertising strategies to increase the traffic to your site. Entrepreneurs, corporate marketing managers, small business owners, and consultants will be given a proven method to turn their commercial Web sites into an online success.

## Your "Members Only" Web Site

The Internet world changes every day. That's why there is a companion Web site associated with this book. On this site you will find updates to the book and other Web site promotion resources of interest. However, you have to be a member of the "101 Ways Insiders Club" to gain access to this site.

When you purchased this book, you automatically became a member (in fact, that's the only way to join), so you now have full privileges. To get into the "Members Only" section of the companion Web site, go to the Maximum Press web site located at *http://www.maxpress.com* and follow the links to the "101 Ways" area. From there you will see a link to the "101 Ways Insiders Club" section. When you try to enter, you will be asked for a user ID and password. Type in the following:

- For your user ID enter: *101ways2e*

- For you password enter: *timetrial*

You will then be granted full access to the "Members Only" area. Visit the site often and enjoy the updates and resources with our compliments—and thanks again for buying the book. We ask that you not share the user ID and password for this site with anyone else.

# 1

# Marketing Principles

With millions of Web sites competing for viewers, how do you get the results you're looking for? When asked if they are marketing on the Internet, many people say, "Yes, we have a Web site." However, having a Web site and Internet marketing are very different things. Yes, usually you need a Web site to market on the Internet. However, a Web site is simply a collection of documents, images, and other electronic files that are publicly accessible across the Internet. Your site should be designed to meet your online objectives and should be developed with your target market in mind. Meanwhile, Internet marketing encompasses all the steps you take to reach your target market online, attract visitors to your Web site, encourage them to buy your products or services, and make them want to come back for more.

Having a Web site is great, but it is meaningless if nobody knows about it. Likewise, having a brilliantly designed product brochure does you little good if it sits in the desk drawer of your sales manager. It is the goal of this book to help you take your Web site out of the desk drawer, into the spotlight, and into the hands of your target market. You will learn how to formulate an Internet marketing strategy and match it with your objectives, your product or service, and your target market. In this chapter, you are provided with an overview of this book and introduced to the importance of:

- Defining your online objectives

- Developing the Internet marketing strategy that is appropriate for your product or service

- Defining your target market and developing your Web site and online marketing strategy with them in mind

## Objectives

Before you even start to create your Web site, you must clearly define your online objectives. What is the purpose of your Web site? Brainstorm. Generate a list of primary and secondary objectives. Every element of your site should relate back to your objectives. When you decide to update, add, or change any elements on your Web site, examine how these changes relate to the primary and secondary objectives you identified. If there is not a clear match between your objectives and your intended changes, you might want to reconsider the changes. It's amazing how many Web sites have been developed without adequate planning or tie in with the corporate objectives.

Some of the most common primary and secondary online objectives include:

- Selling a product or service

- Creating and establishing company identity or brand awareness

- Providing product or corporate information

- Providing customer service and product support

- Generating repeat traffic

- Advertising an event, product, or service

## Selling a Product or Service

Do you intend to sell a product or service that people can order directly from your site? If so, your Web site may require a secure order form and perhaps a sophisticated e-commerce ordering system. Chapter 16 outlines how you might implement an e-commerce system and security for your Web site.

People do not visit Web sites just to fill out the order form. You will need to provide detailed information about your product or service, shipping options, return policies, guarantees, and so on. You will also have to help people find your Web site easily and keep them coming back. This book includes numerous techniques you can use to build traffic to your site and give visitors reasons to return.

## Creating and Establishing Company Identity or Brand Awareness

Another objective might be to create and establish company identity or brand awareness. To "brand" your product, a memorable name and an eye-appealing product logo are necessities. Also, the graphics developed for your Web site must be top-notch and reflect the colors associated with the product logo. A catchy slogan will further promote brand identity. The same branding techniques are also applicable to establishing corporate identity. If building and reinforcing corporate and brand identity are important to you, your Web site must have a consistent look and feel. Likewise, all offline promotional campaigns and materials must be consistent with your online presence.

Based on the success of companies such as America Online, Yahoo, Netscape Communications, Amazon.com, Priceline.com, Infoseek, and Excite, it is apparent that branding a company or product on the Web can occur swiftly. It is amazing how quickly these relative newcomers to the business world have achieved megabrand status. Although they all had significant financial resources, each company used a combination of online and offline advertising to meet their objectives. Their Web sites reflect the branding idea. Each of their sites features a prominent logo, consistent imagery, and a consistent color scheme. Check out the sites of these upstarts who have become big online players if branding is your goal. There is a lot we can learn from them.

## Providing Product or Corporate Information

Some organizations simply wish to provide information on their products or services to a particular target market. Others may want to provide corporate information to potential investors. Information-driven Web sites tend to be text oriented, with graphics used only to accentuate the points being made and to provide visual examples. These types of sites usually have a Frequently Asked Questions (FAQ) section where they provide useful and pertinent information on their company, products or services. If the organization courts the media, it might include a Media Center, which could include all their press releases, a corporate backgrounder, information on key company officials, articles that have been written about the company, and a gallery of relevant pictures that the media can use, as well as a direct link to the company's media person.

## Providing Customer Service and Product Support

Most often, customers will require assistance with the product or service they have purchased. For instance, Dell *(http://www.dell.com)* sells a lot of personal computers. People will surely come to them for after sales service if problems arise with their hardware or if they need help setting up their system.

Dell created a support and service Web site *(http://support.dell.com)* for their customers. The site includes a Frequently Asked Questions database that customers can reference to help solve common problems. Your site might simply require a single page. Other ideas (chat rooms, newsgroups, etc.) presented in the following chapters will also be very applicable to you if your online objective is to provide post sale support.

## Generating Repeat Traffic

Attracting new and repeat traffic to your site is a key factor in establishing an online clientele and increasing sales. How do you attract repeat visitations to your Web site? You must provide content that is current and interesting. A system for changing and updating the content on your Web site must be established. You must also have strategies for submitting to search engines, acquiring links from other sites, developing a mailing list, and having the kinds of features on your site that help form a community. Offering an online seminar would be one example. This book will demonstrate these and many other ideas you can implement to generate traffic to your Web site.

## Advertising an Event, Product, or Service

The objective of some sites is simply to advertise but not to directly sell an event, product, or service. For instance, well in advance of the release of a new film, Hollywood movie studios often establish information sites that include advance multimedia clips from the movie, background information, and details about the actors and actresses. The studios will also issue interactive press releases to the entertainment media. This helps generate interest in the film, and the hope is that people will then want to pay to see the film when it appears in theaters. The following chapters will teach you how to legitimately (i.e., using proper Netiquette) disseminate information quickly across the Internet and build traffic to your site.

Whatever your objectives may be, you must carefully consider how best to incorporate elements in your Web site and your Internet marketing strategy to help you achieve them. Successful marketing on the Web is not a simple undertaking. Before you begin to brainstorm over the objectives your Web site, be certain you have read and studied all information that is pertinent to the market you are attempting to enter. Read everything you can get your hands on, and examine the findings of industry experts.

After you have designed, created, and presented your Web site for the world to see, test your site on a small group of individuals in your target market. Then, after analyzing their feedback, you can tweak your site before engaging a larger audience. For instance, let's say you are a software developer, and you provide an evaluation copy of your software on your Web site for potential customers to download. The people testing your software may be very interested in your product, but perhaps they commented that the download form requires too much information and takes too long to complete. You might want to tweak the form before you promote your software site to a larger audience. Reducing the amount of information people must submit in order to test your software might be the key to obtaining more downloads. Greater distribution of your software would then likely correlate to higher sales.

Another example would be if your home page utilized a lot of Flash and other multimedia effects, and the majority of visitors to your site did not have the latest technology installed on their systems. Given this situation, you might consider simplifying your home page by removing some of the multimedia effects or creating a second version of your home page for people who are not able to use the latest Internet technologies. Thus, everyone who comes to your Web site will then have the opportunity to enjoy your Web site, read your message, gather information about your product or service, and so on.

Once you have tested your site and your marketing strategy, do not stop there. Continue testing and tweaking your online marketing strategy until you find the methods, tools, and techniques that work best. Also, whenever you add something to your Web site or your online strategy, ask yourself, "Is it consistent with my online objectives, my product or service, and my target market?"

In Chapter 2, Web site essentials are discussed in detail to assist you when the time comes to develop your site. You will learn which elements to include on your Web site and how to implement these elements properly in conjunction with your objectives.

## Product or Service

Web sites and Internet marketing strategies will differ depending on the product or service you are selling. A company that markets toys will have to develop a fun and interactive Web site that is attractive to children. The Web site will then have to give children a way to tell their friends about the Web site as well as a reason to return to the site. The toy company might wish to offer an electronic postcard service whereby children can send a colorful and musical message to their friends and tell them about the site.

Another idea would be to provide a "wish list" service. Children could make a list of the toys they want, and this list would be sent to the parents via e-mail. The parents could then make more targeted purchasing decisions and may become loyal to the toy company's site. Likewise, some toy companies offer reminder services that send an e-mail message to visitors who have registered and completed the appropriate questionnaire to remind them of a child's birthday and offer suggestions for gift ideas. Once again, this promotes sales and repeat traffic, and increases customer loyalty.

In another example, a software development company may want to provide downloadable demo versions of their software products and allow people to review their products for a specified period of time before they must make a purchasing decision. When consumers decide to buy the software, a robust e-commerce system will need to be in place to handle the orders.

A travel agency's Web site might include features such as an opt-in mailing list to send people information on weekly vacation specials or a page on the site detailing the latest specials. They might also want to include downloadable or streaming video tours of vacation resorts to entice visitors to buy resort vacation packages. Another idea would be to have a system in place to help customers book vacations, rent cars, and check for available flights. The travel agency might also want to store customer profiles so that they can track where particular customers like to sit on the plane, the type of hotel room they usually book, and their credit card information, to make bookings more efficient for the customer and the agency.

If you are marketing a service online, it is difficult to visually depict what your service is all about. Visitors to your site need some reassurance that the service you are selling them is legitimate and valuable. Therefore, you might wish to include a page on your site that lists testimonials from well-known customers. This will give prospective customers more confidence about purchasing your service.

The bottom line is that the product or service you are selling will determine the direction of your Web site development process and the features that will be included. Remember to think of your online objectives first, then storyboard the site on a sheet (or several sheets) of paper. Once you are satisfied that you have included elements in your site to meet your online objectives, your product or service, and your target market (which we will speak of next), you can proceed with the coding of your site.

## Target Market

This is your target audience—the people to whom you are trying to market your product or service. Determine why people decide to buy your product or service and then focus the development of your Web site to emphasize these elements. What is the most important factor in your potential customers' buying decision? Is it price? product quality? availability? your company's reputation? postsale service and guarantees? These factors will directly determine the tone and content of your site.

Once again, if you intend to market children's products, your Web site will be colorful and the text simple and easy to understand in keeping with what appeals to your target market. Chances are, fun-looking graphics will be used extensively on your site to draw children further into it (see Figure 1.1). If you market financial services, your Web site will require a more professional approach. The

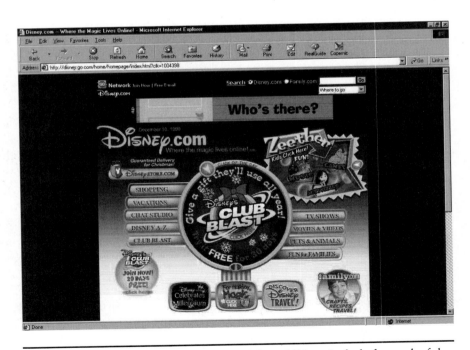

**Figure 1.1.** Web sites designed to appeal to children include fun, colorful images.

graphics will convey a clean appearance, and the text will be informative and written in a businesslike fashion (see Figure 1.2). As this example demonstrates, the content and tone of your site must be tailored to your target market. After all, this is the best way to attract the attention of the people who are interested in purchasing your product or service.

Another aspect of the design of your Web site to consider with regard to your target market is their propensity to utilize the latest technologies and the configuration they are likely to be using. An online business that markets custom-made, streaming multimedia presentations would expect its clientele to be technically inclined. Their clients are more likely to have the latest software, Web browser technologies, and faster machines.

On the other hand, clients of a vendor who sells gardening supplies online might be less likely to have fully embraced the latest technologies. Most people looking for these products will be connecting

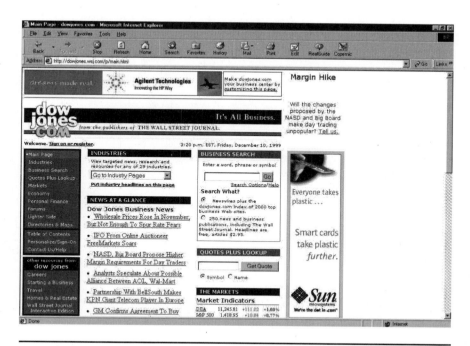

**Figure 1.2.** A business-oriented site incorporates informative text and a clean, magazine-style layout.

from home rather than from their workplace. They may have a slow dialup connection to the Internet, slower machines, and outdated software. They might still be using the Web browser that was originally installed on their system simply because they are uncomfortable downloading the latest version of the browser, are unaware of the more recent version, or are uninterested in downloading a large file. If your target market includes this demographic, you will have to be careful with your use of Java, Flash, and large graphic files.

What does this mean for developing and designing your Web site? Well, streaming multimedia developers could design their Web sites with more graphics and dynamic multimedia effects because their clients expect to be impressed when they visit the developer's site. If gardening supplies vendors designed their site similarly, many of their clients could be alienated because the site would be too slow to load. They might take their business elsewhere. The gardening supplies vendor's site will require a more basic design: less concentration on large graphics and multimedia effects, and more focus on presenting information.

You must know the profile of the people who are interested in your product, service, or information, and develop your Web site to appeal to this target market. This book will describe how you can use a variety of Internet tools and resources to promote your Web site. You will learn how to design your site to achieve higher search engine rankings and how to submit your Web site to major search engines, Web directories, and meta-indexes. E-mail is also an important communication method. Chapter 7 steps you through proper e-mail netiquette and explains the concept of conducting an e-mail marketing campaign to help you reach your target market.

You will also learn about using newsgroups, mailing lists, interactive press releases, affiliate programs, banner ads, online and offline publications, and Webcasting (rich media) to promote your Web site to thousands of potential customers. Once you have absorbed the content of this book and developed an Internet marketing strategy that is focused on your objectives, product, or service and your target market, you will begin to reap the benefits of Internet marketing.

Marketing your Web site can be a full-time occupation. Some organizations have a team of Internet marketing specialists to build, maintain, and promote their site. For others, their online business is a part-time endeavor and they only have an hour or two each week to spend promoting and developing their Web site. Whatever your situation, the better informed your are about Internet marketing, the better chance your online business will have to succeed. Ensure that your site is user friendly and designed with your target market, product or service and objectives in mind. The more you put into the development and implementation of your Internet marketing strategy, the greater the return will be to your online business.

## Internet Resources

**The Top Banana Chat Room for Marketing @ About.com**
Get your marketing questions answered or chat with others

**Network Marketing Weekly Online Newsletter**
*http://www.he.net/~image/nwm/imin.html*
Archive of network marketing newsletters

**Bplans.com**
*http://www.bplans.com*
Business planning resource center

**ConsultHQ**
*http://www.consulthq.com*
Free marketing resources for professionals

**Business Planning Center**
*http://www.businessplans.org*
Business and marketing planning, and business strategy information, advice, and software

**Tilburg University**
*http://marketing.kub.nl/links.htm*
An exhaustive list of marketing-related links

**Marketing Resources, Ltd.**
*http://www.mrlweb.com*
Business-to-business marketing solutions, marketing tips, and a newsletter

# als of Web Site Design

Site design, appearance, functionality, and features are all important aspects to consider before you think about promoting your site. If the site is designed to achieve your marketing objectives, looks good, and and has a layout that is easy to follow, you are ready to open your doors. There are many key factors to consider that may be over-looked in the initial design stages. A great domain name should be chosen, and whenever possible the company's name should be used. Appropriate titles should be located on each page to identify your company and the page content. In this chapter we cover:

- How and why Meta tags should be prepared for each page of your site

- The importance of each page's title, description, and keywords

- Web site features and design guidelines

- Checking out the competition

- The use of graphics

- Top-rated sites

- Encouraging repeat visits

- Incentives for increasing hits

- Corporate identity and your Web site

- Guiding the search engines to you

- Ensuring that your site works with different Web browsers

## Building Traffic to Your Site

The phrase "if you build it, they will come" worked in the movies, but it does not work with your Web site. Building a Web site is just the first step. Driving traffic to your site takes knowledge, planning, time, and effort. This book's focus is on increasing traffic to your Web site. To help you achieve the maximum marketing potential of your site, we cover several topics that relate to your Web site content and design. We recommend that the following Internet marketing tips, tools, and techniques be used in conjunction with your overall Web site design.

## Consider Your Web Site Objectives First

Before you plan your online strategy, and certainly before you start construction of your site, it is imperative to determine your online objectives. What do you want your Web site to accomplish? Do you want to sell directly to your customers? Do you want your site to provide information on your products or services? Do you want to provide customer support and service?

Determine the objectives of your Web site or online presence before you begin to build the site. The most common objectives include:

- Advertising products or services

- Selling products or services

- Providing customer service or support

- Providing useful information

- Reinforcing brand image

- Providing product information cost effectively

Know your objectives and build your site around them. This will ensure satisfaction at the end of the process.

## Presenting Your Web Site Message Clearly

Visitors to your Web site need to know and understand your message instantly from the very first page of your Web site. If not, visitors can leave your site just as quickly as they could press a button on their TV remote control. Your site must load quickly and immediately direct your visitors toward your message. Do you want them to buy? Browse? Provide feedback? Order? In traditional advertisements you need to attract the attention of your audience immediately. This is also the case with your Internet audience. However, unlike traditional advertising, you can deliver more information over the Internet than you can in a 30-second commercial or a half-page print ad. However, you must avoid overloading visitors with information. Too much information on the opening page of your site can appear cluttered and unorganized. As a general rule, keep your message simple and to the point.

## Using Competitor Sites to Your Advantage

Keeping up with the CyberJoneses is very important. Visit your competitors' sites for some ideas. Also visit sites that are listed on hot sites pages. Look at the design of these sites to get a better idea of what you should include in yours. Examine the colors and backgrounds used, see how the information is organized, and look at the features provided. Some good sites to go to for ideas are:

- Cool Site of the Day: *http://cool.infi.net*

- Your WebScout: *http://www.webscout.com*

- Lycos Top 250: *http://www.lycos.com*

- Web Crawler Top 25: *http://www.webcrawler.com*

## Realizing the Potential of Your Domain Name

One of the most important things from an online marketing perspective, often overlooked when developing your Web presence, is your **domain name.** Your Internet domain name is your exclusive Web address, which you can purchase through Network Solutions (*www.netsolutions.com*), an online organization in charge of domain name registration. Having your own domain name provides you with many benefits:

> **Domain name**
> The unique name that identifies an Internet site, of the form *www.sitename.com*

- The name itself can increase traffic to your site.

- Having your own domain name builds credibility for your organization.

- Your presence is mobile when you own your domain name.

- Internet marketing efforts travel with the domain name.

Your domain name should be easy to remember and relate to your online presence. Your company name is usually the best choice and should be used whenever possible.

People will generally try *www.yourcompanyname.com* first when searching for a commercial Web site. If customers or potential customers know your company exists, they will find your Web site quickly and easily if your domain name is your company name. If your company name is not well known, you may choose to use a catchy descriptive phrase or the subject of your Web site as its domain name. For example, imagine that you were searching for information on buying a timeshare and one of your search engine results is a site with

**URL (Uniform Resource Locator)**
An address on the Web

a URL named *www.howtobuyatimeshare.com* with accompanying text of "Free expert advice on buying a timeshare." What are the chances that you would click through to that site? Pretty good. Keep your domain name simple, easy to remember, and related to the subject of your site.

You can register multiple domain names with Network Solutions as well. You might choose this option if there are several business-related keywords you believe potential customers would be inclined to search for. For instance, you might register a domain name for your company's name and a separate domain name for each of the products you are selling. You can have several domain names all pointing to the same Web site. One of the reasons you might consider doing this is that some of the search engines will give your site a higher ranking if the keyword being searched is found in your domain name.

Having your own domain name projects a professional image for your company. One of the benefits of the Internet is that it creates a level playing field for small and medium-sized companies. Having your own domain name projects the image of an established business operating online in a professional manner.

Businesses that develop an online presence without registering their own domain name generally use the domain name of the **ISP** or company that is hosting their site. Your site address would generally have the following:

*http://www.yourISP.com/yoursitename*

This type of address is not mobile, meaning you can't take it with you should you ever want to move your Web site to another host. If you own your own domain name, it is yours as long as you keep your registration fees current with Network Solutions *(http://www.networksolutions.com, see Figure 2.1)*. You then have the option of moving your site to another host without losing your Web address. You can change the host of your site at any time and take your domain name with you. If you allow your ISP or any other party to take care of the domain name registration process, make sure that you are listed as the actual owner of the domain so that you don't run into problems if you decide to move your site. You want to be listed as the both the administrative and billingcontact. This way, Network Solutions will send the invoice directly to you, so you will

**ISP**
Internet Service Provider

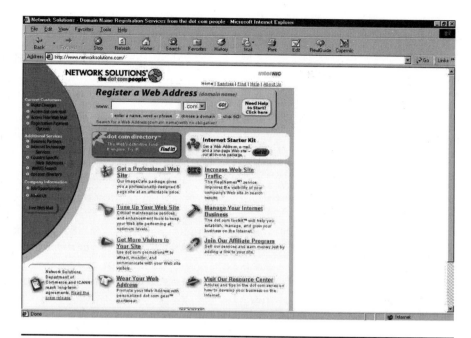

**Figure 2.1.** Network Solutions offers domain name registration services.

never have to worry about forgetting to pay your annual fee. Also, if your ISP goes out of business, they cannot take your domain name with them. In the long run, listing yourself as the administrative contact will help you skirt any potential complications.

It takes a great deal of time and effort to promote your site online. Getting listed in all the search engines and directories, developing links to your site, and getting listed in meta-indexes—all are time-consuming tasks. These listings and links all automatically link the viewer to your site address. If you don't own your address, you can't take it with you if you want to move your site to another ISP or host. If you move you will lose most, if not all, of the momentum gained by your previous online marketing activities. Having your own domain name gives you the option to move your site at any time without having a negative impact on your previous marketing efforts.

When conducting business in an international environment you need the most common top-level domain name, ending in *.com*, which is used around the world. Canadian sites can use *.ca*. However, to be globally recognized you should use the *.com* designation. As mentioned earlier, when a person knows of your company and wants to visit your Web site the first inclination is to check *www.yourcompanyname.com.*

Your domain name must be registered with Network Solutions. Network Solutions provides domain name registration services for the top-level domains: *.com, .net, .org,* and *.edu.* Registering a domain name with Network Solutions can be done through your ISP, or you can do it yourself through the Network Solutions Web site at *www.networksolutions.com.* You can do a search at the Network Solutions Web site to determine whether or not your preferred domain name is available.

The fee for registering your domain name is $70 US for the first two years, and there is a $35 US renewal fee for every year thereafter. Network Solutions' registration fee covers the cost of processing the initial registration and maintaining the domain name record. The renewal fee covers one year of maintenance for the domain name record and is assessed each year on the anniversary of the original registration.

The registration process begins once you have submitted your complete and correctly formatted agreement. Your registration request is processed immediately and you will be notified via e-mail when processing is finished. The complete process generally takes less than 24 hours, with some requests processed in as little as 10 minutes. Network Solutions will mail your invoice to you within a few days. The invoice will name you as the rightful owner and administrative contact for the domain name.

## The Essentials of Your Web Site Design

These are Web site design tips that are relevant to all Web sites:

- Your online and offline corporate image should be consistent.

- Your site should be easy to read.

- Your site should be easy to navigate (include a site map and/ or a search tool).

- Your Web pages should have a consistent layout.

- Your Web pages should be no larger than 50K.

- Have a "What's New" section to let visitors know what has changed on the site.

- Do not overuse **image maps.**

- Avoid "Under Construction" pages (see Figure 2.2) on your site. These look tacky and are of no value to the visitor. When you have information, post it. Until then, don't mention it.

**Image maps** Large single images with clickable "hot spots," commonly used for site navigation

- Your Web site should steer clear of scrolling marquee text. Scrolling marquees are difficult to read and are not compatible with all browsers. Simply post text directly on your pages if you have something important to say.

- Design for various screen widths. Try to accommodate visitors regardless of the screen resolution they use. Twenty percent of Web users still run their systems at 640 pixels wide by 480 pixels high. Keep your image sizes small enough to be fully viewable at this resolution, and use percentage widths in your tables so that your pages are flexible to any screen resolution.

- Use thumbnail graphics where applicable. When you have a page with a lot of large images (e.g., an online photo collection), create small "thumbnail" versions of each image, and give visitors the option of clicking through to the larger version of each image. This is far superior to making your visitors wait for a series of large images to load.

- Include contact information on every page. This includes your address, phone and fax numbers, and especially your e-mail address or a contact form. Make it easy for people to get in touch with you.

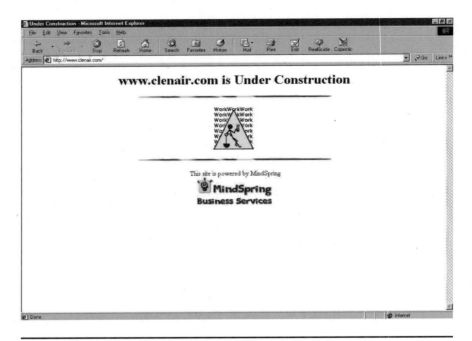

**Figure 2.2.**   "Under Construction."

- Provide security information. Explain to your customers when transactions or exchanges of information on your Web site are secure. This is important if your site will be accepting credit card orders.

- Establish a privacy policy. Tell people how their personal information (e.g., their name, e-mail address, etc.) will and will not be used. This will make visitors more comfortable submitting inquiries to your site.

- Minimize the use of background sounds and autoplay sounds. Some people surf the Web from their office at work and wish to discreetly go from one site to the next. Background sounds and sounds that load automatically can compromise their discreetness. Give your visitors the option to listen a sound, but do not force it upon them. If you do, you could lose visitors forever.

The tone of your text and the design of your graphics will convey your intended image. For example, if your target audience is business-minded, you will want to keep things simple. Minimize the graphics and use just enough text to get your point across and heighten the interest of your audience. On the other hand, a graphic designer will prefer a more graphic-oriented site with some multimedia effects such as Macromedia Flash. Keep your online image consistent with your offline image. Be consistent with the use of logos, corporate colors, and any other marketing collateral associated with your company.

When determining the text content of your site, be mindful of the fact that your own biases may preclude you from placing information on your site that is second nature to you but important data for your visitors. Review all text content on your site to ensure you have not omitted anything crucial.

Also, keep text brief. Almost 80% of Web users scan text online as opposed to actually reading it. Therefore, make your key points quickly and succinctly, and use lots of bulleted lists, headers, and horizontal rules to create visual "breaks" in the content. This will keep visitors interested enough to read the information on your site. If they are faced with huge blocks of text, most visitors will be overwhelmed by the quantity of the information and too intimidated to read your message.

Choose your background and font colors carefully. Using backgrounds that are too busy will obscure your text and will not provide a pleasant viewing experience for your visitor. Only some colors will show up properly on certain backgrounds. A light background with dark text is easiest on the eyes.

White text displays best on black backgrounds, and black text is most readable on white backgrounds. Of course, you can use other color schemes, but choose your scheme carefully as mentioned. There is nothing worse than a Web site that is unreadable. Also, be mindful that some people might wish to print pages from your site. If you incorporate a lot of your text into the actual graphics on your site, the text might be difficult to read when printed. Also, graphic-intensive sites load more slowly. If you have to incorporate text content into your graphics, ensure that it is sensible to do so.

Don't set your text size too small as this is too hard to read. Don't set it too large as this looks like you are shouting!! Also, avoid using ALL CAPS, WHICH ALSO COMES ACROSS AS SHOUTING.

Use the default colors for links whenever possible. Blue text usually indicates an unvisited link. Purple, maroon, or darker blue usually represents a link you have visited, and red is the color of an active link. It should not be difficult for visitors to identify your links. If you decide not to use the default colors, your links should be emphasized in a consistent manner through font size, font style, or underlines.

Ease of navigation is very important to your site. Provide a navigation bar at a consistent location on every page that links to all of the major pages of your site. Make it easy to get from one page to any other. Search engines can index any page from your site, so your home page might not be the first page visitors come to. Never have dead ends where viewers scroll down a page or two of information only to find that they must scroll all the way back up to the top to move on (because you have no links at the bottom of the page). A consistent-looking and well-positioned navigation bar with functioning links is the key to efficient site navigation.

Also avoid dead links. These are links that don't go anywhere and the viewer usually receives a "404—File not Found" error message (see Figure 2.3) from the Web server after clicking on a dead link. Verify periodically that all your links are still active.

Your visitors should be able to get anywhere they want to go on your site in three clicks or less. Develop an effective navigation bar as previously described. If your site is large, you should have an up-to-date site map (explained later in this chapter), which allows visitors to quickly find the information they are seeking on your site.

Keep the design of your site consistent. Font types, headers, footers, navigational bars, buttons, bullets, colors, and so on should be consistent throughout the site to maintain a polished professional look.

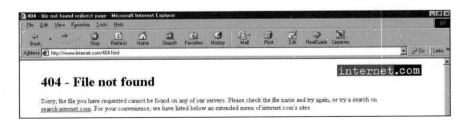

**Figure 2.3.** Broken links result in a "404—File not found" error message.

Your **home page** should be 50K or less, and your home page should be displayed on one or two screens maximum. Studies have shown that visitors will rarely wait beyond 15 seconds to download a site. Test the download time of your site with a 14.4 modem to ensure that it is reasonable for all users.

**Home page**
The main page of a Web site

## Keeping Web Site Graphics in Perspective

Graphics can be pleasant to look at, but be discriminating as you add them to your site. Graphics that are too time-consuming to download may cause visitors to leave your site before they get a chance to see it. Remember that a lot of Internet users are still using 28.8 or 56K modems. The combined size of your text and graphics on any Web page should not exceed 50K.

Some people turn graphics off in their browsers to save time, so you should provide all of your information in text as well as graphics. Use descriptive **Alt attributes** in your image tags. The Alt text will load in place of the images when the graphic does not display for any reason. Visitors who choose not to browse with graphics turned on will have an easier time navigating your site. Also, Alt text is spidered and indexed by a lot of the major search engines. Using keywords in your Alt text in your image tags will improve your ranking in search engines and provide a description of the images in the event they are not loaded. If you use any large files for graphics, audio, or video, warn your visitors by providing some text stating the size of the files.

**Alt attributes** descriptive text associated with respective images on a Web site

You should curb your use of image maps as well. Image maps (see Figure 2.4) are large graphics with clickable "hot spots." Image maps are typically used for navigation. They are useful if your Web site contains five or more major sections. If you do use an image map, make it obvious what portions of the image are clickable and where each link will lead.

Very often, when a large graphic is used for an image map, visitors must wait for the entire image to load before it is apparent where they must click to begin navigating a site. Instead of using a large image map, break the image into smaller images so that visitors will receive

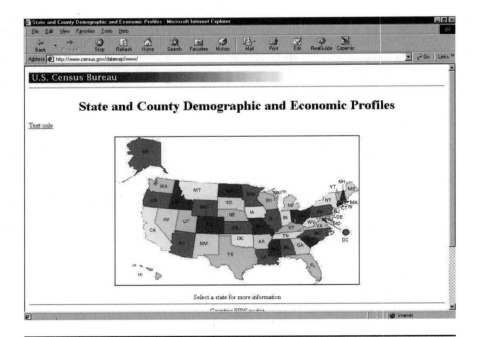

**Figure 2.4.**   A good use of an image map. There are lots of links, and the hot spots are well defined. Each state can be clicked on to obtain more information.

faster feedback from your site without having to wait for a huge graphic to load. Also, always provide an alternate text link navigation system to assist people who surf with their graphics turned off.

## Provide Ease of Navigation with User-Friendly Site Maps

For very large sites (i.e., those sites consisting of 8 to 10 major sections) it is a good idea to include a site map that users can access from any page in your site. Site maps, as shown in Figures 2.5 and 2.6, are usually text-based lists that name all of the site's pages and their content. Site maps make it easy for users to access the information they are looking for without causing them much frustration. In-

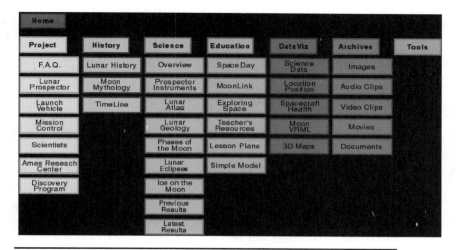

**Figure 2.5.**  Most site maps are provided in a tree structure and provide the user with an easy way to navigate a large site.

clude a link from your main navigation bar to the site map for the easiest possible reference.

## Identify Your Site with Page Titles

Each of the pages in your Web site should be given a title. The title is inserted between the title tags in the header of an **HTML** document. Title tag information identifies and describes your pages. Titles can tell readers where the information contained on a page originated. Most Web **browsers,** such as Netscape, display a document's title in the top line of the screen. When users print a page from your Web site, the title usually appears at the top of the page at the left. When people book-mark your site, the title appears as the description in their bookmark file. These are all reasons why it is important that a page's title reflect an accurate description of the page.

**HTML (HyperText Markup Language)**
The coding language that tells a Web browser how to display a Web page's words and images

**Browsers**
Software programs that let you "surf" the Internet

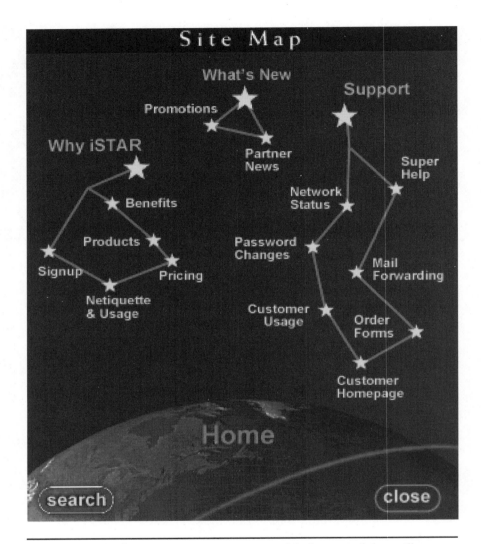

**Figure 2.6.**   Other site maps use a more graphical approach but still provide the user easy access to every page of the site.

Go through each and every page of your Internet site, bookmark each one, and check that your titles represent each page clearly without being lengthy. Longer page titles can dilute the relevancy of your key-words. Keeping your page titles brief (5 to 10 words or fewer) will increase the potency of your keywords and earn your pages higher search engine rankings. The titles should always identify your company.

Examples of appropriate titles are:

- "Progeny Software—Genealogy Software Specialists"

- "Progeny Software—Free Trial Version"

and inappropriate titles are

- "The Best Software Page on the Web"

- "The Software Home Page"

- "Order Form"

Match the keywords you use in your Meta tags with the words you use in your page titles. Search engines check page titles, Meta tags, and page content for keywords. Your pages will be more relevant, and therefore place higher in the search engines, for certain keywords if these keywords appear in each of these three sections. Position your keywords near the beginning of your page titles to increase your keyword relevancy.

## Viewing Your Site Through Browser Eyes

Check your site using different browsers. What viewers see when your site is downloaded depends on what browser they are using. Different browsers will display the same Web site differently. Before you post your site online, check your site with the most popular browsers:

- Netscape Navigator 4.7

- Netscape Navigator 3.0

- Microsoft Internet Explorer 5.0

- Microsoft Internet Explorer 4.0

- Microsoft Internet Explorer 3.0

- America Online 5.0

It is obvious that there are a lot of browsers to consider when designing your Web site. Some people may also be using Netscape 2.0, Mosaic, or a text-only browser. When designing your site, consider your target audience. What browsers will your visitors most likely use? If your intended target audience is everyone and anyone, design for the lowest common denominator. Design for Netscape 3.0 and Internet Explorer 3.0 browsers or higher. Few people continue to use really old browsers, so unless you know your target audience will be using Netscape 2.0 or Mosaic, the 3.0 browser versions are the most appropriate to design for.

America Online bases its browser off of either Netscape or Internet Explorer (depending on who they are currently affiliated with—Netscape or Microsoft). Therefore, if your Web site displays properly in Netscape and Internet Explorer, you can safely assume that AOL users will have no trouble viewing your Web site.

If your audience is more likely to be technically inclined, you can safely design for the latest browser editions. In this case, you might wish to use HTML 4.0, Java applets, Active X, or Flash Media to make your Web site more attractive to your visitors.

Generally speaking, design your pages using HTML 3.2 and minimize the number of slow-loading multimedia elements. This will allow everyone to enjoy your site without having to wait several minutes for each page to load.

**Chat room**
A site where you can chat, in real time, with others

## Choosing Web Site Features to Meet Marketing Objectives

Many features can be incorporated into your Web site. It is important to look at each feature from both marketing and administrative views before deciding to incorporate it into your site. A **chat room** might seem like a nifty feature to have at first blush, but you have to ask the questions, "What is the marketing value to our company in having this on our Web site? Will it increase targeted traffic to our site? Will it encourage repeat visits from our customers and potential customers? Will it result in increased sales?

Assuming that you can justify a chat room on your site from a marketing perspective, you must look at the feature from a financial perspective. What will this feature cost to develop? What will be the ongoing costs of operating this feature in technical resources as well as in human resources? What is your budget? Can these resources provide a better return on investment if spent elsewhere? Would you achieve your objectives more effectively if you put these financial resources into banner advertising or other online marketing activities?

## Customer-Enticing Traffic Builders

The following "traffic builders" are used to attract and invite visitors to your site.

### Free Offers

People love to get something for nothing. Offering something for free is a good way to get lots of traffic to your site. This is great if your objectives include generating lots of general user traffic to your site. Free offers also provide you the opportunity to be linked from the many **Meta-indexes** related to freebies and giveaways. If you are giving something away, you might consider tying it into a registration for your newsletter or mailing list. Some of the things commonly given away include screen savers, icons, software, and games. You should relate giveaways to your company, your products, or your services.

**Meta-indexes** Collections of URLs for related Internet resources

### Online Seminars

Online seminars are generally conducted through live chat sessions. Seminars allow customers and potential customers to interact in a real-time setting with industry experts and celebrities. This can be a great traffic builder.

Live chat sessions will attract people who are genuinely interested in what your business is selling and all topics related to it.

Conducting a seminar will create a more intimate bond between your company and your customers. This encourages repeat business and generates new business as word of mouth spreads and draws more people to your seminars. Eventually, you will have a captive audience to which you can introduce your latest product or service.

### Advice Columns

Advice columns are a great way to increase traffic and to gain the respect of your customers. Many companies answer questions that pertain to their products and industry. They also help their customers solve common problems with expert advice. For example, customers on the Tide Web site can ask questions about how to get certain stains out of their clothes.

### Coupons

Coupons are an effective way to increase traffic to your site. If your coupons are valuable and you change them daily or weekly, you will encourage visitors to return frequently. Kent Building Supplies *(http://www.kbs.com),* a Nova Scotia company, provides weekly coupons on its site. Customers print the coupons and redeem them at the store. This is a great marketing technique for Kent because their customers are encouraged to visit the Web site and the physical storefront as well. A closer bond is created between Kent and their customers, and sales increase as a result.

### Contests

Contests are very popular online, particularly when prizes are involved. To encourage repeat visits you should change the contest regularly or design it in such a way that your visitors can enter often. To get some information about the people who are visiting your site and to help you with your marketing efforts, include a few pertinent questions on the entry form, one of them being "At which e-mail address would you like to be notified of the winner?"

Once the winning candidate is selected, you can send a message to all contest participants to announce the winner. Thank them for their participation and invite them to return to your site. Enticing them with a special offer or a discount on all purchases might be good way to increase traffic to your site. By sending the contestants a message like this, you may generate sales from people who might not have purchased from you otherwise.

### Surveys

Surveys are a popular feature for specific industries. Here, you should make sure the information you are gathering is of value to the industry and promise to provide a copy of the final report to all that participate.

### Interactive Tours

Interactive tours take your visitors on a virtual tour of your offices, your factory, or your Web site. Visitors can find out how a product is made or how your company operates. This is a great way to provide information on the quality of your materials and workmanship.

You can make your interactive tour more interesting by incorporating a contest with the tour. For the purpose of the contest, ask your visitors detailed questions about the tour. They will be more attentive, and they will absorb your message and the information on your site more clearly. If you can make them understand your message, this can lead to sales.

## Guiding the Search Engines with Meta-Information

A common problem faced by Internet marketers is how to influence search engines to index their site appropriately and how to ensure that their site appears when people use relevant search criteria. Many of the interesting and creative sites on the Internet are impossible to find because they are not indexed with the major search engines. The majority (85%) of Internet users employ search engines or directories to find Web sites, which they do by typing in a keyword or phrase that represents what they are looking for.

Retaining a certain measure of control over how search engines deal with your Web site is a major concern. Often Web sites do not take advantage of the techniques available to them to influence search engine listings. Most search engines evaluate the "Meta HTML" tags in conjunction with other variables to decide where to index Web pages based on particular keyword queries.

The Web Developer's Virtual Library defines a Meta HTML tag as follows:

> *An HTML tag used in the Head area of a document to specify further information about the document, either for the local server, or for a remote browser. The Meta element is used within the Head element to embed document Meta information not defined by other HTML elements. Such information can be extracted by servers/clients for use in identifying, indexing, and cataloging specialized document Meta information. In addition, HTTP servers can read the contents of the document head to generate response headers corresponding to any elements defining a value for the attribute HTTP-EQUIV. This provides document authors with a mechanism for identifying information that should be included in the response headers of an HTTP request.*

To summarize this lengthy definition, Meta information can be used in identifying, indexing, and cataloging. This means you can use these tags to guide the search engines in displaying your site as the result of a query.

## Meta and Header Elements

A header without Meta information will look like this:

```
<html>
<head>
<title>Game Nation—Gaming Software Specialists </title>
```

</head>

If you want your site to be displayed properly in search engines, you should create a header as follows:

<HTML>
<HEAD>
<TITLE>Document Title Here </title>
<META NAME="keywords" CONTENT="keyword1, keyword2, keyword3">
<META NAME="description" CONTENT="200-character site description goes here">
<META NAME="robots" CONTENT="index, follow">
<!—Comments Tag, repeat description here?>
</HEAD> indicates the beginning of the header, and the ending of the header is marked by </HEAD>
<TITLE> indicates the title of the page. The end of the title is marked by
</TITLE> which is called the closing tag.

**<META NAME="keywords" CONTENT="...">** tells search engines under which keywords to index your site. When a user types one of the words you listed here, your site should be displayed as a result. A space must be used to separate the words. Do not repeat any of the words more than five times (a lot of the **bots** will not recognize repeat words). You should list the most important words first because some bots only read the first 200 characters. You should create a keywords tag for each page of your site listing appropriate keywords for each separate page.

**<META NAME="description" CONTENT="...">** should be added to every page of your site. It is used to provide an accurate description of the page to which it is attached. Keep the description 200 characters, or it may be cut off when displayed by the search engines.

**<META NAME="robots" CONTENT=" ">** tells certain bots to follow or not follow hypertext links. The W3 Consortium white paper

**Bot**
A program used by search engines to search the Internet for pages to index

on spidering (spiders are defined later) offers the following definition and discussion:
<META NAME="ROBOTS" CONTENT="ALL | NONE | NOINDEX | NOFOLLOW">

default = empty = "ALL" "NONE" = "NOINDEX, NOFOLLOW"

The filler is a comma-separated list of terms:
ALL, NONE, INDEX, NOINDEX, FOLLOW, NOFOLLOW.

*Note:* This tag is meant to provide users who cannot control the *robots.txt* file at their sites. It provides a last chance to keep their content out of search services. It was decided not to add syntax to allow robot-specific permissions within the Meta tag. INDEX means that robots are welcome to include this page in search services.

FOLLOW means that robots are welcome to follow links from this page to find other pages. A value of NOFOLLOW allows the page to be indexed, but no links from the page are explored (this may be useful if the page is a free entry point into pay-per-view content, for example. A value of NONE tells the robot to ignore the page."

The values of INDEX and FOLLOW should be added to every page unless there is a specific reason why you do not want your page to be indexed. This may be the case if the page is only temporary.

<!—Comments Tag, repeat description here?—!> is a tag that is read by the Excite and Magellan spiders. A spider is an artificial intelligence agent that reads all of the information on a page and develops a "page description." The comments tag can be used to trick a spider into displaying an accurate description of your pages. The description that a spider creates without this tag is often not pleasing, and usually doesn't depict what your pages are actually about.

## The Future of Meta Tags

New technologies are constantly replacing existing technologies. The introduction of **XML** may signal the end of the Meta tags and Meta-oriented search engines. XML is a markup language for structured data that allows you to specify both the tags you use and the semantics of these tags. In HTML, both the tag set and the semantics of the tags are fixed.

XML uses a **DTD** to define its tags. Search tools are being developed that search for DTDs when a particular keyword is sought. For instance, if you search for "cars", the XML search engine will seek all DTDs related to "cars". The result is that fewer pages are returned, but the search results are more focused.

A similar search for "cars" in an HTML search engine will return thousands of results barely related to the intended topic. XML search tools will focus on structured data and are more efficient than HTML search tools. HTML Meta tags can be misleading and search criteria varies from engine to engine. This is why Meta-based search engines may eventually be replaced by their XML counterparts as XML becomes a more commonly accepted technology for Web development.

**XML (eXtensible Markup Language)** An emerging tag-based language

**DTD (Document Type Declaration):** Specifies the organization that issued the language specification

## Internet Resources

### Review Your Site

Web Site Garage
*http://www.websitegarage.com*
This is a one-stop shop for servicing your Web site. Here you can run critical performance diagnostics on your entire Web site and ensure browser compatibility by seeing your site in 18 different browsers, platforms, and screen sizes. This speeds up your site by optimizing your images and drives traffic to your Web site. Provided is a comprehensive registration with up to 400 search engines, directories, and award sites. With this tool you can announce news through a Business Wire press release. You can target your industry, target an Internet population, and analyze your Web site traffic with a customizable tracking tool. This site will allow you to run a number of diagnostics on your site for free, including spell check, browser compatibility, load time, link popularity, and HTML design.

### Net Mechanic
*http://www.netmechanic.com*
This site will check your Web site to find broken links, perform HTML validation to make sure the format is compatible with the most common browsers, optimize your images for quicker loading, and monitor your server's performance for speed, checking with different modem speeds. NetMechanic is a free online service.

### Northern Webs
*http://www.northernwebs.com*
Northern Webs' Engine Tutorial is one of the most recognized leaders in exposing the nuances of the various search engines and explaining what makes them tick. See if your site can stand the test of their exclusive Meta Medic!

### Interactive Tools
*http://www.arrowweb.com/graphics/tools.html*
This site includes interactive tools for Web masters and site designers. Use these tools to submit and promote your Web site or to find problems. Utilities are included, such as an encyclopedia, dictionary, complete reference, and search tools.

### Reviews of Relevant Web Site Performance Books
*http://www.connectingonline.com/bookmark/books-15.html*
If you are serious about maintaining an efficiently operating and easy to navigate Web site, here is a link to a few books on the subject.

### How to Build Lame Web Sites
*http://www.webdevelopersjournal.com/columns/perpend1.html*
A tongue-in-cheek article describing the methods you can utilize to achieve a poorly designed Web sites. Don't follow these methods and your site will be fine.

## Meta Tags

### Meta Tags & Search Engines
*http://www.webdigger.com/meta_tags.htm*
Need to improve your search engine standings? Here are a few ideas to get you started: meta tags as well as search engine and Web site design tips.

### Meta Tag Analyzer

*http://www.scrubtheweb.com/abs/meta-check.html*
This will check your Meta tags and your HTML code to help you achieve better placement in search engine results. Let their free Meta Tag Analyzer program check your Meta tags and help analyze your HTML syntax online.

### GoTo.com Search Suggestions

*http://inventory.go2.com/inventory/Search_Suggestion.jhtml*
Enter a keyword into the GoTo.com engine, and this will tell you how many people searched for that keyword. It also generates a list of other related keywords.

### Meta Tag Generator

*http://www.siteup.com/meta.html*
The Meta Tag Generator will automatically generate Meta tags used by search engines to index your pages. SiteUp Internet Promotions offers a free download of the Windows 95 Meta Tag Generator.

### Dr Clue's HTML Guide—Meta Tags

*http://www.drclue.net/F1.cgi/HTML/META/META.html*
This site includes short tutorial on Meta tags in addition to the keywords and description tags. It includes the Meta-Maker.

### How to Use Meta Tags Tutorial

*http://searchenginewatch.com/webmasters/meta.html*

### World of Design

*http://www.globalserve.net/~iwb/search_engine/killer.html*
This is a tutorial for writing Meta tags for higher search engine placement and good descriptions.


## References

### Web Developers Virtual Library

*http://www.stars.com*
A comprehensive illustrated encyclopedia of Web technology, the WDVL is for Web masters and Internet developers. It's a well-

organized gold mine of tutorials, demos, and links to great resources.

### The World Wide Web Consortium
*http://www.w3c.org*
Find out everything you need to know about the past, present, and future of the World Wide Web. This Web site has specifications for every Web-related language. It's a valuable resource for all Web developers.

### Whatis.com
*http://www.whatis.com*
Whatis.com is "definition" paradise. It defines any computer-related word you ever wondered about.

### WWW Meta Indexes and Search Tools
*http://www.fys.ruu.nl/~kruis/h3.html*
This is a Library of Congress Internet Resource page.

### Argus Clearinghouse
*http://www.clearinghouse.net*
The premier Internet research library or meta-index to locate everything you need to find on the Web.

### A Dictionary of HTML Meta Tags
*http://vancouver-webpages.com/META*

## Graphics

### The Gif Wizard
*http://www.gifwizard.com*
You can reduce all your graphics using the Gif Wizard Site Scan Monitor, a free service from Raspberry Hill Publishing.

# 3

# Be Kind to the Search Engines

Let's assume your site is built and you feel you are now ready to submit to the search engines and directories where your site must be found easily by your customers and prospective clients. You need to be listed in as many search engines as possible. Who knows which is the preferred directory or search engine of your potential client? When people conduct Internet searches they rarely go beyond the first few pages of results. You need to appear in the top 20 search results to be noticed. Before you submit to the search engines you have to be sure your site is search engine friendly. In this chapter we cover:

- The key do's of Web site design to accommodate search engines

- The major don'ts of Web site design pertaining to search engines

- Using your competition and industry leaders as guidance

- The all-important content

- The importance of keywords in all aspects of your Web site

## Gaining Visibility on the Internet

A variety of search tools (search engines, directories, spiders, etc.) are currently used to navigate the World Wide Web. Due to the unprecedented growth of the information available on the Internet, there has been an unqualified demand for simplifying this information. As a result, the creation of search tools has catapulted. To maintain a competitive edge, it is absolutely imperative that your Web site be registered with as many search tools as possible, you never know which one is being used by your target market.

A Georgia Tech survey found that people find Web sites using the following methods:

- Links from other sites—88%

- Search engines—85%

- Friends—65%

- Printed media—63%

- Directories—58%

- Signature files—36%

- Television—32%

- Usenet—30%

- Other—29%

- Books—28%

## Search Engines and Their Nomadic Bots

The most common search tool is the search engine. Search engines use programs or intelligent agents, called bots, to actually search the Internet for pages, which they index using specific parameters as they read the content. The agent will read the information on every page of your site and then follow the links. For example, AltaVista's spider continually crawls the Web looking for sites to index and, of course, indexes sites upon their submission. Infoseek uses a spider as well, but their spider does not scour the Web for sites to index. You must submit your site to Infoseek or it will never be listed. Inktomi also uses a spider; however, a user cannot access Inktomi's information directly to search. Instead a user will use other search engines and directories who use Inktomi's search engine technology, such as HotBot, Lycos, and Yahoo. Inktomi is very important in the search engine community, so be sure your site is easily accessible to its spider.

To register with search engines you simply submit your URL on their submission form. This will be discussed in greater detail in the following chapter. Even if your URL is not registered with search engines, most of the major search engines will eventually find you because these bots are continually roaming the Internet looking for new sites to index. There are millions of sites out there, so we suggest you be proactive and register your site to ensure a speedier listing. Once you are registered, the bots will periodically visit your site looking for changes and updates. The following sections discuss what to do and what not to do during Web site design and development to best accommodate the search engines.

## Image Maps

I recommend not using image maps when designing your Web site. An image map is a single graphic or image that has multiple hot links to different pages or resources. Image maps prevent search engines from getting inside your site—you're basically locking the door on many of the search engines. This may result in some of the pages on your site not being indexed, or none of your site being indexed at all. Figures 3.1 to 3.3 demonstrate the use of image maps.

For example, similar to an individual using an old browser, many search engines cannot follow image maps. If you do use image maps make sure that your site is easy to navigate with **hyperlinks**. This will ensure that search engines will find all of your pages and index them. Another tip you should be

**Hyperlinks** Automatic links that connect a word, a phrase, or a picture on one Web page to another Web page

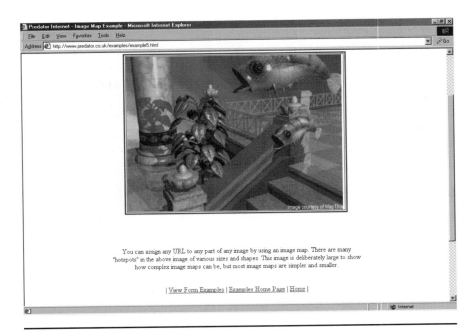

**Figure 3.1.** An example of an image map.

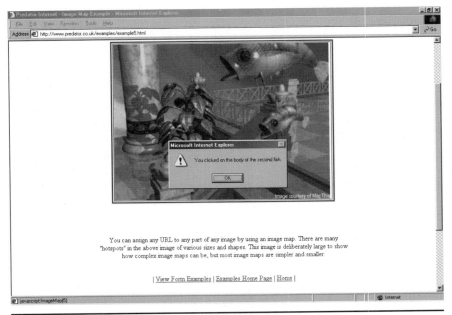

**Figure 3.2.** Notice that clicking on the large fish brings up a window.

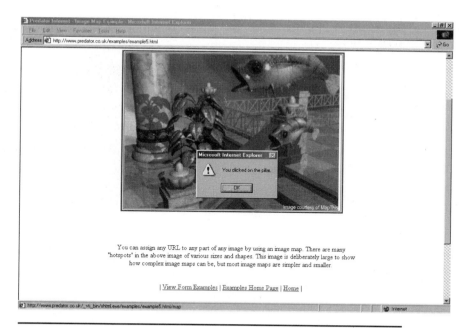

**Figure 3.3.** If you click elsewhere, the pillar for example, you get a different message.

aware of is to create a **site map** that has text links (see Figure 3.4) to all relevant pages within your Web site. Once you have created your site map, submit it to the major search engines. This will help the search engines to index the pages within your site.

## Spamming

Some Internet marketers try various techniques to trick the search engines into positioning their sites higher in search results. These techniques are considered cheating by many Internet users. It is up to you whether you want to risk discovery by the search engines or **flames** from other marketers by implementing them. These tricks do not work with every search engine, and if it is discovered that you are trying to

**Site map**
A Web page that provides links to all major sections of a Web site

**Flames**
Harsh messages to criticize or insult someone for something the person has posted

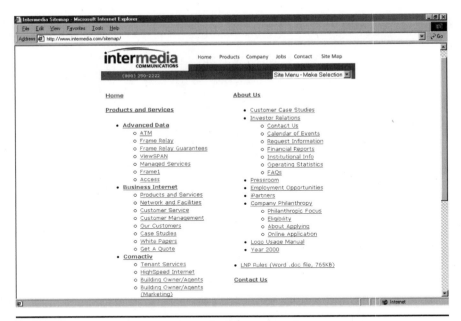

**Figure 3.4.**   An example of a well-done, text-only site map.

dupe the search engines, some may not list you at all. They have been programmed to detect some of these techniques, and you will be penalized in some way if you are discovered. A few of the search engine tricks pertaining to Web site design are as follows:

- Repeating keywords over and over again hidden in your HTML and Meta tags. For example, <!games, games, games, games, games,...>.

- Repeating keywords over and over again by displaying them at the bottom of your document after a number of line breaks.

- Hiding keywords by displaying them in your document using a very small font.

- Repeating keywords in your document by making the text color the same as the background color.

- Making frequent and regular title changes so that the bots think your site is a new site and they list you again and again.

- Changing the name of your site to have a space, exclamation mark (!), or A as the first character so that you come up first in alphabetical lists.

Any time you make significant changes to your site you should resubmit your site to the search engines. Search engines normally revisit on a regular schedule. However, these search engines are growing smarter every day—some monitor how often the site is updated and adjust their "revisit" schedule accordingly.

## Meta Refresh

Have you ever visited a site then been automatically transported to another page within the site? This is the result of a **Meta refresh tag.** A Meta refresh tag is an HTML document that is designed to automatically replace itself with another HTML document, after a certain period of time, as defined by the document author. Now that I've mentioned this, don't use them. Search engines generally do not like Meta refresh tags. Infoseek will not add sites that use a fast Meta refresh. If you do use a Meta refresh tag to redirect users, you should set a delay of at least 7 seconds and provide a link on the new page back to the page they were originally taken from. For example, some people use Meta refresh tags to redirect users from a page that is obsolete or no longer there.

**Meta refresh tag**
A tag used to automatically reload or load a new page

## Frames

From a marketing perspective you should avoid **frames** when developing your Web site. Frames may result in search engines being unable to index pages within your site or improper pages being indexed. Figures 3.5 and 3.6 are examples of frame usage from an HTML tutorial.

**Frames**
Divisions of a browser's display area into two or more independent areas

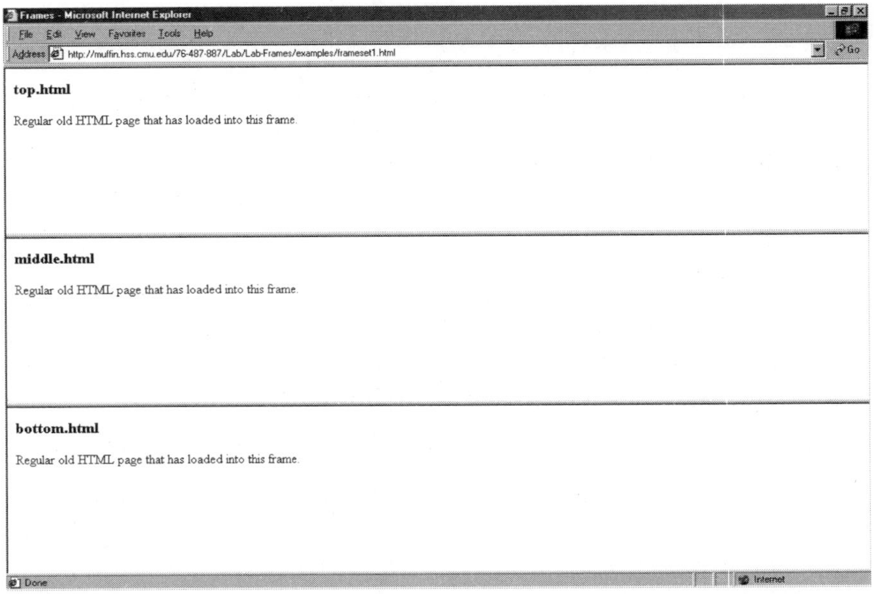

**Figure 3.5.** An example using frames to split a page into three sections.

What I mean by improper pages being indexed is that content pages will be indexed, and when users are directed to these content pages by the search engines they will likely not be able to navigate your site because the navigation frame probably will not be visible. To prevent this, one technique you can use is a Robots Meta tag in the head section of your HTML that does not allow bots to proceed beyond your home page. As a result, you can really only submit your home page, which means you have less of a chance of receiving the high rankings you need on the major search engines. Alternatively you should include textual links to all major sections within your site to accommodate those users who do enter your site on a page other than a home page and to assist the search engines with indexing your site.

Most search engines can only read information between the <NOFRAMES> tags within your master frame. The master frame identifies the other frames. I've found that all too often the individuals who apply frames ignore the <NOFRAMES> tags, which is a *big* no-no. If you do not have any text between the <NOFRAMES> tags, then the search engines that reference your site for information will have nothing to look at. This will result in your site being listed with little or no information in their indexes, or you will be listed so far down in the rankings that no one will ever find you anyway. To remedy this situation, insert textual information that contains your most important descriptive keywords between the <NOFRAMES> tags. This will give the search engines something they can see, and it also helps those users who are browsing with non-frames-compatible browsers. Now that the search engines have found you, you still have a problem. They can't go anywhere. Create a link within your <NOFRAMES> tags to allow search engines and users with non-frames-compatible browsers to get into your site.

Frames are a headache when designing your site to be search engine friendly, and there's plenty more that can be said. For example, if you bookmark a framed site on a page within the site other than the home page, the bookmark will likely only show the home page because the browser is reading from the main frame and the URL of the main frame does not change. To make your life easier and from a marketing perspective it's better to avoid them altogether.

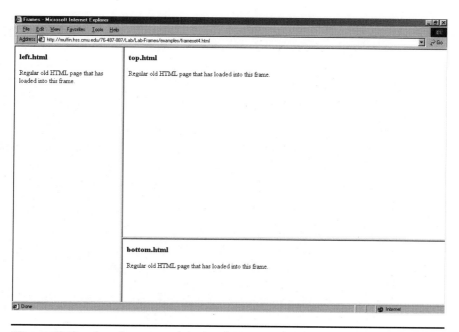

**Figure 3.6.** Another example using frames to divide a page into three sections.

## Splash Pages

A splash page is basically an opening page that leads into a site. Often splash pages consist of a Java or a Flash intro that can be slow to load for some users. If you'd like to see an example, view one of the many feature film sites (See Figures 3.7 and 3.8) out there, they usually have a Flash intro to assist in the promotion of their movie.

Some people use splash screens that consist of an eye-pleasing image and an invitation to enter the site. Many splash pages implement techniques that automatically send you to the home page once you've seen the splash page; others will invite you to "Click to enter" in some form or another. Why do people use splash pages on their sites? For one, they usually look beautiful. Another reason is to provide the user with something to look at while images or content for the home page loads in the background. Individuals also use splash pages as means of advertising. Splash pages are usually very attractive in appearance, but they often lack content relevant to search engines.

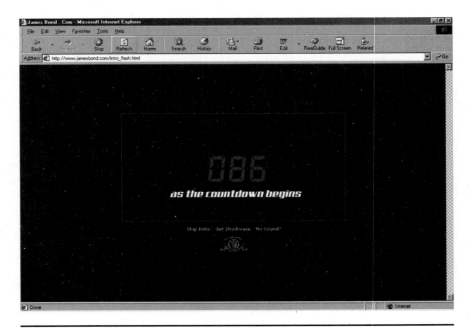

**Figure 3.7.** An image of the flash intro page for the feature film *The World Is Not Enough*.

**Figure 3.8.** An image of the same intro at a later point.

If you do use a splash page on your site, be sure you include the proper Meta tags within your HTML header. This is important so that search engines that use Meta tags can access this information. This ultimately affects your ranking and how your site is displayed to users in the search results. If possible, include a paragraph or statement on your splash page that pertains to your site's content. This can help boost your rankings on some of the major search engines that both use and do not use Meta tags. Some search engines will review your opening paragraph and use this information when developing a description for your site that is presented in their search results. Figure 3.9 shows a nice splash page with an opening paragraph.

**CGI (Common Gateway Interface)** Programs used to enable Web servers to interact with users

## Dynamic Pages and Special Characters

Don't bother submitting pages that consist of **CGI** content or question marks (?) in the URLs. Search engines simply won't

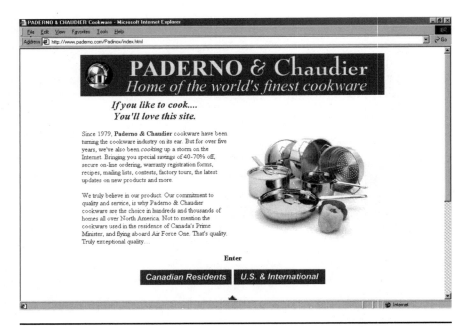

**Figure 3.9.**   Here's an example of a nice splash page with an opening paragraph.

index them. In addition, some search engines such as Lycos will not index sites with the ampersand (&) or percent sign (%) characters (e.g., *http://www.yourdomain.com/default.asp?bcr=1*).

## Use of Tables

**Tables**
Information ar-
ranged in
columns
and rows

Tables can confuse some search engines, so be careful. Also, by using tables you are potentially forcing the content you want search engines to see further down on your page. Because some search engines only look so far, you might be hurting your chances of receiving a high ranking. If you are using tables, place any important information pertaining to the page content above the table if possible to help prevent any potential problems.

Here's an interesting problem some search engines suffer from. Assume you have a Web site, the main color of the background is white, and you have a table on the page with a dark background. If you were to use white color text in the table, some of the major search engines would pick this up as using text on the same color background and ignore your site's submission because it will be considered spam to them. Using tables (see Figure 3.10) is okay, many people do, just be careful with your choice of colors.

## Maximizing Findability with Directories

Directories are often referred to as search engines. Unlike search engines, directories will not find your site if you do not tell them about it. Directories do not use bots or other intelligent agents to scour the Internet for new pages. Web sites must be submitted and the submissions are monitored by human administrators. Some of the more popular directories are LookSmart, Snap, Yahoo (the most popular of all search engines and directories), and the DMOZ Open Directory

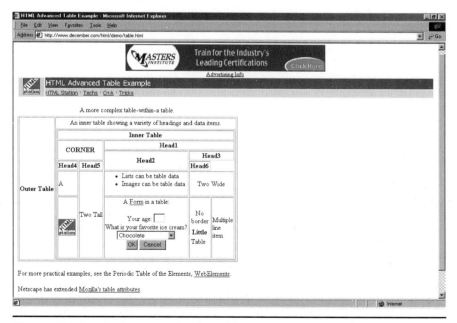

**Figure 3.10.** A nice example of a table.

Project. In general directories do not have near the amount of sites indexed as do the search engines; however, the sites that are indexed are typically more appropriate content wise.

In order to be listed in a directory you need to submit or register your site information and URL address. This is best accomplished by visiting all the directories in which you want to be listed and filling out the required form. The registration forms are all quite similar and generally require information such as your URL, the name of your site, a description of your site, a list of keywords, your contact information, and other information depending on the particular directory. You must complete the form and click on the submit button to complete the registration process. More detail on submitting your site to a directory is covered in the next chapter.

Know your search engines and directories. Each one is different, using different criteria or algorithms to determine which sites rank highly. They also use different mechanisms to provide a description of your site and allow different lengths for a description. See Appendix C for details on popular search engines and directories. These are constantly changing, so to stay current you should follow up with a visit to the search engine and directory Web sites and read their instructions and **FAQs**.

Some directories automatically include the information you have submitted while others review and approve your site for inclusion. The latter can take up to a month.

**FAQ**
Frequently
Asked
Questions

## Keywords Are of Key Importance

Keywords are an important aspect of every Web page because the search engines use keywords in determining your site's ranking and these are the words people are most likely to use when they're searching for your site. When creating your keyword list, don't just use nouns. Think of descriptive words that may be associated with benefits of your products or services. For example, if your site offers information on weight loss, then some of your keywords may be "weight, weight loss, diet, exercise, nutrition," and so on. You can also add some keywords that describe advantages a person may receive from visiting your site such as "thin, slim, attractive, healthy, in shape, etc."

When determining what your keywords will be, always keep the customer or your target visitor in mind. Try to think like they would if they were to do a search for information on your topic. Don't just think about what people would do to find *your* site, but what they would do if they didn't know your company existed and were looking for the types of products and services you provide. If you find this a difficult exercise, then ask around. Talk to both people that know about your business and people that don't. Ask what keywords they would use to find a site like yours.

Start by taking the company's brochures and other corporate marketing materials, as well as the site itself, and indiscriminately highlight any words that individuals might search on if they are looking for the products or services the company has to offer. Record these words in a text document in your word processing program.

Next, edit the list by deleting words that are either too broad (for example, "business") or are not appropriate for keyword purposes. Review each word and ask yourself if someone would search using that word if they were looking for your products and services.

Always use the plural when forming your keywords (adding an "s" forms the plural). If you list "game" as your keyword and someone uses "games" to do a search, then your site will not be found. If you include the word "games" in your keywords and someone requests information on the word "game," then your site will be found because "game" is part of the word "games." Never use both versions because you're then running the risk of spamming the search engines, and you want to be able to use other keywords to increase your chances of achieving high rankings. The only time it is acceptable to use both the singular and the plural is if the plural does not include the singular in its entirety, for example "dairy" "and "dairies" you should list both the singular and the plural as part of your keyword list. It is also important to note that when most people perform their searches they will use the plural version. You're more likely to search for "computers" than you are to search for "computer".

Now, reorganize the remaining keywords in order of importance. By having the most important words first, no matter how many keywords the particular directory will allow, you are ready to submit— simply copy-paste the keywords into their form.

Now you have a good master keyword list. Different directories allow for different numbers of keywords to be submitted. Because you have organized your list with the most important words first, you simply include as many of your keywords as the directory will allow. When a directory will allow multiple submissions for the same URL, you might consider submitting as many times as it takes to include all your keywords. You won't have to change your description or other information every time, just the keywords.

If you plan to submit every page of your site, your master list provides a valuable document. For each page that you are indexing, take a photocopy of the comprehensive list and delete words that are not appropriate for that particular page. Then re-prioritize the remaining keywords based on the content of the page you are indexing. This is then the keyword list for that page. Repeat this procedure for every page you will be indexing.

If you make changes to your Web pages, change the title and keywords contained in the title as well. This will allow you to be re-indexed by search engines.

There is often the question as to whether to include your competitors' names in your keywords. This follows the premise that if someone searches for them they will find you as well. There is, however, an ongoing debate as to whether this is ethical. My position on this issue is NO. Due to the fact that several of the search engines allow for only 200 or less characters for keywords, you would be losing vital space to include keywords that describe or even name their products and/or services. In addition, there have been recent legal battles regarding the use of competitors' keywords within one's keywords.

Your keyword list should be included in your submissions to directories and in a keyword Meta tag. However, to be listed in a higher position in search results you should include your most important keywords in other places as well, such as:

- Your page title

- Your description

- The first 200-250 characters of your page

- Beginning, middle, and end of your page text

- If frames are used, between the <noframes> tags

- In Alt tags

- Keywords Meta tag

- Descriptions Meta tag

- Comments tags

Include a comments tag which has your keywords and your description in it. You can repeat this a couple of times if you wish. It is used by the Excite spider, and if repeated may yield a higher placement in search results.

Some search engines rank sites by how early the keyword appears on the site. The earlier a keyword is mentioned on your site, the higher your site may be positioned in search results. And remember the points made earlier...though you don't want to repeat a keyword hundreds of times (some search engines are on to this), you do want to repeat keywords a number of times on each page of your site. AltaVista, Infoseek, and Webcrawler all like it when different keywords appear relatively close together in the page content.

You can check the effectiveness of your keyword placement and utilization by using Web traffic analysis techniques. This is discussed in depth in a later chapter; however, it also applies to this section. You can use these techniques to look at what sites are referring people to you. You can strip down this information further to view only search engine referrals. By looking at this information you can see exactly what keywords people are using to find you and you can alter your keywords based on this information. Those keywords that prove to be effective keep. Those that provide little or no traffic you can change to something else and see if that's more effective. Refining your keywords is one of the key elements to success—you're letting the search engines tell you what you're doing right and what you could be doing better.

**Spiders and crawlers** Programs that visit Web sites and read their pages to create entries for a search engine index

## Content Tips for Spider and Crawler Discoveries

Although **spiders** and **crawlers** can find your site whether or not you actually submitted it, I suggest you take the proactive approach. Check to see if they have already found your site and if they haven't submit your URL. Methods of checking whether or not your site is already in a search engine's database are discussed in the next chapter.

When a spider adds your page to its database it uses the title found in the <TITLE> tag as the title of your page, hence using good descriptive titles is very important. Different spiders use different methods to index a site. It will index a portion of the page or it will index the entire page. Numerous keywords should be used on your home page to ensure that people who are looking for your type of company will find you. For example, Lycos uses the first 200 characters in the description, yet indexes the 100 most important words on each page. Infoseek takes the first 250 characters of a site for its description.

For your site to be listed higher in search results, you must do a fair bit of research on ranking criteria and adjust your submission accordingly. WebCrawler, for example, will give your site a higher ranking if the word the user is employing as the keyword of the search (vacation, graphics, boats, whatever) appears many times in the first paragraph or so of the page. Print your home page to get an idea of what may be listed for your site after you submit and your site is indexed. Check to ensure that this is an accurate portrayal of your site.

Because spiders will index pages other than your home page, you should go through this process for your entire site. Remember to have good navigational tools on every page of your site—you never know where your prospective customer is going to enter the site! With a good navigation bar the user can get where they want to go on your site quickly and easily.

## Learn from Competitor Sites

Check out your competition. I use the term competition very loosely— I mean your industry leaders (whether or not you compete directly), people who are selling non-competing products to your target market, as well as your direct competitors. Search their names and see what they are using for descriptions and keywords. Next, search using some of your keywords and see what sites receive top ranking. This research will illustrate why they have received such a high ranking—and you can incorporate what you've learned into your Web site or doorway page for that search engine or directory. What do I mean? No one knows exactly how each search engine works, but by searching for your most important keywords and observing what the top ranking sites are using as far as their page content, title tags, description Meta tags, keywords Meta tags, and so on you can formulate a good plan of attack. Remember that if you don't appear in the first two or three pages of search results, it is unlikely the prospective visitor will access your site through the search engine.

Check to see what your competitors have for Meta tags. Not only can you learn from the sites that catch your eye, you can also learn from your competitors' mistakes. After you have done a thorough job of this market research you will be in a good position to develop a description that is catchy and adequately describes your site.

To check your competition's Meta tags in Microsoft Internet Explorer you simply go to their site then click on "View" from your menu bar and in drop down menu select "Source". This will bring up the source code for that page in whatever your default text browser is. For most people this will be Notepad, as shown in Figure 3.11.

Looking for the same information in Netscape is just as easy. From the menu bar select "View" and then select "Page Source" from the drop down menu. The following image is a simplified version of the header portion of the HTML code on a Web site to demonstrate where you should look for keywords.

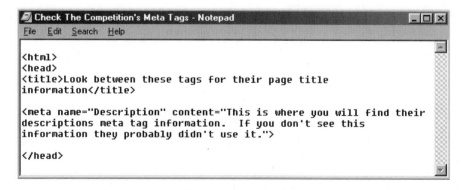

**Figure 3.11.** This is what you should look for in the source code of the site you're viewing.

Another technique you should apply when checking out competing sites is to reverse search the links to their sites. Many search engines now use link popularity in deciding which sites achieve the highest rankings. By looking at who links to your competitors you may be able to get some more links that point towards you, ultimately increasing your site's popularity. If you want to check out who's linking to one of your competitor's sites in AltaVista or Infoseek you simply go to the respective search engine and then enter "*link:competitordomain.com*" in the search field. Web Site Garage and Site Inspector both offer link popularity checking. You can also use one of the many link popularity checkers found on the Web—a couple are mentioned in the resources section of this chapter.

## Marketing Implications of Page Titles

The <TITLE> tag is the first item a search agent reads and many believe that next to site content the title tag is the most important element used in determining your site's relevancy. Make sure every page on your site is titled properly for marketing purposes. D o n ' t just use your company name—use a descriptive title and make sure you include some keywords. Search Engines will retrieve your page, look at your title and then look at the rest of your page for keywords that match those found in the title. As mentioned before, many search engines use title tags in determining your ranking. Among the search engines that use pages titles in their ranking criteria are AltaVista, Excite, Google, HotBot, Infoseek, NorthernLight, WebCrawler, and Yahoo. Pages that have keywords in the title are seen as more relevant than similar pages on the same subject that don't, and may be thus ranked in a higher position by the search engines. However, don't make your title a string of keywords like "cuisine, French cuisine, imported food…" because this will likely be considered spam by the search engines and you will end up worse off in the rankings or removed altogether. Also keep in mind that people will see that title in the search results and they're more likely to click on a site that has a title which flows and is descriptive—not a list.

Keep in mind that when someone bookmarks your site or adds it to their favorites it is the page title that appears as the description. It is important that you keep your page titles under 50 characters in length if possible. Most search engines will not read past 50 characters, therefore you should concentrate on 2 maybe 3 keywords in your title tag.

## Meta Tags

Meta tags are an important part of reaching your search engine goals online. AltaVista, Excite, Inktomi (e.g. Hotbot), Infoseek, Lycos, WebCrawler, NorthernLight, and Google are all examples of search engines that use Meta tags in one form or another. Some search engines use your keyword Meta tag and description Meta tag in determining your ranking in their results. Some search engines also use this information as the source of the description displayed to searchers looking for information. Detailed information on Meta tags can be found in Chapter 2, Web Site Essentials.

As a general rule of thumb, keep your description and keyword Meta tag under 200 characters in length. Some search engines allow for more, such as Infoseek, which allows 1024 characters in their keyword Meta tags. I do not advise you use this many keywords unless you plan on creating a doorway page specifically for that search engine. When you use too many keywords you end up diluting the importance of each keyword, meaning potentially lower rankings in the search engines.

Another rule of thumb is to use lowercase letters when formulating your keyword Meta tag because most search engines are not case sensitive. Only AltaVista and Infoseek are truly case sensitive and most people perform searches using only lowercase letters

It is important not to repeat a keyword more than five times within your keyword Meta tags. Doing so may result in spamming the search engine, which means they'll likely ignore your submission. Not something you want. Another tactic to prevent keyword spamming is to formulate keyword phrases. Instead of using the word "Marketing" over and over again, mix it up by creating phrases like "Internet Marketing, Internet Marketing Consulting, Internet Marketing Research." When you do this be sure to separate the phrases with commas or it will simply look like "Marketing Internet Marketing" —often spam to some of the search engines.

As always with keywords, place the most important words first in your description and keyword Meta tags. This will help you in achieving higher rankings because most search engines consider the first few keywords the most important in their ranking criteria. Also, what if the search engine you're submitting to only looks at the first 30 or so characters? You're ok because you placed the most important keywords first.

## Search Engines' Use of Alt Tags

Some search engines will include information within "alt tags" when ranking of your site. Alt tags appear after an image tag and contain a phrase that is associated with the image. Ensure that your alt tags contain descriptive keywords. This gives your page a better chance of being ranked higher in the search engines' directories. For example:
*<image src="logo.gif" alt="Game Nation - Computer Games Logo">*
You do not want your alt tags to look something like "Game Nation" or "Company Logo" because this does not include any keywords. Be sure you apply proper alt tags to all images on your site to achieve best results. Keep in mind that users who browse with graphics disabled must be able to navigate your site and proper use of alt tags will assist them in doing so.

## Significance of your URL

Where possible apply keywords in your URL. Some search engines give higher rankings to sites that do.
Ensure you own your own domain name. If your site is listed as a subdirectory on your ISP or Web host's domain the search engines will not give you as much creditability. For example, you don't want your site to be *"http://www.yourhostsdomain/companies/ yourcompany.htm"*, you want to be registered under your own domain such as *"www.yourcompany.com"* or *"www.keyword orkeywords.com"*. Google prefers domain names that match the keyword being searched for. Try searching for "mp3" on Google. What are the results? The number one result and likely most of the other top results all include mp3 in their domain name. Try a couple of

other searches as well, maybe "real" for example—I'll bet Real Networks' homepage is the one that comes up first.

Try to use keywords in your sub-pages where possible. For example, if you sell golf clubs then you may want to have a sub-page named "golf-clubs.htm" or "golf_clubs.htm" (it would appear in your URL as http://www.yourdomain/directory/golf_clubs.htm) instead of a generic sub-page named "page1.htm". An important item to remember here is that some of the search engines can't tell two keywords exist if you join the words together in your sub-page like "golfclubs.htm". Be sure you separate the keywords with either an underscore (_) or a dash (-). Using these little tips can go a long way in helping you achieve success among the search engines.

## Site Content Revisited and Other Important Design Factors

To achieve optimum results I recommend you design your site content carefully. You want to apply the most important keywords near the beginning of your page because many search engines weight the content near the start of a site as the most important.

Always have a descriptive paragraph at the top of your Web page. Search engines that do not use Meta tags will use this as their source for a site description and keywords on your site. As well, search engines will use the content found within the opening paragraph in determining the ranking of your site among search results. Again, be sure to use the most important keywords first, preferably within the first 2 to 3 sentences. This is hugely important. Infoseek and AltaVista boost pages that use well-placed keywords near the top of the page content. Make sure that the keywords you use flow naturally within the content of the opening paragraph and relate to content/purpose of your site– you don't want the search engines to think you're trying to cram words in where they don't fit.

Use your HTML <H1>headers</H1> effectively to indicate the subject/content of a particular page. Most people only use them as a method of creating large fonts. Some search engines, including Google, use the content included within the header text in their relevancy scoring.

As you can tell textual HTML content is extremely important to the search engines, which brings me to my next point. Never create a page that is excessive in graphical content. For example, don't display information that should be displayed in text as a graphic file. I've seen this done numerous times. A site may have the best opening statement in the world but the search engines can't use it because the information is presented in the form of a graphic. No matter how great it looks the search engines can't read your graphics for content.

Do not make your homepage excessively lengthy. The longer your page is the less relevant the information on the page becomes to the search engines. I recommend you keep your homepage short and to the point. Of course every technique is not going to work all of the time so you might want to investigate creating doorway pages. AltaVista seems to like pages that are somewhat longer in length.

Little things like how often you update your site can have an affect on how well your site places in search engine results. Spiders can determine how often a page is updated and will revisit your site accordingly. This may lead to higher rankings in some of the major search engines. Remember, you can also resubmit your site manually once you have made changes; however, I don't advise doing so if you already have a high ranking. If the criteria used for ranking a site has changed then you may actually end up worse off.

Before you submit your site, be sure the content on the page you're submitting is completed. Yahoo, for one, will ignore your submission if you have an "under construction" or related sign on your page.

## Internet Resources for Chapter 3

**Search Engine Watch**
*http://www.searchenginewatch.com*
Search Engine Watch is a Web site devoted to how search engines work, search engine news, search engine information, tips on using search engines, and more about search engines. More information than you can stand! Be sure to sign up for the Search Engine Report mailing list.

**Search Engine World**
*http://www.searchengineworld.com*

A great resource for everything surrounding search engines. Plenty of articles, tips, and information to help you achieve online success. This site also has in-depth information on the various search engine spiders.

### PegasoWeb: Web Promotion Portal
*http://www.pegasoweb.com/*
Information on promoting your Web site through search engines, ezines, newsletters, and banner advertising. Tools, resources and services free and fee-based.

### Search Engine Matrix
*http://searchenginematrix.com/*
Learn about search engines and search-engine-positioning to achieve greater positioning within any given search engine.

### Search Engine Forums
*http://searchengineforums.com/bin/Ultimate.cgi*
Information pertaining to search engines and Web site promotion presented in the form of a bulletin board.

### Internet InfoScavenger
*http://www.infoscavenger.com/engine.htm*
Internet InfoScavenger is a monthly newsletter publication devoted to helping busy professionals market their products and services on the Web. Invaluable help, techniques, and tips for top search engine placement.

### WebReference.com
*http://www.webreference.com/content/search*
Search engines and examples, tips, and hints for getting the most out of your search engine, for people who work on the Web.

### Submit It! Search Engine Tips
*http://www.submit-it.com/subopt.htm*
The purpose of this document is to provide you with background information on search engine technology and some Tips on how to get your Web site to appear on the result pages of search engines and directories.

### World of Design—Search Engine Secrets
*http://www.globalserve.net/~iwb/search/*

References to monitor, submit and improve search engine placements and positions.

### Bruce Clay—Search Engine Optimization Tools
*http://www.bruceclay.com/web_rank.htm*
Free search engine optimization, ranking, Web site promotion, keywords advice, and placement material for designers.

### Net Promote
*http://www.netpromote.com/*
Net Promote has Promotion 101, a Web Site Marketing and Promotion Info Center, where you can find all kinds of free articles, resources, tools, and links to help you promote your site. They also offer Web site registration, Web site consultation, press release distribution, site launch, banner advertising, consulting, and more.

### JimTools.com Webmaster's Toolkit Command Center
http://www.jimtools.com/
A number of tools are available on this site that you can use for free. There's information on the search engines, Meta tags, link checker, and a link popularity tool.

### LinkPopularity.com: The Free Link Popularity Service
*http://www.linkpopularity.com/*
A free services that queries AltaVista, Infoseek, and HotBot to check your link popularity.

*Note:* Resources found in the next chapter on search engine submissions are closely related to the information found in this chapter. I recommend reviewing the resources in the next chapter as many contain valuable information on designing your site to be search engine friendly.

# 4

## Search Engine and Directory Submissions

There are an estimated 800 million Web pages on the World Wide Web, so how can you increase your chances of being found? One method is submitting to the many search engines and directories. Once you've optimized your Web site to be search engine friendly, you are ready to face the challenge of submitting to the most important search engines. When I say search engines I'm referring to the combination of search engines and directories. You need to be within the first two pages of search results to ensure your best possible success online. This is no easy feat, and this chapter will provide you with the knowledge necessary to get on the road to success. This chapter covers:

- Search engines, directories, and their ranking criteria

- An in-depth look at Yahoo!'s submission process

- An in-depth look at AltaVista's submission process

- The submission tools available to you

- Search engine and directory submission pointers

## A Closer Look at Search Engines and Directories

The last chapter discussed how search engines and directories differ. In general, search engines have a much larger index and utilize spiders to add sites to their index. In contrast, directories typically have a smaller index and are maintained by humans. When you're submitting to a site, you can usually tell the difference between a directory and a search engine by the information they request. A search engine typically asks for the URL you wish to submit and sometimes your e-mail address. A directory will usually ask for much more, including your URL, the category you wish to be added to, the title of your site, a description, and your contact information.

When you do a search on the Internet, in seconds the search engine has digested what you are looking for, searches the millions of pages it knows about, and responds to your request with appropriate sites ranked in order of importance. Amazing! How do they do it?

Search engines use spiders to index your site. Usually a search engine's spider will index or include the pages on your site once you have submitted the request to be added to their database, but sometimes they can't for a number of reasons. They may have problems with frames on a Web site or image maps, they may simply miss a page, and so on. Even though a number of the spiders out there constantly crawl the Web looking for sites, I suggest you take the proactive approach and submit all appropriate pages on your site to the search engines to guarantee all your important pages are properly listed. Also, before you submit, check the search engine's submission document to be sure submitting more than one page is permitted, because you don't want your site to be rejected. A search engine may also have restrictions on the number of pages you can submit in a single day—perhaps they only allow 5 or 10 to be submitted.

Some of the search engines share technology. For example MSN Search uses Inktomi's technology for some of their results; however, all search engines have different ranking criteria to determine who gets top placement. Some search engines determine how often a keyword appears on the Web page. It is assumed that if a keyword is used more frequently on a page, then that page is more relevant than other pages with a lower usage of that keyword. Some search engines look for the keyword in the title of the Web page and assume that if the keyword is in the title, then that page must be more relevant than those that don't have the keyword in their title. Some search engines determine where keywords are used and assume that pages with key-words in the headings and in the first couple of paragraphs are more relevant. Some search engines use the number of links pointing to a particular page as part of their ranking criteria. Some search engines use information contained in Meta tags; others don't look at the Meta tags at all.

To summarize, search engines all have different ranking criteria, and this is why you receive different results when you search on the same keyword with different engines. For each of the major search engines you should learn as much as you can about their ranking system and adjust your submission or your site's content accordingly. One site that is particularly useful with this information is *http://searchenginewatch.com*.

Some of the more popular search engines are:

- AltaVista (Figure 4.1)

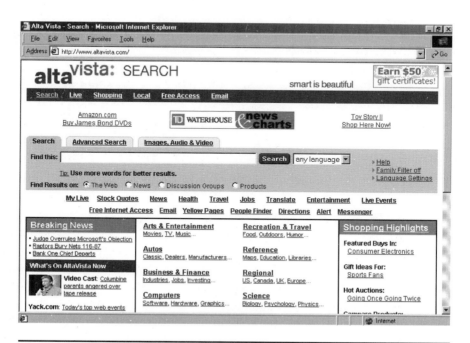

**Figure 4.1.** AltaVista's home page.

- Excite (Figure 4.2)

- Google (Figure 4.3)

- HotBot (Figure 4.4)

- Infoseek/Go (Figure 4.5)

- Lycos (Figure 4.6)

- NorthernLight (Figure 4.7)

- WebCrawler (Figure 4.8)

Let's turn our attention to directories now. Because directories are maintained by human administrators you can expect to wait a longer period of time before seeing your page appear in their index. In general you can expect to wait between two and eight weeks. It

**Figure 4.2.** Excite's home page.

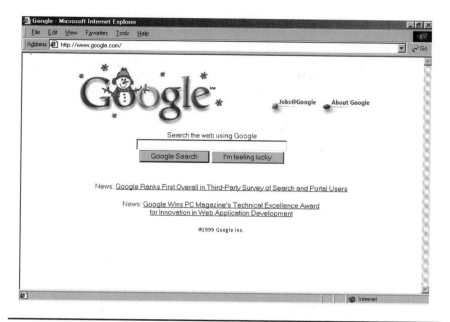

**Figure 4.3.** Google's home page.

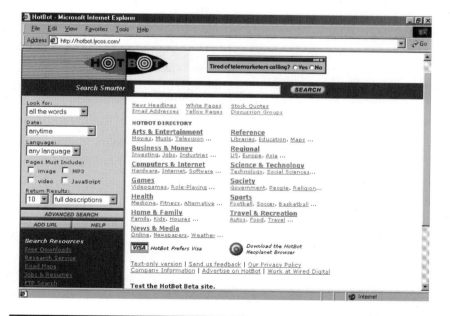

**Figure 4.4.** HotBot's home page.

**Figure 4.5.**   Infoseek/Go's home page.

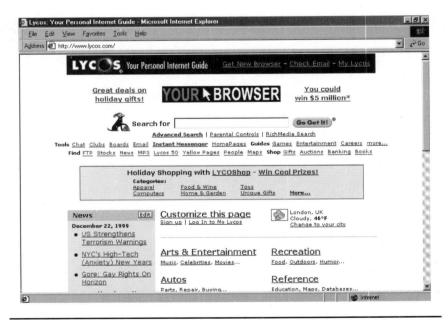

**Figure 4.6.**   Lycos's home page.

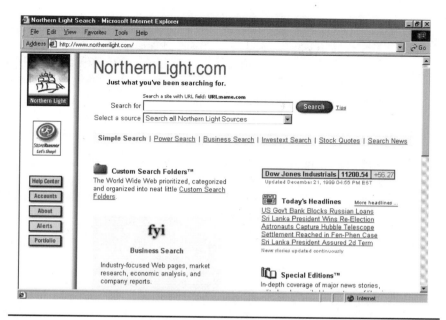

**Figure 4.7.** NorthernLight's home page.

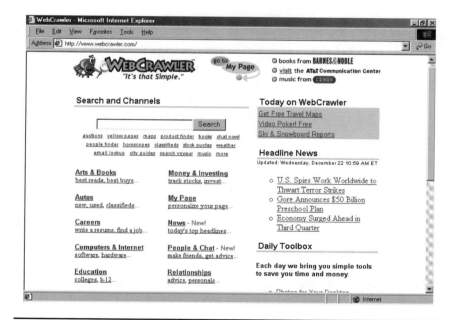

**Figure 4.8.** WebCrawler's home page.

takes longer because the human administrators review every page submitted before adding it to their database. Make sure your page is easy to use, visually appealing, and rich in content, because it is the administrators who decide if your page is worthwhile before they include it.

When you submit to a directory, you will also have to take the time to find the best category for your site. Submitting your site to the wrong category could mean a minimal increase in traffic if no one thinks to look for you in the category you submitted to. Also, your site may not be added if you select an inappropriate category. LookSmart's Travel category contains subcategories including Activities, Destinations, Lodging, Transportation, and so on. These categories are then often broken down further into other categories within the subcategories. The deeper you go, the more specific the category becomes.

Unlike a search engine, your site's position in directories depends much less on Web site design and more on the initial submission process itself, which is why it is important to review each directory's submission procedure and submission tips. You will be asked for a lot more information when submitting to a directory. The title, description, and any other information you give them during submission is what will be used to rank your site.

Here are some of the more popular directories:

- Argus Clearinghouse (Figure 4.9)

- LookSmart (Figure 4.10)

- Open Directory Project (Figure 4.11)

- Snap (Figure 4.12)

- Yahoo! (Figure 4.13)

## Maximizing Exposure with Submission Pointers

Submitting to the search engines and directories is a very time-consuming but extremely important task. Don't rush! Take your time,

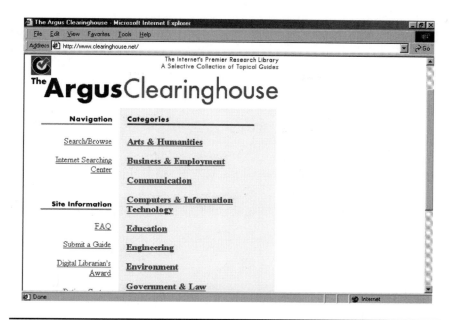

**Figure 4.9.**    Argus Clearinghouse's home page.

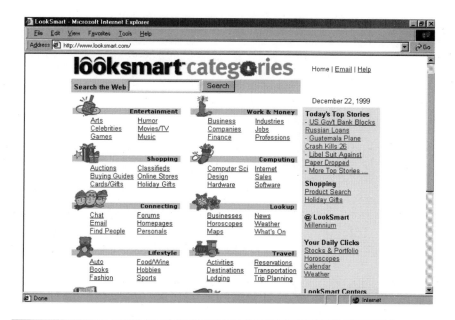

**Figure 4.10.**    LookSmart's home page.

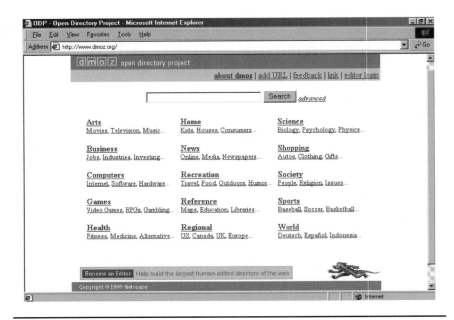

**Figure 4.11.** Open Directory Project's home page.

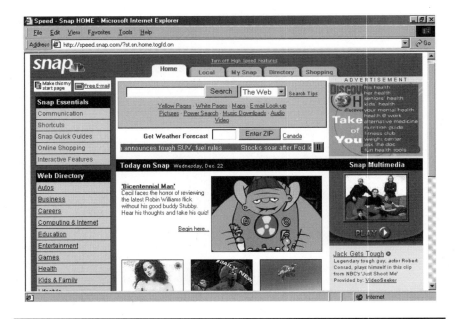

**Figure 4.12.** Snap's home page.

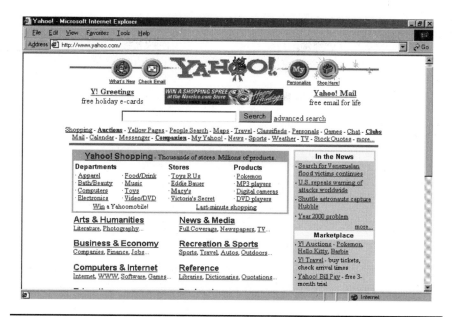

**Figure 4.13.** Yahoo's home page.

do your research, know the ranking strategy employed, and prepare your submission for optimal results. It's very difficult to change your entry once it has been submitted, and the last thing you want is a typo. If the time available for indexing is limited, start by focusing on the most popular search engines and directories for individual submissions, and use a multiple submission site for the less important ones. Remember, 85% of all Internet users use search engines and directories to find what they are looking for.

When submitting to the search engines and directories, take the time up front to develop the submission material carefully. Organize the information in a logical order in a text file. Then when you go to submit you will be able to copy and paste the content to the appropriate fields on the submission form. Be sure to spell check, check, and recheck everything before you start. Spell checkers won't pick up misspelled "works" if that word is also in the dictionary. The information prepared for each page on the site to be indexed should include:

- URL

- Page title

- 10-word, 25-word, 50-word, and 100-word descriptions for the page (different engines allow different lengths of description)

- List of keywords for each page (see "Another Look at Keywords," on page 79 for tips)

- Description of the ideal audience for the site

- Contact information:

  - Company name

  - Contact name

  - E-mail address

  - Company address

  - Telephone and fax numbers

Print the submission forms for the various search engines and directories, and examine them to determine that you have all the information required for submission. Figures 4.14 to 4.17 show some examples of search engine and directory submission pages.

When submitting forms to directories be very careful to fill in every field on the form. Some of the search engines will reject your registration automatically if you have not filled in all the blanks. When you have to choose categories select them very carefully. It would be a shame to have a great product, great price, and a great site, but be listed in a place where your potential customer would never think about looking for you. Read the FAQs or instructions first to ensure that you understand exactly what information they are requesting. Proofread your submission at least twice before you hit the submit button. It isn't quick or easy to change listings if you make a mistake. Your listing may be wrong for quite a while before it gets corrected.

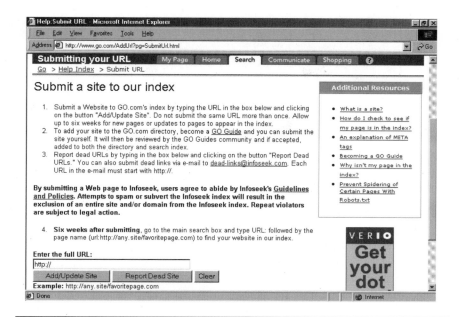

**Figure 4.14.** Go.lcom/Infoseek submission page.

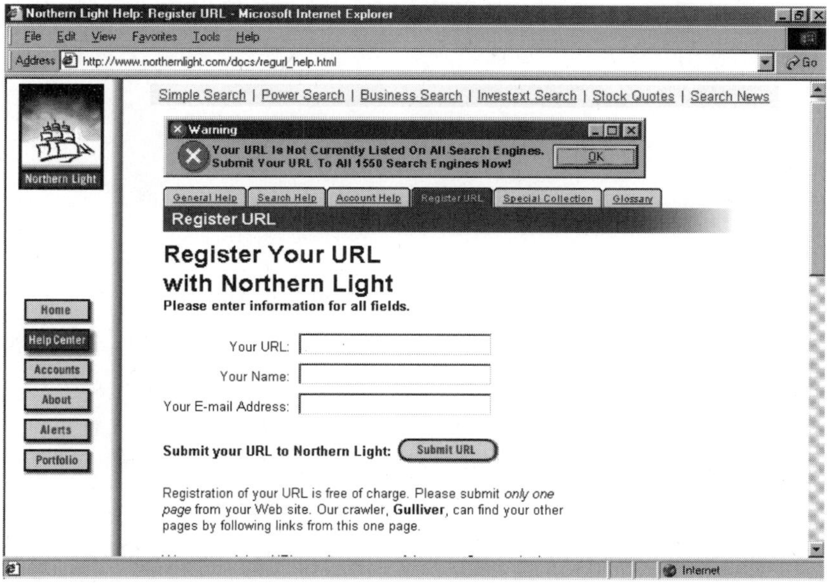

**Figure 4.15.** NorthernLight's submission page.

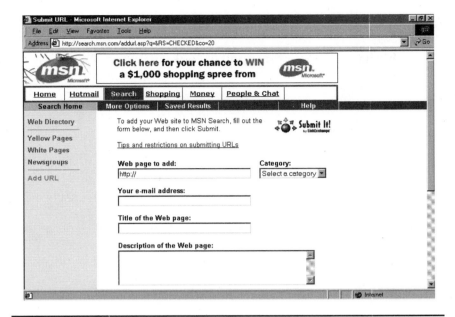

**Figure 4.16.** Submitting to MSN Search.

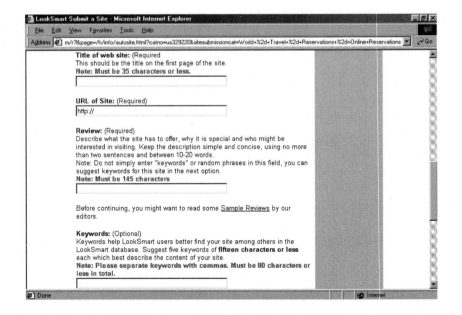

**Figure 4.17.** Submitting to LookSmart.

## Another Look at Keywords

It's important to take another look at keywords. Keywords are the words used by your target customers when they do a search for your types of products and services in the search engines or directories. Your keywords will be used in everything you do and are the key determining factor in how you rank in the search results among many of the major search engines.

As a general rule, you should make sure you use keywords where appropriate. Keywords should be applied in your page titles, headers, Alt tags, keywords Meta tags, description Meta tags, hyperlinks, textual content information, and so on. Another rule of thumb is to apply keywords naturally, so that they flow with the information. For example, a description that is just a list of keywords is likely to get you bumped down in search engine results or removed altogether because some search engines consider this spamming. Last, apply the most important keywords first. Many search engines place greater emphasis on keywords near the beginning of your keywords list, description, and so on.

Be sure to use different keywords and strings of keywords for different pages on your site. Each page is unique, with different content, so by using keywords specific to each page you're increasing your chances of being found by your target audience. If you have the same keywords on every page, you're limiting yourself to the exact same range of keywords.

Review the keywords section in the previous chapter. It discusses how to develop your master keywords list and how to apply it to the appropriate sections of your site. The keywords you want to use are the ones individuals are likely to use when performing a search.

When applying keywords the most important places to remember are:

- Your page title

- Your page content—beginning, middle, and end of your page's text

- Your Meta tags—keywords and description

- Between your <noframes> tag if your site uses frames

- In Alt tags applied to your images

## Great Descriptions Make the Difference

It is a good idea to create a number of different descriptions of varying lengths because the different search engines and directories allow different description sizes. Start off creating a description of 10 words, then 25, then 50, and then 100. Make sure that you use the right length description for each search engine, because you don't want it to be truncated when displayed in search results.

Your description should be compelling. When you get your site to appear in the first 20 to 30 top results of a search, the description is what differentiates your site from the rest. It is the description that will entice the prospective visitor to click and visit—or pass and go to a more exciting site.

Always use keywords in your description. Apply the most important keywords first because keywords used further along in the description are generally given less weight by the major search engines. If possible use keywords in combination with other keywords, but make sure your description flows naturally.

Be sure to use a call to action in your description. It's amazing how many people do what they are told. Perhaps your description could have a line that says "Visit us now and sign up for our free monthly newsletter."

## Get Multiple Listings

One way to get your site listed many times is to submit many times. Because each page on your site is a potential entry point for search engines and each page has a unique URL, you can submit each URL (each page) in the various search engines, directories, and so on. Each page of your site should be indexed to improve your chances of having your site listed in the top 10 search engine results. Because every page on your site is different, each page should have a different title, a different description, and different keywords. In doing this you're increasing your chances of being found by people searching for different criteria and keywords.

It is important to abide by Netiquette. In some search sites the previously discussed practice of submitting multiple times is acceptable and may even be encouraged. In others it is considered abuse and is discouraged. Use your judgment on this one!

## Doorway Pages

Due to the need to be ranked high in search engine results and the enormous competition between sites trying to get listed on search engines, doorway pages have become increasingly more popular. Each search engine is different and has different elements in its ranking criteria. Developing doorway pages allows you to tailor a page specifically for each search engine before submittal to achieve optimal results. Be careful, though, some search engines frown upon doorway pages, so perform a background check before creating and submitting one.

Doorway pages, also known as gateway pages, are pages that lead to your site but are not considered part of your site. Do not include doorway pages on your site's site map! In fact, do not allow any pages within your site to link to the doorway pages you have created. If you do and a search engine spider finds these pages, it will likely consider them spam and you will be removed from their directory or at minimum your current ranking will fall.

Doorway pages are focused pages that lead to your Web site but are tuned to the specific requirements of the search engines. By having different doorway pages with different names (e.g., indexa.html for AltaVista or indexi.html for Infoseek) for each search engine, you can look back and see which page is bringing in the most traffic. Those pages that are not bringing in the traffic can then be edited and resubmitted until you get it right. Make sure that the doorway page you create represents the page it leads to.

The various criteria search engines use in determining their rankings are always changing as the fight for top spot as search engine king (or queen) progresses; however, some general pointers always apply, and they always revolve around keyword use and placement.

Apply keywords or a keyword phrase in your title tag as well as a keyword or keyword phrase in your keywords Meta tag and description Meta tag. Many search engines consider your title tag when ranking sites. If you use a header tag, be sure you apply keywords or a keyword phrase here. Try to keep it a close match with what you use in your keywords Meta tag, descriptions Meta tag, and title tag. Stick with your keywords! Try to use the keywords you used in the preceding steps naturally near the start of the first paragraph on your doorway page. The further down the page the keywords appear, the less emphasis the search engines will place on them. If your doorway page is going to include a graphic or graphics, then be sure to use those ever-important descriptive keywords once more in your Alt tags. This provides users who browse with graphics disabled the ability to understand what graphic you wanted them to see.

Perhaps more important is the fact that a number of the large and popular search engines reference keywords they find in Alt tags when ranking your site. Ensure that you place keywords within your hyperlinks as well. This can also increase search engine rankings! Last, use descriptive keywords throughout the content portion of your doorway page with the most important keywords being applied first. The title and content of your doorway page are the two most important places, so take your time and do it right. For more details on what the major search engines use for ranking criteria, visit the URLs in the resource section of this chapter that relate to search engine feature charts. Also refer to Appendix C.

As one would expect, doorway pages have their drawbacks as well. Doorway pages are often easy to duplicate. Your competition may use your doorway page as a template and tweak/modify it to suit their purposes. If you create a doorway page, be sure not to use a fast Meta refresh tag as discussed in Chapter 3. In addition, if your competition copies and modifies your page to the search engine, it's likely that most of the content will remain very similar. If this is the case the search engine may think you're trying to spam them by submitting duplicate sites and you'll both get removed.

Keywords are the important thing to remember here. When you develop a doorway page, keep the tips that were mentioned earlier in mind. Place the most important keywords and keyword phrases first in your title tag, keyword Meta tags, description Meta tags, opening page paragraph, headers, hyperlinks, and so on.

## A Closer Look At Yahoo!

Yahoo! is the most popular directory among Internet users today. Yahoo! was developed by David Filo and Jerry Yang around April 1994. Today millions of people use Yahoo! every day, and it is definitely a location where you want your site listed.

Yahoo! is not a search engine, it is a directory. Yahoo! has approximately 150 human administrators who review every site submitted. By default Yahoo! displays information contained within its own directory; however, Yahoo! also allows you to perform searches outside its own database by referencing Inktomi's search technology. To view results returned by Inktomi's engine, click on "Web Pages" at the top or bottom of the page once you have performed your search.

Yahoo's directory is broken down into 14 major categories:

- Arts & Humanities

- Business & Economy

- Computers & Internet

- Education

- Entertainment

- Government

- Health

- News & Media

- Recreation & Sports

- Reference

- Regional

- Science

- Social Science

- Society & Culture

Each of Yahoo's 14 major categories are broken down into sub-categories that also contain sub-subcategories. The deeper you go into the categories, the more content specific the directories become. When you are looking for categories appropriate for your site, take your time, because you want to be listed in the best location. If you submit to a category that is not appropriate, the users may not think to look for you there or Yahoo! may not even add your site at all. Check out your competitors and perform some searches using keywords you feel people would use when looking for your products or services. Observe the categories that are displayed. The category or categories you want to be listed in will likely be included in these. Pick the most relevant categories that apply to your page, but keep in mind that when searches are performed the categories are displayed in alphabetical order. Once you find a category you wish to submit to, select "Submit a Site."

Before you go any further, is your site complete? Yahoo! won't add you if you have "Under Construction" signs on your site. Yahoo! likes sites that are complete, contain good and pertinent information, are aesthetically pleasing, and are easy to use. Also, check to see if you're already in their directory. You may not want or need to submit your site if you're where you want to be already. If you are in their directory but want to change the information displayed, then you can fill out a form located at *http://add.yahoo.com/fast/change* that is specifically used for changing information already listed in their directory.

Now that you are ready to submit, take your time to read all of their documentation on submitting. You want to follow their guide to the letter to ensure the best possible chance of being added to their directory. Yahoo! administrators are overwhelmed with submissions and will not take the time to review a site that has not followed their submission directions. Open up your text document where you've saved all of that relevant submission information I mentioned before, it will come in handy here. Fill out their submission form fully and completely. Before proceeding in the submission process, make sure your information is correct and you have made no errors. *You do not want to make mistakes.*

Once you have submitted your information be patient, it takes an average of six to eight weeks for a submission to be reviewed and added to the directory if it's going to be added at all. If you feel you have done everything right, have been waiting for what seems an excessive length of time, and have not been added to their directory, resubmit. If you still aren't added, send a polite e-mail to Yahoo! discussing your situation and request assistance. As a side note, if you're a U.S. commercial company/business then you can pay $199 US for express submission service. This service does not guarantee you'll be listed faster or even that you'll be listed at all, it just means they'll put a priority on reviewing your Web site.

The following are some other tips to remember when submitting your site to Yahoo!:

- Remember, your submission counts for almost everything here, so do it right. Yahoo! is a directory, not a search engine. Designing your site to be "search engine friendly" means very little here.

- Make sure that what you submit is actually what your site is about. Yahoo!'s administrators will review your site, and if they feel the description you provided does not match up with your site, you will not be added to their directory.

- Keep your description to 25 words or less and use descriptive keywords that flow naturally within the description. Yahoo! reserves the right to modify your description if they see fit. You're the only one who knows what information is important to have included in your description, so you probably do not want Yahoo!'s administrators to modify your description, because you may lose an important part of your description, resulting in less traffic. Also remember that Yahoo! does not like submissions that sound like an advertisement—they like concise, pertinent information.

- Submit a short, relevant title, not something like "The Best Gardening Site on the Web." Also, be sure to use descriptive keywords in your title as well. When searches are performed, your page title will be referenced. In addition, when search results are displayed, they are displayed in alphabetical order. If possible, try to generate a title that starts with a letter near the beginning of the alphabet. If the title you submit is not appropriate, Yahoo! may consider your submission spam and your page will be rejected. For example, don't title your site "AAA Gardening Supplies" if that's not the name of your site just to appear near the top of the rankings. Like the description, make sure your title flows naturally.

- When submitting, develop your page title and descriptions to try to use keywords in combination with others as this can also give you a boost. Check out your competitors to see who's on the top and what they're doing right.

- If you're looking for local traffic, then submitting to a regional category may be appropriate for you.

- Don't fill out the submission form using all CAPITALS—they hate that. Use proper grammar and spelling. Before you submit be sure to check and recheck your submission to be sure all is well.

- If your domain name contains keywords, you will benefit here. Keywords in your domain name can help you out when a user performs a search on a keyword that is in your domain name.

- Don't forget to fill out Yahoo!'s submission form exactly as requested! Read their help documentation and FAQs, beginning with "How to Suggest Your Site," (see Figure 4.18) which can be found at *http://docs.yahoo.com/info/suggest.*

## A Closer Look at AltaVista

Originally launched near the end of 1995, AltaVista is the second most popular search tool after Yahoo! and claims to have the largest index of catalogued Web pages at 250 million. AltaVista is a true search engine whose spider, Scooter, indexes Web pages. Scooter is a "deep search" spider, meaning it will visit all pages on your Web site as long as it is given the opportunity to. A fast Meta refresh or a dynamic page developed using CGI can cause problems for Scooter. I

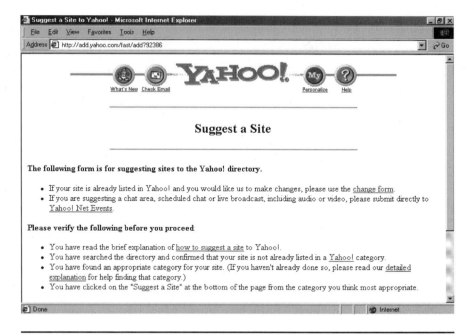

**Figure 4.18.** Submitting to Yahoo!

recommend reading Chapter 3, the search engine friendliness chapter, for more information, because it discusses Web site design and its effects on how your site is indexed by the major search engines. AltaVista also uses the DMOZ open directory project for some of its results, so be sure to submit your site to the open directory project at *http://www.dmoz.org/*.

Before you submit, make sure your page is complete. AltaVista wants quality pages and does not like to index pages that are incomplete or inappropriate. Every search engine wants quality sites indexed, because if they list a lot of "junk" then users will stop returning.

Submitting to AltaVista (see Figure 4.19) is a simple process. All you have to do is click on "Add a URL" from their home page. This will take you to their submission page, where you enter your URL into the designated field. That's it, you're done—the rest relies on your site design.

It typically takes 24 to 48 hours before your site is added to AltaVista's index. Scooter will then periodically revisit your site look-

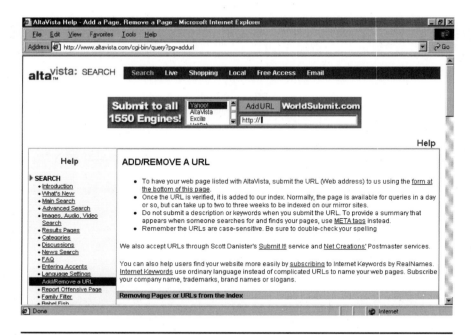

**Figure 4.19.** Submitting to AltaVista.

ing to add new and updated pages. If you feel you have done everything right but are not showing up in their index, then send them a polite e-mail asking if there's a problem and if anything can be done. It could be that your site is not optimized for AltaVista and that is why you're not appearing in the results.

AltaVista uses Meta tags. It will use your description Meta tag to formulate a description of your site, which is then presented to the user when they perform a search. In addition, AltaVista uses your keywords Meta tag and your description Meta tag as factors in determining your site's ranking among its results. Keywords applied in your title are also a factor that affect your page's position. If you do not have a description Meta tag, AltaVista will reference your site's content and formulate its own description based on this. If you do not have a title tag, AltaVista will display "No Title" in the search results, if you're ranked at all. Here are some tips to improve your ranking in Alta Vista:

- Your ranking on AltaVista is determined by your site's design, so be sure to make it easily accessible for AltaVista's spider, Scooter.

- Use keywords in your title, Meta tags, Alt tags, and page content. Make sure the most important keywords are used first because more weight is given to the keywords that appear first. Also, try to use keywords in combination with other keywords because this can boost your ranking.

- AltaVista is a case-sensitive search engine. For any of your keywords that are usually uppercase you may want to include both the upper- and lowercase version of the word in your keyword Meta tag.

- Link popularity can influence your position. If possible, increase the number of links pointing towards your site.

- Search Engine World *(http://www.searchengineworld.com/)* mentions that older pages tend to perform better in AltaVista's rankings, as do pages with a lot of content.

- Do not spam AltaVista, or your ranking will quickly drop or your site may be removed altogether. For example, AltaVista does not like multiple doorways or pages that repeat the same keyword over and over again (e.g., Gardening, Gardening, Gardening Supplies, Gardening, Gardening).

## Effective Use of Submission Tools and Services

There are many multiple search engine submission services available on the Net that will submit your site to varying numbers of indexes, directories, and search engines. They will register your URL, description, and keywords. Check them to see how comprehensive they are before using these services. Here are a couple of sites for you to look at:

**The Postmaster**
*http://www.netcreations.com/postmaster*

This is one of the best URL submission services on the Web.

### Add-Me
*http://www.addme.com*
This site allows you to submit your page to 34 popular sites for free, using one form.

### Submit It!
*http://www.submit-it.com/*
Submit-It! (see Figure 4.20) is one of the oldest and most respected submission services.

### Add Me Too
*http://www.addmetoo.com/*
Add Me Too is a free Web site promotion and search engine submittal service.

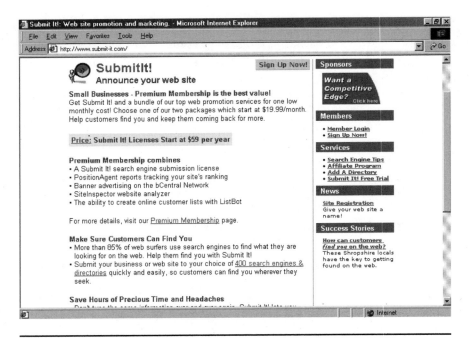

**Figure 4.20.**   You can use Submit It! to submit your page to 400 search engines and directories.

Although these services save a lot of time, it is essential that you be registered accurately in search engines and directories. For the best results, register individually in as many of the top search engines as you can before you resort to multiple submission sites. There aren't that many search engines or directories that have long submission forms, so submit manually to ensure the best results. If you have taken the time to do the work described earlier, submit to the major engines yourself. This way you can take full advantage of the legwork you have done targeting the differences between the engines.

To summarize, each search engine is different. Know the unique qualities of each before you submit, and be sure to check out Appendix C of this book, where details are provided on many of the popular search engines and directories.

## Complete Your Site Before You Submit

Before you submit to any of the search engines and directories, take the time to complete your site. Many of the major search engines and directories are not fond of receiving submissions from people who have pages that are not yet complete. You do not want to spend your time submitting your page only to find out it has not been added because it is "under construction." Also, be sure to validate your HTML before submitting. You want your site to be free of errors to ensure your success with submissions. A few of tools you can use to validate your HTML are:

**Web Site Garage**
*http://websitegarage.netscape.com/*

**SiteInspector**
*http://www.siteinspector.com/*

**W3C HTML Validation Service**
*http://validator.w3.org/*

**NetMechanic**
*http://www.netmechanic.com/index.htm*

**Dr. Watson, v4.0**
*http://watson.addy.com/*

## Is Your Page Already Indexed?

Before you submit or resubmit to a search engine, check to see if your page is already indexed. Perform a search using the most important keywords you think people will use to find your page. Also, perform a search using your company name. If your page is found and you're happy with the results, you will not need to submit or resubmit. In fact, if you do resubmit you could end up worse off because you never know when a search engine is going to change its method of determining what pages receive a high ranking. If you are not listed or not happy with your listing, you can submit your page. If need be, you can edit your page and then resubmit to achieve a higher position. To see if your URL is indexed by AltaVista and Infoseek/Go, enter *url:yourdomain.com/directory/page.html* in the search field of each search engine. Check out the help files for each search engine for more information on how to verify that your URL is included in their index.

## Check Out Your Competition

Using the techniques just mentioned, you can check out your competitors' rankings as well. By looking at the top results you can see what they're doing right to achieve those top placements and learn from them to help you develop a successful submission strategy. You should look at your competition's keywords Meta tag, descriptions Meta tag, page content, page titles, and so on. They may have great keywords you missed. You might want to consider printing off some of their pages or information so that you can use it for reference later. Do not copy their information—you just want to use their information for guidance and reference about what has given their site the high ranking. The top results for your keywords and your competitors can also be analyzed for link popularity, which you can then research to find appropriate links you may able to use to increase your link popularity. This is discussed in the next section.

## The Link Popularity Issue

Now that you know who is appearing at the top of the search results, check out the number of links pointing toward their site. Techniques for this are found in Chapter 10. Link popularity is becoming more and more important among the major search engines, including AltaVista. Google is another example of a search engine that uses link popularity in determining a page's position in its rankings. Perform a search using your most important keywords on Google to see who is appearing at the top of the results. Chances are the sites near the top contain the most incoming links. Look at the links leading to your competitors because they're likely appropriate links for you as well. If so, ask for a link, ask for a reciprocal link, or add yourself to their links if possible to build up your link popularity. This is a time-consuming task, but it will benefit you in the end. Keep in mind that link popularity is good, but link popularity from quality sites is better. Details on finding appropriate link sites, requesting links, and having your link stand out are all covered in Chapter 10.

## Alternative Methods of Promotion

Some search engines, such as GoTo.com (*http://www.goto.com/*, see Figure 4.21), allow bidding for certain keywords. The higher you bid for the keyword or term, the higher your ranking on the search engine will be when someone searches for that keyword. On GoTo, if no one visits your site you are not charged; however, if someone does visit your site you are charged on a per-click-through basis. As you can imagine this can be a costly process to increase your site's traffic, but it's an option you may want to look at. Visit GoTo's site for more information.

Another way of having your site displayed at the top of the search results is to purchase keywords from the search engines and directo-

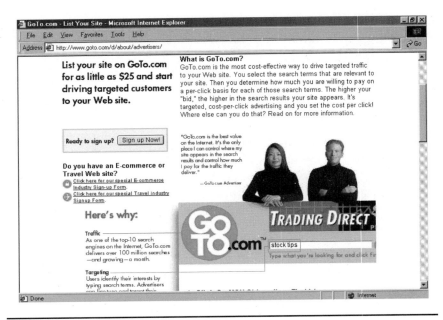

**Figure 4.21.** On GoTo.com you can bid on keywords.

ries. AltaVista (Figure 4.22), Excite (Figure 4.23), and Snap (Figure 4.24) are all examples of search tools that offer this service. When you purchase a keyword or keywords your site will usually be displayed above the search results in the form of a banner advertisement or a "select" link above the other links. A common cost for this service is $85 US CPM (cost per thousand).

## Move to the Top of Search Engine Rankings with RealNames

The RealNames Corporation (*http://www.realnames.com*, see Figure 4.25) provides individuals, small businesses, and corporations with the opportunity to skirt the search engine mind games and instantly achieve top rankings using Internet keywords. In exchange for an annual fee, you can register an Internet keyword that is relevant to your online business from RealNames. Relevant keywords would

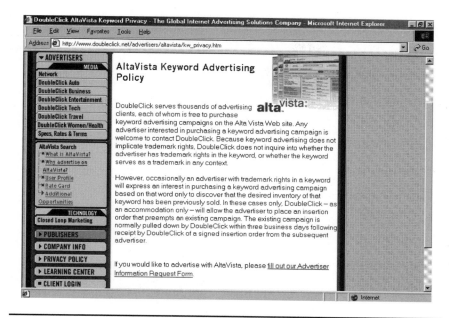

**Figure 4.22.**   You can purchase keywords on AltaVista.

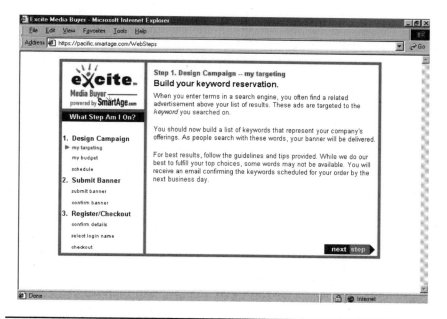

**Figure 4.23.**   Excite also offers targeted keyword advertising.

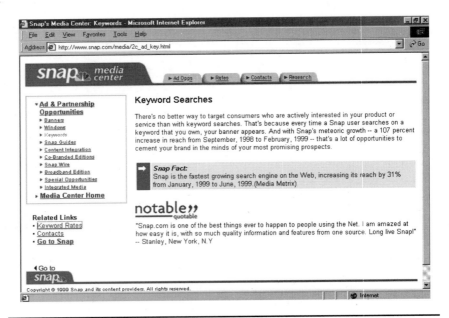

**Figure 4.24.** You can purchase keyword advertising from Snap.

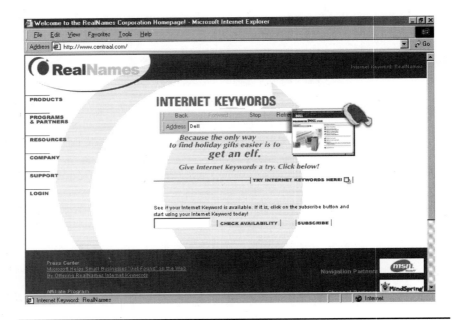

**Figure 4.25.** RealNames issues Internet keywords to deserving registrants.

include your company name, product names, brand names, or slogans.

The objective of RealNames' Internet keywords is to have the most deserving company's Web site appear at the top of the search engine rankings when a user searches on that company's keyword. For instance, if you search for "Microsoft" in AltaVista, the RealNames' result for "Microsoft" is listed above the rest of the search results (Figure 4.26). Clicking on the RealNames link takes you directly to the Microsoft *(http://www.microsoft.com)* home page.

Obviously, Microsoft will have little trouble being found in the search engines anyway, but having a RealNames Internet keyword helps people find them more easily. However, what if your organization is the San Jose Sharks hockey team *(http://www.sj-sharks.com)*? Just imagine how many fan sites and sports news sites the San Jose Sharks would be competing with for high search engine placement. RealNames is a perfect solution for them. Instead of having to guess their domain name or wade through dozens of search results, a user

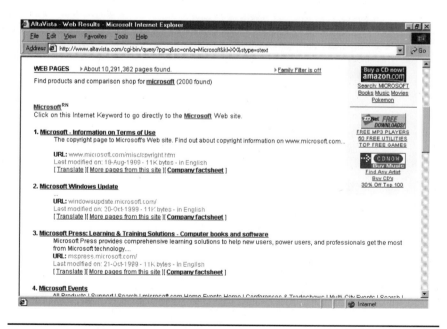

**Figure 4.26.** You can get a RealName for your online business just as Microsoft did.

can simply type *San Jose Sharks* into a search engine like AltaVista. The RealNames result is prominently displayed above the other search results (Figure 4.27), and the user can go directly to the San Jose Sharks' Web site (Figure 4.28).

By registering an Internet keyword with RealNames Corporation, you can generate more traffic to your Web site. As long as you maintain the registration for these keywords, you can have them forever. Keywords are also easier to remember and easier to type than a regular URL.

Individuals and small businesses can register a RealNames Internet keyword for $100 US per year. In exchange, RealNames will issue (pending approval) you a keyword within 72 hours and provide your site with up to 30,000 keyword-driven hits annually. RealNames will also provide you with keyword statistics and traffic reports.

Corporations must contact RealNames for subscription rates because RealNames customizes its services for larger business entities.

**Figure 4.27.**   RealNames makes it easier for users to find a Web site among the clutter of search engine results.

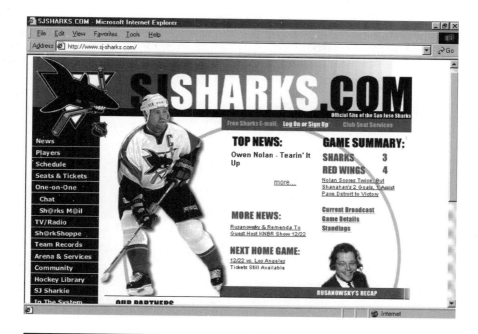

**Figure 4.28.** The official San Jose Sharks Web site is found easily because of their RealName Internet keyword.

RealNames will provide corporations with advanced keyword traffic analysis, marketing statistics, special RealNames promotions, and account management services. Typically, the subscription rate for corporations is determined by a performance-based pricing scheme related to the number of visitors or sales the RealNames keyword generates.

Of course, the scope of the RealNames Internet keyword system is limited by the number of major search engines that support it. Currently, only sites such as AltaVista, LookSmart, GO Network, and MSN Search support the RealNames protocol. Therefore, users of other major search engines like Excite or Lycos will not see RealNames' results. Figure 4.29 shows some of RealNames' distribution partners.

RealNames also has its own criteria and regulations for granting Internet keywords. They prefer that you use keywords that are specific to your company. If you do this, you are guaranteed the

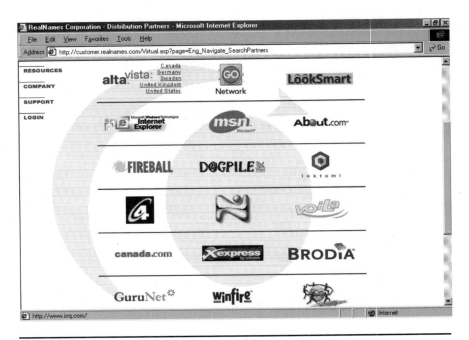

**Figure 4.29.** Some of RealNames' Navigation Partners.

keyword(s). However, what if you want a keyword such as "Cooking"? "Cooking" is a general search keyword. Therefore, no single company, individual, or organization can have exclusive rights to it. However, RealNames will display a list of all Web sites with RealNames closely related to a common search term. Figure 4.30 shows the first page of RealNames' results for "Cooking." There are pages of other sites listed under "Cooking," but some of these sites will earn a few more hits because their registered keyword is closely related to "Cooking."

RealNames is very selective about the Internet keywords they issue and to whom the keywords are issued. To maintain the value of the RealNames directory, RealNames can deny the issuance of a keyword if it suspects any of the following conditions exist:

- Cybersquatting—This is a common problem with domain name registration. People will speculatively purchase a domain name (or keyword in the case of RealNames) in hopes

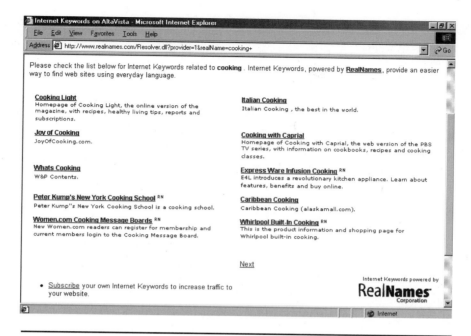

**Figure 4.30.** These sites share a common RealName.

that they can sell it at a considerable price to a more deserving company later.

- Use of others' intellectual property—RealNames will deny anyone but the rightful owner from buying the name of an actual company, brand name, or slogan as an Internet keyword (e.g., you could not register "McDonald's" or "Ford" as a RealName keyword unless you were a representative from either one of these respective companies).

- Misdirection—This situation arises when a commonly known word or phrase is misrepresented and leads visitors to a site containing content that is other than what was expected.

RealNames represents a new use for search engines and allows you to reinforce your company and brand identity. If there are keywords specific to your online business, strongly consider registering one, some, or all of these keywords with RealNames Corporation for increased exposure.

## Don't Spam the Search Engines

If you want to achieve high rankings, then you should avoid spamming the search engines. A common name given to spamming the search engines is Spamdexing. People often use these techniques to try and "cheat" their way to the top of the search engine rankings. What is considered spam (see Figure 4.31)?

- Keyword stuffing, which is repeating the same keyword or keywords over and over again hidden in your HTML and Meta tags.

- Repeating keywords over and over again by displaying them at the bottom of your document after a number of line breaks.

- Submitting multiple pages from the same domain during the same time frame is considered spamming by some search engines, so be sure to do your research and check how many submissions per day from a single domain they allow. Some search engines only want you to submit your home page and allow their spider to do the rest; others say it's okay to submit as much as you want.

> ⓘ Sometimes sites submit a large number of pages to AltaVista hoping to have them show up often on our result pages. They submit pages with numerous keywords, or with keywords that are unrelated to the content of the pages. Some other people submit pages that present our spider with content that differs from what users will see. **We strongly discourage these practices.**
>
> Attempts to fill AltaVista's index with misleading or promotional pages lower the value of the index for everyone and render Web indices and your search experience worthless. **We do not allow URL submissions from customers who spam the index and will exclude all such pages from the index.**

**Figure 4.31.** AltaVista, like many other search engines, frowns upon spamming.

- Submitting identical pages but using different page names will also get you removed if it is discovered.

- Hiding keywords, often called tiny text, is also considered spamming. This is when you place keywords on your page by displaying them in your document using a very small font.

- Repeating keywords in your document by making the text color the same as the background color is considered spam.

- Making frequent and regular title changes so that the bots think your site is a new site and they list you again and again.

- Using page redirects or a Meta refresh can result in your site being eliminated from a search engine's index.

- Using keywords that cannot be found on your page or are unrelated to your page.

- Altering the name of your site to have a space, exclamation mark (!), or A as the first character so that your site is displayed first in alphabetical lists.

## Keep a Record

Keep a record of the directories and search engines to which you have submitted. The information recorded should include the following:

1. Date of the submission

2. URL of the page submitted

3. Name of the search engine or directory

4. Description used

5. Keywords used

6. Password used

7. Notes section for any other relevant information

8. Date listed

## Some Final Pointers

Here are some important final pointers you should keep in mind. Always, always, always read the submission guidelines before submitting. Search engine and directories will also often provide a number of valuable tips that can help you to achieve better rankings.

Periodically review your rankings in the major search engines and directories. To make this manageable, I suggest you make a list of the search engines and directories to which you have submitted. Divide your list into four groups. Every week check your ranking with each of the search engines and directories in one group. If you have dropped in the ranking or don't appear in the first couple of pages of search results, then you want to resubmit to that particular search engine or directory. The next week you check your ranking with the next group. By doing so you can set a regular schedule for yourself, keep organized, and determine which search engines and directories you need to resubmit to and which you do not. Sometimes your site may be removed from an index because the search engine has flushed **its** directory, or maybe it is just one of those things no one can explain—either way you will be on top of things. If you make any significant changes to your site, you may also want to resubmit. You want to ensure your content is fresh.

You may also want to consider submitting to country-specific search engines and directories. Country specific search engines and directories will often give the user the option of searching for sites from a specific country, which may benefit you if you are only looking for an audience in your country. A couple of examples are Canada.com (*http://www.canada.com/*, Figure 4.32) and Yahoo! Sweden (*http://se.yahoo.com*, Figure 4.33).

**Figure 4.32.** Canada.com is a search engine that targets a Canadian audience.

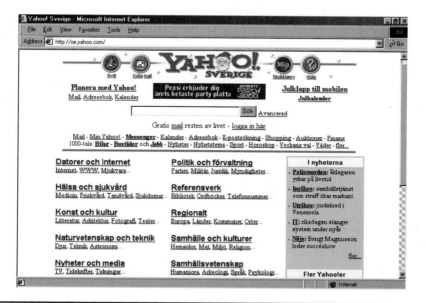

**Figure 4.33.** Sweden's Yahoo! directory.

## Internet Resources

### Web Position Analyzer
*http://www.webposition.com*
Software that tells you where your site is positioned in search results of the 10 most popular search engines. Builds traffic by tracking your search engine positions and helping you improve your rankings.

### Position-It
*http://www.position-it.com*
How to use Internet search engines and directories to skyrocket your Web site traffic using search engine secrets for top positioning.

### Position Agent
*http://www.positionagent.com*
This is a great utility that will automatically check your ranking on 10 top search engines for free.

### Promotion World
*http://www.promotionworld.com/*
Lots of information surrounding online promotion with some good information on search engine submission and preparing your site to be submitted to the search engines. This site also contains some tools you can use to generate Meta tags and check your position on search engines, and a free search engine submission service.

### Search Engine Showdown
*http://www.notess.com/search/*
Detailed analysis of Internet search engines, their features, databases, and strategies.

### Search Engine Tutorial for Web Designers
*http://www.northernwebs.com/set/*
Lots of valuable information on Web site design, search engine ranking methods, and policies.

### The Web Developer's Journal
*http://www.webdevelopersjournal.com/articles/search_engines.html*

A good article on maximizing search engine positioning.

**Browser News**
*http://www.upsdell.com/BrowserNews/stat_search.htm*
A weekly Web-based newsletter that provides a variety of browser news and search engine statistics.

**Promotion 101—Web Site Marketing and Promotion Info Center**
*http://www.promotion101.com/*
A good resource with a search engine placement guide, free tools, and promotion articles.

**CNET features—digital life—how do search engines work?**
*http://coverage.cnet.com/Content/Features/Dlife/Search/ss03.html*
An article about how search engines operate.

## Search Engine Search Features and Submission Charts

**Search Engine Chart**
*http://www.advance-training.co.uk/free/chart.htm*

**Search Engine Features for Webmasters**
*http://www.searchenginewatch.com/webmasters/features.html*

**Search Engine Display Chart**
*http://www.searchenginewatch.com/webmasters/display.html*

**Search Engine Features for Searchers**
*http://www.searchenginewatch.com/facts/ataglance.html*

**Search Engine Comparison Chart**
*http://www.kcpl.lib.mo.us/search/chart.htm*

**Search Engine Feature Chart**
*http://home.sprintmail.com/~debflanagan/chart.html*

**Comparison of Search Capabilities of Six Major Search Engines**
*http://www.cyward.com/chart1.htm*

### Submission Tools

**World Submit**
*http://www.worldsubmit.com/*
World Submit will submit your Web site to 1550 of the World's search engine directories including Yahoo!, what's new sites, and award sites in 90 categories.

**SubmitPlus**
*http://submitplus.bc.ca/*
SubmitPlus (shown in Figure 4.34) helps you promote your Web site with two very effective Web site announcement programs. They offer free and pay services. Before you register your site make sure you check out their "Free Promotion Tools" section for invaluable tips on how to make your Web site ready for the Internet!

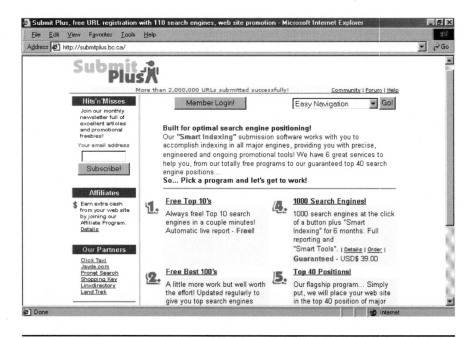

**Figure 4.34.** Submit Plus offers free URL submission with 110 search engines.

## The Broadcaster
*http://www.broadcaster.co.uk/*
Broadcaster search engine submission and announcement services covers all aspects of Web site marketing, promotion, and search engine secrets.

## MetaCrawlers Top Searches List
*http://www.metaspy.com*
Ever wonder what the rest of the world is searching for? Catch a glimpse of some of the searches being performed on MetaCrawler at this very moment (Figure 4.35)!

## WebStepTop 100
*http://www.mmgco.com/4-star.html*

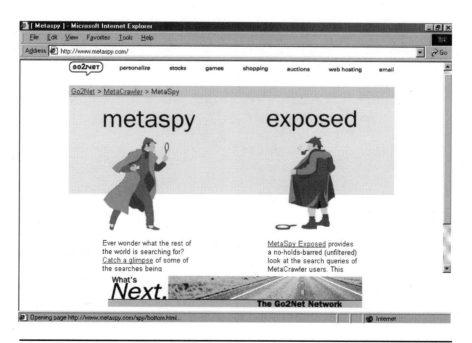

**Figure 4.35.** You can use Metaspy to see what searches are being performed on MetaCrawler at this very moment.

This isn't a standard "link" site, it's much better than that. A listing of hundreds of search engines.

### SiteOwner.com
*http://www.siteowner.com/*
Tools to help individuals submit their site to search engines, develop Meta tags, locate dead links, and so on.

### AAA Internet Promotions
*http://www.web-ignite.com*
One of the first professional Web site promotion services on the Internet, and certainly the most reputable. AAA Internet Promotions manually submits your Web site to search engines and directories. AAA also offers a Partner Program for Web masters and Web site owners. Over 10,000 clients are served, including Price Waterhouse, AT&T, Sony Music, and Warner Brothers.

### Web Themes Internet Consultants
*http://www.webthemes.com*
One of the most active submission and promotion services on the Net. They take a very active role in generating traffic to your site. Web Themes Advertising, Marketing and Promotion and Design, home of The Web Hitman has been promoting new businesses on the Web since 1995. They have experience and the resources to promote your Internet Web site using a variety of tools to accomplish the task. Their Web page promotion services start with your standard professional submission services and extend to extensive programs for increasing traffic on a daily basis.

### Wilson Internet Services
*http://www.wilsonweb.com/webmarket/*
Dr. Wilson's Web Marketing Info Center is a "must visit" site. You'll find links to hundreds of online articles about effective Web marketing and resources for search engine and directory submission. From its beginning in August 1995, this site has become one of the most comprehensive Web marketing sites of its kind. It is a fantastic resource.

### Jayde Online Directory
*http://www.jayde.com/*

The Jayde Online Directory offers a list of places to promote your site organized by type of directory. In addition, be sure to submit your site to the big site database maintained by Jayde.

### Submit-It!
*http://www.submit-it.com*
A very popular Web site promotion tool. You can use Submit It! to register your URL with hundreds of search engines and directories.

### Business@merica
*http://web.idirect.com/~tormall/links.html*
A long list of 2000 places to submit your site. With their Submission King, they will submit your URL to 900 search catalogs and directories for only 4 cents each. You get a full report on all those that post your info. Their list includes the top 100 catalogs such as AltaVista, Lycos, WebCrawler, Infoseek, Yahoo!, and hundreds of others worldwide.

### SOFTSEEK.COM—Search Engine Submission Tools
*http://www.softseek.com/Internet/Web_Publishing_Tools/*
*Search_Engine_Submission_Tools/*
A directory of freeware and shareware search engine submission tools.

### AddMySite.com
*http://www.addmysite.com/*
A free Web site search engine submission service.

### Traffic Boost
*http://www.inetexchange.com/unfair.htm*
The "Unfair Advantage" submission service. Instantly submits your Web site to 500 Internet search engines and directories.

### Net Submitter Pro
*http://www.promotion-expert.com/*
Net Submitter Pro will guide you through the correct ways to prepare your Web page information prior to submission and can submit that information to 500 search engines.

### QuikLaunch Web Site Announcer
*http://www.quiklaunch.com/*

A quick free way to get listed and launched in a number of popular search engines.

### A1 Web Site Promotions
*http://www.a1co.com//freeindex.html*
Over 800 free WWW URL submission and search sites that will take your announcement.

### SubmitWolf Pro
*http://www.msw.com.au/swolf*
With a database of over 2500 sites to promote your URL and hundreds of fully automated submission scripts, SubmitWolf can dramatically increase your site traffic. SubmitWolf is loaded with features. It provides detailed submission reports, and it can generate Meta tags to help search engines correctly index your site. It even enables you to add your own engines.

### Dynamic Submission 2000 Version 4
*http://www.submission2000.com/index1.html*
This software program is a five-star award-winning Web site promotion tool. It will submit your Web site (or URL) to over 800 search engines with just a few button clicks. Enter your Web site details and press a button. This program will automatically submit to hundreds of major search engines within minutes.

### TotalHost Global Submissions
*http://www.totalhost.com/*
Submit your Web site to over 1000 search engines, media outlets, registries, and directories.

*Note:* If you haven't already done so, be sure to review the resources for Chapter 3. The information contained in Chapters 3 and 4 is closely correlated, and their resources tie in well together.

# 5

# Effective Promotional Use of Newsgroups

It is estimated that over 10 million people read newsgroups, making newsgroups an ideal marketing vehicle. The number of newsgroups is always increasing, with over 100,000 different topics now estimated. Using proper netiquette is important. To do this read the FAQ files and rules, "lurk" first, and stay on topic. In this chapter we cover:

- The benefits of using newsgroups in your marketing plan

- Newsgroup Netiquette

- Reading the FAQ files, abiding by the rules, and lurking

- How to advertise if advertising is not allowed

- Developing your Usenet marketing strategy

- Identifying your target newsgroups

- Participating in this online community

- How to respond correctly to messages

- How to start your own newsgroup

- Cross posting and spamming

- Using signature files

## Newsgroups—An Ideal Marketing Vehicle

**News-group**
A discussion group on the Internet that focuses on a specific subject

It is estimated that over 10 million people read **newsgroups.** Usenet newsgroups are hierarchical and are arranged by subject. Each newsgroup is dedicated to a discussion of a particular topic, such as antique cars, home schooling, artificial intelligence, or The Spice Girls. Usenet has been defined as follows:

*Usenet is the Internet's public forum, comprising thousands of newsgroups, each of which is devoted to the public discussion of a narrow, chartered topic such as microbrews, baseball cards, arthritis research, or traveling in Africa.*

Usenet facilitates the exchange of an abundance of information on every topic imaginable. Many newsgroups are tight-knit communities with very loyal residents. Each group's readers are interested in the newsgroup topic, so when you find a newsgroup related to your product or service, it is likely you have found members of your target market.

The number of newsgroups is steadily increasing. Currently it is estimated that there are more than 100,000 topics available. Different newsgroups have varying numbers of readers. Some are read by hundreds of thousands of readers a day, and others see very little traffic. The newsgroups you decide to participate in may be read by a relatively small number of people or have a large number of participants. Large isn't always better. A smaller group may provide you with a better chance of having your message read by your ideal target market. A larger group will provide you with better exposure by sheer volume.

Whether you pick a large group or a small group depends on your objectives and also on your product or service. For example, even though a posting to *alt.politics* may be seen by 300,000 readers, if what you are trying to sell is reproduction Model T Fords, it will not likely generate more potential business than a posting to a Usenet group such as *rec.antiquecars.misc* with only 1000 readers. Not to mention that if your posting to *alt.politics* is inappropriate for that group, you will have done more harm than good. Newsgroup readers do not appreciate messages unrelated to their topic posted to their newsgroup, especially if these are advertisements.

If you use an online service, you can still participate in newsgroups because they have similar services. CompuServe has forums or special interest groups, AOL has forums and clubs, and Prodigy has forums and bulletin boards. The same rules regarding participation, acceptable messages, and marketing activities generally apply. Not only are newsgroups helpful marketing tools, they can also help you identify competitors and trends in your industry, find valuable information from experts in your field, and perform market research activities.

## The Benefits of Newsgroups

There are many ways online marketers can benefit from participating in newsgroups:

- **Reaching prospective customers.** You can immediately reach thousands of your targeted potential customers with a single message.

- **Communicating with existing customers.** You can provide your loyal customers with valuable information.

- **Market research.** You can use newsgroups to find out the latest trends, customer needs, what people are looking for, and what they are talking about.

- **Reputation building.** By answering people's questions and helping to solve their problems you will build your reputation as an expert in the field.

- **Increased Traffic.** You can direct people to your commercial Web site if you do it in an informative way.

## Thousands of Newsgroup Categories

Newsgroups are organized into different types of discussions or categories. Each of the major categories has lots of individual newsgroups in which you can participate. Major newsgroup categories include:

- **alt**   Discussions on alternative topics

- **biz**   Discussions on business topics. You may find groups that allow advertising here

- **comp**   Discussions on computer related topics

- **misc**   Discussions of miscellaneous topics that don't have their own categories

- **news**   Discussions on Usenet news and administration

- **rec**   Discussions on recreation topics

- **sci**   Discussions on science

- **soc**   Discussions on social issues

- **talk**   Making conversation

Each of the major categories has a number of subgroups, and each of the subgroups has a number of sub-subgroups. For example under the *rec* major group you will find a subgroup *rec.sports*. Here the discussion revolves around all kinds of sports. Under the subgroup *rec.sports* you will find sub-subgroups and sub-sub-subgroups, for example,

*rec.sports*

*rec.sports.hockey*

*rec.sports.hockey.NHL*

*rec.sports.hockey.NHL.BostonBruins*

As you can see, the longer the name the narrower is the discussion that is taking place.

## Target Appropriate Newsgroups

With the large number of Usenet newsgroups that currently exist and the additional groups that are being introduced every day, it is a formidable task to identify appropriate newsgroups for your company's Internet marketing activities. First, you need to determine which newsgroups your prospective customers frequent.

Look for a close fit between a newsgroup and the product or service you are offering. For example, if your company sells software that aids genealogical work, then one appropriate newsgroup for your business might be *soc.genealogy.methods*. Try finding newsgroups that your target market may enjoy reading or ask your clients or customers which newsgroups they participate in or find particularly interesting. Find and make note of all appropriate newsgroups that might be of interest to your target customer.

There are many ways to find appropriate Usenet newsgroup listings: More than 54,000 mailing lists and newsgroups are located at the Liszt Web Site, *http://www.liszt.com*. You can also do a search using the newsgroup functions of the two leading browsers, Netscape Navigator and Microsoft Internet Explorer. Be sure to check out Appendix B for more information on newsgroups.

Most newsreader programs have a search capability. Search the newsgroups for keywords that relate to your target market, your product, or your service to identify possible appropriate newsgroups for your marketing effort. Another good place to start is Deja.com *(http://www.deja.com)*. Here you can conduct a keyword search of the Usenet Newsgroups. The search results are displayed in chronological order, with the results at the top being the most recently used. You should choose keywords appropriate for your target customer or client. These methods will identify a fairly large list of potential newsgroups that may be included in your marketing activities. A benefit of the Deja.com site is that you can post to the newsgroups directly from the site. You don't have to go through alternative software to do so.

If your company specializes in providing exotic vacations to Mexico, you may want to search Deja.com for keywords like "Mexico, vacation, travel, tropical, resorts, beaches," and so on to find potential newsgroups for your marketing effort.

Once you have done your preliminary research and compiled a long list of what you think are the most appropriate newsgroups related to your target market, you are ready to investigate further and qualify your list. The next step is to go to the Usenet Info Center Launch Pad at *http://sunsite.unc.edu/usenet-i/home.html*. There you can look up the newsgroups on your list. From this site you will be able to find out where the FAQ files for each newsgroup are located. The FAQ files will usually provide information on the newsgroup's stance on advertising. Info Center Launch Pad will also provide you with details on the number of people participating in the group.

## Read the FAQ Files and Abide by the Rules

**Charter**
Estab-
lished
rules and
guidelines

Read the FAQ files, **charter** and rules about posting and advertising for each of your target newsgroups. It is very important that you abide by all the rules. If the FAQ files do not mention the group's stance on commercial advertising and announcements, then go back to Deja News. Conduct a search based on the group's name and charter. This will tell you where the newsgroup stands on commercial activity.

## Lurking for Potential Customers

Once you have narrowed your potential newsgroup list, you will want to visit each and every one to determine if the participants of the newsgroup are, in fact, potential customers. Spend time **lurking.** Monitor the types of messages that are being posted. Is there likely to be an opportunity for you to contribute? Are the participants your target market? Research the newsgroup to ascertain if it will appeal to your customers. The name of the newsgroup may not reveal what the newsgroup is about, so take your time and make sure.

## Tips on Posting Messages

After you have become familiar with the rules of your selected newsgroup, have spent some time **lurking**, and have decided that the newsgroup is one where your target market is participating, you may begin to post messages. Remember to abide by the rules! If the rules do not allow advertising, then do not blatantly post an ad. To take full advantage of the newsgroup you have to gain the trust of its members. With one wrong message you could outrage all of the potential customers who participate in the newsgroup.

**Lurking**
Browsing
without
posting

It is a good idea to run a test before you post a message to a newsgroup. Doing a test will show you how the posting works and prevent you from making a mistake when it comes to the real thing. For a test mechanism go to the newsgroup *misc.test*.

Becoming a respected member in a newsgroup is a way to promote yourself as well as your company. In time you may forget that you began reading the newsgroup to promote your business. You will find yourself reading newsgroups in order to participate in stimulating discussions. You will be discussing anything and everything about the newsgroup subject. Only mention your Web site when you find an appropriate opportunity to bring your business knowledge into the conversation.

Newsgroups exist for specific purposes. They can be designed for discussions, news announcements, postings related to particular topics, and even buying and selling goods. They may have hundreds of messages sorted and available for access at any point in time. Newsgroup participants will decide whether to open or pass up your posted message based on the words in the subject area. Make your subject short and catchy so that your message will be read and not passed over. Try to put the most important words of the subject first. This is a very critical part in posting a message to a newsgroup. Some people adjust the screen to see only the first few words in the subject area. When deciding on the text for the subject area, think about what keywords someone would use to search for information on the content of your message. The worst thing that you can do is post a message to a newsgroup with no subject at all. This will definitely receive no attention and is basically a waste of your time.

Start your message with a short description of how it relates to the group's main topic. People are looking for answers to specific questions, so it is rude to jump into the conversation with a topic that doesn't match the one in the subject line. You should attempt to get your message across right away. You should get to the point of your message in the first sentence. By doing so you will catch the reader's attention, and ensure that they will read the entire message.

Message length should be short, no longer than 24 lines. Messages should briefly discuss main points and ask if readers would like to have more information. Once people show an interest in the information you are offering, your message can be as long as needed.

When responding to a message in a newsgroup, you have the option of responding to the individual who posted the message privately or responding through the newsgroup. Determine which is more appropriate under the given circumstances. If your message will be of value to the entire group or will appropriately promote your company's capabilities, then post the response to the newsgroup for all to see. If you think that your company has a solution for the individual and would like to provide details to the "target customer," but feel that it would not benefit the other members of the group, then deliver a private response. Sometimes you may choose to do both. Whichever approach you take, make sure that you respond as quickly as possible so that the first message is still fresh in the mind of the recipient.

## Tips to Ensure Your Messages Will Be Well Received

Here are some basic rules to help you post well-received messages.

### Keep to the Newsgroup Topic

Make sure you always stay on the newsgroup topic of discussion. People participate in specific newsgroups because of that subject and don't appreciate off-topic postings.

### Stay on the Thread

When responding to a message, use the Reply option to stay on the same thread. When you reply without changing the subject line, your message will appear immediately below the message you are responding to in the newsgroup. This makes it easy for others to follow the discussion. A good example can be seen in Figure 5.1.

### Make a Contribution

Informed, quality responses to people's questions will give you credibility with the group and reflect well upon you and your company. If you post positive and informative information, visitors will return to the newsgroups and look for your posts.

### Don't Post Commercials or Advertisements

Advertising is not welcome in most newsgroups, and many charters specifically disallow the posting of ads. Read the FAQ files before

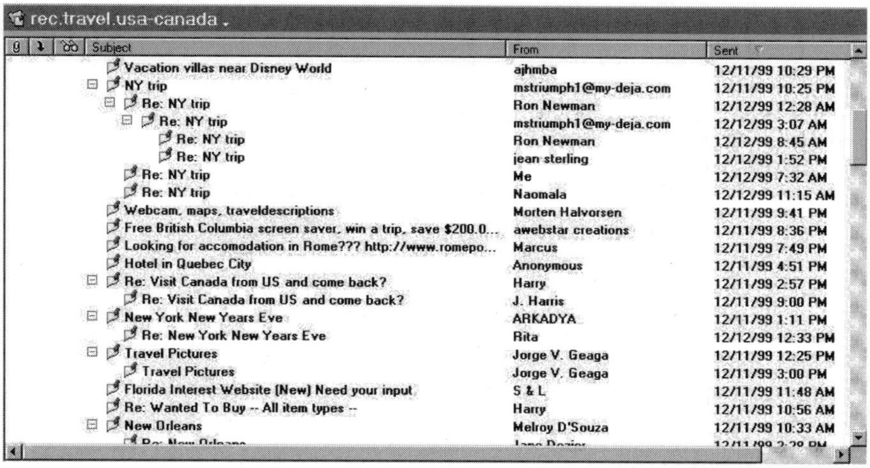

**Figure 5.1.** It is very important to stay on thread. As you can see in this travel newsgroup, the NY trip messages are staying on thread. The messages have been replied to keeping the same subject line.

posting a message. If the newsgroup does not allow commercial messages or ads don't post them.

**You Don't Have to Have the Last Word**

Don't post gratuitous responses in newsgroups. Never post a message with just a "Thanks" or "I like it" if you have nothing else to contribute. If you feel such a response is warranted or would like to discuss the issue privately, send a private e-mail to the person to convey your appreciation or opinion.

## Signature Files as Your E-Business Card

**Signature file, sig.file**
An e-business card, usually attached to e-mail

A **signature file**, or **sig.file** as it is commonly referred to, is your e-business card. It is a short message at the end of an e-mail. Most, if not all, e-mail programs allow for the use of a signature file. Sig.files can be attached at the end of your message when you post to a Usenet newsgroup or a mailing list, even if the group does not allow advertising.

You can use your sig.file in a number of clever ways. Sig.files can be simple—only listing phone numbers and addresses—or they can be virtual ads for your company. They can be very useful in providing exposure for your company. You can use your sig.file to offer some substantial information, such as letting people know about a special event, informing people about an award or honor your company has received, or promoting a specific product or service your company has to offer.

You can design and use different sig.files for posting to different newsgroups. A particular sig.file may be appropriate for one newsgroup but not for another. Always ensure that the message in your sig.file is appropriate for its audience.

Keep your sig.file short. Usually four to eight lines is a good size. There is nothing more annoying than a sig.file that is longer than the text of your message to which it is attached, or one that resembles a brochure.

Sig.files should include the following:

- Contact name

- Business name

- URL

- Address

- E-mail address

- Telephone number

- Fax number

- A brief company tag line or a company slogan

This is an example of what a sig.file looks like:

---

Jane Doe, Marketing Assistant
jdoe@bug.com
Sunnyvale Volkswagen
101 Main Street
Woodstock, NY, 10010
Toll Free Tel: (800) 555-1001 Fax: (800) 555-1000
"www.bug.com"

---

For a complete discussion of sig.files and how to use them, see Chapter 6.

## Newsgroup Advertising Hints

Newsgroups have been developed for different audiences and different topics. Some newsgroups are dedicated to posting advertisements. If advertising is appropriate for your company, the following newsgroup types might be included in your Internet marketing strategy. Most of the newsgroups that allow advertising are readily identifiable. The newsgroup name itself might include one of the following:

- biz

- classified

- for sale

- marketplace

Again, read the FAQ files and lurk to determine if the newsgroup is appropriate for your target market before you post. Use a short, catchy subject line with keywords at the beginning—the subject will determine whether your message warrants a read or a pass. Avoid all CAPITALS. This is equivalent to shouting on the Internet. Stay away from !!!!, ****, and @@@@, and other such symbols.

When you have found a newsgroup whose participants include your target market but the newsgroup does not allow advertising, don't despair. By responding to queries or providing information that is of genuine interest to the newsgroup, you have the opportunity to attach your sig.file. A sig.file can be as effective as an ad if it is designed properly. Your message should offer substantial information to the discussion (a thinly veiled excuse to get your sig.file posted will not be appreciated). If your information is relevant and of value to the participants of the newsgroup, the fact that your sig.file is an advertisement will not matter—in fact it may add credibility to the information you have provided and enhance your company's reputation.

## Cross Posting and Spamming

Cross posting is posting identical messages to a number of relevant newsgroups. Doing this is considered to be inappropriate because of the number of common users in associated newsgroups. Spamming is posting identical or nearly identical messages to irrelevant newsgroups without care or regard for the posting guidelines, the newsgroup topic, or the interests of the group. Cross posting and spamming will annoy the readers of the newsgroup. Doing these things will reflect badly on you and your company, and prevent you from achieving your online marketing objectives.

If you disobey proper newsgroup etiquette you may quickly learn what a flame is. A flame is a reply that may be posted into a newsgroup, or sent to you by e-mail that contains extremely negative feedback.

In the worst cases, people have been sent e-mail that contain 100 copies of a 16 MB file, which could take your computer hours to download or even crash your server. Although these acts are very immature, you must remember to obey newsgroup etiquette to make sure that this does not happen.

Sometime in your online postings, no matter how careful you are, someone is bound to get upset. Accept this as fact and learn how to handle flames appropriately. Be sensitive to complaints. Learn from them, but do not worry unnecessarily. If someone posts a message that reflects badly on your company, you have three options: defend your comments in the newsgroup, send the person a private e-mail, or do nothing. Responding to the person via e-mail is the most appropriate response, even though in most cases your message will be ignored.

## Earning Respect with Newsgroup Netiquette

Following are ten rules for Netiquette. Incorporating them in your newsgroup posting will gain you respect by the other participants:

1. Don't use CAPITALS. They are akin to shouting on the Internet.

2. Don't post ads where they are not welcome.

3. Do provide valuable, on-topic information for the newsgroup.

4. Don't be rude or sarcastic.

5. Don't include the entire message you are replying to in your response. Only quote relevant sections of the original message.

6. Do a thorough review of your message before you post. Check your spelling and grammar. Check your subject; it should be short and catchy with the keywords first.

7. Do provide an appropriate sig.file.

8. Don't post messages that are too lengthy. Online communication tends to be one screen or less.

9. Don't spam or cross-post.

10. Don't post replies that contribute nothing to the discussion ("I agree" or "Thanks").

## Have Your Own Newsgroup

You can start your own newsgroup if you feel it is warranted and appropriate. All group creation requests must follow set guidelines and are first met with discussion. If you need help, you can always find a body of volunteers who are experienced in the newsgroup creation process at *group-mentors@acpub.duke.edu*. They assist people with the formation and submission of good newsgroup proposals.

### The Discussion

A request for discussion on creation of a new newsgroup should be posted to *news.announce.newsgroups* and *news.groups*. If desired, the request can also be posted to other groups or mailing lists that are related to the proposed topic. The name and charter of the proposed group and whether it will be moderated or unmoderated should be determined during the discussion period.

### The Vote

The Usenet Volunteer Vote Takers (UVT) is a group of neutral third-party vote takers who currently handle vote gathering and counting for all newsgroup proposals. There should be a minimal delay between the end of the discussion period and the issuing of a call for votes. The call for votes should include clear instructions on how to cast a vote. The voting period should last for at least 21 days and no more than 31 days. Only the votes that are mailed to the vote taker will be counted.

### The Result

At the completion of the voting period, the vote taker must post the vote tally to the applicable groups and mailing lists. The e-mail addresses and names (if available) of the voters are posted along with the tally. There will be a five-day waiting period, beginning when the voting results actually appear. During the waiting period there will be a chance to correct any errors in the voter list or the voting procedure. In order for a proposal to pass, 100 more YES/create votes must be received than NO/do not create votes. Also, two thirds of the total number of votes must be in favor of creation. If a proposal fails to achieve two thirds of the vote, then the matter cannot be brought up for discussion until at least six months have passed from the close of the vote.

The following locations will help you should you wish to create your own newsgroup:

- How to Format and Submit a New Group Proposal: *news. announce.newgroups, news.groups*

- How to Write a Good Newsgroup Proposal: *news.announce. newgroups, news.groups*

- Usenet Newsgroup Creation Companion: *news.groups, news. announce.newusers, news.answers*

## Internet Resources

### Newsgroups
*News.newusers.questions*
*News.announce.newusers*
*News.newusers*
These provide information to new Usenet users on posting, finding appropriate newsgroups, netiquette, and other frequently asked questions new users are faced with.

### Reference.COM Search
*http://www.reference.com*

Reference.com has searchable directories of newsgroups and mailing lists. Newsgroups are archived, but mailing lists are only archived and searchable with the permission of the list owner.

### Deja.com—The Source for Internet Newsgroups!
*http://www.deja.com*
The Web site where you can read, search, participate in, and subscribe to more than 50,000 discussion forums, including Usenet newsgroups. Deja.com is a resource for finding people, getting noticed, and getting answers to all sorts of questions. You can find discussion forums on any topic imaginable.

### Liszt of Newsgroups
*http://www.liszt.com/news*
A complete listing of newsgroups organized by different categories. Has listed over 30,000 newsgroups and is the largest directory of newsgroups on the Web.

### How to Advertise on Newsgroups
*http://www.nsmi.com/noflames.html*
How to Advertise on Newsgroups shows step-by-step techniques to follow so you won't get blacklisted. Everything you need to know about how to advertise in newsgroups and mailing lists without getting flamed.

### Creating Newsgroups
*http://www.fairnet.org/fnvol/training/newsgrp.html*
All you need to know about how to create your own newsgroup.

### Public News Servers
*http://login.eunet.no/~kjetilm/news.htm*
Free access to newsgroups/NNTP servers.

### Open Newsserver Search
*http://www.muenz.com/sdienst/html/sgroup_e.html*
English/German search engine that finds open news servers that carry newsgroups matching your search terms.

### Newsgroups
*http://www.engl.uvic.ca/OnlineGuide/News/newsGroupsWel.html*

Introductory information called the Online Guide.

### NIC—Master List
*http://www.engl.uvic.ca/OnlineGuide/News/newsGroupsWel.html*
See this master list for a description of newsgroups.

### Downloading Free Agent
*http://www.forteinc.com/getfa/getfa.htm*
Free Agent furnishes newsreader software.

### Talkway
*http://www.talkway.com*
This membership site attempts to provide a friendlier interface to the arcane structure of Usenet newsgroups.

# 6

## Utilizing Signature Files to Increase Web Site Traffic

A signature file is a short memo at the end of your message. You can use your signature file in a number of clever ways, from just giving out phone numbers and addresses to offering some substantial information. Sig.files can be used to let people know about a special event or to inform people about an award or honor your company has received. In this chapter we cover:

- The appropriate size of sig.files

- Content and design of sig.files

- Creating signature files to add statements to your messages

- The benefits of sig.files

### Presenting Your E-Business Card

A signature file, or sig.file as it is commonly referred to, is your e-business card. It should be attached at the end of all your e-mails, those that are sent to individuals and especially those that are sent to Usenet newsgroups and mail lists. Most if not all e-mail programs allow for the use of a signature file. If yours doesn't, you should consider switching e-mail programs because sig.files can be very effective in drawing traffic to your Web site when used appropriately.

You can use your sig.file in a number of different ways, starting with providing basic contact information such as phone, fax, e-mail, and URL. You should provide every way possible for the recipient to reach you, not only the way in which you would like to be contacted. It is the recipients' choice if they would rather call than e-mail you. Some people also have a "Click here" link on their sig.file that takes you directly to their Web site. This is a nice idea, but you must also remember to include your URL so that they will have it. Sometimes people will just print their e-mail to take home that night, and it can be really hard getting to a Web site trying to click on a piece of paper. You should also include details offering more substantial information about your company and its products and services. You can tell your readers about a current sales promotion, where you will be located at a trade show, a special event you are hosting, or an award your company has received. Sig.files are readily accepted online and, when designed properly, comply with Netiquette.

## How to Develop Your Signature File

In preparation for designing and developing your sig.file, you should decide what information you want to include and what you want your e-business card to look like. Create your sig.file using Windows Notepad and save it as a text file (that's with a .TXT extension). If you are using Netscape or Internet Explorer, the following are the steps to develop your sig.file:

### *Microsoft Outlook Express 5:*

1. On the menu bar click "Tools."

2. On the drop down box click on "Options."

3. Click on the "Signatures" tab.

4. Click on "New" to create your sig.file.

5. Click on "Add sig.file to all outgoing messages."

*Netscape Messenger:*

1.  On the menu bar click "Edit."

2.  Click on "Preferences."

3.  Go to the folder named "News Groups Folder."

4.  Go to the folder named "Identity."

5.  Choose a file to create your sig.file in. Be sure to always use a text file because you do not know what the other person is using, so you do not know how your file will appear on their screen. After you have developed your sig.file, send an e-mail message to yourself with it attached to see what it looks like. Make sure to check and double check for typos, errors, or omissions.

**Tag line**
Advertising message, usually included in your signature file attached to e-mail

One of the most important elements from a marketing perspective is the **tag line.** Does your tag line give the reader a real and compelling desire to visit your Web site?

If you are using one of the online services, there are different ways to develop your sig.file:

*America Online:*

1.  Click on "Mail Center" on the toolbar.

2.  Click on "Set up Mail Signature."

3.  Click on "Create," type in the name of the sig.file, and create the sig.file using the different options available.

4. Set the default to "On" so that your sig.file is added to your outgoing mail.

### CompuServe:

1. Click on "Mail Center" on the toolbar.

2. Click on "Set up Mail Signature."

3. Click on "Create," type in the name of the sig.file, and create the sig.file using the different options available.

4. Set the default to "On" so that your sig.file is added to your outgoing mail.

### Prodigy:

- Prodigy uses Microsoft Outlook Express for their e-mail service, so follow the instructions given earlier for Outlook Express.

## The Do's and Don'ts of Signature Files

It is a good idea to develop several signature files to use with different groups of recipients. You can use an appropriate sig.file for each different group you are targeting. You should update your sig.file often to reflect current marketing related information.

Some e-mail programs allow a maximum of 80 characters per line for sig.files. You should design your sig.file to fit well within the limits of all programs. Use no more than 70 characters per line to be assured that your sig.file will be viewed as you have designed it no matter what reader is being used.

Some people get really innovative in the design of their sig.files. They often include sketches, designs, or logos developed by combining keyboard numbers and punctuation. An example of this is "John Doe" of "Game Corporation," who is in the game software business.

>>>>>>>>>>>>>>>>>>>>>>>>>>>>>>>>>>>>>>>>>>>>>>>>>>>>>>>>>
John Doe, Director of Marketing          jdoe@gamecorp.com
                                              Tel: (800) 555-0008
 I GAME CORP I                              Fax: (800) 555-0009
 I     ___     I                                   290 Young St.
 I I           I I          "Free Trial Version @   New York, NY
 I_I____IIII___I_I          www.gamecorp.com"              81010
GAME CORP.
>>>>>>>>>>>>>>>>>>>>>>>>>>>>>>>>>>>>>>>>>>>>>>>>>>>>>>>

Including graphics in your sig.file is not a good idea. This may look quite nice on your screen, but when you send it to other people who have a different e-mail program or different screen resolutions, it could look quite different on their monitors. You should stay away from using icons or sketches in your signature files.

Check out sig.files attached to messages you receive or those posted to newsgroups to see what you like, what you don't, and what suits you best. You can always build a sig.file, test it on your colleagues, and then decide whether you will use it or not.

The use of signature files offers a number of benefits to your company. If you use sig.files appropriately, you will be able to promote your company and your online presence in the following ways:

- The use of sig.files will increase your company's online exposure. By merely placing a sig.file at the end of a posting to a newsgroup, your company name may be seen by thousands of people. A great tag line with a call to action will encourage people to visit your site.

- Like any advertisement, the design and content of your sig.file can be used to position your business and create or complement a corporate image.

- Using your sig.file can enhance the reputation of your company based upon the e-mail that it is attached to. If your postings to newsgroups and mailing lists are helpful and continually appreciated, this will become associated with your company name.

- Using appropriate sig.files, as shown below, will signal to the online community that you are a member that respects proper netiquette.

| Sig.file DO's | Sig.file DON'Ts |
| --- | --- |
| Do list all appropriate contact information | Don't list prices of any kind |
| Keep it short, say 4 to 8 lines | Don't use a sales pitch |
| Keep it simple | Don't use too many symbols |
| Provide an appropriate and professional tag line | Don't list the company's products or service |

## Sig.files to Bring Traffic to Your Web Site

The major benefit of sig.files is that they can attract visitors to your Web site. Use your signature file as a mini advertisement for your company and its products and services (called sigvertising). With sigvertising you can go beyond offering the basic contact information. Use your sig.file as a tool to bring traffic to your Web site. Instead of simply listing your company's phone number and URL, give the reader some insight into your company and a reason to visit your Web site. Use some of the following tips to increase the traffic to your Web site:

- **Announce a sale or special offer.** Briefly mention that your company will be having a sale, or inform people that there is a special offer available on your Web site.

- **Offer something for free.** Inform readers of free information or samples that they can access if they visit your site.

- **Announce an event.** If your company is organizing or sponsoring a special event, inform people through your sig.file and invite them to your site for more information.

- **Announce a contest.** If your site is holding a contest, tell readers that they can enter by visiting your site.

- **Announce an award or honor.** If your company or your Web site has received special recognition, tell people about it through your sig.file.

Sig.files are accepted online in e-mail, newsgroups, mail lists, and discussion groups. However, be cautious when developing your sig.files to ensure that they will be well received. Sig.files that are billboards, or sig.files that are longer than most of your text messages, are to be avoided. Sig.files that are blatant advertisements will definitely not be appreciated. The online community reacts unfavorably to hard-sell advertising unless it is done in the proper forum. Here is an example of a sig.file that may offend Internet users.

xxxxxxxxxxxxxxxxxxxxxxxxxxxxxxxxxxxxxxxxxxxxxxxxxxxxxx
**Are you in need of a reliable vehicle?**
If you are, come on down to Sunnyvale Volkswagen!
We have the best deals in town and will beat any of our
competitor's prices on new and used cars!
Money back guarantee!
Great deal on a 1995 Diesel Jetta.....$ 2995.
Talk to Jane Doe about our new lease incentives!
101 Main Street, Woodstock, New York 10010
Tel: (800) 555-0000
Cell: (800) 555-1010
Fax: (800) 555-1020
www.bug.com
xxxxxxxxxxxxxxxxxxxxxxxxxxxxxxxxxxxxxxxxxxxxxxxxxxxxxx

Another mistake that people make is that they try to make their sig.files too flashy or eyecatching. Using a lot of large symbols may catch people's eye, but the impression it leaves will not be memorable. Here is an example of what not to do.

```
☯☺☺✉☺☺☺✉☺☺☺✉☺☺☺✉☺☺☺✉☺☺☺✉☺☺☺☯
☯  !Sunnyvale Volkswagen !                                    ☯
☯  !Jane Doe, Marketing Assistant !                           ☯
☯  ! jdoe@bug.com !                                           ☯
☯  232 Main Street                    ☎800) 555-0000 ☯
☯  Woodstock, New York ☖             🖨 (800) 555-0002 ☯
☯  30210 🖃
☯                    "Test drives @ www.bug.com"              ☯
☯☺☺✉☺☺☺✉☺☺☺✉☺☺☺✉☺☺☺✉☺☺☺✉☺☺☺☯
```

Here are some examples of what sig.files should look like.

```
====================================================
              Sunnyvale Volkswagen
          Jane Doe, Marketing Assistant
                 jdoe@bug.com
101 Main Street                      Tel: (800) 555-0000
Woodstock, New York, 10010           Fax:(800) 555-0002
      "Our once a year sales event is on now @ www.bug.com"
====================================================
```

```
_____

              Sunnyvale Volkswagen
          Jane Doe, Marketing Assistant
                 jdoe@bug.com
101 Main Street                      Tel: (800) 555-0000
Woodstock, New York, 10010           Fax: (800) 555-0001
      Charity Telethon sponsored by Sunnyvale Volkswagen
              info available @ www.bug.com
_____
```

```
✉_____✉
Jane Doe    ✉    Marketing Assistant    ✉    Sunnyvale Volkswagen
      "Enter to win a new 1999 Bug @ www.bug.com"
      101 Main Street, Woodstock, New York, 10010
              (800) 555-0000 jdoe@bug.com
✉_____✉
```

>>>

**Jane Doe, Marketing Assistant**
**Sunnyvale Volkswagen**

101 Main Street                                       jdoe@bug.com
P.O. Box 101                                       Tel: (800) 555-0000
Woodstock, New York 10010               URL: www.bug.com
"1999 Winner of the Best Dealership Award"

>>>>>>>>>>>>>>>>>>>>>>>>>>>>>>>>>>>>>>>>>>>>>>>>>

**Jane Doe, Marketing Assistant**                 **jdoe@bug.com**
**Sunnyvale Volkswagen**
101 Main Street                                 Tel: (800) 500-1000
P.O. Box 101                                    Fax: (800) 500-1002
Woodstock, NY 10010                          URL: www.bug.com
**"Test Drives @ www.bug.com"**

## Internet Resources

**123 Promote**
*http://www.123promote.com/workbook/plan1.htm*
E-mail guide to e-mail styles, e-mail mail-merging, e-mail autoresponders, e-mail autoreminders, e-mail Netiquette, e-mail headers, signature files, announcements, press releases, business administration, free designs, mailing list announcements, newsgroup announcements, office automation, mass e-mailing, publicity, form letters, form folders, e-mailed databases, programs, and software.

**Coolsig.com**
*http://coolsig.com*
Over 70,000 people have shown their good taste by signing up to get coolsig delivered by e-mail. It comes once or twice a week, and like everything good in life, it's free.

**Webnovice.com**
*www.webnovice.com/sig_files.htm*

Everything You Wanted To Know About Signature Files…But Didn't Know Where To Ask.

### Using Signature Files
*http://www.emtech.net/links/signaturefiles/sld001.htm*
Using signature files, how to create them, and what to include.

### Internet Strategist
*http://www.techdirect.com/strategy/sigfiles.html*
What to do and not to do on sig.files and mailing lists. Learn how to create your personal sig.file and what the different types are used for.

### SquareOne Technology: How to create an e-mail signature?
*http://www.squareonetech.com/signatur.html*
How to create a sig.file with Notepad and import it to use with all your mail messages.

### Signature Files
*http://www.smithfam.com/news/n8.html*
Signature files are an absolutely vital way of promoting your Web site. Learn how to market your product on the Internet from the leading Internet marketing experts, and it is all free.

### GNOFN Help: How to Make and Maintain a Signature File
*http://www.gnofn.org/info/help/ppp/makesig.html*
A tutorial on designing and developing your signature file.

### Esther's Massive Signature File Collection
*http://www.contrib.andrew.cmu.edu/~moose/sigs.html*
A massive collection of sig.files to review the good, the bad, and the ugly.

### 32bit.com
*http://www.32bit.com/hyper95/get/internet/798.html*
A tutorial on adding links in signature files in Netscape 3.x and 4.x.

### Signature Museum
*http://huizen.dds.nl/~mwpieter/sigs/*
The Signature Museum is a gallery of signature files sorted by category. At this site you will also find a list of other sites that provide examples of lots and lots of signature files.

# 7

## The E-mail Advantage

E-mail is rapidly becoming one of the most crucial forms of communication you have with your clients, potential customers, suppliers, and colleagues. E-mail is now a widely accessible and generally accepted form of communication. CyberAtlas *(http:// cyberatlas.internet.com)* has reported that there are 435 million active e-mail accounts in the world. There are enough e-mail addresses for each person in North America to have his or her own account.

In the online community e-mail is an extremely efficient way to build and maintain relationships. As a marketing tool, e-mail is one of the most cost-effective ways to maintain an ongoing dialogue with your audience. In this chapter we cover:

- Strategies for creating effective e-mail messages

- E-mail Netiquette

- Information access with autoresponders

- Customer service and e-mail

- E-mail marketing tips

- Sending HTML versus ASCII (text-based) e-mail messages

## Making the Connection

E-mail is a communication medium, and, as with all forms of communication, *you do not get a second chance to leave a first impression*. E-mail must be used appropriately. People receive large amounts of e-mail each day, and the tips in this chapter will help to ensure that your e-mail is taken seriously.

One of the greatest benefits of e-mail is the speed with which you can communicate. E-mail takes seconds rather than weeks to send a message around the world. The cost of this form of communication is negligible compared to making a long-distance phone call or sending a fax. The economies of scale are significant. One e-mail message can be sent to millions of people across the globe simultaneously. This type of mass mailing is done at a fraction of the cost and a fraction of the time (and internal resources) it would take with **snail mail**.

All kinds of files can be sent via e-mail, including sound, video, data, graphics, and text. With an **autoresponder**, information can be sent to customers and potential customers 24 hours a day, 7 days a week, 365 days a year in response to their online requests.

**Snail mail**
Slang term for the regular postal service

**Autoresponder**
Program that automatically responds to incoming e-mail —an electronic fax-back system

## Effective E-mail Messages

Most people who use this medium get tons and tons of e-mail, including their share of junk e-mail. The following tips will increase the effectiveness of your e-mail communication.

## The Importance of Your E-mail Subject Line

The subject line is equivalent to a headline in a newspaper in terms of attracting reader attention. It is the most important part of your e-mail message because this phrase alone will determine whether or not the reader will decide to open your e-mail or delete it.

When you receive e-mails, what do you use to determine which e-mail to read first or at all? The subject line of course! Never send an e-mail message without a subject line. Subject lines should be brief, with the keywords appearing first. The longer the subject line is, the more likely it will not be viewed in entirety.

Effective subject lines will:

- Be brief, yet capture the reader's interest

- Build business credibility

- Attract attention with action words

- Highlight the most important benefits

- Always be positive

- Put the most important words first

Effective headlines should grab the reader's attention, isolate, and qualify your best prospects, and draw your reader into the sub-headlines and the text itself. Remember to avoid SHOUTING! Using CAPITALS in your subject is the same as SHOUTING AT THE READER! DON'T DO IT!!

## E-mail "To" and "From" Headings Allow You to Personalize

Use personal names in the "To" and "From" headings whenever possible as this creates a more personal relationship. Most e-mail programs allow you to attach your personal name to your e-mail address. If you don't know how to do this, look at the help file of the e-mail program you are using.

### Blind Carbon Copy (BCC)

Ever receive an e-mail message in which the first screen or first several screens was a string of other people's e-mail addresses to which the message had been sent? Didn't you feel special? Didn't you feel the message was meant just for you? This sort of bulk mailing is very unpersonalized, and most often each recipient will delete the message without looking at it.

It is advisable to use the BCC feature when sending bulk or group e-mails; otherwise, every person on the list will see that this e-mail was not sent just to him or her. The e-mail recipients will see the list of the other recipients first and not the intended message. They will be required to scroll down past the list of recipients to get to your message. This is not the best way to make friends and influence people. Make sure that you know how to use the blind carbon copy function in your e-mail program.

> **BCC**
> Blind
> Carbon
> Copy

Even better than blind carbon copy is using a software application that can send personalized messages to each recipient in your database. E-mail applications like this are far more flexible than the blind carbon copy method because there is no limitation on the number of messages you can send, and the field merge capabilities enable you to create a more personalized message.

Before you send any "live" bulk e-mail, do a test with a number of your colleagues and friends to make sure you are using the program and features effectively and that all of their addresses do not appear by mistake in each message.

### Effective E-mail Message Formatting

The content of the message should be focused on one topic. If you need to change the subject in the middle of a message, it is better to send a separate e-mail. Alternatively, if you wish to discuss more than one topic, make sure you begin your message stating "I have 3 questions" or "There are 4 issues I would like to discuss." People are busy, they read their e-mail quickly, and they assume you will cover your main points within the first few sentences of your message.

E-mail is similar to writing a business letter in that the spelling and grammar should be correct. This includes the proper use of upper- and lowercase lettering, which many people seem to ignore when sending e-mail. However, e-mail is unlike a business letter in that the tone is completely different. E-mail correspondence is not as formal as business writing. The *tone* of e-mail is more similar to a polite conversation than a formal letter, which makes it conducive to relationship building.

In general, you should:

- Keep your paragraphs relatively short—no more than seven lines.

- Make your point in the first paragraph.

- Be clear and concise.

- Give your reader a call to action.

- Avoid using fancy formatting such as graphics, different fonts, italics, and bold, because many e-mail programs cannot display those features.

- If your e-mail package doesn't have a spell check feature, you might want to consider composing your message first in your word processing program. Spell check it there and then cut and paste it into your e-mail package.

- Choose your words carefully. E-mail is a permanent record of your thoughts, and it can be easily forwarded to others.

- If you want to be really careful, test the e-mail in a number of the popular packages to ensure your message will be received in the intended format.

## A Call to Action

When you give your readers a call to action, it's amazing how often people will do as they're told. I'll give you an example through something we did at Connex Network. We ran a series of 10 Internet marketing workshops for a large organization. Their staff and selected clients were invited to participate in any, some, or all of the workshops. Their clients could include up to three employees. Since the workshops extended beyond noon, lunch was provided.

Since Connex Network was responsible for organizing and managing the project, we needed to know the approximate number of people who would be attending each of the workshops to organize the luncheons. When we contacted each company's representatives by e-mail looking for participation RSVPs we conducted an experiment. We sent half the representatives one version of the message and the other half a slightly different version. The only difference between the two messages was that in one, we had a call to action. In that message we asked "RSVP before Wednesday at noon indicating if you will be attending as we must make arrangements for lunch," and in the other this same line read "Please let us know if you are planning to attend as we must make arrangements for lunch".

There was a 95% response rate from the group who received the first message. This is because we gave people a call to action and a deadline, and they felt obligated to respond more promptly. Meanwhile, less than 50% of the people in the second group responded to our message. What does this tell us? To improve your response rate, give your readers a call to action when you send them e-mail. People will respond when told to do something, they act with more urgency when there is a deadline.

## Appropriate E-mail Reply Tips

Do not include the entire original message in your replies. This is unnecessary, aggravating to the original sender of the message, and often takes too long to **download**. However, use enough of the original message to refresh the recipient's memory. Remember to check the "To" and "CC" before you reply. You would not want an entire mail list to receive your response intended only for the sender. The same applies for selecting "Reply All" instead of "Reply."

**Download** Transmission of a file from one computer to another

### Always Use Your Signature Files

As discussed previously, signature files are a great marketing tool. Always attach your signature file to your online communication. (See Chapter 6 for information on signature files.) Also, ensure that the signature files are appropriate for the intended audience.

### Discerning Use of Attachments

If you are sending a fairly large volume of data, you may want to send it as an attached file to your e-mail message. However, only include an e-mail attachment if you have the recipient's permission to send an attached file. You would never consider going to someone's home, letting yourself in, finding your way into their living room, and then leaving your brochure on the coffee table. However, people do the online equivalent of this when they send an unsolicited attachment. The attachment is sent across the Internet to the recipient's computer and is downloaded and stored on the recipient computer's hard drive. This is considered quite rude and, in most cases, unwanted.

Also, unless the recipient of your e-mail is aware of the file size and is expecting it, don't send an attachment that is larger than 50K. Although your Internet connection might be a cable modem or a T1 line and a 3 MB file is sent in seconds, the person who is receiving your message and attachment might be using a 14.4 Kbps modem and a slow machine. If you send a 3 MB file, it might take the person with the 14.4 Kbps modem two hours to download the file. Needless to say, he or she won't be too pleased.

Another factor to consider when sending an unsolicited attachment is that the attachment you are sending may be incompatible with the operating system or the software the recipient has installed on their system. Someone using a Macintosh with Corel WordPerfect installed may not be able to read a Microsoft Word 2000 document sent as an attachment. Thus, you will have wasted your time sending the file and the recipient's time downloading the file.

Finally, it is a well-known fact that e-mail attachments can act as carriers for computer **viruses**. You may unknowingly send someone an attachment with a virus, and even if the file you send is virus-free, you may still take the blame if recipients find a virus on their system just because you sent them an attachment. Basically, avoid sending

**Viruses**
Programs that contaminate a user's hard drive, often with unwanted results

e-mail attachments of any variety unless you have the recipient's permission. Be mindful of the size of the file you intend to send, compatibility with other platforms, and computer viruses. One alternative to sending a large attachment is to post the file on a Web server, and in your e-mail message, direct users to a URL from which they can download the file.

## Before You Click on "Send"

There are a number of things you should do before you send an important e-mail, especially if it is going to a number of people. Send a test message to yourself or a colleague so that you can check that the word wrap looks good, that the text is formatted properly, and that it displays as you want it to. Check that there are no typos, errors, or omissions.

## Expressing Yourself with Emoticons and Shorthand

In verbal communication you provide details on your mood, meaning, and intention through voice inflections, tone, and volume. You also give clues about your meaning and intention through facial expression and body language. E-mail does not allow for the same expression of feeling. The closest thing we have to this online is the use of **emoticons.**

The word "emoticons" is an acronym for "emotions" and "icons." Emoticons are combinations of keyboard characters that give the appearance of a stick figure's emotions. They have to be viewed sideways and are meant to be smiling, frowning, laughing, and so on. Emoticons let you communicate your meaning and intentions to your reader. For example, if your boss gives you an assignment via e-mail and your response is, "Thanks a lot for unloading your dirty work on me," your boss may become upset at your obvious defiance. But if you replied with this: "Thanks a lot for unloading your dirty work on me :-)," your boss would understand that you were jokingly accepting the assignment.

**Emoticons**
Symbols made from punctuation marks and letters that look like facial expressions

Emoticons enable you to add a little personality and life to your text messages. However, their use is not universal and should generally not be used in business correspondence. Some of the more commonly used emoticons include

| | | | |
|---|---|---|---|
| :-) | Smiling | :-@ | Screaming |
| :-0 | Wow! | :-p | Tongue wagging |
| ;-) | Wink | (-: | I'm left handed |
| :-V | Shout | :-o | Wow! |
| :-& | Tongue-tied | :-r | Tongue hanging out |
| ;-) or ;-< | Crying | :-# | My lips are sealed! |
| :-* | Oops! | :-S | I'm totally confused. |
| 8-0 | No way! | :- | Skeptical |
| :-< | Sad or frown | ~~:-( | I just got flamed! |
| %-0 | Bug-eyed | :\ | Befuddled |
| :-D | Laughing, big smile | }:-> | Devilish, devious |

E-mail shorthand is used in newsgroups and other e-mail to represent commonly used phrases. Some common abbreviations are:

- BTW   By the way

- IMHO In my humble opinion

- IMO   In my opinion

- IOW   In other words

- JFYI   Just for your information

- NBD   No big deal

- NOYB None of your business

- TIA   Thanks in advance

- PMFJI Pardon me for jumping in

- OIC   Oh, I see...

- OTL   Out to lunch

- OTOH On the other hand

- LOL   Laughing out loud

- LMHO   Laughing my head off

- ROFL   Rolling on the floor laughing

- BFN   Bye for now

- CYA   See ya!

- FWIW   For what it's worth

- IAE   In any event

- BBL   Be back later

- BRB   Be right back

- RS   Real soon

- WYSIWYG   What you see is what you get.

- <g>   Adding a grin

Since e-mail shorthand is most commonly used in newsgroups and chat rooms, you will be most successful when using these acronyms with others who are familiar with them.

## Using Automated Mail Responders— Mailbots and Infobots

Automated mail responders act like fax-back systems. They send requested information via e-mail automatically to the person that made the request. You can ask your Internet Service Provider (ISP) for details on autoresponder services they may offer. Alternatively, you can also do a search on "mailbots" or "autoresponders" to find any third-party companies that can provide you with these services.

You can make information on your company, your products, your services, and your marketing materials easily accessible 24 hours a day, 7 days a week, 365 days a year through mailbots. Examples of information that you can easily provide through this service are:

- Catalogue and price lists

- Brochures

- Reviews and testimonials

- Press releases

- Newsletters

- Annual reports

- Award announcements

- Sample reports

These types of information could be placed on your Web site. However, you may choose to promote them by way of an autoresponder so that you can obtain customer data prior to providing the customers with the information they are requesting from you. Ask them for their e-mail address, mailing address, phone number, and answers to any marketing-related questions you may have. This type of data can be useful for targeting individuals in a future e-mail marketing campaign.

Autoresponders can also be used to personalize and build relationships. Provide outstanding customer service. For instance, even if you are out of the office, you may set an autoresponder personal note might consist of something like the following:

*Thanks for your e-mail. Sorry, I am out of town and not able to access my e-mail on a regular basis. If your message is time sensitive, please contact my assistant Lynn at 902-*

*468-2578 or via e-mail at lynn@connexnetwork.com. She has my itinerary and telephone numbers where I can be reached. I'll be back in the office Monday and will catch up on correspondence at that time.*

*Regards*
*Susan*

Obviously, it would be better to be able to respond immediately, but if you are unavailable, an "out the office" message such as the preceding one is an example of outstanding customer service. You are letting your customers know that they are important to you even though you are unavailable.

Autoresponders also provide an excellent means of promoting your company. Each time someone sends you a request for information, include a short marketing blurb in the autoresponder that includes the requested information. This marketing technique will not be viewed as unsolicited e-mail because the person asked for it. Change the autoresponder message until you find the one that generates the best response. Autoresponders are easy to set up and easy to change, so your marketing message can be modified in an instant. See the Internet Resources at the end of this chapter for more information.

## E-mail Marketing Tips

Be prepared. You will receive a number of e-mails requesting information on your company, your products, your locations, and so on, from people who have seen your e-mail address on letterhead, ads, business cards, and sig.files. Don't wait for the first inquiry before you begin to develop your company materials. Here are some tips. Following them will make you more prepared to respond.

### Brochure and Personal Note

Have an electronic brochure available that you can easily access and send via e-mail. Try to send a personal note in your e-mail along with any material requested.

### Gather a Library of Responses

You will have different people asking a number of the same questions, and over time you will be able to develop a library of responses to these frequently asked questions. You can save a lot of time by copying and pasting the answers to FAQs into your e-mail responses. Again, always make sure to personalize your responses.

### Have More Than One E-mail Account

**GIF**
Graphic
Image
File

By having a number of different e-mail accounts you can develop databases of all the people who have sent you a message—sorted by their interests. (You will know their interests by which mailbox they choose to send an e-mail to.) For example, you may be able to tell that a person is interested in your virus scanners but not your game software, or interested in your information on making animated **GIFs** but not in your virus archive.

The tactic of using separate e-mail accounts and filtering them into different mailboxes can be used for many marketing purposes other than developing e-mail lists. An example would be to place the same advertisement in three different magazines. Associate a different e-mail address with each ad, and determine which ad generates the best response by reviewing the number of responses sent to the different e-mail addresses. You will then know in which magazine to advertise in the future for the best response.

### Have More Than One E-mail Folder

You want to be able to target your customers based on their interests and past purchases as much as possible. The more you can personalize your message to your target audience, the greater success you will achieve with your Internet marketing campaigns. Organizing your e-mail inbox into distinct folders will assist you in sorting your customers from your potential customers and further identifying these individuals by their interests.

For instance, if your online business sells books, music, and electronics equipment, create a separate folder in your e-mail program to contain all of the e-mail inquiries you have received from people interested in books. Then, create other folders for people who have written you about certain music CDs, electronics equipment, and so on. In the future, you will be able to market to these individuals directly based on their specific, expressed interest from the past. This is the crux of opt-in e-mail marketing.

### Run an Opt-In E-mail Marketing Campaign

An opt-in e-mail marketing campaign is perhaps the best means to reach your target audience. "Opt-in" refers to the fact that people can willingly subscribe and unsubscribe from your e-mail list. This is important because if people do not want mail from you and you send them unsolicited e-mail, you could be accused of spamming. Spam is the scourge of the Internet and a pet peeve of many people. If it is reported to your ISP that you are sending unsolicited bulk e-mail, you could lose your Internet account.

Only send mail to people who have expressed prior interest in your business, and allow them to unsubscribe themselves from your mailing list if they choose. As mentioned earlier in this chapter, you can use the blind carbon copy method or a specialized e-mail application to conduct an e-mail marketing campaign. Most e-mail marketing software packages will permit you to easily add or subtract new subscribers from your mailing list. These applications also create more personalized messages than can be achieved using blind carbon copy.

## Following Formalities with E-mail Netiquette

When writing e-mails, remember these points:

- Be courteous...remember your pleases and thank-yous.

- Reply promptly...within 24 hours.

- Be brief.

- Use lowercase characters. Capitals indicate SHOUTING!

- Use emoticons where appropriate.

- Check your grammar and spelling.

- Use attachments sparingly.

- Do not send unsolicited bulk e-mail.

## Reply Promptly

People expect an answer the same day or the next day at the latest. E-mail communication is like voice mail. If you do not respond within 24 hours, you send a very clear message to your clients, potential clients, and colleagues: "Your communication is not important to me." Respond within 24 hours even if the message is, "Sorry, I can't get to this immediately. I'll try to have a reply for you by the end of the week." This may be a response you will want to save in a readily available file from which you can copy and paste it into an e-mail message. A prompt reply is better than no reply at all. The people writing you for information will appreciate the fact that you felt their messages are important enough to respond to immediately.

## The Heart of Customer Service

Although most customer correspondence via e-mail is very pleasant and businesslike, you will occasionally encounter people who are displeased with the service they have received from you. Very often, a series of courteous, prompt e-mail responses can turn a disgruntled customer into a customer for life. Taking a potentially disagreeable situation and reversing it to a positive one is the heart of customer service. Following is a real example of how a client turned such a situation around. This excerpt was provided to me by Donna Ross of the Shambhala Sun at a recent seminar and has been included with the permission of Donna and the *Shambhala Sun* magazine *(http://www.shambhalasun.com)*. The name and address of the subscriber have been changed.

Customer 1st Message:
Dear Shambhala Sun Folk:
I sent in a change of address form back a few months ago, but I have
not been receiving the latest issues of your magazine at my new ad-
dress. The last one I received was the January 1999 issue at my old
address. So let's try again:
Name:
Joe Subscriber
Old Address:
100 Some Street
Anaheim, CA
92999
New Address:
49494 Another Street
San Jose, CA
92000
My home phone number is (999) 999-9999.
Thank you for your help and consideration on this matter.
Sincerely,
Joe Subscriber

Shambhala Sun Response:
Dear Joe:
We do have your new address in our system. Your May issue should
be arriving there any minute now. I will send you the missed March
issue in this evening's mail. I notice that we have the city for your
new address listed as Laguna Hills. In your e-mail, you have it as San
Jose. Please let me know which of the two is more accurate. Thanks.
Donna Ross
Shambhala Sun Subscriptions

Customer 2nd Message:
How did you know? The May issue arrived in my mailbox this very
day! As I was just in a fairly bad auto accident and am laid up, it is
most welcome. Thanks for your speedy reply.
Sincerely,
Joe Subscriber

Shambhala Sun Response:
Actually, it is my job to know. :-)

Sorry to hear you are hurt. Heal well.
Donna Ross
Shambhala Sun Subscriptions

Customer Final Message:
Thanks Donna for your concern. It's no surprise that Shambhala Sun has folks like you working there. Consider me a subscriber for life.
Sincerely,
Joe Subscriber
P.S.—Although my car was totaled, I am doing fine and healing quickly.
End of Correspondence Thread

As has been clearly demonstrated by the example, the value of strong customer relations is immeasurable. If you take great care to respond quickly and courteously to your customers' (even when they're not happy) e-mail messages, you can win them over for life. Nothing exceeds the value of a lifetime customer.

## HTML or Text Messages?

E-mail messages are commonly sent and encoded as regular ASCII text. However, HTML mail is steadily making inroads into the e-mail world. Many e-mail clients are capable of sending HTML encoded messages, (see Figure 7.1) but should you use this format or just stick to text?

Susan,

Here is the information you requested. Please let me know if you require any further assistance.

Raland Kinley
Connex Network Inc.
http://www.connexnetwork.com
************************************

**Figure 7.1.** An example of an HTML message.

The benefit of sending an HTML formatted message is that you can effectively send a message that acts and appears like a Web page. It's like a colorful brochure and is much more attractive than a plain ASCII text message. The only drawback of HTML mail is that a lot of e-mail clients cannot properly decode the HTML. Thus, the message is converted to ASCII, loses its formatting, and looks unappealing. Your recipients will be inclined to delete such poorly formatted messages.

If you have ever received an e-mail message that contained a line of hyperlink text such as "Click here to visit our Web site," this is one example of an HTML message. An e-mail client that can decode HTML will permit you to click on the highlighted text and access the Web site. If your e-mail client only understands ASCII formatted messages, the hyperlink might not work.

To ensure that URLs you insert in an e-mail message always display as hyperlink text, simply type the full URLs into your message. For instance, type

Click on the link below to visit Connex Network: *http:// www.connexnetwork.com*

Most e-mail clients will recognize the "http://" as the beginning of a hyperlink.

Regardless, if you want to try using HTML formatting in your e-mail correspondence, let your recipients decide which type of message they prefer. Send HTML formatted messages only to the people who prefer it and ASCII messages to the rest of your recipients.

Some e-mail software packages can send both an HTML and an ASCII text version of an e-mail message at once. If your software has this capability, then you can send either type of message without any concern.

## Internet Resources

### E-mail Netiquette
*http://ultra.santarosa.edu/net/email/netiquette.html*
This document is from David Harris, author of Pegasus Mail, a popular PC and MAC e-mail package designed to help get the most from your e-mail.

### Everything E-mail
*http://everythingemail.net/*
Information and links to make your e-mail account more productive and fun! Resources, guides, and glossary to make things easier for you to understand. Extensive Web site dedicated exclusively to e-mail and e-mail services.

### 123 Promote
*http://www.123promote.com/workbook/plan1.htm*
E-mail guide to e-mail styles, mail merging, autoresponders, autoreminders, Netiquette, headers, signature files, announcements, press releases, business administration, free designs, mailing list announcements, newsgroup announcements, office automation, mass e-mailing, publicity, form letters, form folders, e-mailed databases, programs, and software.

### A Beginner's Guide to Effective E-mail
*http://www.webfoot.com/advice/email.top.html*
Help in writing the e-mail you need. Formats and why you need e-mail are all explained in detail.

### Neophyte's Guide to Effective E-mail
*http://www.webnovice.com/email.htm*
This site goes through, step-by-step, the important issues you should keep in mind from start to send.

### I Will Follow.com E-mail Tips
*http://www.iwillfollow.com/email.htm*
This site offers advice to beginners on all aspects of using e-mail.

### Internet Marketing Newsletter
*http://www.arrowweb.com/graphics/news/ap12.html*
"The Secrets of E-mail Marketing Success," an article by Lesley Anne Lowe.

### Windweaver
*http://www.windweaver.com/emoticon.htm*
Recommended emoticons for e-mail communication.

### Dave Barry's Guide to Emoticons
*http://www.randomhouse.com/features/davebarry/emoticon.html*
Good resource for emoticons and shorthand. His site has an Emoticon Gallery with lots of examples (3069 at last count) and an area where you can make your own.

### EmailAddresses.com
*http://www.emailaddresses.com*
A directory of numerous free e-mail services including POP accounts, e-mail forwarding, newsletters, and so on.

### EEF's Extended Guide to the Internet
*http://www.eff.org/papers/eegtti/eeg_286.html*
This Unofficial Smiley Dictionary is only one of many different collections by various "editors" you'll come across at many places on the Net.

### Aaron's Emoticons
*http://www.teleport.com/~rhubarbs/faces.htm*
Another extensive source of emoticons.

### CyberAtlas
*http://cyberatlas.internet.com*
CyberAtlas is your guide to online facts. The site provides readers with valuable statistics and Web marketing information, enabling them to understand their business environment and make more informed business decisions.

### E-mail—The Mining Company
*http://email.miningco.com/internet/email/*
Updated weekly, this site consists of articles and links to e-mail resources on many topics: beginning e-mail, finding people, free e-mail, greeting cards, privacy, and much more.

# 8

# Effective Mailing List Promotion

Internet mailing lists are quick and easy ways to distribute information to a large number of people. There are thousands of publicly available online lists. You can also create your own Internet mailing lists to keep your clients and prospects informed of company events, product announcements, and press releases. In this chapter we cover:

- How to identify appropriate publicly accessible mailing lists (discussion lists)

- Subscribing to the mailing list

- Writing messages that will be read

- Mailing list Netiquette

- Creating your own mailing list

## Connecting with Your Target Audience

Discussion mailing lists are publicly available and focused on a particular subject matter. Participating in a discussion list relevant to your line of business can help you attract new customers. Discussion lists are organized hierarchically by subject matter in a way similar to Usenet newsgroups. Likewise, the membership rate of each discussion mailing list varies. People subscribe to particular lists to participate in that list and receive all of the postings that are sent to the group, generally because they have an interest in the topic. When you post a message to a mailing list, the message is sent out to everyone who has subscribed to the list by e-mail.

Discussion mailing lists are quick and easy ways to distribute information to a large number of people interested in a particular topic. The difference between discussion mailing lists and newsgroups is that anyone on the Internet can visit newsgroups at any time and read any articles of interest, whereas a discussion list delivers all messages posted directly to the subscribers' e-mail.

*Note:* Only discussion list subscribers can receive these messages. Newsgroups can be viewed by anyone with access to a news server. All they have to do is log onto the news server and enter the name of the newsgroup they wish to peruse, and they can view all postings made to that group. To subscribe to a discussion list, you have to send a subscription message to the list administrator and request permission to join the mailing list. Thus, newsgroup postings can be viewed anonymously, but permission is required to view postings to mailing lists.

## Types of Publicly Accessible Mailing Lists

Publicly accessible mailing lists can be one of several types, each with varying degrees of control. Following is a discussion of the major types of lists.

### Moderated Discussion Lists

This type of list is maintained by a "gatekeeper" who filters out unwanted or inappropriate messages. If you try to post an advertisement where it is not permitted, your message will never make it out to the list of subscribers. Similarly, flames (i.e., publicly chastising another list member) are screened out. The gatekeeper will also keep the topic of discussion on track if a few members get off-topic.

### Unmoderated Discussion Lists

An unmoderated list is operated without any centralized control or censorship. Most lists are of this type. All messages are automatically forwarded to subscribers. Unmoderated lists tend to have more blatant advertisements and flame wars because there is no gatekeeper to guide the discussion. It is then the responsibility of the list members to police their own actions. Otherwise, the list could end up being a landfill for spammers, or a lot of members will simply leave the list if a few individuals choose to ridicule them.

## Targeting Appropriate Discussion Mailing Lists

There are thousands of publicly available lists online and a number of sites that provide lists of mailing lists. Three of the most popular and comprehensive are:

- The Liszt at *http://www.liszt.com* (Figure 8.1)

- The List of Publicly Accessible Mailing Lists at *http://www.neosoft.com/internet/pam/* (Figure 8.2)

- Tile.net at *http://tile.net/lists* (Figure 8.3)

There are also companies online that specialize in providing targeted e-mail lists. One such company is Post Master Direct Response at *www.postmasterdirect.com.* This Company rents e-mail lists of people who have requested information on a particular topic. However, these differ from the discussion mailing lists that we described earlier in this chapter. E-mail lists are simply that—lists of e-mail addresses. If you subscribe to one of these lists, you are not entering into a discussion, you are placing yourself on a mailing list that will receive e-mail advertisements. However, from a marketing perspective, e-mail lists can be useful tools if they are targeted.

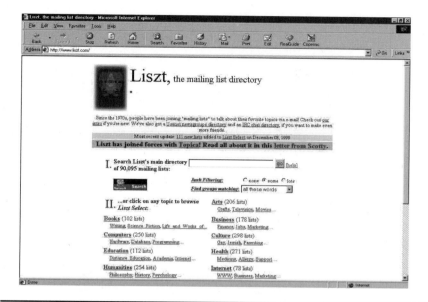

**Figure 8.1.** The Liszt has indexed over 90,000 publicly available mailing lists.

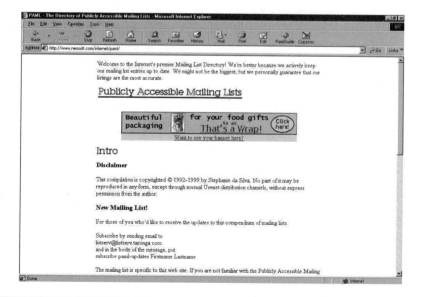

**Figure 8.2.** The List of Publicly Accessible Mailing Lists.

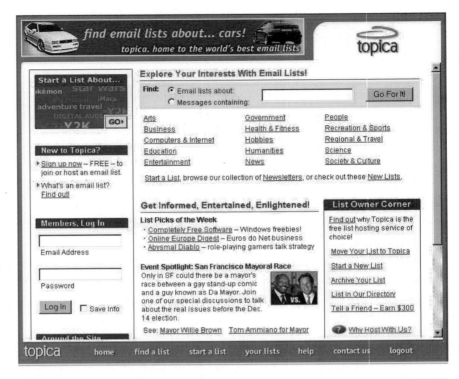

**Figure 8.3.**   The Tile.net offers more publicly accessible mailing lists.

**Bulk e-mail**
Group of
identical
messages e-
mailed to a
large num-
ber of ad-
dresses at
once

**Spam**
Sending the
same mes-
sage to a
large num-
ber of
people who
didn't ask
for it;
sending
people
annoying
mail

Another option is to develop your own mailing list. This concept will be discussed in the next chapter. Still another option is to purchase **bulk e-mail** lists. This is a questionable practice because it involves **spam**. Bulk e-mail lists are generally sold without the permission of the addressees, much like junk mailing lists. The recipients did not ask to be put on a mailing list. They are not aware of the fact that they are on a list and often do not appreciate being sent unsolicited e-mail. Another drawback is that usually these lists are not targeted. By using bulk e-mail lists you run the risk of not reaching any of your target market. You also risk annoying those addressees who under other circumstances may have been interested in what you were trying to sell.

The correct choice depends on the market you are targeting. Some people use the shotgun approach to reach as many people as possible. We've all received those e-mails that say, "Reach 5 million with our mailing list available for $29.95." After all, one of the major benefits of the Internet is reaching large numbers of people quickly. There is no excuse for this kind of "marketing." Even if someone is marketing a product with broad-based appeal, it does not grant them a license to spam the world with their marketing message. If it isn't "opt-in," don't send it. Nobody is going to be too impressed if they receive spam. Either the message will be deleted without being read, or some of the recipients of the spam could complain to the sender's ISP and have the sender's Internet access revoked.

The best approach is to choose a list whose subscribers fit your target market as closely as possible. For example, if you are selling Geographic Information Systems to municipalities, a shotgun approach is a waste of both your time and resources. By using bulk e-mail you raise the ire of thousands of recipients of your e-mail, destroy your corporate image, and potentially damage your professional credibility. In this case, a much smaller targeted list should be used to get a much higher-quality response rate. Less is better.

## Finding the Right Mailing List

Whether you join a publicly accessible discussion mailing list or choose to purchase an opt-in e-mail list from one of the many online sources, you want to find a mailing list whose members are your target market. You will have to do your homework here, because there are thousands of mail lists to choose from.

There are various meta-indexes of publicly available mailing lists where you can search by title or by subject. Some of these sites provide detailed information on the mail lists, such as their content and the commands used to subscribe. We have provided information on a number of these resources in the Internet Resources section at the end of this chapter.

Once you have identified mail lists that have your target market as members you will subscribe to those lists. To confirm that the list is appropriate for your marketing purposes, lurk a while to monitor the discussion taking place. Once this has been confirmed, you can begin participating in the list by providing valuable content. If advertising is not allowed, abide by the rules.

## Subscribing to Your Target Mailing Lists

*Liszt, title.net/lists,* and the Internet Publicly Available Discussion Mailing Lists are great resources and will provide you with not only a huge list of accessible mailing lists but also specific instructions for joining the particular lists you are interested in. Most lists are subscribed to by sending an e-mail to the given address with "subscribe" in the subject or the body of the message. There are variations on this theme, so you must check the instructions for joining each specific mailing list. After you subscribe you generally will receive an e-mail response with the rules, FAQs, and instructions on how to use the list.

For the most part, all of the rules for posting to newsgroups apply to mailing lists as well. Read the rules carefully and abide by them. A lurking period should be considered before you post a message. This will help you observe what types of messages are posted and the commonly accepted practices for that particular group.

### List Digests

These are compilations of many individual messages sent to each subscriber as one bulk message. Many digests contain a table of contents. The good thing about a digest is you do not receive as many separate e-mails and your mailbox doesn't become clogged up. Also, the digest administrator chooses all or only the best postings to include in the list digest. Therefore, blatant advertisements, flames, and postings containing repetitive subject matter are filtered out. In an unmoderated list, you would receive every single message posted to the list. Most of these postings would not be of interest to you and would be deleted anyway. The digest format simplifies things so that you get the information you need without wasting a lot of time.

## Composing Effective Messages

As discussed in the previous chapter, your e-mails must be carefully prepared before you post to a mailing list. Remember to make your subject line relevant, keep your messages short and to the point, and always include your sig.file. If you are unsure whether your posting is appropriate for the group, you can simply send a test message to the moderator asking for advice.

Unlike newsgroups, the members of mailing lists receive all the messages directly into their mailbox every day. Some people prefer to receive the postings in *digest form*; that is, all the messages for that day are compiled into one e-mail sent to the recipient at the end of the day. The digest provides, at the beginning of the e-mail, a listing of all the messages with the "From" and "Subject" identified, followed by the complete messages. Just as individuals who visit a newsgroup don't read all the messages, subscribers to publicly accessible discussion lists do not read every posting. They decide which messages to review based on the subject line. Thus, the content of the "Subject" field is extremely important.

You must never repeat the same or similar messages to a mailing list as you might do in a newsgroup. Once members of a mailing list have seen your posted message, they will not appreciate seeing it again, whereas a newsgroup has different readers all the time and similar postings are acceptable if they are timed appropriately. The following tips on mailing list postings will assist you in becoming a respected member of their online community:

- Make sure that your messages are "on the subject." List subscribers don't want to hear announcements unrelated to their topic.

- You should be a regular contributor to your list before making any commercial announcement. If your mailing list does not allow advertising (most do not) use your sig.file. Sig.files are generally accepted. Ensure that you make effective use of your tag line to get your mini-ad into discussion mailing lists where blatant advertising is not permitted. (See Chapter 6 for advertising when advertising is not allowed.)

- Track and record your responses when you use a new mailing list. You should have a call to action in your posting, encouraging the readers to visit a specific page on your site or to send e-mail to an e-mail address designated solely for this purpose. Only by employing an appropriate mechanism to track responses will you know with any certainty which mailing lists are successful and which are not. It's amazing how well calls to action work. For some reason, people tend to do what they're told.

- Set reasonable and achievable goals. As a benchmark, in most e-mail marketing campaigns a 1% to 3% response rate is considered a good response. However, if your mailing list is very targeted and you are offering something of interest or value to a particular group, your response rates should be significantly higher.

## Building Your Own Private Mailing Lists

You may want to build your own mailing lists. Generating your own mailing lists is often beneficial because of the many marketing uses the lists have. They can be used to maintain an ongoing dialogue with existing customers regarding updates, support, specials, and so on. They can also be used to communicate with current and prospective customers through distribution of corporate newsletters, price lists, new catalogues, product updates, new product announcements, and upcoming events.

You can use a number of methods for soliciting and collecting e-mail addresses, including an online guestbook or other type of registration form to be filled out on your Web site. However, you must provide people with an incentive to leave their e-mail address with you.

Place a form with a "Subscribe here" button on your site where visitors can sign up for the mailing list. Terminology such as "Sign up now to receive our free newsletter" or "Click here to receive our reliable information newsletter" might be useful in convincing people to subscribe. Having people register for your mailing list by offering an informative newsletter is a great way to stay in touch with your target market. If you have valuable information that your customers and potential customers want, they will gladly give you their e-mail address to obtain your newsletter.

A prime example of this would be John Audette, who moderates the prestigious Internet-Sales Discussion list, which publishes the I-Sales Digest and is sent daily to more than 7000 subscribers in over 65 countries. John operates an Internet marketing company and needed to find a way to reach his target market. The I-Sales Digest now boasts a strong online readership and is the perfect environment to learn about Internet marketing. All 7000+ subscribers gladly divulged their e-mail address to join the I-Sales community. You can accomplish similar feats if you decide to administer your own newsletter. Others provide freebie incentives such as T-shirts, software, or games. If you sign up for the newsletter at Lobster Direct (*www.lobsterdirect.com*), your name will be put in the draw for live lobsters.

Encourage customers and potential customers to subscribe to your electronic newsletter through traditional marketing techniques including press releases, offline newsletters, advertising, letters, and so on. If you use hardcopy direct mail, you can design a response system that requests the e-mail addresses through a fax-back, business reply card, or 1-800 number, or by asking respondents to go to your Web site or e-mail you directly. You can also ask people to sign up for your mailing list through newsgroup and mailing list postings, signature files, and other advertising.

You can boost your response rate by guaranteeing that responders' e-mail addresses will be kept confidential and not sold to anyone else. People are concerned about the privacy of the information they provide you with. If you cannot assure them that your company will use their e-mail address solely for your correspondence with them, they will not feel comfortable giving their e-mail address to you. Provide people with your private policy statement. Make them feel comfortable about divulging their e-mail address to your business.

Don't ever add someone's name to your mailing list without his or her permission. People really resent receiving unsolicited mail, even if you give them the option to unsubscribe. However, one method of obtaining more e-mail addresses is to suggest to your subscribers that they recommend your mailing list to a friend (or a few friends). Let your subscribers spread the word about your mailing list. If your list provides useful information, your subscribers will recommend the list to their friends. Some of these people will then subscribe and tell their friends about your mailing list, and so forth. Word of mouth is a powerful force on the Internet. See Chapter 9 for details on the "how to" of setting up your mail list.

## Starting Your Own Publicly Available Mailing List

To create your Internet mailing list, first you must give it a name that reflects the discussion that will take place and is enticing for your target market. Draft a FAQ file or charter containing information on what the list is all about. Develop guidelines for participation.

You will need to find a place to host your mail list. Many ISPs host mail lists, or you can use one of the many online mail list hosting services. For lists and links of hosting service providers check out Vivian Neou's site at *http://www.catalog.com/vivian/mailing-list-providers.html.*

You should create a Web page for your list to provide information about the list as well as its charter and guidelines. You should provide an opportunity to subscribe from the Web site as well. This will add credibility to your mailing list.

Once the list is up and running you will have to advertise it so that people will actually subscribe. You can promote your list by participating in newsgroups that relate to your mail list topic. Remember not to post blatant ads where advertising is not allowed. Contribute to the newsgroup with your postings and use a tag line in your signature file to promote your mail list. You can also trade e-mail sponsorships with other mailing lists for promotion purposes.

There are a number of places to appropriately announce your list. One recommendation is the Internet Scout's New List, which you can find at *http://scout.cs.wisc.edu/scout/new-list/index.html.* Net Happenings is another announcement resource for new Internet resources. Gleason Sackson, the moderator of this list, has a huge following. To subscribe to Net Happenings, send an e-mail to *majordomo@is.internic.net* with "subscribe net-happenings" in the message area.

Get your mail list linked from the many lists of lists on the Internet. We have provided some of these in the Internet Resources at the end of this chapter. Make your list worth reading by ensuring that you and others have valuable information on the topic to share.

## Escape the Unsolicited Bulk E-mail Trend

Bulk e-mail is any group of identical messages sent to a large number of e-mail addresses at one time. In some cases bulk e-mail lists have been developed from opt-in lists, and the names are continually filtered through all of the universal remove lists. These lists are often categorized by subject and provide an acceptable marketing vehicle. If you are using opt-in e-mail lists and removing unsubscribe requests from your database, this is considered a legitimate e-mail marketing campaign.

However, many bulk e-mail lists have been developed by unscrupulous means, and the people on the lists have no interest in or desire to receive unsolicited e-mail. Unsolicited bulk e-mail is the single largest form of e-mail abuse we have seen to date.

Over the last couple of years, more and more businesses on the Internet focus on services and software products catering to the bulk e-mail market. Software products have been developed that collect e-mail addresses from Usenet newsgroups, online service members' directories and forums, bots that look for "mailto:" codes in HTML documents online, publicly available mailing list subscribers, or even your site's visitors. Service companies that collect e-mail addresses and perform bulk mailings abound today on the Internet. Be very careful when considering bulk e-mail for online marketing purposes.

## Internet Resources

### Lists of Mailing Lists

#### Search the List of Lists—Mailing Lists
*http://www.catalog.com/vivian/interest-group-search.html*
Search one of the largest directories of special-interest group e-mail lists (also known as listservs) available on the Internet.

#### Liszt, the Mailing List Directory
*http://www.liszt.com*
A very big directory of mailing lists—over 90,000 to date. The Liszt has organized its lists into subject categories. The Liszt provides details on how to subscribe to each of the mailing lists in its database and provides information on content as well.

#### List of Publicly Available Mailing Lists
*http://www.neosoft.com/internet/paml*
The List of Publicly Accessible Mailing Lists is posted on this site and once each month to the Usenet newsgroups *news.lists.misc* and *news.answers*. The Usenet version is the definitive copy—this Web version is generated from the database and uploaded several days

after the Usenet version is posted. They continually post to Usenet so that the PAML will be archived at *rtfm.mit.edu*.

### Reference.com
*http://www.reference.com/*
Reference.com makes it easy to find, browse, search, and participate in more than 150,000 newsgroups, mailing lists, and Web forums. Reference.com does not break their listings down by subject categories, but you can do a keyword search. Information is provided on content as well as on subscribe commands. Reference.com allows list owners to archive their content for free. A clipping service is also available—you enter search criteria and Reference.com forwards incoming mailing list messages that match.

### The List Exchange
*http://www.listex.com/imark.html*
The Internet's one-stop mailing list resource. It links to a number of list sites and sites with information on building your lists.

### L-Soft's CataList
*http://www.lsoft.com/lists/listref.html*
CataList, the catalog of listserv lists! From this page, you can browse any of the 19,516 public listserv lists on the Internet, search for mailing lists of interest, and get information about listserv host sites. This information is generated automatically from Listserv's Lists database and is always up-to-date.

### The Internet Mailing List Network
*http://www.listsnet.com/*
ListsNet comprises a directory of publicly available mailing lists with browse and search capabilities. The mailing lists are categorized by subject and subtopics.

### Internet Marketing Mailing List
*http://www.o-a.com*
The Online Advertising Discussion List focuses on professional discussion of online advertising strategies, results, studies, tools, and media coverage. The list also welcomes discussion on the related topics of online promotion and public relations. The list encourages shar-

ing of practical expertise and experiences between those who buy, sell, research, and develop tools for online advertising, as well as those providing online public relations and publicity services. The list also serves as a resource to members of the press who are writing about the subject of online advertising and promotion.

### Usenet Newsgroup
*news.lists*
Gives you the list of new Usenet Newsgroups, up-and-coming ones as well as the most popular ones.

### AOL, Prodigy, and CompuServe
All have their own areas where you can search for mailing lists.

### HTMARCOM
A mailing list that discusses high-tech marketing. To subscribe send the message "subscribe htmarcom your name" to the e-mail address *listserv@usa.net*.

### I-Sales Digest
*http://www.mmgco.com/isales*
Formed in November 1995, the goal of the Internet Sales Moderated Discussion List is to provide a forum for meaningful and helpful discussion of online sales issues by those engaged in the online sale of products and services. The list is moderated by John Audette, president of Multimedia Marketing Group, Inc.

## E-mail List Builder Programs

### The Direct E-mail List Source
*http://www.copywriter.com/lists/index.htm*
Thousands of e-mail lists where you can advertise without spamming.

### Elmed Targeted Email Software
*http://www.yug.com/tools/itools.htm*
Information on, and links to, many e-mail marketing tools and software programs.

### Campaign email marketing software
*http://www.arialsoftware.com*
This is e-mail marketing software used to conduct legitimate e-mail marketing campaigns. Campaign can import your contact database information and send personalized e-mail messages to all of your contacts.

### MailKing
*http://www.mailking.com*
MailKing is similar to Campaign in that it can import your contact database information and send personalized e-mail messages to all of your contacts.

### Web Crumbs
*http://www.thinweb.com*
Web Crumbs gathers the e-mail addresses of visitors to your Web site. This intelligent program can also manipulate what the visitor sees based on rules. Downloadable demo available from this site.

### ListBot
*http://www.listbot.com/*
ListBot makes starting your own free e-mail list quick and easy. Use a ListBot e-mail list to stay in touch with friends and family, notify customers of new products and specials, find out who is visiting your Web site and send updates, let your clubs, teams, classes, and so on talk by e-mail, create a forum for discussing favorite topic, publish an electronic newsletter, or connect any group of people by e-mail.

### ONElist
*http://www.onelist.com/*
ONElist is a free e-mail community service. The ONElist service empowers you to explore and create e-mail communities where you can share views, ideas, and common interests with others. Create your own mail list today.

# 9

# Establishing Your Private Mailing List

Private mailing lists exist in many different forms (discussion lists, newsletters, moderated or unmoderated lists, and digests) and are a tremendous vehicle for building relationships and a sense of community with your target market. You have seen how you can join a publicly accessible mailing list, but what if you wanted to establish your own private list? In this chapter we cover:

- Why you should administer your own list

- Choosing the right type of mailing list

- Selecting the right host for your mailing list

- Establishing your list

- Advertising your mailing list

- Potential troubleshooting issues

## Why Have Your Own Mailing List?

There are numerous reasons why it would be appropriate to administer your own list. In fact, some of the same reasons that make it imperative to join someone else's list are also benefits for running a list of your own. Running a mailing list of your own can be beneficial in other ways:

- Learning from others

- Networking, creating new business relationships

- Establishing yourself as an expert in your field

- Keeping yourself updated on the current trends in your field

- Permission-based marketing

- As a potential source of revenue

### Learn from Others

In any given field of business, science, or art, there is always someone else who knows something that you do not. By administering your own discussion list, you are inviting other experts in your field will join your list and divulge their knowledge and insight. You can learn valuable lessons and acquire useful techniques from this exchange of information and apply these techniques to your own business.

Obviously, you can learn a lot from simply joining another person's discussion list. However, if you are the list administrator, you establish the guidelines for conversation and the topics appropriate for discussion. Therefore, you can focus your mailing list on the topics that are most applicable to your business and that interest you the most. Someone else's list might occasionally discuss issues that are not as relevant to your field. By having your own list, you can make the topics of discussion as narrow or as broad as you wish.

## Networking

Having your own list permits you to network closely with others in your industry. Very often, new business relationships and opportunities develop when people with similar interests are brought together. Utilize your discussion list to facilitate the creation of these sorts of relationships. It could be that you find new business partners, establish new clients, or start another business venture.

## Establish Yourself as an Expert

By moderating your own industry-specific mailing list and offering your advice to members of your list, you will establish yourself as an expert in your field. Thus, you can quickly earn the respect and admiration of your peers and develop new business contacts and clients as a result.

## Keep Yourself Up To Date

Participants in your publicly accessible mailing list can bring new ideas and innovations relevant to your industry into focus. Discussing or moderating the discussion of these innovations will make you more knowledgeable and keep you abreast with the latest buzz in your industry.

## Permission-Based Marketing

Subscribers have willingly given you their e-mail addresses, and they are interested in the issues discussed. You have acquired their permission to send them e-mail, and you have established yourself as a respected member of the industry. Your mailing list's participants are exactly the type of people you want to market your product or service to because they are a captive audience in your target market.

Ariel Poler of Topica (*http://www.topica.com*), (Figure 9.1) a site that provides a central directory for creating and subscribing to electronic mailing lists, figures that discussion mailing lists provide a window into a user's passions. For instance, tennis enthusiasts will join

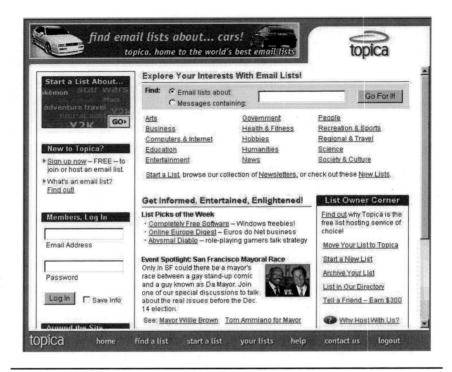

**Figure 9.1.** Topica is a free Internet service that allows you to easily find, manage, and participate in e-mail lists.

mailing lists about tennis and music lovers will join lists that cater to the types of music they enjoy. Thus, discussion lists are able to accomplish what all marketers wish to achieve, and that is to attract the target market. Poler said, "There's a business here in applying the classic audience aggregation model." Basically, your mailing list brings together the people who are keenly interested in your product or service. This is permission-based, opt-in, e-mail marketing. You are able to market without spamming, and the marketing is targeted.

## Potential Source of Revenue

Once your list becomes established and has many subscribers, you may be able to sell advertising to people interested in marketing to your list members. Needless to say, a mailing list becomes an excellent revenue source as its credibility and membership expand. In the end, the time and effort you exert  nurturing your list to prominence will pay for itself and more. If you are already a member of a publicly accessible mailing list, take note of the number of advertisements that appear in each posting you receive from the list. Administer your own list and earn advertising revenue for yourself.

## Choosing the Right Type of Mailing List

Before you can proceed with your private mailing list, you must decide the format for your list. The format you choose will depend on how much discussion you wish to generate and the amount of time and resources you can devote to administering to the list. Following are the mailing list formats you have to choose from. Many of these were discussed in the previous chapter as well:

- Discussion list

- Announce list (newsletter format)

- Open forum

- Closed forum

- Moderated list

- Unmoderated list

- Digest format

### Discussion List or Newsletter?

The discussion list is the most common type of mailing list because this format best fosters conversation between individuals interested in a particular topic. For instance, the VEGLIFE discussion list will attract people wishing to discuss aspects of vegetarian lifestyle. They exchange nutritional information, recipes, restaurant suggestions and health tips. If you want to create an interactive support community such as the VEGLIFE group has, a discussion list would be a good option. A discussion list encourages an open forum in which the conversation is multidirectional. List members speak directly to you, you can speak to them, and they can converse with each other.

An announcement/newsletter format is appropriate when you desire the conversation to move in one direction: from you (the list owner) to the subscribers. Announcements, press releases, and news articles would fit well into a newsletter format. With the newsletter format, it is easier to advertise as well, because you control the content of the newsletter. If you only intend to provide information and not to stimulate discussion, choose the newsletter format.

### Open or Closed Forum?

Mailing lists that are "open forum" allow anyone with a valid e-mail address to subscribe to the list. If you are promoting an online business indirectly through your mailing list, apply an open forum format in order to appeal to a broader spectrum of individuals. For instance, anyone can visit your Web site and subscribe to your list if it has an open forum.

**Intranet**
An internal Internet not accessible to the public

"Closed forum" mailing lists restrict access to an exclusive group of people. Closed forum lists are great for corporate **intranets**, where the topics of discussion cannot be revealed to the public. In this situation, you would not allow just anyone to visit your site and subscribe to your list.

### Moderated or Unmoderated?

A moderated list (as discussed in Chapter 8) allows you (the list administrator) to forward the best postings to the group and filter out inappropriate messages. This means more administration time on your part because you are responsible for reading (and sometimes editing) every post that comes in and then forwarding the good posts to all of the group members. However, moderated lists tend to stay on topic, and spam and flames are stifled before they can cause trouble. This keeps your mailing list more topical, more friendly, and more conducive to generating conversation.

With an unmoderated list, all postings are automatically forwarded to everyone on the list whether the messages are appropriate or not. This reduces your administration time, but it increases the chances of having your mailing list go off-topic or turning into a spam repository. When a mailing list is regularly off-topic, it is less useful and subscribers may lose interest. For the purposes of creating an online community, you will be best served by having a moderated mailing list.

### The List Digest Format

This is the most compact and "digestible" format for an Internet mailing list. Your readers will appreciate it because they will receive one message daily or every couple of days containing all or the best recent postings instead of having to download every message sent to the list. Of course, this means more work for the discussion list administrator to edit and compile the digest. Some **list server software** can generate digests for you, but ideally, you should seize control. It's your digest after all.

**List server software**
An application installed on a publicly accessible server that manages messages sent to and from a mailing list

## Selecting the Right Host for Your Mailing List

Who will host your mailing list? Ask yourself this question once you have decided which format you want your list to assume. You have two options:

- Host your own mailing list

- Find a mailing list hosting service provider to host your list

### Hosting Your Own List

If your organization has the bandwidth and a computer available to use as a list server, you could host your own mailing list. By this, we mean that your server will handle all of the incoming and outgoing mail related to your mailing list. Be aware that the e-mail resulting from an Internet mailing list can become voluminous. Ensure that your connection to the Internet and the list server you are using are robust enough to handle the traffic. Otherwise, your list server could crash, your list will not be delivered, and messages sent to the list could start bouncing. Also think of what other features besides the format of the mailing list you would be interested in. Carefully select your list server software to ensure it accommodates the features you are looking for. Other features to consider are:

- **Automatic problem-solvers.** Some list server software can help you send automated responses to commonly asked questions. If technical support is your business or if most responses to your newsletter are repetitive in nature, select a list server application with this feature.

- **Archives.** Some list server programs can save and compile past messages into a handy archive that can be accessed over the Web. This database of responses can provide valuable information to your customers, but it can eat up a lot of space on your server. You might also wish to write a script to make the archive searchable.

- **Importing an existing list of addresses.** Make sure the list server software you choose can import your existing e-mail contact list from whichever file format you have saved it in. If you have to reenter all of your contact information into the list server software by hand, a lot of time will be wasted.

- **Virus protection.** You might be interested in selecting a list server application that automatically filters out e-mail file attachments. This will prevent anyone from sending a virus to your entire mailing list.

Our Internet Resources at the end of this chapter indicate a few of the popular list server applications you can install and configure on your mail server to help you administer your mailing list. Consider all of the features you require to implement and administer your mailing list while deciding which software suits your needs.

### Find a Mail List Host Service Provider

A lot of companies host their mailing lists with an ISP. Quite often, your regular Internet Service Provider will gladly host your list for you for an additional fee. However, some ISPs are reluctant to host Internet mailing lists due to the high volume of traffic they can generate. This reluctance to host mailing lists has opened a door of opportunity for mailing list hosting service providers.

Mailing list hosting service providers will charge approximately $15 to $30 US per month for their hosting services. Some providers offer this service for free, but the features they offer might be too restrictive. There may be subscriber limits or limited customer support if something goes wrong. Choose a list host that can offer you all of the features you require without charging you too much or imposing too many restrictions. Also, ensure that your list host performs regular backups of its list server. If their server ever crashes, you do not want to lose posted messages or your subscriber list. The following URL provides a list of Internet mailing list hosts you can select from:

*http://catalog.com/vivian/mailing-list-providers.html*

## Establishing Your List

### Give It a Name

The first step is to select a name for your mailing list. Keep the name brief and descriptive so that it is memorable and gives a clear indication about the primary topic of discussion. Most list owners use one-word names. Hyphens or underscores can be included in your list's name to connect two or more words.

### Draft Your Charter

Write a succinct and concise series of paragraphs stating the purpose of your mailing list, the scope of its topics, and the rules of conduct.

Let your subscribers know why you created the mailing list, and keep its scope narrow enough that the list will be useful. Establish the ground rules for what is an acceptable post, and indicate the consequences of straying from the list's charter. In your charter, specifically take a stand on the following issues:

- Appropriate and inappropriate advertising to the list

- Your stance on flaming

- Your stance on obscene language and other forms of offensive writing

To protect yourself, you should also caution subscribers about the potential for viruses to be sent to the mailing list. Although viruses on lists are rare, you should recommend that subscribers install virus-protection software on their systems to scan their hard drives on a regular basis. Finally, keep your mailing list's charter short. Nobody wants to read a lengthy document.

## Write a "Welcome Aboard" Message

Create a greeting message that is automatically sent to new subscribers. Most list server software can send a message to people as they subscribe. In the greeting message, include:

- Your charter

- Instructions for posting to the list

- Directions for where list members can go for help

- Unsubscribing and subscribing information

- Your contact information

Keep the greeting message short and descriptive, and encourage users to archive the message for future reference.

### Create a FAQ File and a Companion Web Site

Post a list of Frequently Asked Questions (with answers) on a companion Web site so that subscribers can easily find answers to common questions. This will reduce the number of instances where subscribers post the same questions to the mailing list. Long-time subscribers quickly tire of reading the same old questions over and over again. Also, post your charter to your Web site, and include a form on the mailing list's site to allow new subscribers to join.

### Before You Go Live...

Work closely with your technical staff or your ISP (if you outsource the mailing list hosting) to ensure that all the features of the mailing list are in proper working order. Enlist your colleagues to help you test your mailing list. Have them subscribe, post a message to the list, unsubscribe, proofread your charter and FAQ, and verify that the companion Web site works and loads properly into various browsers. Once you are satisfied that your list is fully operational, start advertising it and seek out new subscribers.

## Advertising Your Mailing List

There are numerous tools online to help you promote your mailing list. Here are just a few of them:

- Register your mailing list with The List of Lists *(http://catalog.com/vivian/interest-group-search.html)*, Topica, Liszt, tile.net *(http://tile.net/lists)*, and the Publicly Accessible Mailing Lists index *(http://www.neosoft.com/internet/paml)*.

- Publicize your mailing list in postings to other mailing lists and newsgroups if it is appropriate. There is a moderated mailing list devoted to helping new list owners promote their list. To subscribe, send a message containing the line "subscribe new-list firstname lastname" to *listserv@vm1 .nodak.edu.*

- Submit the companion Web site for the mailing list to all of the major search engines. Of course, following the tips presented in this book will help you achieve higher search engine rankings.

- Invite your friends and colleagues to join your list.

- Remember to mention your mailing list in your e-mail signature file. This is an easy way to promote the list.

Some other promotional activities include the following:

- Do not subscribe anyone to your mailing list without their expressed permission to do so. This would be spamming. We have already discussed this point in great detail. Spamming is wrong, so don't do it.

- Stay active. Actively participate in your own list. Offer advice when you can and encourage conversation between subscribers. Never allow the conversation to die. If posts to your mailing list get stale, subscribers will quickly lose interest.

Of course, you will be an active participant in other ways as well. You are going to be the person responsible for enforcing the charter and keeping the discussion on-topic. Deal with inappropriate posts swiftly, snuff out flame wars and prevent spamming.

How busy you are with your mailing list will depend on how popular the list is and vice versa. The amount of promotional work you perform for your mailing list is directly correlated to the number of subscribers you will attract. Of course, you will have to spend time helping people subscribe and unsubscribe, find the FAQ file, and so on, because not everyone is able to figure it out without help. There are a lot of aspects to having your own list. Tending to every aspect will keep you occupied. If you ever need advice about administering your mailing list, here is an excellent newsgroup you should inspect: *comp.mail.list-admin.policy.*

## Potential Troubleshooting Issues

Besides setting up your list and promoting it, you will face numerous troubleshooting issues as a mailing list administrator. If you have an ISP hosting your list, they will handle some of these tasks. If you host your list, then the troubleshooting responsibility rests squarely on your shoulders. Here are some of the issues to be wary of:

- Bounced mail

- Malformed commands sent to the list server software

- Flames

- Spam

- Bossy subscribers

- Practical jokes

- Viruses

- Server crashes

### Bounced Mail

As a mailing list owner, you will often have to deal with undeliverable mail. These are messages that were sent to subscribers but were returned to your server for whatever reason. It's possible that a particular recipient's mail server was down or the mailbox was full. Bounced mail is an inevitable event.

Your list server software can likely be programmed to handle returned mail automatically. Otherwise, the bounced message will have to be deleted by hand. Some list server applications send regularly scheduled probes to all subscribers on your list. These probes are simply e-mail messages sent to test whether a subscriber's e-mail account is still active. If the probe message is returned, the subscriber is assumed to no longer be an active list member and is removed from the list. Either you or your ISP will handle returned mail, depending on your hosting arrangements.

### Malformed Commands Sent to the List Server Software

Despite providing clear and concise instructions in the footer information of all postings and in the FAQ file for subscribing and unsubscribing, some people will still make mistakes. List server software must regularly cope with incorrectly formatted subscribe and unsubscribe messages. Some software will bounce these malformed messages back to the sender or forward a copy of the message to you for correction. Ideally, your list server software should be modified to automatically handle malformed commands. Unless the software you install on your list server can parse the invalid subscribe and unsubscribe requests automatically, the best you can do is clearly state the list instructions in your charter and on your Web site and deal with the poorly formatted messages as they occur.

### Flames

Most people are good-natured most of the time, but occasionally, someone will lose their cool and flame another subscriber. Regardless of the reason for the attack, you must stop flames immediately before they become uncontrollable. Send a private note to the offending person, repeat the antiflame policy in your charter statement, and insist that they cease the attacks. If this person persists with flame mail, remove him or her from the mailing list.

### Spam

No matter what, do not allow spam to overrun your mailing list. Spammers know that posts to mailing lists are distributed to all the subscribers. Therefore, mailing lists are prime candidates for a good spam attack.

If you moderate your mailing list, you can easily filter out the junk mail before it hits all of your subscribers. Some list management applications can filter out spam if the subject line reads something like "Quick $$$ for you!" Write a well-defined spam policy in your charter statement, and send a private message to people who break the rules. Immediately remove continual offenders from the list. If you are able to determine the spammer's ISP, file a complaint with them. Chances are, the ISP will revoke the spammer's Internet account.

## Bossy Subscribers

Occasionally, a subscriber will act as the great purveyor of justice and scold others who break the rules of the charter. Although their intentions may be grounded in good faith, do-gooders like this can instigate a series of inflammatory posts. To avoid a problem of this nature, suggest to your subscribers that they privately file complaints to you if someone abuses the charter rules instead of bogging down the entire list.

## Practical Jokes

Pranksters can occasionally tamper with your list and subscribe third parties without their consent. Thus, you end up looking like a spammer when your mailing list is sent to people who never actually subscribed. To avoid situations like this, ensure that your list server software is able to send an autoresponder message to ask new subscribers to confirm their subscription. This will prevent anyone from being inadvertently subscribed to the mailing list.

## Viruses

We mentioned earlier in this chapter that you should caution subscribers to be very conscious of attachments sent to the list because these may contain viruses. If your list server software cannot screen out attachments, suggest to your users that they simply delete any attachments sent to the list. This will prevent widespread virus contamination. Consider using list server software that can screen for attachments in the first place. If your list host's software does not provide this feature, consider switching to another host.

## Server Crashes

Mailing lists are hosted on a computer, other computers connect this computer to others, and so on. All systems are connected when they are on the Internet. Your server may crash from time to time. If this happens and your mailing list is inaccessible, subscribers might become grumpy. The best tactic is to send your subscribers a written apology as soon as the server is up and running again. Switch your service provider if you find your list server crashes frequently.

## Where to Go from Here

In this chapter, we discussed reasons why you might want to administer your own mailing list, deciding what type of list is best for your needs, how you can set up your mailing list, and other issues you will likely face once your list goes live. Private mailing lists are prime marketing vehicles if you manage them correctly and actively promote them. You can reach out to your target market with a mailing list. This technique of permission or opt-in e-mail marketing is the key to your success. If you have something to offer to people in your industry and it is feasible for you to establish and administer a mailing list, give the idea strong consideration.

## Internet Resources

### LISTSERV
*http://www.lsoft.com/*
LISTSERV e-mail list management software is renowned for its flexibility, scalability and performance. Start your own Internet mailing discussion list.

### Lyris—E-mail List Server
*http://www.lyris.com/*
Lyris is a powerful e-mail list server that automatically delivers your newsletters, announcements, and discussion lists.

### MailWorkz
*http://www.mailworkz.com*
Broadc@st HTML facilitates your online communications campaign; from building quality customer lists through designing and sending your key messages, to handling the responses and requests for more information.
Dynamic product!

### Majordomo
*http://www.greatcircle.com/majordomo/*
Majordomo is a program that automates the management of Internet mailing lists. Commands are sent to Majordomo via electronic mail to handle all aspects of list maintenance. Once a list is set up, virtually all operations can be performed remotely, requiring no intervention upon the postmaster of the list site.

### Macjordomo
*http://leuca.med.cornell.edu/Macjordomo*
Here is an excellent list server application for the Macintosh platform.

### E-mail List Management Software
*http://www.catalog.com/vivian/mailing-list-software.html*
This is a list of e-mail list management software packages provided by Vivian Neou.

### Internet Mailing List Providers
*http://catalog.com/vivian/mailing-list-providers.html*
This is another resource provided by Vivian Neou. Find yourself an Internet mailing list provider if you are unable to host your own mailing list.

### An Introduction to "Mailing Lists"
*http://www.petidomo.com/mailinglists.html*
This provides an excellent resource for setting up your own mailing list. Also described is Petidomo—mail list server software.

### Mailing Lists and Discussion Groups
*http://www.augsburg.edu/library/aib/listserv.html*

This is another introduction to using listserv software and joining mailing lists and discussion groups.

### Top 10 Rules for Moderating a Mailing List
*http://www.skylist.net/mailing-lists/josh-top10.html*
Check out these 10 quick pointers if you decide to administer a mailing list of your own.

### ListQuest.com
*http://www.listquest.com/*
Use this site to find discussion lists of interest to you and promote your own Internet mailing list.

# 10

# Develop a Dynamite Links Strategy

The more appropriate links you have to your site, the better! Expand your horizon by orchestrating links from related Web pages to increase your traffic. In this chapter we cover:

- Developing a link strategy

- How to arrange links

- Getting noticed—providing an icon and tag line hypertext for links to your site

- Link positioning

- Tools to check your competitors' links

- Using links to enhance your image

- Web rings and meta-indexes

- Getting links to your site

- Reciprocal link pages

- Associate programs

- How links can enhance your search engine placements

## Links Have an Impact

Developing your link strategy is one of the most crucial elements involved in Internet marketing. It is a very time-consuming task, but it is time very well spent. Links are important for two reasons:

1. Appropriately placed they can be a real traffic builder.

2. A number of the frequently used search engines use link popularity as one of their ranking criteria. The more links to your site, the more popular it is, so the number of links you have to your site can significantly impact your placement with the search engines.

## Links Have Staying Power

When you post a message to a newsgroup where you promote your Web site through your brilliant contribution and your signature file, you will receive increased traffic while the message is current and being read by participants in the newsgroup. As time passes your message appears further and further down the list until it disappears and then your traffic level returns to normal. The same goes for a promotional effort in a mail list. You can expect increased traffic for a short period of time after your mail list posting, but as soon as everyone has read your posting and visited your site, traffic levels return to normal.

This is not the same for links. Traffic from links does not go away as easily as other forms of Internet marketing. Links generally stay active for a long period of time. When you have a link to your site placed on another Web site, people will see it and be enticed to click through to visit your site. As long as the site that hosts your link has new traffic, you will continue to receive traffic through it. The beauty of links is that in three months time that link will still be there, and people will still be clicking through!

Links are very important because if you have links placed appropriately on a high-traffic Web site, they can turn into traffic builders for your Web site. They are also important because they can have a major impact on your search engine ranking in some of the major search engines, because some search engines use link popularity in their ranking criteria. These search engines include:

- AltaVista *www.altavista.com*

- Excite *www.excite.com*

- Google *www.google.com*

- Go/Infoseek *www.infoseek.com*

Once your link strategy is implemented and you begin to see an increase in the number of sites linking to your Web site, your will see your ranking in the previous mentioned search engines improve. For more information on search engines and their ranking criteria, see Chapter 4.

## Everything Links to You

The more **links** you have to your site, the better chance you have that someone will be enticed to visit. However, a quid quo pro usually applies, and this means providing reciprocal links, giving people the opportunity to leave your site with the click of a button. To minimize this "flight effect," make sure you place outbound links two or three layers down in your site. Never place outbound links on your home page. You want your visitors to come into your site and see everything you want them to see and do everything you want them to do before they have the opportunity to go elsewhere.

Regularly test all of the links from your site to ensure they are "live" and going to the appropriate locations. Dead links reflect poorly on your site. There are tools available online that can

**Links**
Selectable connections from one word, picture, or information object to another.

help you determine whether or not you have dead links. These tools include Link Cop at *www.linkcop.com*, Net Mechanic at *www.netmechanic.com*, Web Site Garage at *www.websitegarage.com*, and SiteOwner.com at *www.siteowner.com*. These tools analyze your page, detecting any dead links that may be on your site. Each of these tools will be discussed in more depth in the Internet Resources section at the end of this chapter.

## Strategies for Finding Appropriate Link Sites

Ideally you should be linked from every high-traffic site that is of interest to your target market. You have to develop a strategy to find all of these sites and arrange links.

The first place to start is with the popular search engines. Most people use search engines and directories to find subjects of interest on the Internet. Most of the people searching never go beyond the first 20 to 30 results the search engine returns. Thus, these top 20 to 30 sites returned by the search engines must get a lot of traffic. Make sure you search relevant keywords in all the popular search engines and directories, and investigate these top sites for appropriate link sites. Some of these sites will be competitors and may not want to reciprocate links. The best opportunity for links is with noncompeting sites that have the same target market. I suggest you take your most important keywords, do a keyword search in the 20 most popular search engines and directories, and review the top 30 sites in each for potential link sites.

Another strategy to find appropriate link sites is to see where the leaders in your industry and your competitors are linked. I use the term "competitors" very loosely. It would include your direct competitors, your industry leaders, companies selling noncompeting products to your target market, companies selling similar types of products or services to your target market, and companies that compete with you for search engine ranking. See what your competition is doing. Determine where they are linked from, and decide whether these are sites that you should also be linked from. Learn what they are doing well, and also learn from their mistakes. You should be linked everywhere your competition is appropriately linked and then some.

## Explore These URLs

There are many tools on the Internet to help you identify a Web site's links. This is a great way to research where your site could be linked from, but isn't—yet!

When determining which sites you should be linked from, you first have to develop a lengthy list of competitors. A competitor can be any business or site that offers the same products or services as you do or anyone targeting the same demographic as you. Since the Internet creates a level playing field for all businesses, you are also competing against people in other countries. Someone using a search engine to find information on services that your company can provide may see results from companies from all across the world in the top 10 results.

Once you have developed your extensive list of competitors and have gathered their URLs, you must then find out what sites they are linked from. Tools have been developed to assist you in finding who is linking to your site. In most cases you enter your URL, and then these tools provide you with the list of sites linking to your URL. However, these tools can be used just as easily to determine which sites are linking to your competition and industry leaders by entering *their* URL instead of your own.

The more organized you are for this exercise the better. I suggest that you:

1. Gather an extensive list of competitors and their URLs.

2. Choose the tool or tools from the next section that you are going to use for this exercise.

3. Enter the first competitor URL to find the sites linking to it.

4. Copy and Paste the results into a Word, Notepad, or other file that you can access later.

5. Enter the next competitor URL to find the sites linking to it.

6. Copy and Paste the results into the same Word, Notepad, or other file, adding to your list of potential link sites.

7. Repeat steps 5 and 6 until you have found all the sites linking to your competition. When this is done, you have your Potential Link Sites list.

8. Now develop a link request (see the next section for details) and keep it open on your desktop so that you can Copy and Paste it into an e-mail when you find a site you'd like to have a link from.

9. Next visit each and every one of the potential link sites to determine whether the site is one that is appropriate for you to be linked from. If the site is appropriate, then send your link request. If the site is not appropriate for whatever reason, delete it from your list.

10. Follow through and follow up. Follow through and provide an appropriate link to those who have agreed to a reciprocal link. Follow up to make sure that they have provided the link as promised to your site, that the link works, and that it is pointing to the correct page on your site.

## Tools to Identify Your Competitors' Links

The following tools can be used to obtain a list of locations on the Internet that are linked to your competitors' Web sites:

**Web Site Garage**
*http://www.websitegarage.com*
This site (Figure 10.1) has a link popularity summary that tells you all of the sites linking to a particular URL. When you visit this site, enter your competition's URL into the URL check query. The results will include a diagnosis of the site, including the link popularity. You then have the option of viewing all sites linking to that Web site.

**AltaVista**
*http://www.altavista.com*
To find out where your competitors are linked using AltaVista, simply enter the competitor's URL in the search area like this:

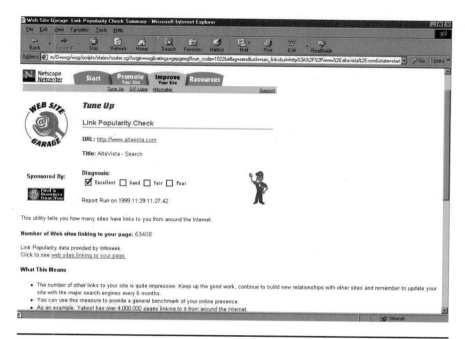

**Figure 10.1.** Web Site Garage provides many valuable tools. Their Link Popularity Check can be used to find who has linked to you from around the Internet. It can also provide valuable information on where your competitors are linked.

*link:yourcompetitorsdomain.com*. This will return all pages in AltaVista with a link to your competitor's Web site.

### Hot Bot
*http://www.hotbot.com*
Enter your competitor's URL in the search box and change the default from "all the words" to "links to this URL." When you type in the URL, remember to include *http://* The results will contain all Web sites linking to your competitor's Web site.

### WebCrawler
*http://www.webcrawler.com/WebCrawler/Links.html.*
Enter your competitor's URL into the search query box to find out how many links are provided to that page. WebCrawler provides the names of all the referring sites.

**Infoseek**
*http://www.infoseek.com*
Go to the Infoseek home page, and click on the "Advanced Search" link. Select "WEB Advanced Search." Under "search the Web for pages in which the:" choose "hyperlink" in the first drop-down menu. Select "must" in the second drop-down menu and "phrase" in the third drop-down menu. Then key in the URL you want to find in the space provided. Click on "Search," and the results will show listings, with descriptions, of the sites that provide a link to your selected URL.

**Excite and Other Search Engines**
Just enter your competitors' URLs and see what comes up. (Be sure to include the http://). If anything, the search query will include all Web sites that are indexed that contain the URL searched.

## Other Potential Link Strategies

Another strategy for finding potential competitors is to visit the many different search engines and do a search on the keywords you feel people would search on if they were looking for your site. The top results can also be considered your competition. You should add them to your list, and repeat the procedures discussed earlier to find out where they are linked from, and to see if they are appropriate links for your site.

Now you have a starting list of sites you want to link from. Your next activity is to request the link. Remember that although this is a time-consuming exercise, it is also one of the most important activities. Developing a strong link strategy is critical if you want a large volume of traffic to your Web site and if you want high placement in those search engines that give heavy weighting to link popularity.

## Winning Approval for Potential Links

Now that you have a list of Web sites you would like to be linked from, the next step is to identify the appropriate company contact from whom to request the link. Usually this can be found on the site. Titles such as Webmaster@ or any variation on the theme are usually a pretty safe bet. If the site does not have an appropriate contact, then try *feedback@*. You can either send the request there or ask for the e-mail address of the appropriate person.

If you cannot find an e-mail address on their Web site, and you feel that you will benefit a great deal from being linked on their Web site, you can visit Network Solutions (*www.network solutions.com*) to find out contact information for that domain name. Click on the *"WHOIS Lookup"* link and submit the URL in the WHOIS search to do a search on the domain in question. The results will include the contact, both technical and administrative, for that Web site. The technical contact will most likely be the person that you are looking for, because that person is the one that most likely looks after the Web site. The administrative contact is usually responsible for the renewal of the domain name, and the billing contact is usually the bill payer for the domain name.

Generally, a short note with the appropriate information in the subject line is most suitable. Your note should be courteous, briefly describe your site's content, and provide the rationale for why you think reciprocating links would result in a win-win situation. It doesn't hurt to compliment some aspect of the site that you think is particularly engaging.

It is a good idea to develop a generic "link request" letter that you can have on hand when you are surfing. You should always keep this letter open on your desktop when surfing the Internet so that you can quickly and easily copy and paste the letter into an e-mail. If you don't have a link request ready and you find a site that you are interested in requesting a link on, you usually jot the site down as a reminder to go back to request a link. Quite often it doesn't happen. But if you have the request open on your desktop, when you find a site that is appealing from a link perspective, you can simply copy and paste the link request into an e-mail, do a little editing or customizing, and hit the "Send" button.

Here is an example of a link request e-mail.

*Dear Web Site Owner,*

*I have just finished viewing your site and found it quite enjoyable. I found the content to be very valuable, particu-*

*larly (customize here). My site visitors would appreciate your content as I think we appeal to the same demographic. My site, http://www.mysitename.com, focuses on (my site content) and would likely be of value to your visitors. If you have no objection, I would like to add a link to your site.*

*Sincerely,*
*John*

When you get a response, it will usually say that they would appreciate the link to their site and will offer to provide a reciprocal link. To facilitate this you should either have the HTML for the link ready to send or have it available on your site, or both.

Make sure to follow through and follow up. If you said you would provide a reciprocal link, follow through and do so within 24 hours. Follow up to make sure that your site has been linked from theirs, the link works properly, and it is linked to the appropriate page on your site.

Then remember to send a thank-you. Since they are doing you a favor by adding your site to their Web page, you should strive to develop a good relationship with them. This way they may be more generous with the link that they give you. They may place it higher on the page, or even offer you the opportunity of having a small graphic link on their page, which would be dynamite for increasing traffic to your site. These graphic links will be explained in more detail later in the chapter.

Another way to get links is to ask for them on your site. In a prominent location on your site, place a link that says something like, *"Would you like to provide a link to this site? Click here."* Link this message to a separate page that holds several options for links. You can provide viewers with several different sizes of banner ads they could place on their Web site. You can also provide them with a thumbnail icon, the HTML, and your tagline, which they could simply copy and paste into the HTML code on their Web site. Quite often if you offer viewers these opportunities for links, you will have a better chance of receiving these enhanced link features. If you make it easier for them to add the link they would be more willing to provide the link, for they can do it at their convenience. Figure 10.2 shows an example of a site that provides the relevant coding and images for people who to provide a link to this site.

You might want to consider offering an incentive to people who will provide you with a link. It could be something that can be downloaded or a free sample of your product in exchange for a link. This also provides you with another opportunity to market your site because you are giving something away for free, and thus you can be listed on the many Internet sites that identify sites for freebies. Another tactic that you can use is that viewers who provide a link to your site will be included in a draw for a prize.

Meta-indexes and **Web rings** are other sources for links. For a complete discussion of meta-indexes and Web rings, see Chapters 12 and 20 respectively.

**Web rings**
Interlinked Web sites

You may need to prompt sites to provide promised links. If you have made an arrangement for a link and, on following up, find that the link is not there, it is appropriate to send an e-mail

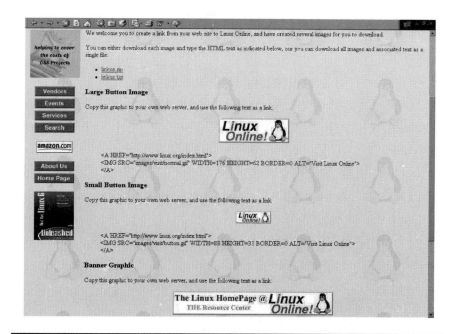

**Figure 10.2.** By providing the HTML text and icons on your site you can make it very easy for a viewer to add your link to their site. It is best to supply them with the option of placing a text link, small button, a large button, or a banner advertisement on their Web site.

reminder. When sending the follow-up e-mail, include your icon, HTML, URL, and any other information that may be helpful.

## Making Your Link the Place to "Click"

There are links and then there are links. Usually links are your company name hypertext-linked to your home page, and your company's site link is listed with a number of other companies' links. Sometimes, if you are lucky, there is a brief description attached to the link.

You should take a proactive approach with linking arrangements. Explore every opportunity to have your link placed prominently and, if possible, to have it *differentiated* from the other links on the page. Figure 10.3 shows you how having an image associated with your link can make your link stand out amongst all of the other links.

Once you have an agreement with a site willing to provide a link, you should ask if you could send them an icon and the HTML for the

**Figure 10.3.** By adding a small graphic to your link, you can definitely make your link stand out from the others.

link. The **icon** (GIF or JPG format) should be visually pleasing and representative of your company. Within the HTML, include a tag line that entices people to click on the link. With the icon or logo, the tag line, and your company's name, your link will stand out from the rest. Since another Web site is going to be generous in providing a link to your site, your image should only be a thumbnail, for you don't want to take up too much space on their Web site. This image could be your corporate logo or a graphic which is used in the current promotion for one of your products or services. By having this image and tag line strategically placed on a Web site, the chances that a viewer will click through to visit your Web site are much higher. Here is an example of what it should look like:

> **Icon**
> An image that represents an application, a capability, or some other concept

<IMG SRC= *"your gif/tif/bmp name"*>
<A HREF= *"http://www.yourdomainname.com"*>Catchy tag line here </A>

## To Add or Not to Add with Free-for-All Links

There are thousands of free-for-all links on the Net. These sites allow you to add your URL to a long list of links, but they provide little in the way of traffic unless you can have your link stand out from the rest. One advantage you can get from being linked from these sites is in search engine ranking. As mentioned previously, some search engines use the number of links to your site in their ranking criterion.

## Add Value with Affiliate Programs

Another way of benefitting from links to your Web site is by developing an associate program. Associate programs (also called reseller or partnership or affiliate programs) are revenue sharing arrangements set up by companies selling products and services. When another site agrees to participate in your associate program, it is rewarded for sending customers to your business. These customers are sent to your site through links on your associates or affiliates Web site. By developing and offering this type of program, you generate increased revenue and increased links to your site. Associate programs will be explained in more depth during Chapter 14.

## Maintaining a Marketing Log

Record all new links to your site in your Internet marketing log. It is important to maintain this log and review it on a regular basis. You must periodically check to make certain that links to your site are operational and going to the appropriate location. Along with the URL where your site is linked from, you should also keep track of all contact information you may have gathered when communicating with the Web master.

## A Word of Caution with Link Trading

You must be aware when trading links that all links are not created equal:

- If you provide a prominent link to another site, make sure you receive a link of equal or greater prominence.

- Be aware, when trading your links with sites that receive substantially less traffic than you do, that you will probably have more people "link out" than "link in" from this trade. Consider trading a banner ad and a link from their site for a link from your site, thus making it more of an equal trade. If their site has more traffic than yours, don't mention it unless they do.

- Never put your outbound links directly on your home page. Have your outbound links located several levels down so that visitors to your site will likely have visited all the pages you want them to visit before they link out from your site.

- Sometimes when people update their site, they change the Internet address or delete a page altogether. If you have placed a link on your page to that page, and one of your viewers tries to link out to that page, and receives an HTTP 404 error, this reflects badly on your site. You should always check your Web site for dead links.

# Internet Resources

## Tools That Check for Dead Links

### Web Site Garage
*http://www.websitegarage.com.*
This site has a dead link check in its Web site diagnosis. It has a link popularity tool as well, which tells you how many links a particular site has pointing to it and also from where a URL is linked.

### Net Mechanic
*http://www.netmechanic.com*
To find out if you have any dead links with Net Mechanic, simply enter your URL into the query box and view the results. The site will generate a detailed report, which will outline whether or not you have any dead links, and if so where.

### Site Owner
*http://www.siteowner.com*
When using Site Owner, you can check your site for various Web site criteria. To check for dead links you must enter your URL into the query box, then select "Dead Link." The results will outline any dead links that are on your site.

## Reciprocal Link Information

### Virtual Promote
*http://www.virtualpromote.com/guest6.html*
This tutorial covers how to promote traffic to your Web site with reciprocal links. This is a free service for all Web site developers who want to learn more about announcing their Web site and promoting more traffic to the Internet.

### Free-for-All Link Sites

#### Mega Linkage List
*http://www.netmegs.com/linkage/*
An exhaustive listing of over 1500 directories, classified ad sites, little-known search engines, FFA pages, and more...all compiled for you alphabetically. Although there are some dead/broken links here, a large majority are active, and you will be hard-pressed to visit each one.

#### Entrepreneurial Trend
*http://www.angelfire.com/ct/suremoney/page2.html*
Links to hundreds of places to list your site! Free-for-all link pages and search engines. Free classifieds and message boards. Free news-letters and reciprocal links.

#### Auto Link/Master Link
*http://www.career-pro.com/autolink/index.cgi?autolink*
AutoLink allows you to type in your site's URL, and with one click automatically list it on over 350 FFA pages, directories, and search engines. MasterLink is a brand new tool, and you must see it to truly appreciate this new concept in Web site promotion. Highly recommended.

#### Link-O-Matic
*http://www.linkomatic.com/index.cgi?10000*
It allows you to submit your URL to over 450 quality promotional sites with one click, driving traffic to your Web site and saving you loads of time.

#### FFA Net
*http://www.ffanet.com/links/list.pl*
This page has a detailed listing of thousands of free-for-all link pages. It also offers you the opportunity to set up your own free-for-all link pages on the FFA network.

# 11

# Winning Awards/
# Cool Sites and More

There are literally hundreds of Cool Sites, Sites of the Day, Hot Sites, and Pick of the Week Sites. Some of these sites require you to submit; others are selected based on such things as:

- Awesome graphics

- Dynamite content that is useful and interesting

- Uniqueness

- Fun features

If you are selected for one of these sites, it can mean a huge increase in the number of hits to your site. You must be prepared for the increased traffic flow as well as the increased demand for online offerings. In this chapter we cover:

- Where to submit your site for award consideration

- How to win Site of the Day—tips, tools, and techniques

- Getting listed in What's New

- Posting your awards on your site

- Hosting your own Site of the Day

## It's an Honor Just to Be Nominated

There are sites that find and evaluate other sites on the Internet and recognize those that are outstanding by giving them an award. The award sites are generally very discriminating in terms of which sites are selected to be the recipients of their award. They have established criteria defining what is considered "hot" or "cool" and base their award selection on those criteria. Figure 11.1 shows a variety of awards.

What's New Web sites are designed to inform Internet users of new sites and updates to existing sites, and are often selective in which new sites they will promote. The owner of each site also selectively chooses awards for Site of the Day, Week, Month, and Year. As discussed earlier, some of these sites require you to submit an announcement or site description, and the awards are granted based on criteria such as graphics, dynamic content, uniqueness, and the "fun" quality

**Figure 11.1.**   A collage of some of the more popular awards.

of your site. Other sites grant their awards based solely on the personal likes and dislikes of the owner of the site and do not adhere to any criteria at all.

Some awards are taken just as seriously as the Academy Awards. The Webby Awards have a very comprehensive nomination procedure. The following information regarding their process is available on their Web site:

### How to Win a Webby—Web Site Nomination Procedure

*The International Academy of Digital Arts and Sciences (IADAS) is responsible for nominating and awarding each year's Webby Award and People's Voice Award winners. The 1999 awards were given out in 24 different content categories, including: Arts, Commerce, Community, Education, Fashion, Film, Finance, Games, Health, Humor, Living, Music, News, Politics, Print and Zines, Radio, Science, Sports, Tech Achievement, Travel, TV and Weird. The site plans to expand the number of categories for The 2000 Webby Awards; possible new categories Kids, Services and Webcast. Nominees are selected by the International Academy of Digital Arts and Sciences' nominating committee for each category. Comprised of 240 journalists, experts, critics, scholars, or new-media professionals, the committee for each category collaborates to select five Webby Award nominees. The Academy now accepts web site nominations in exchange for a $50 fee.*

When you win an award you post the award on your site for all to see. The award icon is usually a link back to the site that bestowed the honor on you.

## Choosing Your Awards and Submitting to Win

There are different levels of prestige associated with each of the different award sits. Some are an honor to receive. Some are highly competitive because of the number of submissions they receive.

Some awards are easier to receive than others, such as those from commercial sites that give out awards in an attempt to increase the traffic to their own site. Traffic increases because the award is a graphic link displayed on the winner's site that visitors can follow back to the award giver's site. Other Web masters give out awards to anybody and everybody who makes a submission. The award is granted with the sole purpose of building traffic.

The bottom line is that awards are valuable assets. The average Web user cannot tell which awards are the prestigious ones and which are given to anyone that submits. So, submit for any awards that you choose to, as long as your site is ready. (A sample submission form is shown in Figure 11.2.)

Where you place these awards is important. If you win a lot of awards, you will be expected to place a promotional graphic and a link on your home page for each award you win. Your home page can become quite cluttered and load more slowly as a result. If you have

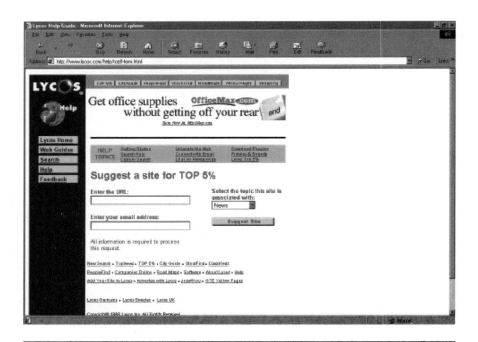

**Figure 11.2.**   Sample award submission form. This one is for the Lycos Top 5%.

been fortunate enough to be in this situation, consider developing an awards page with a link from your navigation bar to house them.

Another item to determine before you submit for an award is whether the huge amount of new traffic will benefit your site. If you sell T-shirts emblazoned with WWW cartoons, then any traffic is good traffic, and awards will benefit your site. On the other hand, if you are a marine biologist specializing in red tides in the Arctic, then the traffic that "Site of the Day" would bring may be more of a hindrance than a help in marketing your services. Always determine if the marketing tools and techniques will increase hits from your target market before deciding whether to include them in your online marketing strategy.

Getting mentioned on one of the Cool Sites lists is probably the single biggest way to draw traffic to your site. The traffic they send to your site is like a flash flood—fast and furious. Be careful what you wish for—you might just get it! The traffic will be swift and plentiful after you win one of these awards. Be prepared! Have a plan that you can implement on a moment's notice. If you offer something free from your site, ensure you can access a huge volume of whatever it is and ensure you have a plan to distribute quickly. If you offer a free download from your site, plan to have a number of alternate **FTP sites** available to your visitors. If you have a "call in" offer, ensure you have a telephone response system in place and staff to handle the huge volume of calls you may get. You will need a plan to handle the huge volume of e-mails you will get as well.

What's New sites accept submissions for sites that they review. The best of the best are then placed prominently on their home page for all to see. It is considered to be quite an honor to develop or own a site that has been selected by some of the more discriminating What's New sites.

Once you have decided that the type of traffic that comes along with winning the award fits with your marketing strategy, you should make sure your site has the makings of a winner and then submit to as many award sites as you can.

> **FTP (File Transfer Protocol)** The simplest way to exchange files between computers on the Internet

- First, make a list of the URLs of these award sites.

- Understand the submission form and guidelines. Review a number of forms to determine the common information requested.

- Develop a document with the answers to the various questions from which you can copy and paste into the different submission forms (this will save you time).

- Submission forms will capture the following types of information:

  - URL

  - Title of your site

  - Contact person (name, e-mail, phone, address)

  - Owner of the site

- Submission guidelines will tell you what types of sites can be submitted (i.e., some awards do not accept personal pages; others do not include commercial sites). The submission guidelines will also tell you what meets their definition of "Cool" or "New" and what doesn't.

- Some award sites require that you display their award icon on your site. Posting an award on your site can provide a number of positive results—including enhanced credibility.

There are different levels of prestige associated with each of the different award sites. Some are an honor to receive, such as a Starting Point Hot Site (*http://www.stpt.com, see Figure 11.3*) award. These awards are highly competitive because of the number of submissions they receive.

## What's Hot and What's Not in the Name of Cool

Most of the award sites will provide you with their selection criteria. Some award sites look for and base their selection on valuable content; others look for innovative and unique capabilities. Sites vary on what they consider "Hot" or "Cool," but they are fairly consistent on what doesn't make the grade, as summarized next.

**Figure 11.3.** Starting Point's Hot Site Awards are very competitive.

| What's Hot | What's Not |
| --- | --- |
| Awesome graphics | Single page sites |
| Great, original content | Single product promotion |
| Broad appeal | Offensive language or graphics |
| Fun feature | Lengthy download time |

## Posting Your Awards on Your Site

If you have managed to collect a few awards for your Web site, you will want to display them somehow. After all, any award is a good award, and the award site that granted you a particular award will expect you to display it in return for the recognition. Posting the awards on your home page might not be the best idea, though. For one, the additional graphics that will have to be downloaded will slow the load time for your home page. Second, by posting the awards on your home page, you are placing links leading out of your site on the first page. Thus, you are giving people the opportunity to leave your site before they have even had a chance to explore it. Where should you post your well-deserved awards then? Simply create an "Awards" section on your Web site. Here, you can list all of your awards without adversely affecting the load time of your home page or losing traffic.

## Becoming the Host of Your Own Awards Gala

You can also create your own award program in order to draw traffic to your site; however, this requires a huge amount of work to maintain. You will need to work at it on a daily or weekly basis, so you must be committed to it. Be sure there is a benefit from a marketing perspective before you design and develop your own award program. You must also be prepared to conduct your own searches at the outset to find sites to promote if the quality of sites being submitted to you is poor.

- You will first have to develop the criteria you will use in your site selection.

- You will have to develop several Web pages related to the award (information on selection criteria, submission forms, today's or this week's award winner, past award recipients page, etc.) in order to promote the award. (Ensure that you stipulate you are looking for submissions from commercial sites or personal pages and what criteria will be used in judging the submissions.)

- You will have to have your award icon developed. Have this icon link back to your site. The award distinguishes the winner, thus the link will probably be displayed prominently on their site. This is a great traffic builder.

- Finally, you have to announce the award and market, market, market.

## Internet Resources

### Awards

#### Webby Awards
*http://www.webbyawards.com*
The Webby Awards have been embraced by the online community as the leading creative honors for digital media. The awards recognize the most creative and innovative Web sites of the year and the talented editorial, technical, and design teams behind them.

#### Best of the Planet Awards
*http://www.2ask.com*
Called the people's choice award, where you can decide who's best.

#### Best of the Web Awards
*http://botw.org/*
This award aims to highlight those places that best show the quality, versatility, and power of the World Wide Web.

#### PC Magazine's Top 100 Web Sites
*http://www.zdnet.com/pcmag/special/web100/index.html*
A list of top sites listed in five categories, everything from amazing online stores to essential computing resources, with a couple of stops along the way for fun and entertainment.

#### High Five Award
*http://www.highfive.com*
Each week they review well-designed Web sites and discuss how to make your site become a killer.

#### People Chase
*http://www.rainfrog.com/pc/*

Award-winning sites become part of the People Chase Web ring. Web site design and content are judged to determine the winner.

**Jayde.com**
*http://www.jayde.com/goldlnks.html*
Awards the Gold Diamond Award to sites with great style, design, and content. Jayde.com also has an award for commercial sites.

## What's New

**Yahoo!**
*http://www.yahoo.com/new*
Yahoo!'s "what's new" on the Web.

**Netscape What's New**
*http://www.netscape.com/netcenter/new.html*
Netscape features a few new Web sites every day and gives them a rating. You can submit your site to Netscape for review.

**What's New Too**
*http://newtoo.manifest.com*
New announcements are posted to this site within 36 hours of submission, and the list, which is lengthy, is updated daily.

**Whatsnew.com**
*http:www.whatsnew.com*
This is a seven-days-a-week, continuously updated, fully searchable directory of new Internet Web sites.

## Hot Sites/Cool Sites

**USA Today Hot Sites**
*http://www.usatoday.com/life/cyber/ch.htm*
USA Today scours the Web for sites that are hot, new, and notable. Visit their daily list to find some of the best sites the Web has to offer. They look for sites that may stretch the design envelope and show

where the Web is headed…sites that offer something unusual or unexpected, or something just plain useful.

### Starting Point Hot Site
*http://www.starting-point.com*
Votes are taken from their What's New section for sites worthy of a Hot Site Award.

### Lycos Top 5%
*http://www.lycos.com/help/top5-help.html*
Lycos Top 5% is the oldest and most prestigious Web site directory. Each site in the Top 5% directory includes a detailed review describing its editorial and visual merits.

### 100 Hot Web sites
*http://www.100hot.com/*
Directory of Web sites based on Web traffic and organized by category.

### The All Original Web Site Awards
*http://www.oliveplace.com/originalwebs.html*
Awards for Web sites that are completely original in their design, graphics, and content. No clip art allowed!!!

### A Comprehensive Guide to Receiving Web Site Awards for Free
*http://www.fonesave.com/websave/freeawards.htm*
Includes links to submission pages for award sites plus links to other free Web resources.

### Cool Site of the Day
*http://www.coolsiteoftheday.com*
Cool Site of the Day is a wildly popular Internet award site that features interesting, provocative, and irreverent Web sites from around the world.

### Cool Central Site of the Hour
*http://www.coolcentral.com*
Delivers the best new Web sites the moment they are discovered. Featuring Cool Central Site of the Moment and Hour, and Nick Click, Private…Eye.

### CoolStop
*http://www.coolstop.com/*
The Best of the Cool Award consistently recognizes truly outstanding sites in terms of design, originality, and content.

### Netscape What's Cool
*http://home.netscape.com/netcenter/cool.html*
Netscape's picks of the coolest Web sites.

### Virtual Reference Meta-Index of Award Sites
*http://www.refdesk.com//textcool.html*
A listing of different sites that host site of the day, hot sites, and so on.

### The Bottom 95%
*http://www.dartmouth.edu/~jaundice/bottom95/*
If your Web site has never received a top 5% award, the bottom 95% could be for you.

### Web Pages That Suck
*http://www.webpagesthatsuck.com*
Keep your site from being nominated to Web Pages That Suck, and you are probably doing well. However, you can learn a lot from Web Pages That Suck about how to properly design your site from a marketing perspective.

## Tools

### Free Links Award Sites
*http://www.freelinks.com/awards.html*
This is a free service to aid and simplify your Web site promotion efforts. You can also find information on databases, search engines, and link pages where you can list your site for free.

### Links2Go: Site Awards
*http://www.links2go.com/topic/Awards*
Find links to dozens of award sites.

# 12

---

# Maximizing Promotion with Meta-Indexes

Meta-indexes are intended to be useful resources for people who have a specific interest in a particular topic. Meta-indexes are a large and valuable resource to reaching your target audience and should be utilized to their full potential. In this chapter we cover:

- What meta-indexes are

- Why meta-indexes are useful

- How to make the link to your site stand out

- How to create your own meta-index

## What Are Meta-Indexes?

Meta-indexes are lists of Internet resources pertaining to a specific subject category and are intended as a resource for people who have a specific interest in that topic. These lists, like the one for Internet

Shopping Sites shown in Figure 12.1, consist of a collection of URLs of related Internet resources and are arranged on a Web page by their titles. The owners or creators of meta-indexes put a lot of effort into compiling these lists and are eager to find new sites to add to them. They will often list your site for free because they desire to have the most meta of the meta-indexes—they strive to have the largest of the large indexes and more sites means a larger index. So if you come across a meta-index that is associated with the topic of your site, feel free to ask for a link.

Some of these meta-indexes have a "Submit to add your site" area; for others you have to develop an inclusion request e-mail and send it to the owner of the site. In your inclusion request e-mail, you would let the owner know that you had visited the site and feel that your site would be appropriate to be included. Give the reasons you think your site appropriate and request the link. You should provide the HTML for the link as well. Review the techniques discussed in

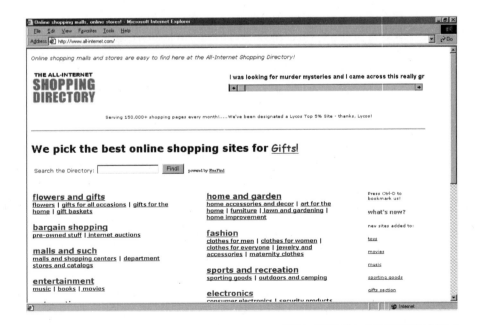

**Figure 12.1.** All-Internet Shopping Directory, a meta-index of malls, stores, products, and services on the Web.

Chapter 10 to have your link stand out with the graphical icon, hypertext link, and tag line.

Meta-indexes are directed at a specific topic, such as "pets" or "cars." Meta-indexes provide easy access to a number of sites on a specific topic, and they are a great way to draw targeted, interested people to your Web site. In addition, some users may rely on meta-indexes as their only search effort. They may not use a search engine to perform a query on Mexican resorts, for example, if they know a certain meta-index contains 200 sites on Mexican resorts. Meta-indexes can increase your chances of being found by people who are interested in what you have to offer. You may want to consider placing a banner ad on one or some of the meta-indexes you find, given that the target audience you want to reach will be the people using these indexes. Choose carefully, though, you don't want to buy a banner ad on a meta-index that is not up to par and doesn't provide you with the traffic you want to acquire. Take your time and investigate the meta-index before advertising on it. Does it appeal to the eye? Is it of good quality? Are there a lot of dead links? Is it updated frequently? Does it have sufficient traffic?

## How to Find Appropriate Meta-Indexes

Now that you know what a meta-index is, how do you find one? You might be browsing on the Web and happen to come across one. If you do, bookmark it for future use or add it to a document that you can look at and print off at a later time. A better way to find meta-indexes is through the search engines and directories on the Web.

When you're looking for meta-indexes we recommend you create a more focused search by adding an extra word such as "directory," "list," "index," "table," "resource," "reference," or "guide." By adding one of these words in conjunction with another word, for example, "travel," you're increasing your chances of finding appropriate meta-indexes. Performing a search on "travel" alone will return far less targeted results. Looking for a travel directory alone may not work for you. Why? A search for a travel directory on the search engines often means looking for all sites that contain the words "travel" and all sites that contain "directory." You should refine your searches to achieve more accurate results. Some general techniques using the words travel and directory as examples you can apply in your search for meta-indexes are:

- Entering *travel directory* generally means, Look for all sites containing the words "travel" or "directory," but try to gather those sites with "travel" and "directory" together.

- Entering *"travel directory"* (with quotation marks) often means, Look for all sites containing the words "travel" and "directory" next to each other.

- Entering +*travel directory* generally means, Find all sites with the word "travel" and preferably the word "directory" as well.

- Entering +*travel* +*directory* generally means, Find all sites with both words.

Search engines look for information in different ways and allow different techniques to be applied in order to narrow or broaden the search criteria. This information can be obtained by looking at the respective search engine's help page (Figure 12.2).

Many search engines and directories have or give you the option to use an "advanced" search or search "options" page that present you with the ability to perform more detailed searches without using the parameters outlined above. Yahoo! (Figure 12.3) and Infoseek (Figure 12.4) are two such sites.

## Enlisting Meta-Indexes for Optimal Exposure

To ensure that you are taking full advantage of meta-indexes, do the following:

- Source appropriate meta-indexes

- Request a link

- Provide the details necessary

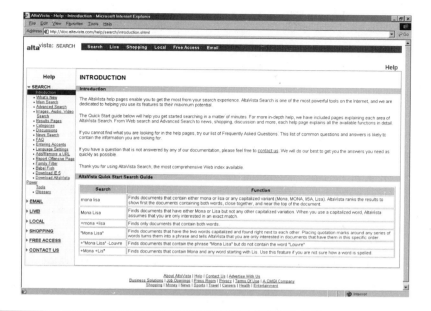

**Figure 12.2.** AltaVista's help page and quick search guide.

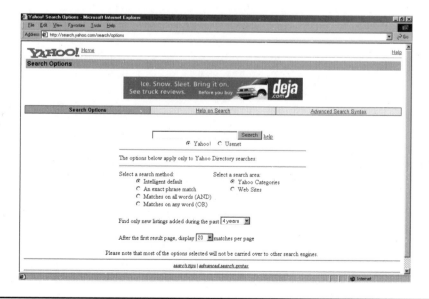

**Figure 12.3.** Yahoo's advanced search.

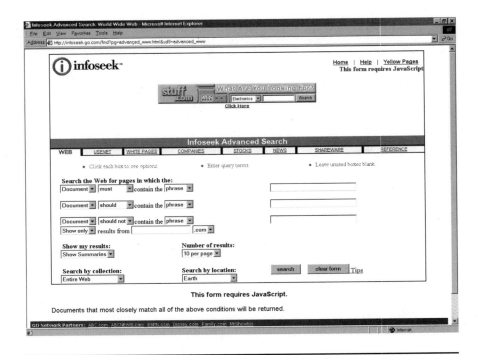

**Figure 12.4.** Infoseek's search options.

- Look at sponsorship or banner advertising opportunities

Meta-indexes can be arranged by subject (sites that provide information on book publishing) or by geography (tourist sites in Alaska). As mentioned before, the major search engines are a good place to start. For example, to find tourist sites in Alaska, conduct a search by entering *+Alaska+tourist+directory*. Once you find a good list and start to check the links, you will likely find other lists through the first list. Bookmark or keep a record of the meta-indexes you like for future reference.

If you are not sure if your site will be accepted by a certain meta-index, send a request anyway. Meta-lists draw more traffic when they provide more resources to their readers, so list owners may be fairly lenient on what's acceptable and what's not.

When requesting a link to your site send an e-mail with "site addition request" in the subject area of your message. Include the following in the body of the message:

- URL

- Description of your site

- Why you feel your site is appropriate for the list

- Your contact information in your signature file (see Chapter 6)

Once you have identified indexes that appeal to your target market, determine whether additional opportunities might exist for sponsorship or purchasing banner advertising on the site. Meta-indexes that relate to your market are a great place to advertise because they are accessed by your target customers.

Keep in mind that the compilers of meta-indexes are motivated by noncommercial reasons and are under no obligation to add your site to their list or process your request quickly. However, because of the banner advertising revenue potential, more and more meta-index sites have a commercial focus.

To make your link stand out among the many others listed, inquire about adding a prominent link or icon to the meta-index page along with a short tag line, in addition to your company name. If you provide the GIF and the HTML, the meta-index owner may be happy to include it.

## Review the Work of Some Meta-Index Giants

**AlltheEarth.com—Online Shopping and Business Directory**
*http://www.alltheearth.com/* (Figure 12.5)

**GIS Resources on the Web**
*http://www.gsd.harvard.edu/~pbcote/GIS/web_resources.html* (Figure 12.6)

**Scout Select Bookmarks**
*http://www.ilrt.bris.ac.uk/mirrors/scout/toolkit/bookmarks/ index.html*

**Craft Site Directory**
*http://www.bobbilynn.com/directory.html* (Figure 12.7)

**Figure 12.5.**   Directory of shopping and business-related sites.

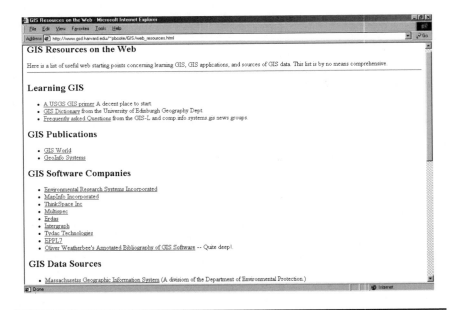

**Figure 12.6.**   GIS resources of the Web.

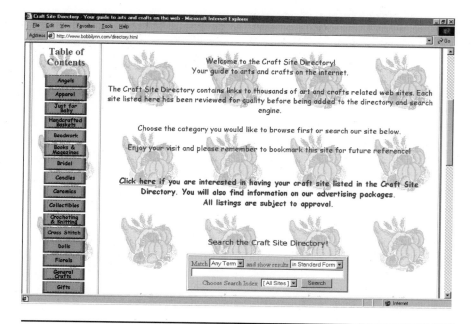

**Figure 12.7.** Index of craft sites by category.

**Australia Travel**
*http://www.anzac.com/aust/aust.htm* (Figure 12.8)

**Achoo Healthcare Online**
*http://www.achoo.com/* (Figure 12.9)

**Hotels and Travel on the Net**
*http://www.hotelstravel.com/homepage.html* (Figure 12.10)

## Internet Resources

**WWW Meta-Indexes and Search Tools**
*http://www.fys.ruu.nl/~kruis/h3.html*
A Library of Congress Internet resource page.

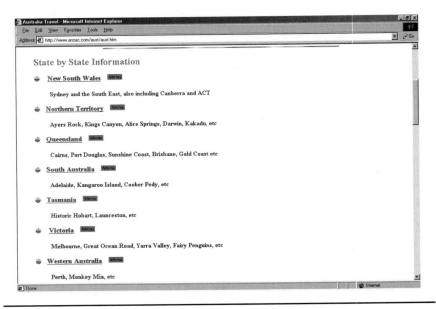

**Figure 12.8.** Meta-index of Australian travel-related sites.

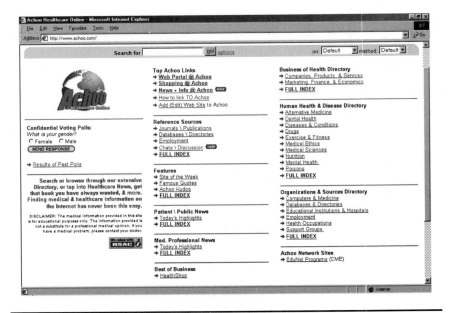

**Figure 12.9.** Directory of healthcare-related sites.

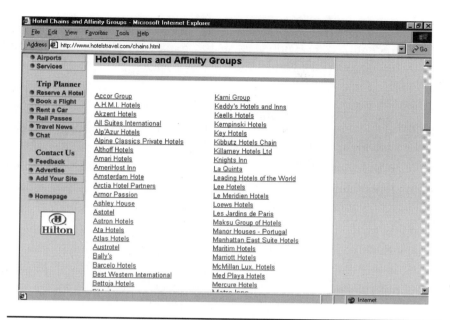

**Figure 12.10.** A list of links to all kinds of Web sites for Hotel Chains, worldwide.

## Argus Clearinghouse
*http://www.clearinghouse.net*
The premier Internet research library (or meta-index) to locate everything you need to find on the Web.

## The Ultimate Directory—Infospace
*http://www.infospace.com*
InfoSpace calls itself the Ultimate Directory! You'll find yellow pages, white pages, classifieds, shopping sites, investing information, government listings, chat rooms, and much more.

## Virtual Library
*http://vlib.org/Overview.html*
The Virtual Library is the oldest catalog of the Web, started by Tim Berners-Lee, the creator of the Web itself. Unlike commercial catalogs, it is run by a loose confederation of volunteers, who compile pages of key links for particular areas in which they are expert. Even

though it isn't the biggest index of the Web, the VL pages are widely recognized as being among the highest-quality guides to particular sections of the Web.

### W.E.D. The World E-mail Directory
*http://www.worldemail.com/*
WED World E-mail Directory has estimated access to more than 18,000,000 e-mail addresses and more than 140,000,000 business and phone addresses worldwide. One of the fastest-growing engines for people, businesses, and organizations.

### Essential Links: Portal to the Internet
*http://www.el.com/*
Essential Links to the Internet and the World Wide Web. Essential Links is a portal to the Internet portal sites, news headlines, search engines, Web directories, references, and utilities.

### @LinkPad
*http://www.referthem.com/pad/links.htm*
A meta-index of meta-indexes. This site has indexes ranging from advertising, e-zines, and e-mail to Web graphics and real estate.

# 13

## Productive Online Advertising

There have been numerous studies on banner advertising over the last couple of years. Some say banner advertising works; others are not so positive. I find it very interesting that such a blanket statement can be made. It really depends on what your objectives are, what type of ad you develop, and your ad placement strategy. Advertising online provides visibility—just as offline advertising does. You must develop a banner advertising strategy that works with your product, your marketing objectives, and your budget. In this chapter we cover:

- Your online advertising strategy

- Advertising opportunities on the Web

- Banner ad design and impact on click-throughs

- Banner ad sizes and locations

- Placing classifieds

- Tips to creating dynamite banner ads that work

- The cost of advertising online

- Measuring ad effectiveness

- Banner ad exchange networks

- Using an online advertising agency

- Sources of Internet advertising information

## Expanding Your Exposure Through Internet Advertising

Today Internet advertising is being recognized in the advertising budgets of businesses around the globe. Banner ads are a way to create awareness of your Web site and increase the traffic to it. Your Web site is your online presence. Banners are placed on the sites that your target market is likely to frequent, thus encouraging this market to click through and visit you!

The Internet offers many different advertising spaces. Banner ads can be placed on search engines, content sites, advertising sites, and online magazines. The choice of where your ad is displayed is based on the objectives you wish to achieve with your online advertising strategy.

There are a number of advantages to online advertising:

- The response from these ads can be easily measured within one day.

- The amount of information that can be delivered, if your Web site is visited, far surpasses that of a traditional advertising campaign.

- The cost of developing and running an online advertising campaign is much less than using traditional media.

Traditionally, advertising used to be handled by a PR/Advertising company who would come up with your marketing concept. Businesses, as clients, would review and approve (usually after several attempts) the concepts before they were ever released to the public eye. The PR/advertising firms would be responsible for developing TV, radio, and print ads for the businesses. They would come up with the media buy strategy after reviewing appropriate publications, editorial calendars, pricing, and the discounts that they would receive for multiple placements. The ads were then gradually released over the period of the campaign, and finally viewed by the public. At the end of the campaign the PR/advertising company would evaluate the success of the marketing campaign. This is very easy to evaluate if the objective of the campaign was to achieve x number of sales, but it is much more difficult if the goal of your campaign was to generate brand awareness.

Today online banner ads are developed in much less time and are placed on Web sites very quickly. Web traffic analysis software can tell you the next day if the banner ad is working or not by tracking the number of visitors who clicked through and visited your site through the ad. This provides you with the opportunity to change the site on which you are advertising or to change the banner ad to see if it will attract a greater audience.

Nielsen Net Ratings (*http://www.nielsen-netratings.com/*) (Figure 13.1) offers great up-to-date resources to find out who is doing the most online advertising. You can check this resource to find the top 10 banners displayed on the Internet each week and the top 10 advertisers online. Since everyone is eagerly trying to be number one, these figures change weekly.

## Maximize Advertising with Your Objectives in Mind

When developing your advertising strategy, you will need to determine the objectives of your advertising campaign. The most common objectives for an online advertising campaign include:

- Building brand awareness

- Increasing Web site traffic

- Generating leads and sales

You have a number of choices to make, such as what type of advertising to use and where to advertise. These choices should be made based on your objectives. If it is your objective to increase over-

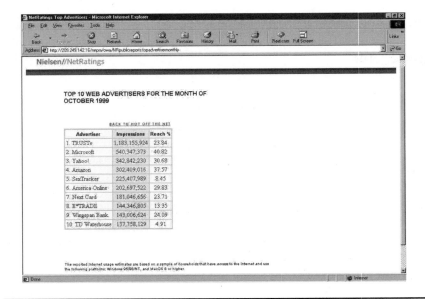

**Figure 13.1.** Nielsen NetRatings provides you with continuously updated statistics on who is doing the most advertising on the Internet. They can also provide you with the top 10 most viewed banner ads on a weekly or monthly basis.

all brand recognition, a nicely designed banner ad on one of the high-traffic search engines would be effective. If you would like to develop leads and find new clients, then a more targeted approach should be taken such as placing a banner ad on a high-traffic Web site that is frequented by your target market.

When deciding how to proceed with your advertising strategy, consider how many people you want to reach. Do you want a high-quality response from a small number of very targeted people, or do you want to reach a mass audience of grand proportions?

Think about the people you are targeting. If you sell dentistry supplies to dental practices, then you want to target dentists and hygienists. It would not make much sense to put an ad on Yahoo! when you could advertise on a site about new medical discoveries in dentistry.

Always keep your budget in mind when you are devising your online advertising strategy. There are many ways to stretch your advertising dollar. If you have the time you can find appropriate sites to trade banners. You can also participate in banner exchange programs.

## Online Advertising Terminology

### Banner Ads

Banner ads are small advertisements that are placed on a Web site. Companies usually develop their banner ads, find appropriate sites for placement, and then either purchase or trade banner space.

### Click-Throughs

When a viewer clicks on a banner ad with the mouse and goes to the site advertised, it is called a "click-through." Sometimes banner advertising prices are determined by the number of click-throughs.

### Hits

Hits to a site are the number of times that another computer has accessed that site (or a file in a site). This does not mean that if your site has 1000 hits, 1000 people have visited it. If your home page has a number of graphic files on it, this number could be very misleading. A hit is counted when the home page main file is accessed, but a hit is also counted for every graphic file that loads along with the home page. So if a person visits 6 pages on a site and each page has 4 graphics, at least 30 hits would be generated.

### Impression or Page Views

When someone views a banner ad, it is called an impression. Banner advertising prices are often calculated by impressions. If a person visits a page 6 times, this will generate 6 impressions.

### CPM

Cost per thousand impressions, or CPM, is a standard advertising term. CPM is often used to calculate the cost of banner advertising. If the CPM of banner advertising on a site was $40 US and the number of impressions the ad had was 2000, then the advertiser would have to pay $80 US for displaying the ad.

### Keywords

You can purchase keywords on search engines. This allows your banner ad to appear when someone does a search on the keyword that you purchase. This is very good for zooming in on your target market.

### IP Numbers (Geotargeting)

Purchasing IP numbers is one of the latest trends in Internet marketing. Every device that connects to the Internet has its own, unique IP number. These are assigned centrally by a designated authority for each country. We are now seeing search engines sell IP numbers to help businesses pinpoint their target demographic. For example, John Doe is building a new home in Utah and is searching for a company selling lumber in his area. Dooley Building Supplies, a lumber company in Utah, happens to be marketing over the Internet, and as part of their banner advertising campaign they have purchased banner ads by keyword and by IP address. Simply stated, they have said they only want their banner ad to appear when the keyword "lumber" is searched on by individuals whose IP address are within a certain range (the range being those existing in Utah). When John Doe does his search on the word "lumber," the Dooley Building Supplies banner ad is displayed at the top of the page holding the search results. Someone in Michigan searching for lumber will see a different banner ad.

## Jump on the Banner Wagon

Banner advertising is the most common and most recognized form of online advertising. Banner ads are available in various sizes, but the most common banners are displayed at roughly 468 × 60 pixels. See Figure 13.2 for some of the more popular banner ad sizes. Banners usually have an enticing message or call to action that coaxes the viewer to click on it. "What is on the other side?" you ask? The

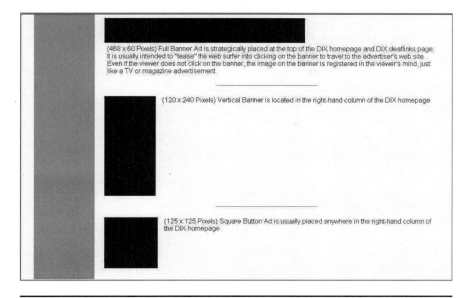

**Figure 13.2.** There are many different marketing resource Web sites available online that can provide you with the different size possibilities for your banner ads.

advertiser's Web site, of course. Banner ads can also be static, just displaying the advertiser's logo and slogan, or animated with graphics and movement.

If you use an advertising or PR company to develop your offline ads, quite often they will provide you with a library of different banner ads that you can use for your online advertising campaign. If you choose not to use an advertising or PR company, you can outsource the banner ad creation activity to another company or create your own.

The banner ad is designed to have a direct impact on the number of click-throughs it will achieve. There are a number of resources online to assist you in developing dynamic banner ads. The Banner Generator at *http://www.coder.com/creations/banner* allows you to create banners online at no charge. The Media Builder at *http://www.mediabuilder.com/abm.html* provides you the opportunity to develop animated banner ads directly from their site. Other resources to assist you in designing and building banner ads are identified in the Internet Resources section at the end of this chapter.

There are a wide variety of banner sizes available. You should consult with the owners of the Web sites on which you want to advertise before creating your banner ad or having one created professionally for you.

The objective of your banner ad is to have someone click on it. Do not try to include all of your information in your ad. A banner that is too small and cluttered is difficult to read and is not visually appealing. Many banners simply include a logo and a tagline enticing the user to click on it. Free offers or contest giveaways are also quite effective for click-throughs because they tend to appeal to the user's curiosity.

## Exploring Your Banner Ad Options

*Static banners* are what the name suggests. They remain static on the same Web page until they are removed. Your banner ad will be visible on that particular page until your reader moves to another page. *Animated banners* are banners that move on a Web site. Animated banners are usually in GIF format (Graphics Interchange Format) and contain a group of images in one file that are presented in a specific order (see Figure 13.3a-c). When using animated banner ads you can choose to loop the file so that the banner will continue to move between the images in the files, or you have the option to make it stop after a complete cycle.

*Rotating banners* are banner ads that rotate among different Web pages on the same site. Some rotating banners rotate every 15 or 30 seconds, so a visitor may see several ads while remaining on the page. Other rotating banner ads rotate every time there is a new visitor to the page. Rotating banners are commonly used in high-traffic Web sites.

*Scrolling banners* are similar to modern billboards. Here the visitor will see a number of billboard ads, scrolled to show a different advertisement every 10 to 30 seconds.

## Banner Ad Tips

Follow these tips to ensure that your banner ad will achieve your marketing objectives:

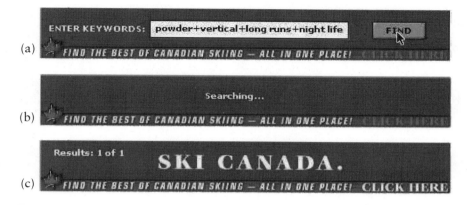

**Figure 13.3.** (a) This is the first stage in the animated banner ad. It catches visitors' attention, and makes them think that the banner is doing on a search on popular keywords related to skiing. (b) This is the second stage in the animated banner ad. It acts as though the banner is doing a search on the keywords put into the query box. (c) This is the final stage in the animated banner ad. It acts as though the search has been completed and now takes its opportunity to promote skiing in Canada. This is great, because by the time they are ready to promote Canadian skiing, they have the viewer's full attention.

- Make sure that your banner ad is quick to load. If the Web page loads in its entirety before the banner, then the viewer may click away before ever seeing it. Ideally you should have a real fast banner ad on a relatively slow-loading site. This way your viewers have nothing to do but read your banner ad while they are waiting for the site to load. You should always try to keep your banner ad size under 10K.

- To see how big files are when using any version of Internet Explorer you must follow these steps:

  - Right-click on the banner ad.

  - Select "Properties."

  - In the Properties window you will see a "Size" line, which will tell you the banner size.

- To see how big files are when using any version of Netscape Navigator you must follow these steps:

  - Right-click on the banner ad.

  - Select "View Image," and the banner ad will appear on a page of its own.

  - Right-click on the banner and select "View Info." Another page will pop up and give you the information on the banner ad size.

- Keep it simple! If your banner contains too much text, animation, or too many colors and fonts, this will cause viewers to experience information overload. Viewers will not be encouraged to read or click on your banner.

- Make sure your banner ad is legible. Many banners on the Internet are nicely designed, but difficult to read. Use an easy-to-read font with the appropriate size. Be careful in your choice of color.

- You should always use Alt tags for those visitors who surf the Internet with their graphics turned off or cannot see your banner ad for whatever reason.

- Make sure your banner ad links to the appropriate page in your site. It is not uncommon to click on an interesting banner only to find an error message waiting for you. This is very annoying to Internet users and counterproductive for your marketing effort.

- Check your banner ads on a regular basis to verify that the link remains active and is pointing to the appropriate page on your Web site.

- If you are using animated banner ads you should limit your ads to two to four frames.

- You should always include a call to action such as "Click here." It is amazing how many people will do what they are told. You still have to make your ad interesting and one that grabs their attention. Don't simply say "Click here," give your audience a compelling reason to do so.

• Test your banner ads with the different browsers, the different versions of these browsers, and at different screen resolutions to make sure that they look the way you want them to.

• If you know absolutely nothing about advertising and graphic design, do not try to create a banner on your own. Go to a professional. If you do design your own banner, get a second opinion and maybe a third.

## Interesting Banner Ads

The following are more technologically advanced forms of banner advertising. They are interesting to the viewer because they have attributes that are unique or different in some way. These attributes may be more apt to grab the viewers attention, and entice them to click on the banner ad.

**Expanding Banner Ads.**   An expanding banner ad (see Figure 13.4a-b) is one that looks like a normal banner ad, but expands when you click on it, keeping you on the same site rather than transporting you to another site on the Internet. Usually these say "Click to Expand," and the viewer then can learn more about what it is that the banner is promoting. Some of the more advanced expanding banner ads have e-commerce capabilities, which allow you to actually order products from the banner, without actually ever going to their Web site.

**Animated Banner Ads.**   Animated banner ads contain a group of images in one file that rotate in a specific order. These banner ads are more likely to receive a higher click-through than a normal banner ad, because with moving images on the Web site your chances of the viewer reading the banner are increased. These banners also offer you the chance to deliver more information to the viewer than a normal banner ad, for you can show different files, which contain different data. You should limit your banner ads to two to four frames to

**Figure 13.4.** (a) This expanding advertisement for Investors Business Daily displays the product, but then prompts the viewer to expand the banner ad. (b) When the banner expands it explains more about the product, and actually gives the visitor a chance to subscribe directly from the banner ad. This incorporates e-commerce and banner ad technology together.

keep your load time fast and to make sure your viewers read your information before they continue to surf the Internet.

**Banners Containing Embedded HTML.**   Lately we are seeing an increase in banner ads containing embedded HTML (see Figure 13.5 and 13.6). This allows viewers to choose commands from a drop-down menu that relate to the Web site the banner ad is promoting. These banners are great because instead of making viewers click through and then have to navigate through your site, like a conventional banner, these will direct your viewers to the page of interest on your site.

**Interstitial** ads are advertisements that appear in a separate browser window while you wait for a Web page to load. Interstitial ads are more likely to contain large graphics, streaming presentations, and more applets than a conventional banner ad. Studies have found that more

**Figure 13.5.** Trip.com advertises using banners with embedded HTML, which allows viewers to choose a specific vacation destination from a pull down menu, and then find out what travel opportunities are available for them. This is great because the viewer can go directly to the page of interest on the Trip.com site instead of searching through the entire site.

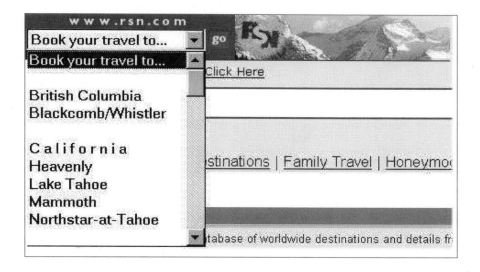

**Figure 13.6.** Another embedded HTML banner, showing different opportunities for the viewer to choose from.

users click on interstitial ads than on banner ads. However, some users have complained that interstitial ads slow access to destination pages.

**Java and Flash** banner ads allow you to use rich media in your advertisements. By using Java and Flash technology you can incorporate animation and sound into your banner advertisement. Although Java banners are more technologically advanced and offer more features, they also take much longer to download and risk not being viewed.

Flash was designed to generate faster-loading Web sites, online animation, and advertising. If you want to incorporate rich media into your banners, you may want to go Flash because you want your visitors to see your banner ads as quickly as possible.

## Location, Location, Location

As with all types of advertising, the location of the ad is extremely important. There are any number of targeted sites where you can place your banner ads. Always ensure that your banner advertising location is consistent with your objectives.

### Search Engines

If your goal is to reach as many different people as possible, high-traffic search engine sites are where you should be. Cost per thousand impressions is usually $20 to $50 US. If your target market is more selective, then a more targeted buy within the search engine is appropriate. Targeted buys can include tying your banner ad to specific keywords (i.e., every time the keyword is used in a search your banner ad would appear). Targeted ads generally range in CPM from $40 to $90 US but are quite often worth the extra price because of the correlation to the targeted buyer. If you owned a bed and breakfast and purchased "Bed and Breakfast" as a keyword, whenever someone searched for "Bed and Breakfast" your banner would appear.

### Content Sites

If your objectives include bringing interested people from your target market to your site, then advertising on appropriate content sites would be extremely effective. These are sites that concentrate on a specific topic. The CPM of advertising on content sites ranges from $25 to $50 US depending on the traffic volume they see and the focus of their visitors.

## Banner Ad Price Factors

The price of banner ad space varies from site to site. Banner ads are often sold based on the number of impressions or number of click-throughs. As stated earlier, an impression is an ad view, and click-throughs are the actual clicking on the banner. The price per impression should be less than the price per click-through. Banner ad CPM is between $10 and $90 US depending on the site you are advertising on—how targeted the audience is, and how much traffic it receives. Search-engine banner ads CPMs range between $20 and $50 US. Keyword advertising CPMs range between $40 and $70 US. The cost to run a geotracking campaign can be very costly. For example, Excite *(http://www.excite.com)* charges approximately $10,000 for the purchase of an IP address. The click-through pricing is somewhere between $0.20 and $1.20 per click-through, again depending on the site and the traffic. Before you sign anything, make sure that you understand what you are paying for. Based on industry standards, Ad Resource *(http://www.adresource.com)* has average CPM advertising rates that are updated quite frequently.

When site owners charge per impression, there is usually a guarantee that your ad will be seen by a certain number of people. The burden is on the seller to generate traffic to their site. When the charges are per click-through, the responsibility is on you, the advertiser, to design an ad that will encourage visitors to click on it. Sites that charge per impression are more common than those that charge per click-through.

There are obvious advantages to the advertiser when paying per click-through. They don't have to pay a cent for the 10,000 people that saw their banner but did not pursue the link. Sites that do not have a large volume of traffic often charge a flat rate for a specified period of time.

## Make Sure They Can See Your Banner

A major thing that is often overlooked is the fact that some people surf the Internet with their graphics turned off. Not a big deal, right? What if you purchased a banner ad? They are not going to see it, so why will they click through? A easy way to make sure that the viewer still knows that your banner is there is to attach a Alt tag to your banner. An Alt tag is a small piece of HTML code that is added to a Web site. It tells the browser what is supposed to be displayed if the graphic cannot be viewed. It is here that you should develop a clever tagline that will still entice the viewer to click through to your Web site. Remember that it is important to include an Alt tag on all of the graphics on your Web site.

## Banner Ad Placement: Where Should Your Ad Be?

As it is for an advertisement in a newspaper or in a magazine, the location of your banner ad on a Web site is very important. A past study by graduate students at the University of Michigan has showed us that by placing a banner ad on the lower right-hand corner, next to the scroll bar, you receive a higher click-through rate. This is because when people scroll down the page, their eyes are in the bottom corner, so they see your ad. The study also showed us that placing a banner ad a third of the way down the page received a 77% higher click-through rate than those placed at the top. It is very common for the search engines to place their banners a third of the way down the page for prime advertising exposure.

When placing a banner ad you must always go back to your objective, which is to increase the traffic to your site. You should always do research on a Web site before you place an ad on it. You want to find out if it receives high traffic, for you don't want to pay for an ad that will not be seen by anyone. You should try to place an ad on a site that is aimed to your target audience. You want to make sure that your banner is as appealing as possible and includes a call to action that will entice the visitor to click through.

## Making It Easy with Online Advertising Networks

If your objective is to reach a large number of users through a wide variety of sites, Internet ad networks may be appropriate. Ad networks have a wide range of different Web sites that people look at every day. If you are going to join an ad network, you are known as an advertiser.

You have to supply your banners to the ad network and determine how you want them to promote you. B2B Works (*http:// www.b2bworks.com*) is an example of a very popular ad network (see Figure 13.7). B2B Works has well over 70 different industries in its network and is emerging as an ad network leader. It can target a specific industry of your choice or advertise your banner to a mass audience. For a more targeted audience your CPM will be higher. Even though you have to pay a little more initially, it will save you in the long run.

The benefit of joining an ad network is that they not only target your audience, they also provide you with real-time reports that indicate the success of your banner ads. This allows you to evaluate the success of your current banner ad campaign and offers you the chance to change your marketing strategy if you are not happy with your results. Maybe you want to take a different approach, or maybe a different banner design might work better for you. Whatever it may be, the data that the ad network can provide you with is very beneficial to determining the strength of your banner ad campaign.

**Figure 13.7.** B2B Works is one of the world's largest ad networks, offering its advertisers the opportunity to target their audience using the B2B Works Web site network, which covers over 70 different industries.

You can also join an ad network as a publisher. Publishers are the Web sites that banners are placed on. If you have a Web site and would like to make some additional online revenue from your site, you can join an ad network, and they will place banner ads on your site, and pay you for the usage of this space. Very similar to an affiliate program, or banner exchange, by joining an ad network you can dramatically increase your online revenue. A detailed list of ad networks is listed in the Internet Resources section at the end of this chapter.

## Saving Money with Banner Exchange Programs

Banner exchanges work much as you would expect (i.e., your ad is placed on other sites in exchange for someone else's banner ad placed on your Web site).

To register with a banner exchange you often have to go through a qualifying process. What this means is that your site has to meet certain minimum standards. Once you have passed the test, the banner exchange will provide you with HTML code to insert into pages of your site where the banner ads will appear. Every time this HTML is accessed, a random banner ad appears for the viewer to see.

This process is monitored and tracked. Each banner that is accessed from the exchange and displayed to a visitor earns you some sort of credit or token. These credits or tokens are used within the banner exchange like a bartering system. The credits you earn are exchanged for having your banner displayed on another site.

Sometimes some of the credits you earn go to the banner exchange itself, as a fee for managing the process. The banner exchange will sell the credits to paying advertisers or use them to promote the exchange. Some banner exchanges will allow you to focus your exposure on your target market.

When determining which banner exchanges to belong to, look for restrictions. When banner exchanges have no restrictions, you never know what could be loading to your pages. Don't join banner exchanges without size specifications for the banners. Your site could be displaying huge 150- × 600-pixel banners that make your visitors wait while they load. Ensure that the load time of every banner displayed on your site will be reasonable.

Applying to join a banner exchange is very easy. For example, we will use LinkExchange (*http://www.linkexchange.com*). To apply to join MSN's LinkExchange program you have to follow a few short steps (Figures 13.8, 13.9, and 13.10). First you have to agree to their Terms and Agreements of participating in the program. Next you have to fill out a few forms containing your personal, and Web site, information. Then simply submit this information to LinkExchange, for their review. If you are accepted they will contact you, and give you the appropriate HTML code that you will need to place on your Web site to be able to start the program.

LinkExchange offers you the chance to promote your banner ad on over 450,000 different Web sites across the world. In exchange you must agree to display the LinkExchange HTML on your site. This HTML will enable LinkExchange to display different banner advertisements for

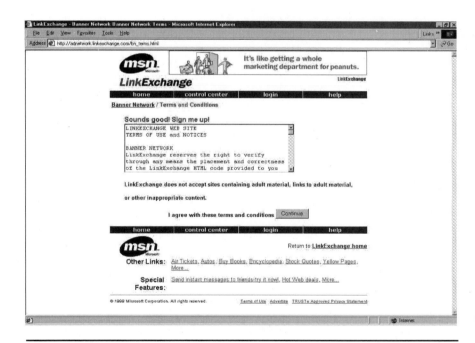

**Figure 13.8.** The first step in signing up for the LinkExchange program is accepting the terms and conditions of the program. By doing so you fully understand not only what is involved in the program, but also what you cannot do.

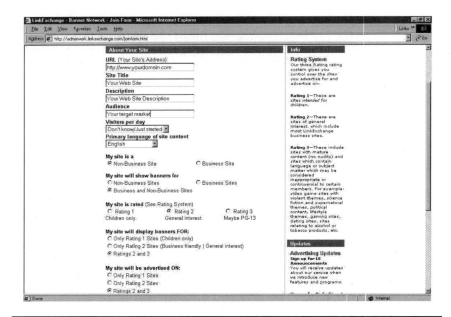

**Figure 13.9.** The second step in the LinkExchange program is very easy. You simply fill out some personal information about yourself, then some about your Web site.

LinkExchange sponsors and LinkExchange members on your site in return for the free service that they are providing you with. You will have your banner ad displayed once for every two banners you display on your Web site. This can generate a lot of exposure for your site.

Here are some of the other popular online banner exchange programs. A more complete listing is available in the Internet Resources section of this chapter.

- Net-On: *http://www.net-on.se:81/banner/index.html*

- SmartClicks: *http://www.SmartClicks.com*

- BannerSwap: *http://www.bannerswap.com/*

- Banner-X-change.net: *http://banner-x-change.net/*

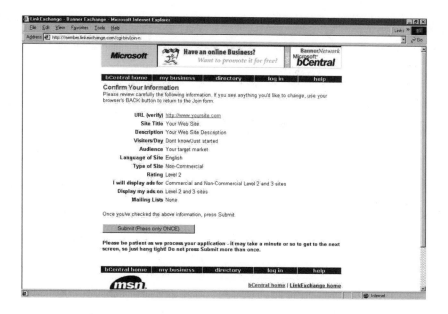

**Figure 13.10.** The third step is to review your information to make sure that it is correct and then submit the information for review. If you get accepted to the program, you will be contacted by MSN and they will give you all the information that you will need to immediately set up your exchange program. This is a very easy way to promote your Web site. You can apply in a matter of minutes.

## Bartering for Mutual Benefits with Banner Trading

Using this technique requires you to barter with other Web sites to trade banners with their sites. If you are browsing the Internet and find a site that you think appeals to your target market, then ask for a trade. Send the Web master an e-mail outlining your proposition. Include the reason why you think it would be mutually beneficial, a description of your site, where you would place their banner on your site, and where you think your banner might go on their site.

When you make arrangements like this, be sure to monitor the results. If the other site has low traffic, then more visitors may be leaving your site through their banner than are being attracted. Also, check the other site regularly to make sure that they are still displaying your banners for the duration agreed to.

## Tips for Succeeding with Classified Ads

Classified ads are also displayed on the Internet on various Web sites. Some sites offer to display classified ads for free; others will charge a small fee. Here are some great tips for creating effective classified ads:

- **Headlines.**   The headline of your ad is very important. The subject line determines how many people will read the rest of your ad. Look at the subject lines of other ads and see what attracts your eye.

- **Entice.**   Use your classified ad to get people to request more information, not to make immediate reservations. You can then send them a personalized letter outlining all of the information and make a great pitch to attract an order.

- **Be Friendly.**   Your classified shouldn't be formal and businesslike. Make your ad light and friendly.

- **Call for Action.**   Do not only offer information about what you are selling. Call the reader for action; for instance, to order now!

- **Do Some Tests.**   Run a number of different ads and use a different e-mail address for each one. This way you can determine which ad receives the most responses. You can then run the best ad in a number of different places to find out which place gets the biggest response.

- **Keep a Record.**   Keep records of your responses so that you will know which ads were the most successful.

## Form Lasting Advertising with Sponsorships

Sponsorships are another form of advertising that usually involve strong, long-lasting relationships between the sponsors and the owners of the sites. Sponsors may donate money, Web development, Web hosting , Web site maintenance or other products and services to Web site owners in this mutually beneficial relationship. By sponsoring Web sites on the Internet, you can achieve great exposure for your site. People appreciate sponsorships and will look at banner ads that are from a sponsor. The benefits of sponsorships on the Internet are that you can target a specific audience, you usually get first call on banner ad placement, and you show your target market that you care about their interest. Overall, by sponsoring sites on the Internet, you have the opportunity to get directly in the face of your target market.

There are a number of different ways in which you can advertise online through sponsorships. The following is a list of the more common forms of online sponsorship:

- **E-Zines and Newsletters.** An example of this would be Nike sponsoring a Golf Digest e-zine.

- **Content Sites.** An example of this would be DuPont sponsoring a Nascar Racing Web site.

- **Online Chat Sessions.** An example of this would be CDNow sponsoring a chat on the Ultimate Band List.

- **Events.** An example of this would be a search engine such as AltaVista (Figure 13.11) or Google sponsoring the Search Engine Strategy '99 seminar.

## Commercial Links

Another form of online advertising is commercial links. A number of targeted sites provide a lengthy list of URLs related to a specific topic. These sites will often provide your listing for free but charge a fee to have a

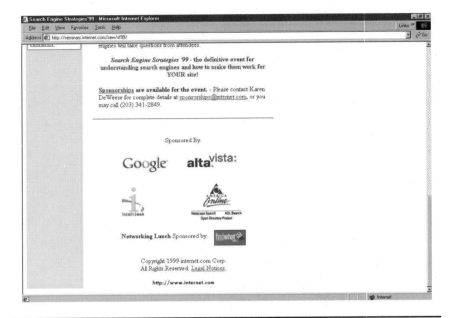

**Figure 13.11.** AltaVista, Google, and others were all sponsors of the Search Engine '99 seminar in California. Sponsoring events like this is a great way to promote your site to a large group of people from all over.

hypertext link activated from their site to yours. There are also Web sites where you can be listed if you don't have a Web site and would prefer to only have your business name and phone number or e-mail address listed. These are great sites, especially because they are targeted toward your demographic. An example of this would be Franchise Solutions (*http://www.franchisesolutions.com*). This site (Figure 13.12) has a database of franchise and business opportunities targeted toward entrepreneurs wanting to open their own business. If you are a franchisor and are interesting in expanding your business, you would want to have a link on this Web site because your target market will visit a Web site like this.

## Sponsoring a Mailing List

Another online advertising opportunity is presented by mailing lists. Mailing lists provide a very targeted advertising vehicle. Mailing

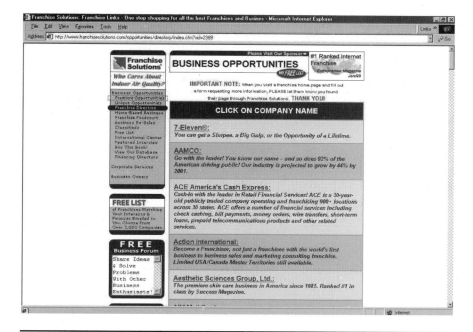

**Figure 13.12.** Franchise Solutions is a fine example of a commercial Web site that offers companies a chance to purchase links on their site. If you are a franchiser, you would want to be on sites like this because they share the same target audience.

list subscribers are all interested in the list topic and are therefore potential clients, if you select the mailing list appropriately. The rates for sponsoring lists are quite low. The cost would be determined on a price-per-reader basis and is usually between 1 and 10 cents per reader. Subscribe to the lists that have appeal to your target market and read the FAQ files to determine whether advertising or sponsorship opportunities exist for each mailing list. If the mailing list allows sponsorship, contact the mailing list administrator to inquire about the cost of sponsoring and, if it is reasonable, check availability and sponsors. All of the members of the mailing list have subscribed and want to be on the list; therefore, it is likely that they will read this e-mail. This is an excellent opportunity for you to expose your products and services to these potential consumers. A good example of this would be Trip.com sponsoring a mailing list about different vacation destinations around the world. Readers are interested in the topic, so they may be encouraged to click through and book a trip.

## Online and Offline Promotion

Your advertising strategy shouldn't be limited to online activities. It is important to integrate your offline advertising strategy to include promotion of your Web site. For more information on offline promotion see Chapter 21.

## Internet Resources

### Banner Ad Tools

**The Banner Generator**
*http://www.coder.com/creations/banner*
The Banner Generator is a free service to let you create graphical banners for your Web pages.

**The Media Builder**
*http://www.mediabuilder.com/abm.html*
Create your own custom animated banners right here. No fancy plug-ins or hard thinking required.

**Animation Online**
*www.animationonline.com*
Create your own animated banner in minutes for free from this site.

**Animated Communications**
*http://www.animation.com*
Another online resource to build your own animated banners in minutes.

**Creative Connectivity**
*http://www.crecon.com*
Home of the Instant Online Banner Creator.

## Online Advertising Agencies

### MMG The Online Agency
*http://www.mmgco.com/index.html*
MMG specializes exclusively in online media planning, buying, tracking, and reporting. They combine state-of-the-art technology with expert knowledge to place advertising for clients in the right place, before the right audience, at the right time, and for the right price. For companies with quarterly online advertising budgets of $100,000 or more.

### Thielen Online
*http://www.thielenonline.com/index.htm*
Full-service advertising agency, located in Fresno and Sacramento, California, with strategic online marketing and complete Web site development capabilities.

### Lunar Group Interactive
*http://www.lunargrp.com/*
Lunar Group Interactive is a full-service advertising agency with expertise in traditional mediums, as well as one that embraces the future of marketing. Clients include Casio and Imtech.

## Ad Networks

### Flycast Communications
*http://www.flycast.com*
Flycast Communications the leading provider of Internet direct-response advertising solutions. They strive to help companies get the best return on investment for their marketing dollar.

### B2B Works
*http://www.b2bworks.com*
B2B Works has well over 70 different industries in its network and is emerging as an ad network leader. It can target a specific industry of your choice or advertise your banner to a mass audience.

### 24/7 Media
*http://www.247media.com*

24/7 Media is a top-reach network of branded sites in a vast variety of categories. This allows their advertisers to zone in on their target market and get the results that they want from their online marketing efforts.

### ValueClick
*http://www.valueclick.com*
ValueClick is the Internet's largest results-based advertising network. They use a cost-per-click model, which enables participants to pay only for the viewers that click through to their Web site.

### DoubleClick
*http://www.doubleclick.com*
The DoubleClick ad network goal is to provide solutions to make advertising work for companies on the Internet. They offer five different types of services to help advertisers prosper on the Internet. They will enable you to market globally and locally. They can help you to build brand awareness, or to close the loop on your target market. DoubleClick also offers its clients the opportunity to participate in the e-commerce world by offering online sales technology to their advertisers who would like to sell products online.

## Banner Exchanges

### The Banner Exchange
*http://www.bannerexchange.com*
When you register, you agree to show banners on your site. Each time a banner is displayed on your site you receive half a credit. For every full credit you accumulate, your banner will be shown on the Banner Exchange network of Web pages.

### LinkExchange
*http://www.linkexchange.com*
Free banner advertising on over 450,000 Web sites. Support for over 3000 geographic regions and subject categories, and over 30 languages. They also provide reports and statistics about the people who visit your site.

### Smart Clicks
*http://www.smartclicks.com*

Free banner exchange with automatic or manual targeting, animation allowed, real-time reporting and much more!

### BannerExchange.com
*http://www.bannerexchange.com*
The BannerExchange.com offers you the opportunity to advertise on their growing network of Web sites. They will display your banner on a 2:1 display ratio.

### GSAnet
*http://bs.gsanet.com*
GSAnet Banner Swap is unique in that it offers up to a 1:1 display ratio to members depending on where you locate the banner on your Web page(s). In addition, small sites (sites with few visitors) see an even greater ratio due to what are called "charity banners."

### LinkMedia
*http://www.linkmedia.com/network*
LinkMedia Free Exchange is a free service for the Internet Community. As a member of the LinkMedia Free Exchange, you will receive free banner advertising on other member sites. In return, you will display banner ads on your site.

## Banner Advertising Price Information

### Ad Resource
*http://www.adresource.com*
Web advertising, marketing resources, and secrets. Ad Resource offers an extensive price guide about Internet advertising, including what the Top 100 sites are charging. This site also has a large number of Web advertising related links.

## Online Advertising Education

### Nielsens Net Ratings
*http://www.netratings.com*
Nielsens Net Ratings provides you with continuously updated statistics on the top advertisers on the Internet, and which banner adver-

tisements are the most commonly viewed on the Internet. They also offer a wide range of other Internet related statistics that may prove important to your marketing needs.

### Website Promoters Resource Center
*http://www.wprc.com*
The focus of the Website Promoters Resource Center is to stay on the cutting edge of the developing Web site promotion industry. If you are looking for resources to help conduct your own promotional campaign, or seek to hire a professional staff to conduct it for you, this is a good place to start.

### Four Corners Effective Banners
*http://www.bannertips.com/*
This site is dedicated to the study of all things banner-like, including banners, click-through ratios, banner advertising, banner link exchanging, and so on. You'll learn how to improve your banners and increase your site traffic. The best part is that this entire site is free!

### Mark Welch's Web Site Banner Advertising Site
*http://www.markwelch.com/bannerad*
A great site about ad networks, brokers, exchanges, pay-per-click and pay-per-sale (commission) ads, counters, trackers, software, and much more.

### Advertising Age Magazine
*http://adage.com/news_and_features/deadline*
This advertising industry publication always has interesting articles on advertising online.

### Internet Advertising Bureau – Online Advertising Effectiveness Study
*http://www.mbinteractive.com/site/iab/study.html*
The IAB Online Advertising Effectiveness Study is the most comprehensive and projectable test of online advertising effectiveness to date. With 12 major Web sites and over 16,000 individual users taking part in the test, the study ranks as the largest, most rigorous test of advertising effectiveness conducted to date in any medium.

# 14

---

# Affiliate Programs

It began in 1996 when Amazon.com (*www.amazon.com*) began to pay Web sites for referring customers to their site. If you joined Amazon's affiliate program and properly coded a link on your Web site that directed a visitor to the Amazon.com Web site, and the visitor then decided to purchase an item, you received a percentage of that sale. Today we see many sites following in the footsteps of Amazon.com. These affiliate programs, also known as associate programs and referral programs, are now very common in the Internet marketplace.

There are many different affiliate programs available on the Internet. These programs all vary in terms of reliability, quality, and the amount of commissions offered. E-tailers have these programs to develop repeat business and increase sales. A side benefit to having an affiliate program is that every affiliate provides a link to your site, which in turn improves link popularity, which in turn improves search engine ranking in a number of the popular search engines. On the downside, developing and implementing the affiliate program takes time and effort, and you have to be competitive with other affiliate programs to encourage participation. In this chapter you will learn:

- How to distinguish between the different types of affiliate programs

- How to pick the appropriate affiliate program for your Web site

- Tips to succeed with affiliate programs

- The benefits of affiliate programs

- How to start your own affiliate programs

- Important features for affiliate-tracking software

- Affiliate program resources

## Affiliate Programs: Increase Traffic to Your Web Site

To understand the opportunities available, you must first understand the different types of affiliate programs. All pay for referral business but in different ways. Before you decide to participate in an affiliate program, you must first look at your objectives, your products and services, and your target market, and then decide whether an affiliate program is appropriate for your site. Once this has been affirmed, you then choose the type of program that works for you.

## Commission-Based Affiliate Programs

The most common type of affiliate program is the commission-based program. The commission-based program offers a Web site a chance to make a percentage of sales resulting from the referral. Commissions typically range from 1 to 15%. Some programs offer a two-tier commission structure, and some offer an increased amount of commission for those who have higher-traffic sites. Some examples of commission-based affiliate programs include:

- Amazon.com:  (Figure 14.1)

- CDNow: *www.cdnow.com*

- Beyond.com: *www.beyond.com*

## Flat-Fee Referral Programs

The flat-fee referral programs will pay a Web site a fixed amount for every new visitor who links from the referring site to the host site and takes certain predefined actions. The required action is quite often

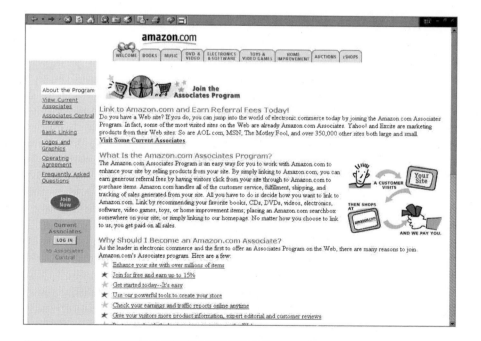

**Figure 14.1.**   Amazon.com was one of the first Web sites to offer an affiliate program and now has one of the largest affiliate programs on the Internet.

making a purchase on the host site. Other flat-fee programs do not require the purchase of an item. The predetermined actions might be downloading a free demo, ordering a catalog, requesting a quote, or another action desired by the host site. A good example of this is JobMatch.com (Figure 14.2). You can post your resume on the JobMatch.com Web site to increase your employment opportunities. If you join the JobMatch affiliate program and place a link on your site that encourages a viewer to post a resume on the JobMatch Web site, you will receive a commission. Below you will find links to JobMatch and two other companies that offer flat-fee affiliate programs from their Web site.

- JobMatch: *http://www.jobmatch.com/*

- Bach Systems: *http://www.bachsys.com/*

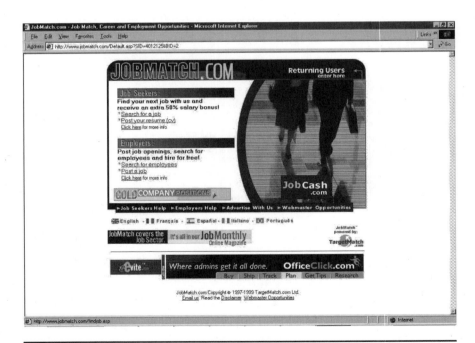

**Figure 14.2.**   JobMatch.com has a unique affiliate program offering its affiliates money for every person who posts a resume on the JobMatch.com Web site. This is an excellent example of a flat-rate referral program.

- Dash: *http://www.dash.com/wmintro.asp*

## Click-Through Programs

A click-through program is one in which affiliates receive a fee for every unique visitor who clicks through on the host's banner ad that has been placed on their Web site. There are many click-through programs available on the Internet. For example, ValueClick (*www.valueclick.com*) is a click-through program that eliminates the problems of finding individual advertisers and allows you to place various banner advertisements on your Web site. Whenever a visitor links out from your site through one of these banner ads, you receive a flat fee. Some other popular click-through programs are:

- PennyWeb.com: *http://www.pennyweb.com/*

- Teknosurf Adwave: *http://www.teknosurf.com/*

## Selecting an Affiliate Program That Is Right for You

The first thing that you should do when deciding whether to start an affiliate program is to ask yourself if this fits in with your Web site objectives and if the program is something that would be of interest to your target audience. Click-through programs can serve to increase traffic to your Web site as long as your banner ad is designed with your target market in mind and the banner ad is placed on sites that are of interest to your target market. Commission-based and flat-fee affiliate programs can go further in having the referred visitors do what you want them to do when they get to your site. The referring site knows that they only receive their commission when a certain action has been taken by the visitor, whether that action be a purchase, a quote request, or something else. The referring site has a vested interest in having the referred visitor take that action and is in a position to suggest or recommend that the visitor take the desired action.

## How to Succeed With Your Affiliate Site

You may have an affiliate program, but are you really doing all that you can to exploit it? There are several things that you can do to be successful with an affiliate program. You should go out of your way to help make the links stand out on your affiliates' sites. Provide different-sized icons that grab visitors' attention and are designed with the target market in mind. Also prepare the proper HTML coding and a tagline linking to your Web site, and you will help your affiliates get the attention of their visitors. You can also inspect your affiliates' Web sites regularly to determine whether or not there is anything you can do to help them add value to the links on their pages. You could offer them advice about where they should locate their links if they have them in an obscure place on their Web site. Remember that you don't run their Web sites, so make it clear that you are simply offering advice and not trying to run their site.

You should also make sure that you, the affiliate program administrator, do your best to be prompt with reporting and referral payments. People will not want to participate in your program if you are late with payments or don't provide them with detailed reports of their referrals from the last reporting period. By sticking to the program schedule and doing the best you can for your affiliates, you will not only keep your affiliates happy, you will also advance the interests of your affiliate program.

## Benefits of Affiliate Programs

There are many benefits to having your own affiliate program. There are also some not so obvious advantages that you can benefit from. By creating your own affiliate program you may generate a significant increase in traffic to your Web site. When your affiliates place links on their Web sites linking to your site, you will increase your link popularity. This generates a significant amount of traffic to your site, but also helps to increase your search engine rankings. Some of the major search engines use link popularity in their search engine ranking criteria. Once you have successfully launched your affiliate program and have developed a wide sales force on the Internet, you may be surprised with the amount of new traffic you have coming to your Web site.

Your greatest advantage is the opportunity to expand your sales force to thousands of people. If you run a good affiliate program, your sales force could consist of people all over the world, thus expanding your target market into different cultures your personal sales force might have otherwise not been able to penetrate.

## Starting Your Own Affiliate Program

If you have a product or service that you are trying to sell online, you should consider starting your own affiliate program. It is an easy way to generate a wide sales force for your products or services, while continuing to retain most of the profits. But what is involved in starting your own affiliate program?

First you must decide which type of program you want to offer to your affiliates. If you expect a high amount of interest in your affiliate program, perhaps click-through and flat-rate programs are not for you. Your program could be very successful in getting visitors to your site, but they may actually never purchase your products/services. With a commission-based program, you don't pay affiliates for referrals that did not produce any sales. Your affiliates have an incentive to recommend specific products to encourage the sale.

The second, most important step in setting up your affiliate program is deciding which type of tracking software you are going to use to monitor your affiliate program. This is important, because like any other part of your Web site, you want it to be as user friendly as possible. You should make it easy for your affiliates to verify how well they are doing with your program. There are three options for tracking your affiliates' success.

### Develop Mirror Sites for Each of Your Affiliates

This is one of the original ways of tracking affiliates. It is a more cost-effective way to track your affiliates, yet very time-consuming and has a number of faults. What you actually have to do is set up a mirror site for each of your affiliates. This is a separate page for each of your affiliates to use when directing consumers to your site.

For example, let's say that you are developing your mirror page for your first affiliate. Your site is *http://www.yourdomain.com*, but you can assign your first affiliate the URL of *http://www. yourdomain.com/index1.html*. Your first affiliate would be indexed as affiliate number one, and all sales that came from his mirror page would be traced to that affiliate. You would repeat this process for the next affiliate, and so on.

The problem that occurs when using mirror sites to track your affiliates is that they are aimed more specifically at people who have only one product to sell. If you have more than one product, you would have to design multiple mirror pages for your affiliates, and this would be very time-consuming. With more pages for each of your affiliates, it may become confusing when tracking sales due to sheer volume. When changes are made to any of the pages (e.g., a graphic is updated), you would have to modify the graphic on each of your affiliates' mirror pages. This is very time-consuming. If you don't host your site on your own server, you would also have to be concerned with the cost for hosting. With more pages on your ISP's server, you will have to pay more, and if each of these pages is receiving high amounts of traffic (as you hope), you will have to pay for more bandwidth.

## Pay an Affiliate Program Service to Track Your Affiliates Success

Another avenue you can explore when starting your own affiliate program is to pay an affiliate program service to track your affiliates' traffic and their activities. The affiliate program service can provide everything you need to have a good affiliate program. Full tracking services provide real-time statistics for your affiliates so that they know how they are doing with sales, and the tracking service takes care of the accounting side as well. They calculate the amount due to your affiliates at the end of every reporting period. The affiliate program service providers charge a fee for their services.

Some of the more popular affiliate program services are:

- ClickTrade: *http://www.clicktrade.com*

- Affiliate Shop: *http://www.affiliateshop.com* (Figure 14.3)

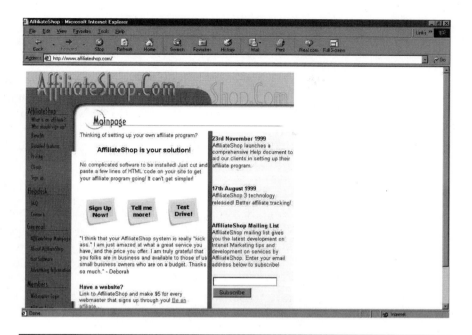

**Figure 14.3.** AffiliateShop.Com is just one of many affiliate service providers available if you want to start your own affiliate program. They will manage your program and make tracking your affiliate sales easy, which can save you a lot of time.

These services take care of everything for you from developing and implementing the program to providing you with activity reports. However, if your objective for starting your affiliate program was to make more money, you might want to do a few calculations to determine the cost. With the affiliate program service, you not only have to pay your affiliates, you also have to pay for the tracking service, which in turn cuts into your profits.

## Purchasing Affiliate Tracking Software

If you want to avoid the problems involved in tracking your affiliates, your best bet is to purchase affiliate tracking software. Companies have developed comprehensive tracking software that can allow you to provide maximum service to your affiliates. Depending on what features you would like to provide to your affiliates, the cost of tracking software ranges anywhere from $300 to $15,000.

There are many varieties of affiliate-tracking software. Some software programs are quite unsophisticated and offer very few features, and others offer them all. There are some features that you should watch for when purchasing your software. They can help you to run a very smooth affiliate program and can save you a lot of time. Here are some of the more important features available:

- **Automated Signup.**   You should always look for this feature because you want to make it as easy as possible for your affiliates to sign up for your program. It should not take them days to officially sign up for your program. They should be able to do so automatically. You want them to get started as quickly as possible, so as soon as they sign up, they should automatically be sent all information that you feel necessary for them to quickly incorporate your program on their Web site.

- **Automated Tracking System.**   This is one of the most important features that you must look for. You want to make sure that your software is capable of tracking all sales made so that you can reward your affiliates with the appropriate commission. You don't want to have to calculate which Web sites the sales came from at the end of the month. You want to be able to let the software do all of the tracking for you and at the end of the reporting period provide you with a report outlining payment due to your affiliates.

- **Automatic Contact Systems.**   You should be able to contact all of your affiliates whenever you find it necessary. Some software allows you to send messages to all of your affiliates at the click of a button. It compiles their e-mail addresses in a database.

- **Real-Time Statistics.**   Real-time statistics allow your affiliates to view their current sales statistics. This will let them know how many people clicked through from their site and how many of those people actually purchased something. This is a very good feature because it is important to keep your affiliates informed about their current sales status in your program.

- **Variable Payment Option.** Another important feature that you should look for is the variable payment option. Some forms of affiliate software will only let you work with so many variables, meaning the fixed fee, percentage, or flat rate per click-through that you multiply by the referral from your affiliates' sites. Some software is only designed for certain types of programs. You might purchase software designed to calculate payments for a click-through program. If you wanted to have a commission-based program that pays a percentage of sales resulting from each click-through, this software would not be good for you. It would not be able to comprehend and manipulate data to calculate the payments, for it is incapable of using the percentage of sales variable. You should remember to check this out before you purchase any software.

- **Automatic Check Payment.** As soon as your affiliate program is up and running, and you have developed an extensive list of affiliates, it can become a hassle to write checks at the end of each payment period. Some software comes equipped with an automatic check payment option that allows your computer to print off the checks payable at the end of the payment periods. This can make your affiliate program run very smoothly and can also save you lots of time.

- **Automatic Reporting Period Statistic Distribution.** Some of the more advanced affiliate tracking software will automatically e-mail each of your affiliates at the end of the reporting period, which is usually one week. This keeps your affiliates informed as to how much success they are having with your program, and allows them to adjust their marketing strategy to help them to succeed with your program.

Some of the more popular affiliate tracking software programs available to people wanting to start their own affiliate program are:

**AffiliateLink**
*http://www.affiliatezone.com*
AffiliateLink enables you to do everything from signing up affiliates to checking on both administrative and individual affiliate statistics.

**Affiliate Program**
*http://www.theaffiliateprogram.com/entry.htm*
This affiliate tracking software allows you to manage all of your affiliate members and track impressions, click-throughs, and online sales.

## The Amazon Example

Amazon.com is a pioneer in the affiliate program game. For this reason, we will now walk through how they have set up their affiliate program. The Amazon.com affiliate program model is a good one for you to follow if you intend to establish an affiliate program of your own.

Amazon describes their affiliate program as follows (the following excerpt is taken directly from *http://www.amazon.com*):

> *The Amazon.com Associates Program is an easy way for you to work with Amazon.com to enhance your site by selling products from your site. By simply linking to Amazon.com, you can earn generous referral fees by having visitors click from your site through to Amazon.com to purchase items. Amazon.com handles all of the customer service, fulfillment, shipping, and tracking of sales generated from your site. All you have to do is decide how you want to link to Amazon.com. Link by recommending your favorite books, CDs, DVDs, videos, electronics, software, video games, toys, or home improvement items; placing an Amazon.com searchbox somewhere on your site; or simply linking to our homepage. No matter how you choose to link to us, you get paid on all sales.*

As Amazon describes it, the affiliate program sounds easy for both the affiliate and Amazon. Upon further inspection, we can see that this is the case. Prospective affiliate members can link through to the Amazon affiliate program information page directly from Amazon's home page (see Figure 14.4). You should also make your affiliate program this easy to find on your site.

Like Amazon, you will need an information page or section of pages explaining the details of your affiliate program to visitors. The Amazon.com information page (shown in Figure 14.1) is well written and walks potential affiliate members through a series of steps that describe the details of the program (what the affiliate program is, the commission rate, how commissions are paid, and so on). Current affiliate program members can also log in to their account from this page and inspect their sales statistics. Ensure that you provide a place on your site for potential affiliate members to log in and find provide adequate information about your affiliate program so that potential they understand its potential.

Next you will require a signup form for your affiliate program. Figure 14.5 displays a portion of Amazon's associate program appli-

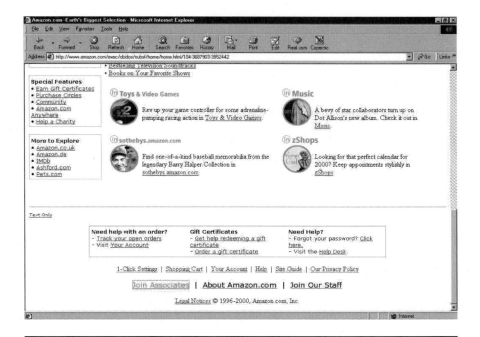

**Figure 14.4.** Visitors can access the Amazon.com affiliate program directly from Amazon's home page.

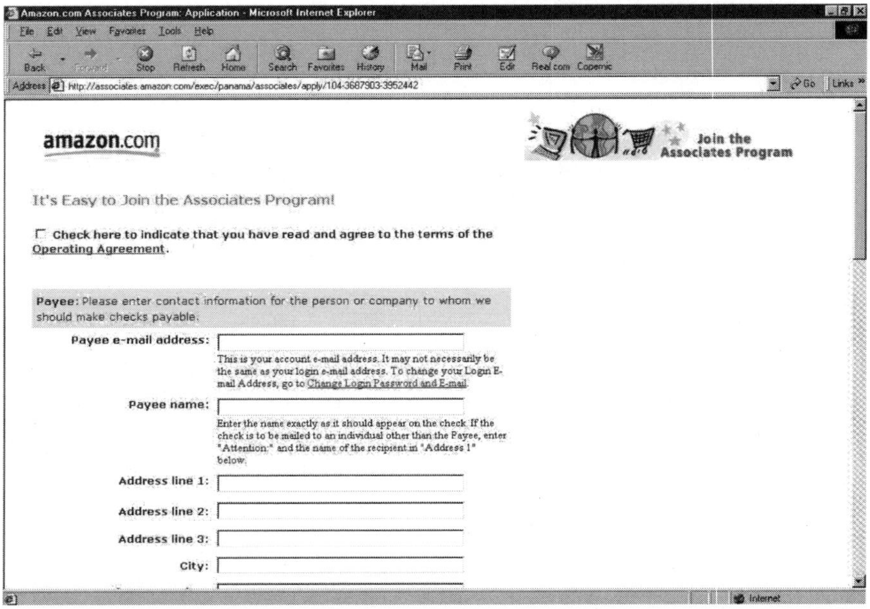

**Figure 14.5.** Like Amazon.com., make it easy for new members to join your affiliate program by providing a concise application form on your site.

cation form. Only ask applicants for necessary information. This will keep the length of your signup form brief and encourage more new members to join.

Once a person completes and submits the affiliate program application form, Amazon immediately sends the linking code to the new member to include on their site. Connex Network is a member of the Amazon affiliate program, and when we joined, we were sent the following code:

```
<url1>
<A   HREF="http://www.amazon.com/exec/obidos/ASIN/
1885068379/connexnetworkinc">Title of book or image goes here
</A>
```

As you can see, the URL to the Connex Network affiliate page is quite lengthy. However, there is no need to memorize it. The affiliate member (in this case Connex Network) simply has to copy and paste this linking text into the HTML code of the pages of their site. As described earlier, provide affiliate members with tips on where to include and how to present the affiliate link on their site. On the Connex Network site, we simply link to our Amazon affiliate page by inserting the linking text around a graphic of the book we're selling (see Figure 14.6). The affiliate link is prominently displayed on our site, so if visitors want to purchase the book, they click on the book graphic and are linked through to Amazon.com, where they can proceed with the transaction (see Figure 14.7).

Thus, Amazon receives the sales request, processes the order, and delivers the book to the customer, and Connex Network receives a 15% commission from the order. Amazon sends Connex a weekly sales report and a check for the commissions earned after our affiliate sales reach a certain level.

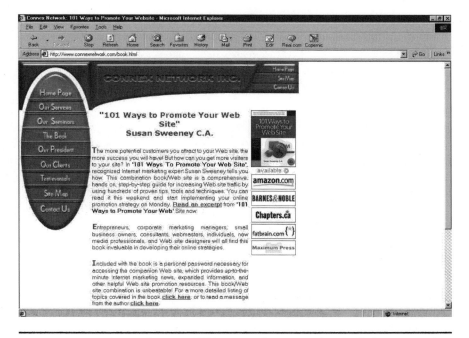

**Figure 14.6.** Persuade your affiliate members to make the link to your site prominent, as Connex Network *(http://www.connexnetwork.com)* has done with their Amazon.com affiliate program link.

**Figure 14.7.** Visitors to your affiliate members' sites can link through to your site. The affiliate members receive a commission for each sale they generate. In this image, a visitor has clicked through from the Connex Network site to the Amazon.com site. Connex Network will receive a commission if a sale is made.

Once again, the point of presenting this example of how the Amazon affiliate program operates is to give you some ideas for what you should include in your affiliate program and how you should present the information. With this example and the other details provided in this chapter in mind, you should now be sufficiently informed to initiate an affiliate program of your own.

## Internet Resources

AssociatePrograms.com
*http://www.associateprograms.com/*

The AssociatePrograms.com directory helps you find the best associate programs—also known as referral, partner, revenue sharing or affiliate programs—to earn money from your Web site.

### Refer-it.com
*http://www.refer-it.com*
Refer-it.com is the authoritative guide to Internet affiliate programs, associate programs, and referral programs. Refer-it is a great resource for merchants with affiliate programs and Web masters with affiliate Web sites.

### AssociatePrograms.co.uk
*http://www.associateprograms.co.uk/*
A UK guide to affiliate marketing and associate programs. Listings and ratings of many programs by category. Fox Tucker, Managing Director. Includes headlines, tips, advice, and free weekly news update.

### Associate-It
*http://www.associate-it.com/*
Claims to be the "Web's biggest directory of associate programs."

### I-Revenue.net
*http://www.I-Revenue.net*
Claims to be one of the largest affiliate program directories on the Internet.

### ClickQuick: Affiliate and Pay-per-Click Program Reviews
*http://www.clickquick.com/*
ClickQuick provides in-depth reviews of Web master affiliate, associate, and pay-per-click programs that offer opportunities to make money on the Internet. Also reviews of banner ad networks and helpful articles on improving affiliate program performance.

### CashPile.com
*http://www.cashpile.com/*
Comprehensive directory/search engine for revenue sharing (affiliate, associate, referral, and bounty) programs.

### AssociateCash.com
*http://www.associatecash.com/*
AssociateCash.com reviews different associate and affiliate programs and rates them. Learn which affiliate programs earn Web masters money.

## More Popular Affiliate Programs

### Amazon.com
*www.amazon.com*
A pioneer in the affiliate program industry, Amazon.com claims to have the earth's biggest selection of products, including free electronic greeting cards, online auctions, and millions of books, CDs, videos, DVDs, toys and games, and electronics.

### CDNow
*www.cdnow.com*
CDNOW is the world's leading online music store.

### Reel.com
*www.reel.com*
Reel.com is one of the biggest places online to buy movies.

### Barnes and Noble
*www.barnesandnoble.com*
BarnesandNoble.com offers a wide selection of books, and has over 120,000 Web sites participating in their affiliate program.

### Tunes.com
*www.tunes.com*
Steal Our Sites is Tunes.com's affiliate program. Tunes.com is the Internet's definitive music hub, combining the Web's largest collection of music content with programming and content from RollingStone.com, TheSource.com, and DownBeatJazz.com.

# 15

# The Cybermall Advantage

Cybermalls are Internet shopping centers that contain "stores" related to a specific topic. Some of the more successful malls are those that concentrate on a specific type of product or service category. These cybermalls often do not bring in tremendous amounts of traffic, but they do bring in targeted, interested people, looking for a specific type of product or service. The Hall of Malls is one site that provides a list of cybermalls you can search to determine if there are any that are appropriate for your company. In this chapter we cover:

- Can your site benefit from being linked in cybermalls?

- Cybermall features

- Types of cybermalls—which is best suited to your business?

- Where to look for cybermalls

- Discounts and coupons to lure customers

- Selecting the appropriate cybermall

- What will it cost?

- Checking visitor statistics

## The Advantages of Internet Shopping Centers

**Cybermalls**
Internet
shopping
centers

**Cybermalls** are collections of commercial Web sites on the Internet. There are literally thousands of cybermalls, and they are growing in popularity. Cybermalls provide an arena where people can shop online via the Internet. As in traditional malls, cybermall merchants benefit by receiving more traffic due to the promotional power of, and services offered by, the mall owner. These malls are accessed by the consumer through a common Internet address.

Some cybermalls will design, build, and host your Web site, and offer ongoing maintenance of your site for a fee that is comparable to that charged by other Web developers and service providers. Other malls simply provide a link to your site on another server. If you already have a Web site and choose this option, the charges are generally a lot less.

## When Are Cybermalls Appropriate?

There are many different reasons that businesses choose the cybermall route. Some businesses choose to participate in a cybermall and also offer their products or services from their own site. Some businesses choose to participate in a number of different cybermalls. Any one of the following may provide sound reasoning for their business decision.

- *You don't have a credit card merchant account.* Some financial institutions charge a premium for small-business merchant accounts if the business is going to be selling online, or they may even refuse to provide a merchant account for online vendors. The cybermall may provide merchant accounts or merchant account services to its tenants.

- *You don't know how or don't have the time to work on building traffic to your site.* In a cybermall the onus is on the mall to perform online and offline marketing activities to increase the traffic to their site. Your site will benefit from the general traffic that comes through the mall doors as long as your product is of interest to the incoming mall visitors.

- *You don't have a secure server.* The fact that a cybermall has a secure server may be reason enough to locate your online business there. If you are going to be selling online you need a **secure server**, and the volume of business you are going to do may not warrant the purchase price and expertise required to set up your own secure server.

**Secure server**
A server allowing secure credit card transactions

- *You can locate your online storefront in a niche mall that caters to your target market.*

- *You don't have credit card validation.* Many malls provide electronic commerce or **e-commerce solutions** for their tenants. Credit card validation online means that once the purchaser provides the credit card number as payment, the transaction is then authorized and approved by the financial institution. The transaction amount is automatically deposited into the bank account of the vendor, minus, of course, the credit card commission and usually the credit card validation charge.

**E-commerce Solutions**
The buying and selling of goods and services on the Internet

- *You don't have shopping cart capability.* Shopping carts online allow mall visitors to drop items into their shopping cart as they travel through an online store or cybermall with the click of their mouse. When they have finished their shopping, they can review and edit their invoice online. They may decide they wanted two copies of that CD rather than one, and can make the change with one keystroke. Or they may delete a few items when they see that the total of the invoice is more than they were planning to spend. When the online invoice reflects exactly what they want, they complete the transaction by providing their credit card for payment. Where a business does not have the technical or financial resources to put shopping carts on its site, a cybermall might provide this valuable service.

## Cybermall Categories

Cybermalls can be organized in a number of ways. These are described next.

### Geographic Region

All of the tenants are located in the same geographic region. Many of these cybermalls are provided by an ISP for its clients. In many cases participation in these types of malls is done to provide easy access through a variety of means for the customer, to build name recognition with the local customer base, and as a means of advertising and cross-promotion.

### Products and/or Services

All of the tenants provide similar types of products. These types of cybermalls are of interest to the same target market. A model airplane cybermall would consist of a number of merchants all providing products or services related to model airplanes. Other cybermalls that would fit into this category would be computer software cybermalls, electronics cybermalls, environmentally friendly products cybermalls, and vacation malls. Figures 15.1, 15.2, and 15.3 illustrate some of the cybermalls available.

### Industry

All of the tenants would be in the same industry. A financial services industry cybermall would provide a wide range of different products

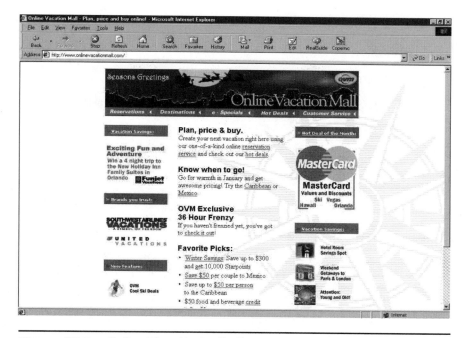

**Figure 15.1.** Online Vacation Mall allows you to order airline tickets, make hotel reservations, book your car rental, and order attraction tickets from one location.

and services such as insurance products and services, banking products and services, investment products and services, and accounting services and products.

## Unrelated Products and Services Catering to One Demographic

Some cybermalls have tenants that provide a variety of unrelated products and services. There should always be some common theme that ties the visitors together for target marketing purposes. A children's cybermall that has vendors providing everything from clothing to books to gifts to toys would be a good example of this type of cybermall. A seniors' cybermall could include a wide range of very different products and services of interest to that demographic.

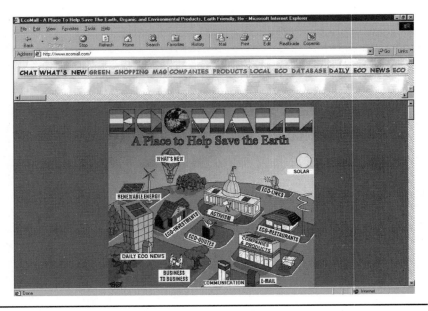

**Figure 15.2.** EcoMall provides you with everything green.

**Figure 15.3.** This coolshopping.com site is a general mall offering everything from candy to cars.

## Typical Cybermall Products and Services

Most of the items you would find in your local shopping malls are appropriate for a cybermall. Some businesses that are not typically found in retail shopping centers because of the space requirements, such as car dealerships, are also appropriate for cybermalls. Products and services that are popular in cybermalls today include:

- Software

- Books

- Computers

- Electronics

- Gifts

- Games

- Clothing

- Travel

- Arts and collectibles

- Automotive

- Food

- Health and fitness

- Housewares

- Financial products and services

- Professional services

- Sports and recreation

- Specialty shops

Some malls choose to concentrate on a specific niche, such as the one shown in Figure 15.4. The niche can be a type of product or service category. These malls bring in very targeted, interested people looking for a specific type of product or service. A number of cybermalls focus on niche categories such as new automobiles, used automobiles, antique or collector automobiles, environmentally friendly products, tourist resorts, electronics, magazines, coins, stamps, and software.

## Selecting the Right Cybermall

Before you commit to a cybermall that is going to host your site, you should check out a number of things in your evaluation pro-

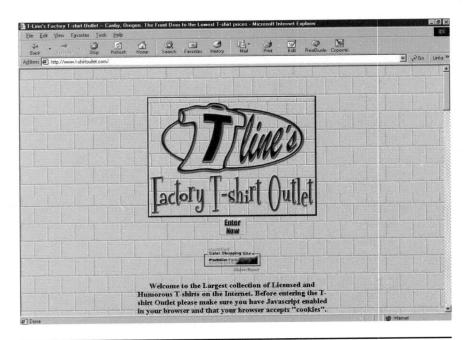

**Figure 15.4.** The Factory T-Shirt Outlet is a storefront that focuses on one product but provides a range of services such as gift-wrapping, delivery, and a dressing room.

cess. Choosing a successful mall is tricky, but if you use the following guidelines you will be better equipped to make the right decision.

## High-Speed Access

The cybermall merchant should have a high speed connection. If access is slow, the visitors will not wait. This is very similar to traditional retail outlets. If the line at the cash register is too long, customers will not wait and will shop elsewhere.

## Home Page and Interface

A good cybermall should have a good-quality, attractive home page with consistent navigation throughout the site. It is great if there is space for specials, coupons, or other advertising that you might choose to participate in.

## Domain Name

The mall you choose should have a logical and easy-to-remember domain name.

## Hardware

The cybermall's server should be reliable, state-of-the-art, fast, and have lots of capacity to handle the anticipated volume. There should be technicians available to provide technical support and quickly resolve any problems that occur.

## Categories

Before choosing a mall, make sure that your business fits within one of the categories in the mall. Don't join a mall that is targeting a different demographic than yours.

### Online and Offline Promotion

Make. sure that the mall you choose is promoted both online and offline. Many of the malls only promote online. The cybermall owner should be able to provide you with details of their Internet marketing strategy to increase the traffic of their targeted market to their site.

### Site Maintenance Activities

Successful Web sites must be updated on a continual basis. Ensure that the mall provides software tools to make it easy for you to maintain your own site or, if the mall provides the updates, that their fees regarding changes are not too expensive.

### Traffic

Obtain details on mall traffic and the number of unique visitors to the home page of the mall, if possible. Any other count of hits may include hits to the pages of merchants in the mall, which would be misleading. Talk with other merchants residing in the mall about their traffic, as well as their experience with the mall itself (fee increases, hidden costs, server downtime, etc.). Many progressive malls now provide their tenants with access to their Web traffic analysis.

### Secure Server

Ensure that the mall has a secure server allowing you to offer secure credit card sales transactions. Most consumers will not purchase online without it.

### Credit Card Merchant Account

Merchant accounts for the popular credit cards are usually difficult to obtain for businesses with only a virtual presence. If you don't have a merchant account, you will want to choose a mall that offers this service.

## Promotions

Find out what type of promotional efforts the mall is involved in. Many malls indicate that they promote extensively but ensure they are actually targeting shoppers *not merchants*.

## Commission Fees

Some malls charge a commission on every sale. Check the details on all commissions, transaction fees, and other charges. If the mall is responsible for all the traffic to your site, it should be compensated for this activity either through your monthly rental charge or a commission on sales. If you are making an effort to promote your site yourself and the traffic to your site is a result of your marketing efforts, it is unreasonable for the mall to expect to be compensated for each and every transaction on your site.

## Cybermall History and Reputation

Find out how long the mall has been in existence. Talk to existing tenants and past tenants about their experience.

## Other Features and Services Provided by the Cybermall

Cybermalls may include a variety of other products and services to their tenants, as shown in Figure 15.5. When comparing cybermalls make sure you are comparing apples with apples. Some additional features and services provided by cybermalls might include supplying mailing lists and autoresponders, or providing chat rooms and bulletin boards.

# Cybermall Features

Cybermalls may provide a number of features to their tenants as well as to the tenant's customers.

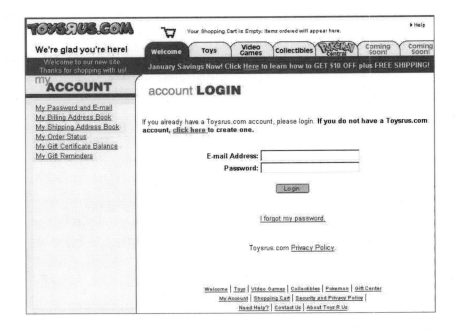

**Figure 15.5.**   Toys R Us allows you to register your billing information and ship to addresses to expedite your check-out process.

## Electronic Shopping Carts

Shopping carts, like the one shown in Figure 15.6, are commonplace on the Internet. They enable users to click on items they would like to purchase from various mall vendors and put them in their shopping cart. At the end of their online shopping trip they have an opportunity to review the contents of their cart as well as the invoice. Purchases can be edited before an order is placed.

## Secure Ordering

Most cybermalls offer a secure server and encrypted transactions for their tenants' online transactions. Technology is advancing rapidly in the area of e-commerce, and the cybermalls are among the first Web sites on the Internet to make use of the latest capabilities. Some malls now offer online charge card authorization and automatic deposit for their tenants.

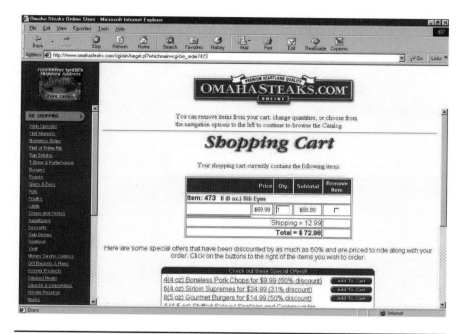

**Figure 15.6.**  Omaha Steaks provides a shopping cart to facilitate your purchase.

## Search Capabilities

Many cybermalls will provide a site search capability to assist shoppers with finding the items they are looking for.

# More than One Cybermall?

It may be appropriate to join more than one cybermall, especially if you have your own site and are just paying a monthly fee for the link from your storefront in the mall to your site. If you decide that this is appropriate for your business, you should have some mechanism in place to track the traffic to your site to determine which malls are effective. This can be accomplished quite easily these days with all the Web traffic analysis tools that are available. See Chapter 22 for a full discussion of Web traffic analysis.

## Cybermall Pricing

Malls charge their tenants in a variety of ways. If you choose a mall that hosts one page as a storefront and a link from that storefront to your site on a different server than the cybermall, the charge is generally a flat fee per month. If your Web site is hosted by the cybermall, you may be charged on a flat-fee basis, your charge may be a basic fee with add-ons, or you may be charged on a commission-on-sales basis. The variable charges are generally either on a commission or set fee per transaction basis.

Cybermall charges to be linked to their storefront can be anywhere from $25 a month to over $1,000 a month, which includes services and a number of features provided by the host.

## Where to Look for Cybermalls

To find cybermalls, you can use the search engines. A number of meta-indexes of cybermalls can be found online. There are cybermall Web rings that can be researched and also cybermalls of cybermalls. There are all kinds of locations and sites listed in the Internet Resources at the end of this chapter to assist you in finding the appropriate cybermall for your business.

## Enticing Customers with Coupons and Discounts

To increase the traffic to your cybermall site you can post coupons either as banner ads or as links from other sites. The sites you choose to host these banner ads or links should be those that appeal to your target market, or you might consider purchasing a keyword from a search engine. See Chapter 13 for advice on appropriate banner advertising.

You can also use online coupons, which can be printed from your site, to increase the traffic to your offline locations. If your customers know they can check your weekly coupons or sales, it will encourage repeat visits from your target customers. You might also consider trading coupons with other online vendors who offer noncompeting products to the same target market.

## Internet Resources

### The Most Frequently Shopped Malls on the Internet
*http://ourworld.compuserve.com/homepages/asappub/CYBER.HTM*
Listing the more commonly visited cybermalls on the Internet.

### The Hall of Malls
*http://nsns.com/MouseTracks/HallofMalls.html*
The most comprehensive listing of all known online malls located on the Net.

### MallPark
*http://www2.mallpark.com*
Thousands of online merchants by shopping category! Instant searching. Secure order forms, shopping carts, merchant accounts to accept credit cards, and merchants can link for free.

### The Cybermall.com Directory
*http://www.cybermall.com*
Evaluation of hundreds of online malls and selection of only what they determine are the very best. Malls cannot purchase a listing on this site (unlike other directories) and are selected exclusively because they provide you with a positive home shopping experience. You get access to the better shopping malls without fighting through hundreds of them. The categorical listings include brief site reviews to help you find the quality shopping sites you want without all the work.

### Malls.com
*http://malls.com*
Besides providing a range of products and services from their mall, Malls.com provides a huge meta-index of all the malls on the Net at

*http://malls.com/metalist.html.* This list is a great starting point when doing your cybermall research.

### eMall
*http://www.emall.com*
This is a great location for organic and natural foods. They have a Complete Health Online Store, a Spice Merchant section with the flavors of Asia, fine teas, and sun-roasted Mexican coffees.

### ShopNow Market
*http://www.internet-mall.com*
ShopNow Market's Merchandising Program gives you two key components to successful online marketing: strategic positioning and targeted, focused traffic generation programs. You'll benefit from their partnerships with high-traffic sites such as Yahoo! and PC World as well as from an aggressive advertising and marketing campaign designed to drive hordes of shoppers to this portal—and to your business. They provide Merchant Listings with options ranging anywhere from an Entry Tenant position with a listing on the department level for just $25 a year to virtually owning the category with top-level placement and other "spotlight" positioning as a $995 per month Anchor Tenant. They provide àla carte programs for banner, sponsorship, and e-mail advertising. They also offer sponsorship and promotional packages.

### Internet Plaza
*http://internet-plaza.net*
This site is actually a "cybertown" with addresses for each category of product/service they provide. They have Card and Gift Drive, Fashion Blvd., Finance Street, Home and Garden Row, Career Way, Sport and Recreation Street, Travel Avenue, BookEnd, Gourmet Lane, Health Care Place, Impression Avenue, Industry Parkway, and Kids Alley. Neat site!

### Access Market Square
*http://www.icw.com/mall.html*
Access Market Square has an occasion (birthday, anniversary, etc.) reminder service that also provides personalized gift ideas. They also have a great search engine that allows you to enter names of items,

brand names, product types, or store names. They provide a wide variety of products by category, including art, audio/video, automotive, books, clothes, computers, electronics, flowers, food, health, jewelry, music, sports, travel, and others. Access Market Square uses VeriSign for secure ordering capabilities.

### American Shopping Mall
*http://www.greenearth.com*
The American Shopping Mall has been rated among the topmost visited sites on the Internet by *PC Magazine*. They profess to be one of the busiest virtual shopping malls on the World Wide Web with over 32 million visitors last year and over 50 million visitors since their opening in 1995.

### iMall
*http://www.imall.com*
This is an electronic commerce enabler of small and medium-sized businesses allowing them to cost-effectively engage in electronic commerce through the use of iMall's proprietary e-commerce tools and services. iMall offers its electronic commerce services directly to merchants, as well as through partnerships with leading ISPs, Web hosting firms, and financial service companies with an Internet focus. The company professes to operate the largest shopping mall on the Internet, with more than 1600 hosted storefronts and millions of visitors monthly.

# 16

# E-commerce

You have established your Web site and you have been busily promoting it with your target market in mind. Now, you want to make it easy for people in your target market to become your customers. They should be able to purchase your product or service online without a lot of effort. How will these transactions be handled? In this chapter, we discuss:

- The e-commerce concept

- E-commerce on the rise

- Features of e-commerce Web sites

- Web trust: The challenge of e-commerce

## E-commerce: We've Just Begun

E-commerce is a rapidly growing sector in the world's economy. The reason this is happening is simple. In the year 2000, eStats predicts that 92% of Internet users will use the Net to "shop around." In turn, 45% of all Internet users will purchase products or services online. Forrester Research predicts the e-commerce revenue to exceed $6.5 billion US in year 2000, while eStats believes consumers will spend $11.1 billion US online in year 2000 (see Figures 16.1 and 16.2).

No matter which figures you believe, revenues from e-commerce are growing at a rate of 50% to 100% each year. Implementing an e-commerce system on your site might generate more sales and make your business more profitable.

In the recently conducted America Online/Roper Starch Cyberstudy, 1000 adult Americans were surveyed to see how they use the Internet, how it is affecting their lives and society, what prompts their activity online, and their thoughts about its future impact.

Online shopping exhibited the most dramatic increase among Internet activities: 42% of Internet consumers regularly or occasionally purchase goods and services online. This figure is up from 31% in 1998. This increase may be fueled partly by the fact that 54%

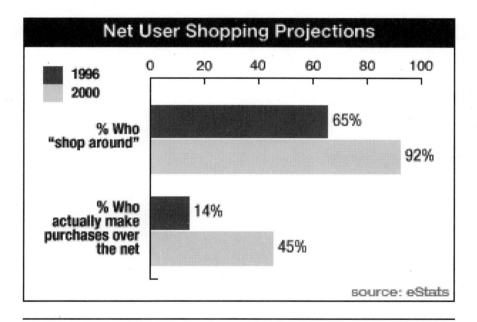

**Figure 16.1.** eStats estimates that almost half of online shoppers purchase goods and services online.

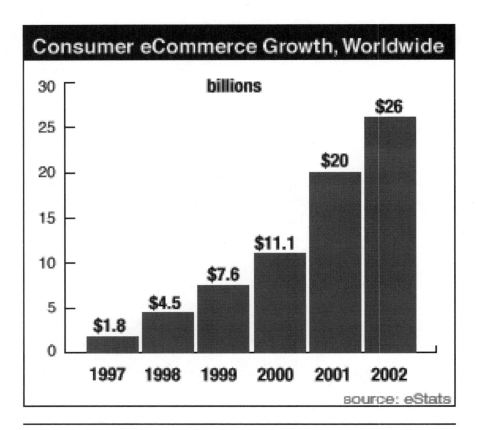

**Figure 16.2.**   eStats reports that the growth of e-commerce is already upon us.

more women (37% compared to 24% in 1998) were shopping online in 1999.

The survey also demonstrated that Internet consumers are becoming more mainstream. Online consumers are generally more affluent and educated than the population at large. In 1999, more women (55%) than men (45%) were new to the Internet. Also, 30% of new Internet consumers were college graduates in 1999. This compares to 43% of 1998 newcomers, and 23% of the population at large. The median household income of 1999 newcomers was $41,250, compared to a national average of $38,900, and the median income among 1998 newcomers of $53,000.

As can be seen, the typical Internet user has purchasing power, and almost half of them are active online consumers. The average Internet user is also becoming more mainstream. As time moves on, this trend will continue as more of the world's population goes online. E-commerce is bound to grow as people continue to become more comfortable with the Internet and online shopping.

The preferred means of conducting transactions on the Internet is the credit card. To convince customers to disclose their credit card and personal information online, you will require a secure, reliable, and convenient e-commerce system. Otherwise, your potential customers can quickly take their business elsewhere with the click of the mouse or a few keystrokes.

## Further Evidence of E-commerce on the Rise

The top E-commerce retailer, Amazon.com, has managed to see a 50% increase in the number of buyers from its site. Amazon.com processed orders from approximately 1.8 million home-based buyers in November 1999. Buy.com and eToys.com both saw significant sales gains as well, but not to the level that Amazon.com experienced. Winning the home-based market is the key to success for these businesses focused on e-commerce. Following are PC Data Online's complete estimates for the Top 20 Web retailers for the month of November 1999:

*Top 20 Web Retailers Among U.S. Home Users November 1999 (total home users in brackets)*

1. Amazon.com (1,805,000)

2. buy.com (876,000)

3. eToys.com (403,000)

4. barnesandnoble.com (362,000)

5. iprint.com (331,000)

6.  drugstore.com (316,000)

7.  planetrx.com (286,000)

8.  landsend.com (283,000)

9.  ticketmaster.com (261,000)

10. mothernature.com (239,000)

11. gap.com (228,000)

12. gateway.com (160,000)

13. SmarterKids.com (152,000)

14. cdnow.com (139,000)

15. enews.com (109,000)

16. officemax.com (101,000)

17. 1800flowers.com (97,000)

18. petopia.com (86,000)

19. chipshot.com (85,000)

20. kbkids.com (84,000)

*Source: PC Data Online*

## What Is E-commerce?

The term "e-commerce" is widely used, but e-commerce represents different things to different people. To some people, e-commerce is simply having a Web site with a toll-free number customers can call to place an order. Other people think e-commerce is having a Web site that enables customers to submit their credit card information online, even though their orders may then be processed manually just like a fax or telephone order.

Still others believe that e-commerce means being able to place a secure online order, having immediate credit card verification, and having a fully integrated back-end database that dynamically updates and informs the customer of the latest prices and whether or not an item is in stock. The point is, how you define e-commerce and how you implement e-commerce on your site will depend upon your business and the type of products or services you currently (or intend to) market on the Web.

For instance, a software development company that sells a downloadable software application (i.e., has no physical boxed version) has no inventory per se. Therefore, they would not require a back-end inventory database to be integrated with their e-commerce system. All they might need is an e-commerce system that automatically verifies credit card information. On the other hand, if you have an online business that intends to sell books and you want to become the next Amazon.com, you will require a full-blown, full-featured e-commerce system to compete with the Amazon.coms of the world. Otherwise, potential customers will shop at Amazon.com because their e-commerce system is more convenient and easier to use. We discuss the features of an e-commerce site in the next section.

## Features of E-commerce Sites

The consumer is king (or queen). This statement is especially true in the e-commerce realm. For instance, if you were gift shopping and visited an offline bookstore, you might browse through the aisles for a few hours, pick out a few books you wanted to buy, and take them to the cashier to pay for them. If you asked the cashier whether the bookstore offered gift-wrapping or shipping services, the response from the vendor would probably be "no, we don't provide those services." You would be satisfied with this and make the purchase anyway. You would then take the gifts home, wrap them, and ship them to their destination.

Online it's a whole different world. You have higher expectations. Often you are shopping online for the convenience, and you expect the online merchant to meet your needs. You expect the online merchant to deliver what you want, when you want, and how you want.

If you are making the same gift purchases in an online bookstore, you expect to be able to have them gift-wrapped and delivered to any address you desire. It defeats the purpose somewhat if you have to have the books delivered to your address only to turn around and ship them someplace else. If you are purchasing the books as gifts, you want to have them gift-wrapped. Again, it defeats the purpose if you have to have the books sent to your address so that you can gift-wrap them and then reship. Shopping online is all about consumers: their convenience, their shopping experience, and their expectations. If you don't provide what they want the way they want it, another vendor is just a click away.

Not all possible features of an e-commerce site are applicable to every business, but if you intend to be competitive online, you must give your consumers want they are looking for. You might have something they want, but if they cannot conduct transactions easily on your site and if your competitors offer more point-of-sale service, people will leave your site and shop at another site that is easier to buy from. This section focuses on some possible e-commerce features that you might want to include on your site. Decide which features are most applicable to your business, and implement them into your e-commerce system.

## Shopping Carts

An e-commerce shopping cart is an excellent feature for sites selling multiple products or services. The online shopping cart system operates much like an actual shopping cart. You can add items to your cart as you please, and you can remove items just as easily. As customers add and subtract items from their shopping cart, a running total of their purchase choices is dynamically updated.

Figure 16.3 demonstrates how an online CD vendor's shopping cart system operates. Notice the customers have the power to add and subtract items from their cart. They can also modify the quantities of the items they wish to purchase, continue shopping, or proceed to the "checkout counter" at any time. In all ways the customer has the same options with the online shopping cart as they do with a cart in an actual storefront. The customer is in control.

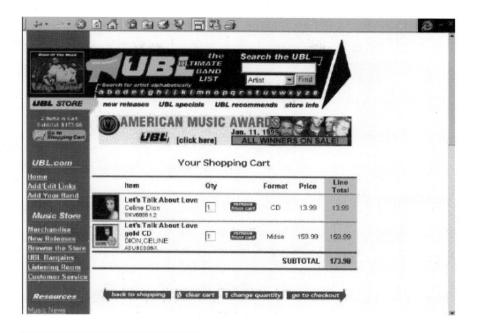

**Figure 16.3.** UBL *(http://www.ubl.com)* offers an example of an online shopping cart system.

## Database Integration

To create a one-to-one, personal relationship with each of your customers, you will require specific information about them. Generally speaking, a database is the best place to store customer data. This facilitates easy referencing of information for a particular customer on demand.

Wouldn't it be great if you could tie in your customer database to your Web site? This is exactly what major e-commerce companies are doing today. For instance, Amazon.com *(http://www.amazon.com)* will save each customer's profile. This makes it more efficient to order from Amazon.com in the future because the customers do not have to reenter their personal information for each order. You enter it the first time, and that's it. Each customer is issued a user name and password that permits access to that customer's Amazon.com account at any time. This database integration enables the vendor to implement loyalty programs, volume discounts, and other features affected by a consumer's history.

Aside from linking your customer database to your Web site, it is possible to link into your inventory database as well. Doing so can instantly inform customers if the items they want to purchase are in stock or if they have to be back-ordered. Figure 16.4 demonstrates this e-commerce feature.

## Gift-Wrapping

A well-run e-commerce site should allow its customers to have each item they purchase gift-wrapped. Many online vendors such as Amazon.com offer gift-wrapping services. If you wish, you can purchase a Christmas present or birthday gift, and Amazon.com will

---

Please review what we have in stock today, then fill out your Bill-To and Ship-To Addresses. Once you have entered this information, click **Continue Checking Out**.

### Items In-Stock

| Item | Qty | Format | Price | Adj Price | Line Total |
|------|-----|--------|-------|-----------|------------|
| Let's Talk About Love Celine Dion SNY68861.2 | 1 | CD | 13.99 | 13.99 | 13.99 |
| SUBTOTAL | 1 | | | | 13.99 |

### Item Temporarily Out-Of-Stock

Note: The item shown below is temporarily out of stock. You may choose to backorder this item. Additional charges for gift wrap and sales tax will be calculated and applied at the time the item is shipped.

| Item | Qty | Format | Price | Adj Price | Line Total | Back-order? |
|------|-----|--------|-------|-----------|------------|-------------|
| Let's Talk About Love gold CD DION,CELINE ADUBCD06X | 1 BkOrd* | Mdse | 159.99 | 159.99 | 159.99 | ○ Yes ○ No |
| SUBTOTAL | 1 | | | | 159.99 | |

*BkOrd: The item marked BkOrd is a Backordered item that is temporarily out of stock. It is a regularly stocked item. If you choose to backorder this item, it will be sent to you as soon as it is restocked.

**Figure 16.4.** E-commerce systems can be linked to a company's database to identify out-of-stock items and for tracking promotions.

gift-wrap it for a nominal fee. This convenience can be a great time-saver for your customers and an additional source of revenue for your business.

Amazon.com has two tiers of gift-wrapping service. Basic gift-wrapping costs $1.95 per parcel. This includes a choice of gift-wrap and the option to attach a personalized message to the gift. However, for $4.95, Amazon.com gives their customers fancier gift-wrapping options. Thus, Amazon.com upsells its gift-wrapping service for increased revenue.

Remember: The consumer rules. For some people, gift-wrapping services are a requirement of an e-commerce site. If your site does not have it, your customers can leave your site at the click of their mouse and order from another site that offers gift-wrapping. If I am shopping for a birthday gift online I will only shop where this service is offered, because I would not send a birthday gift that was not suitably gift-wrapped.

## Shipping Options

Having a variety of shipping options is a popular e-commerce feature. For example, people might be on your site doing all their holiday shopping. They want to be able to identify different "ship to" addresses for different items in their basket. A well-run e-commerce site should allow customers to have each purchase gift-wrapped and shipped directly to the address of their choice (Figure 16.5). It is more convenient for them to specify a different shipping address and have your company mail the gifts to the intended recipients than for the customers to have to transport or re-send the gifts themselves.

Aside from allowing for unique shipping addresses for each parcel, good e-commerce sites offer a number of different delivery options as seen in Figure 16.6. Permit your customers to choose the level of service they desire. Give them the options of next-day delivery, airmail, or surface mail. If they want their parcels delivered quickly, they will gladly pay for it. E-commerce sites are great if you're one of those last-minute shoppers—you can do your shopping in minutes, make your purchase, have it gift-wrapped, personalize your card, and have your gift delivered the next day.

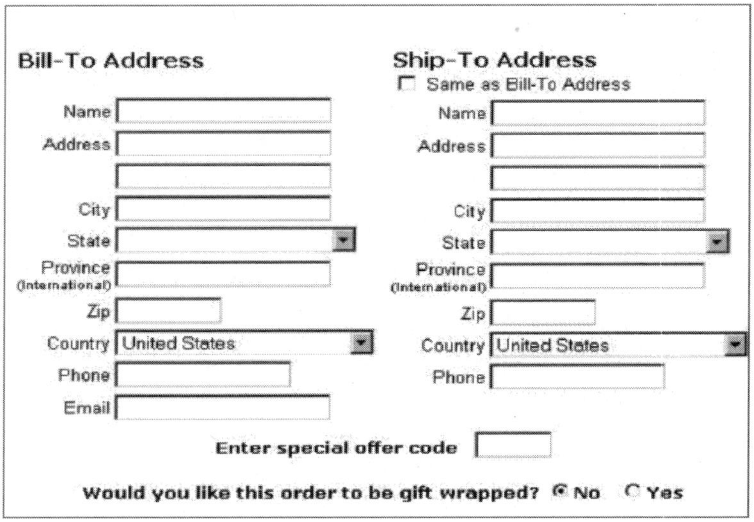

**Figure 16.5.** Ideally, an e-commerce site will allow you to specify separate shipping addresses for each parcel. Also, you can track promotions by accepting promotional codes from customers.

**Figure 16.6.** Offer different levels of shipping service with each order.

## Tracking Promotions

Tracking your promotional efforts is easy with e-commerce. You can include a special, unique promotion code with each advertising campaign you run. Then, set up your order form to accept promotion codes from your customers. This will allow you to track which ads are more successful. To convince people to enter the promotion codes, offer them an incentive such as free shipping, or 10% off. The feedback you receive from your advertising campaigns is valuable, and promotion codes are a great way to gain it.

## Reminder Services

Another useful technique employed by e-commerce sites is a reminder service. I find the reminder service to be an especially great feature. I travel a lot, hate to shop, have my extended family living in several different areas in two countries, and am terrible at remembering birth dates. Online stores that have reminder services frequently get the sale.

One online toy store provides a great reminder service. The toy store allows me to register dates that I want a reminder about. They ask me for the date, the significance of the date (birthday, holiday, graduation, etc.), the name of the child, the relationship to me, the age, the sex, and the kinds of toys that might interest them. Finally, I choose the number of days prior to the event that I want to receive the reminder e-mail, and that's all there is to it.

Now, 10 days prior to my niece Mykhala's birthday, the online toy store sends me a reminder notice. It generally reads something like this:

*Dear Susan,*

*Your niece Mykhala will be having her 9th birthday in 10 days. Mykhala likes Barbies. We have a great assortment of Barbies that may be of interest including the new Millennium Barbie for only $30. Click on any of the Barbies below for more information.*

This reminder message is very targeted. Chances are, I will click on one of the Barbies and go to the vendor's site. There I will likely order the Millennium Barbie doll or something else, have the item gift-wrapped in the paper of my choice, personalize the birthday card, choose my shipping option, and complete the transaction. My customer profile (including my credit card number) will already be on file because I have purchased there before. They have made it very easy for me to purchase from them. The reminder e-mail draws my attention to the toy store, the transaction is completed quickly, and best of all I am not late with Mykhla's birthday gift. I'm hooked! Using a reminder service is easy, and it quickly builds loyalty between the consumer and the online vendor. Consumers get what they want, and the vendor generates repeat business.

We will see all sorts of variations on this theme over the next year. This year I received e-mails from online toy stores where my children had completed their Christmas Wish List. There are bridal and gift registries developing extensive promotional campaigns as well.

## Putting It All Together

As can clearly be seen, there are a lot of steps to the e-commerce process. There are many decisions to be made. The services you offer in your offline store may be quite different than the services you offer online. Although it may be quite acceptable to not provide gift-wrapping in your offline book store, it may be a necessity online.

Unless you are a coding genius yourself, you will likely require e-commerce software, a Web development firm, or your ISP to customize an e-commerce system that works for your business. The methods used to reach an effective e-commerce solution will vary depending on your business, your products and/or services, and the expertise of the particular contractor you are working with.

Please keep in mind that customized e-commerce solutions can be rather expensive to have designed and maintained. If your business is a small start-up operation, if you develop and manage your own Web site, or if you have a limited budget for this project, you may want to start small and add e-commerce components as your business or your budget grows. Companies such as Amazon.com and CDNow (*http://www.cdnow.com*) have had years to design and refine their e-commerce presence. These enterprises are also well capitalized and can afford their own in-house e-commerce team. However, if you have a product or service that a lot of people want, the e-commerce system will pay for itself.

E-commerce is the buzzword in today's business world. Despite all the excitement surrounding e-commerce, Internet transactions represent only a small fraction of retail sales. However, online revenue is expected to increase rapidly, and you are well advised to do everything you can to reap some of the benefits from e-commerce. If you make it easy for your customers to buy your products and encourage repeat business, your Internet-based company will succeed. Remember, word of mouth remains a powerful marketing vehicle in the E-commerce environment, and the customer rules.

## Web Trust

Online privacy has been a major issue with e-commerce ever since the day e-commerce began to propagate across the Internet. Thanks to recent innovative technologies, consumers are feeling better about the security measures many e-commerce sites now employ. Although consumer fear of conducting online transactions has dissipated to some extent, there are still a lot of folks who need convincing. This section addresses the issues surrounding consumer confidence and e-commerce security.

### The Challenge of E-commerce*

*This section was written and provided compliments of Stefan Gashus, CA. Stefan owns and operates a professional services firm that specializes in e-commerce consultation, information technology, and insurance services. He represents CA4IT (http://www.ca4it.com), which specializes in the needs of the IT contractor. You can visit Stefan's informative Web site http://www.gashus.com for more information on security issues related to e-commerce on your site.*

Technology alone will not drive e-commerce; trust among the parties involved is also necessary. Even the most sophisticated Web site will not inspire consumers to buy if consumers do not feel they can trust the merchant company behind the Web site. Consumers must trust the vendor, or in the very least, believe they have some recourse against the vendor if their order is not fulfilled correctly. A vendor needs to project integrity and credibility to win the sale. This has always been the case in business, and the challenge of e-commerce is to gain the trust of people you have never met and possibly never will.

Common sense tells us not to trust people or companies we don't know, so how will companies assure potential customers to engage in e-commerce? Gaining credibility from brand recognition the company may currently hold will certainly help, but how long will the company's brand be perceived as "the best"? The new economy of e-commerce has dramatically altered the costs of doing business, has squeezed margins, and has reduced many of the barriers of entry for new competition. As e-commerce continues to shift the balance of power toward the consumer, brand management will become even more synonymous with quality control and sound business practices. The new economy has begun to level the playing field among competitors, making consumers more in control of what and how they buy, while providing them with a range of selection never before enjoyed.

For less-established brands, a means to create trust with online customers is essential. To compete and maintain customer loyalty, and trust, all brands need to clearly define their business practices and outline their commitment to offer quality, price, and superior customer service. Building trust is a function of integrity and competence, and above all, an exercise of judgment. Of course, building trust with consumers or business partners is a complex matter, both on organizational and social levels. A successful e-commerce business will implement strategic initiatives to achieve and monitor customer trust, satisfaction, and loyalty. In other words, a useful e-commerce plan will strive to place the company ahead of its competitors by utilizing the Internet to improve customer service and quality.

## Web Seals of Assurance

Web Seals certifying that a particular Web site practices "good" e-commerce have become more common in recent years. The Cheskin

Research Group produced a study in January 1999 that established that placing a seal of assurance on a merchant's Web site can be effective in increasing consumer confidence in the merchant, its technology, and the network behind it.

The value of a Web seal is derived from any increase in online sales that can be attributed to consumers being more comfortable in dealing with the merchant who displays the seal. In other words, consumers may come to trust the merchant because they already trusts the organization behind the seal. This concept has been referred to as third-party trust. However, it is unlikely consumers will be heavily influenced by a mere rubber stamp that a merchant has paid to have placed on its Web site.

In many respects, the Web seals being used on the Internet today are extensions of traditional assurance services provided by not-for-profit organizations and the public accounting and auditing professions. The more common Web seals are Trust-e, BBB online, VeriSign, and WebTrust. A good example of all four seals can be found at *http://www.altusmortgage.com/safety.htm.*

### BBB online

*http://www.bbbonline.org*

The Better Business Bureau, a not-for-profit organization sponsored in part by Dun & Bradstreet, instigated its seal program in 1997. The BBB Web seal can also be obtained online, with a registration fee of $75 and annual registration of approximately $150 for a business with revenues under $1,000,000. Records are maintained for any customer complaints, and members must remain in good standing to continue displaying the seal. BBB also provides a seal for Web sites targeted at children under 13.

### Truste

*http://www.truste.org*

Truste is a not-for-profit organization established in 1997 and is based in Silicon Valley. The Truste seal demonstrates that a Web site has disclosed its business policy with respect to privacy and that management has agreed to a process of arbitration, in case of any consumer complaints or disputes. The Web seal can be obtained by registering online and paying an annual fee of approximately $300 for a business with annual revenues under $1,000,000.

**VeriSign**

*http://www.verisign.com*

VeriSign is the leading certificate authority, providing online businesses with the infrastructure necessary to encrypt Internet transmissions. VeriSign, Inc. (Nasdaq: VRSN), is a darling stock that, after a 2 for 1 stock split, has moved from $11 to $143 in 1999. VeriSign creates public and private keys or digital certificates that work in conjunction with Microsoft and Netscape browsers. The digital certificates enable SSL (secure socket layer), a connection on the Internet between a server and a browser that is protected by encryption.

When a server is registered with VeriSign (Figure 16.7) and has been issued a digital certificate, which resides on the particular server, a Web site located on the server may display the VeriSign Secure Server Seal. The VeriSign Web seal signifies that a digital certificate has been issued and that the Web site is capable of sending and receiving encrypted information. The annual cost of the Secure Server Seal starts at

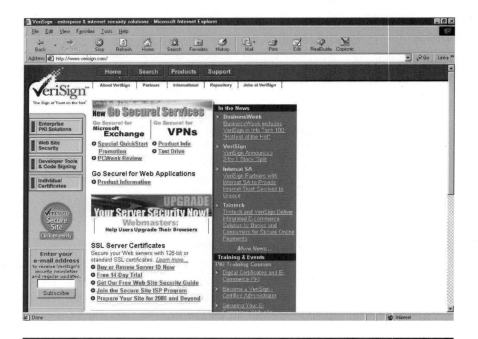

**Figure 16.7.** VeriSign *(http://www.verisign.com)* enables businesses to implement encrypted Web site security to allow for secure credit card transactions.

approximately $1300 and includes Lloyd's of London insurance, which protects VeriSign Server certificate customers against economic loss resulting from the theft, corruption, impersonation, or loss of use of a certificate damages due to a digital certificate not working correctly. The following certificate authorities also provide digital certificates: Entrust, Thawte, GlobalSign, Government of Canada (Internal).

## WebTrust

*http://www.cica.ca/cica/cicawebsite.nsf/Public/SPASWebTrust*
WebTrust is the highest level of assurance that can be obtained from a Web seal. The American Institute of Certified Public Accountants (AICPA) and the Canadian Institute of Chartered Accountants (CICA) initially developed the WebTrust standard in 1997. These organizations represent the public accounting and auditing professions, and are renowned for setting standards that help regulate financial reporting for the stock markets and government. Standard setting for the Internet is of course no less important, and the standards and criteria for WebTrust provide for an in-depth investigation of a business's Web site and business practices.

A WebTrust seal includes a VeriSign secure server digital certificate and costs $2000 per year. In addition, an independent Certified Public Accountant (CPA) or Chartered Accountant (CA) must be involved in the process of acquiring the WebTrust seal, and will also charge an hourly fee. The time spent by a CA and CPA should be valued, because they can also impart valuable professional advice with respect to business practices and business strategy.

The CA or CPA broadly examines the e-commerce entity no less than every three months. The WebTrust audit covers the three major areas of e-commerce: (1) transaction security, (2) protection and use of confidential information, and (3) disclosure of business practices. Disclosure of business practices includes disclosure of how customer disputes will be resolved, and The National Arbitration Forum (*http://www.arb-forum.com*) has assisted in the design of a program for e-commerce and specifically WebTrust. The decision to invite a CPA or CA to review a business's Web site clearly demonstrates the business's commitment to consumer's concerns. Only CPAs and CAs are personally accountable and liable for the assurance they provide.

## Security Matters

There is no doubt that SSL technology protects Internet transmissions by encryption. The real question is what happens to the information once it is decrypted and residing on someone's private network somewhere? There is a risk that highly skilled network hackers, or novices, will attack. Experts agree that the only truly impenetrable networks are those with the connection to the Internet turned off! A business's internal controls always have inherent limitations because they are always subject to human error, fraud, or being overridden by management. Therefore judgment must be exercised in implementing controls for protecting a network from unauthorized use. Every network security program needs to consider the costs of protection and performance against the benefits of further security.

Between the Internet and a private network resides a firewall, or proxy. The firewall can be thought of as a gap between two networks, filled with something that lets only a few selected forms of traffic through. There is a growing number of types and configurations of firewalls, each of which can be easily reconfigured or bypassed. This places significant responsibility on network administrators and management to ensure that the company's control procedures are in fact effective. Testing firewalls can be expensive and can only be performed at a particular moment in time. It is always possible that a firewall will be improperly reconfigured after the test. Rather than trust the firewall itself, it is much more practical for consumers to place their trust in someone who is accountable for security practices. This is why business practice disclosure is vital to successful e-commerce, because it sets up boundaries and accountability in return for trust.

## Who Will Consumers Trust?

Considering the proliferation of franchised businesses in recent years, consumers clearly look for familiarity and consistency in many of their buying decisions. Trusted Internet search engines or Internet infomediaries, who provide consumers with a service of finding particular merchants online, can provide an element of trust and assurance for dealing with the merchant if they themselves are trusted. Internet service providers that host merchant sites may also be able to provide additional assurance for consumers. Brands will continue to play an important role of signifying quality and assurance to consumers, because of their known business practices.

For all the players in e-commerce, it is advisable to take the concept of third-party trust very seriously. The organizations that can win the trust of consumers, and keep it, should be very successful.

Forrester Research estimated the total amount of dollars lost to fraud with Internet transactions versus other types of transactions. Internet transactions had far fewer instances of fraud.

### *DOLLARS LOST TO FRAUD PER $1,000 IN REVENUE TRANSACTIONS*

| Types of Fraud | Dollars per $1,000 Lost |
|---|---|
| Cellular phones | $19.83 |
| Toll calls | $16.00 |
| MasterCard | $1.41 |
| Expected Internet fraud | $1.00 |

Consumers want transactions to occur instantly on the Web. This helps to reduce anxiety and gives them more confidence about conducting business on your site. In the end, efficiency and security represent good customer service. The better your customers are serviced, the more likely the possibility of having repeat business from your clients.

After all, the consumer is truly in control in the Internet world. Not only is a strong e-commerce system "nice to have" these days, it's imperative. Consumers have many more choices in an online shopping environment than they do in a shopping mall in the physical world. Therefore, your e-commerce system had better be up to the standards of your customers, or they will take their business elsewhere. The following section describes some of the e-commerce features you should consider for your business.

## Internet Resources

### Related Links

**Internet.com's Electronic Commerce Guide**
*http://ecommerce.internet.com*
Includes links and information for companies seeking an e-commerce environment.

**ECNow**
*http://www.ecnow.com/Internet_Marketing.htm*
Thirty Internet marketing techniques to implement for your business.

**Electronic Commerce Modeling Language**
*http://www.ecml.org*
A collaborative effort by several large players in the e-commerce industry to develop a universal format for wallets and merchant Web sites.

**Electronic Commerce Resource Center**
*http://www.ecrc.ctc.com*
ECRC serves as a catalyst for a vast network of small and medium-sized enterprises to adopt electronic commerce.

### Resources

**Mercury Web Technologies**
*http://www.mercurywebtech.com*
Features a variety of resources and information to help you launch your business on the Web.

**Forrester Research**
*http://www.forrester.com*
Provides statistical analysis of technology change and its impact on business, consumers, and society.

### eMarketer
*http://www.estats.com*
Aggregates, filters, organizes, and analyzes the statistics, news, and information that businesses need to succeed on the Web.

## Successful E-commerce Sites

### Amazon.com
*http://www.amazon.com*
Books, music, toys, electronics, e-cards, auctions, and so on.

### Barnesandnoble.com
*http://www.barnesandnoble.com*
Books, music, software, and magazines.

### Ebay
*http://www.ebay.com*
The best-known and largest auction site on the Web.

### CDNow.com
*http://www.cdnow.com*
One of the original music and video vendors on the Web.

### Travelocity
*http://www.travelocity.com*
Book vacations, business trips, flights, rent cars, and so on.

### The Gap
*http://www.gap.com*
Designer clothing at your fingertips.

### L.L.Bean
*http://www.llbean.com*
More clothing and specialty items.

### Dell.com
*http://www.dell.com*
Customizable computer solutions.

**Gateway**
*http://www.gateway.com*
Customizable computer solutions.

**Egghead.com**
*http://www.egghead.com*
One of the largest software vendors on the Web.

**E-Trade**
*http://www.etrade.com*
Online brokerage services.

## Merchant Accounts

**VeriSign**
*http://www.verisign.com*

**Carefree Community Solutions**
*http://www.carefreesolutions.com*

**RealTime Commerce Solutions**
*http://www.realtimecommerce.com*

**Business Solutions Merchant Account Services**
*http://ourshops.com/paycard*

# 17

## Keep 'Em Coming Back

There are many little things that will spice up your Web site to "keep 'em coming back." Learn the tips, tools, and techniques to get visitors to return to your site again and again. In this chapter we cover:

- Attractive Web site content

- How to have your own What's New page, Tip of the Day, and Awards page

- Hosting online seminars

- Ensuring you are bookmarked

- Cartoons, contests, jokes, and trivia

- Calendar of events and reminder services

- Interesting bulletin boards

- Online chat sessions, workshops, and discussion groups

- Special guests or celebrity appearances

- Giveaways, awards, and surveys

- Offline tactics for promotion

## Encourage Repeat Visits

Just as you would want customers to visit your place of business frequently, so too in cyberspace you want customers and potential customers to visit often. The more often people visit your site, the more likely they are to purchase something. You want to ensure that the techniques you use to get repeat traffic are appropriate for your target market. For example, if you are having a contest on your site targeted toward children, you would not want to give away a bread maker as the prize. That would be okay if your target market  is families or homemakers. You would want to offer something of interest to the market you are targeting. If your target is business professionals, then something like a Palm Pilot that they could use in their everyday business would be appropriate. If your target market is skiers, then a weekend in Vail might be appropriate. You should always remember your objectives when doing any form of online marketing, because you don't want to do something inappropriate that might drive your target audience away from your site.

## Use a What's New page for Repeat Hits

A What's New page can mean different things to different sites. For some, this page updates the users with the summaries of the most recent features and additions to a particular site, as in Figure 17.1. You should have your What's New page accessible from your home page so that when people visit your site they will not have to search through your entire site to find out what is new. If visitors repeatedly find interesting additions in the What's New section, in whatever context you use it, they will come back to your site on a regular basis to check out what's new. Without this they may visit and search through your site and find that nothing was new and they just wasted 20 minutes looking for anything new. Here, too, you can ask if visitors

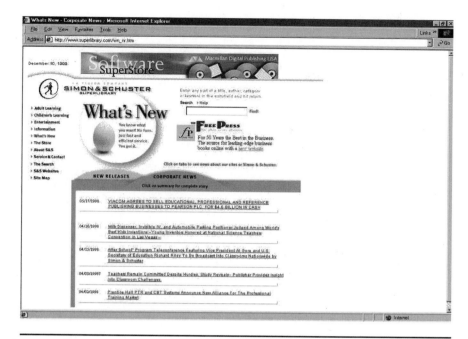

**Figure 17.1.** You can use a What's New page to tell users about updates to your site and about what's going on in your company.

would like to be notified when you've added something to the What's New section via e-mail. It's all about getting their permission to send them e-mail and therefore include them in your community.

For others, What's New may be What's New in their industry or What's New in their product line. Whatever it is, you should always make sure that it is of interest to your target market. You can also ask your visitors if they would like to be notified when updates are made to your Web site. This once again gives you permission to e-mail them and present them with new information that will make them want to come back to your site again.

## Free Stuff—Everyone Loves It

Giving items away for free is a great way to increase traffic—everybody likes a freebie. If you give something away each week, you are sure to have a steady stream of repeat traffic. When you have freebies or giveaways on your site, your pages can also be listed and linked from the many sites on the Internet that list places people can receive free stuff. To find these listings of free stuff, simply go to a search engine and do a search on "Free Stuff Index" or "Free Stuff Links." You will be overwhelmed by how many people are giving things away online.

You don't have to give something away to everyone. You could simply have a draw every week. You could then ask entrants if they would like you to notify them of the winner, which again gives you permission to e-mail them. An example of a site that has a monthly draw is Lobster Direct (*http://www.lobsterdirect.com*). Lobster Direct is a site that ships live Nova Scotia lobster anywhere in North America the next day via FedEx. They have a draw for a lobster dinner for four every month. So, every month many people enter their draw for their chance to win the free lobster. When the draw is done, Lobster Direct e-mails everyone to inform them of the winner, but takes the opportunity to remind them of the monthly specials. This certainly can't hurt sales.

If you want to bring only people from your target market to your site, then don't give away mainstream things like screen savers, shareware games, utilities, and so on. Try to give away something that only people interested in your industry would want. If you don't care what traffic comes your way, and any traffic is good traffic, then give away useful things that everybody needs. Try to have your logo and URL displayed on the item. For example, a neat screen saver can be made that displays your logo and URL. When this is made available as a download, there are no handling or shipping charges associated with it. If your freebie is something that has your URL on it and is something that is generally kept around a computer, it reminds and encourages people to visit your site. A mouse pad with your URL would be a good example.

## Give a Taste of Your Product with Sample Giveaways

Use a traditional marketing approach and give away free samples of your product from your Web site. After giving away the samples, follow up with an e-mail. Ask the people who received a sample what they thought of it, if they had any problems, and if they have any questions. Direct the samplers back to your Web site for more information and discounts on purchasing the regular version of the product. If you have a number of products, you might consider alternating your free samples. Ask if visitors would like to be notified by e-mail when you change your free sample. This gives you permission to e-mail the visitors on a regular basis to remind them about the sample. You also get to update them with new information regarding your Web site, your products, or your company. This will entice them to visit your site again. Make sure you include your signature file in your e-mail message.

## Resisting a Deal Is Hard with Coupons and Discounts

Offer coupons and discount vouchers that can be printed from your site. You can change the coupon daily or weekly to encourage repeat visits. People will come back to your site again and again if they know they will find good deals there. This is a great strategy to use in conjunction with a free sample giveaway. If people liked the sample, give them a coupon and they may purchase the regular version at a discount. If they like the regular version, they may purchase it again at full price or recommend the product to a friend. You can also ask people if they would like to be notified by e-mail when you update the coupons on your Web site. This, once again, gives you the opportunity to present them with new information about your business. Offering coupons is a great idea if you have a physical location as well as a Web site. These can be your loss leader to get customers to come in to your store.

You can develop a coupon banner ad, shown in Figure 17.2, that links to your site, where the coupon can be printed. The banner ads should be placed on sites frequented by your target market. You can trade coupons with noncompeting sites that target the same market that you do. Your coupon on their site links to your site, and their coupon on your site links to their site.

By offering coupons from your Web site you also cut down your overhead cost because people are printing the coupons off on their

**Figure 17.2.** The banner for storecoupon.com looks like a coupon, which would entice people to click for more information.

own printers, thus not using your paper. Remember that you should have terms and conditions on the coupons that are available for printing. For example, you should have an expiration date. Someone could print off a coupon, then visit your store in a year and try to use it. You should try to have the expiration date close to the release of the coupon. This will entice the visitor to use the coupon quicker, and then come back for more coupons.

Today we are seeing an increase in the amount of coupon-related sites that are appearing on the Internet. CoolSavings.com (*http://www.coolsavings.com*) is an online coupon network where businesses can advertise and place coupons for their products and services, as seen in Figure 17.3. The service is provided to businesses in the United States only, and they have been operating since 1997. Sites like this are a good way to promote your business, for they receive a high amount of traffic. CoolSavings.com has been a household name since they launched their national advertising cam-

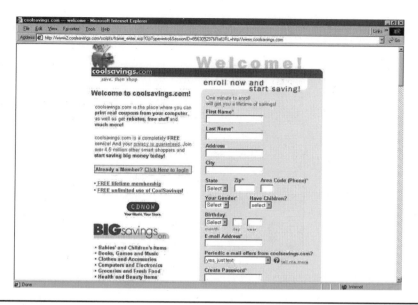

**Figure 17.3.** CoolSavings.com offers coupons from businesses to people all over the United States.

paign during 1999. If you offer coupons from your site, it would benefit you to be listed on these sites. If you are not aiming for a national appeal, you should search to find out if there are coupon networks in the geographic location that you are targeting (see Figure 17.4). There are other coupon sites, which will be listed in the Internet Resources section at the end of this chapter. There are meta-indexes to sites with coupons or discounts from which you can be linked for greater exposure.

## A Calendar of Events Keeps Visitors Informed

A comprehensive, current calendar of events related to your company or your industry will encourage repeat visits. A sample calendar is shown in Figure 17.5. Your calendar should always be kept up to date and be of value to your readers. A calendar of events for a band might show their scheduled appearances. A calendar of events of what

**Figure 17.4** The Coupon Network targets people in the province of Nova Scotia by offering coupons for that geographic region.

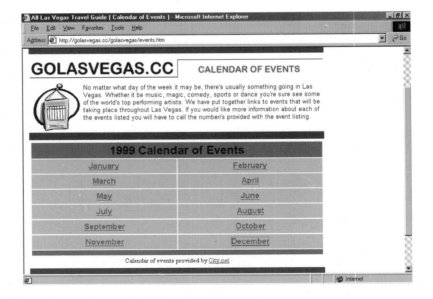

**Figure 17.5.** You can use a calendar of events to keep your audience informed of what's coming up in the future.

is going on in your business community is very appropriate for a Chamber of Commerce or Board of Trade site. This will encourage a lot of repeat traffic as long as it is current and complete. Calendars of events are also appropriate on community sites, because these are accessed often by the community and they can stay posted on what is going on.

## Lure Customers with Contests and Competitions

Contests and competitions are great traffic builders. Some sites hold regular contests on a weekly or monthly basis to generate repeat visitors. Holding contests is also a great way to find out about your target market by requesting information on the entry form.

What type of contest you hold depends upon your Internet marketing objectives. If you want to attract as many people as possible to your site regardless of who they are, then offer items such as money, trips, cars, computers, and so on as in Figures 17.6 and 17.7. If you would like to attract potential customers from your target market, then give away something that relates to your products and industry.

You could simply request that people fill out an electronic ballot including their name, address, phone number, and e-mail address to enter the contest. If you want to find out something about the people entering, ask them to answer a question about your products. If the prize is one of your products, consider asking entrants to write a short essay outlining why they would like to have the product you are giving away. You can award the winner or winners with the product and follow up with the other entrants. These people may be in a position to buy your products, and you will have gained some valuable knowledge from the essays submitted.

If your product is appropriate for a prize that would be of interest to many different types of people, you might consider finding contest sites that might like to offer your product as the prize on their site. This will generate brand awareness for your product. You could have it set up on their site so that it shows a picture of your product with a link to your site. The contest site should be more than happy to do this because you are offering to give him/her something for free that adds value to their site.

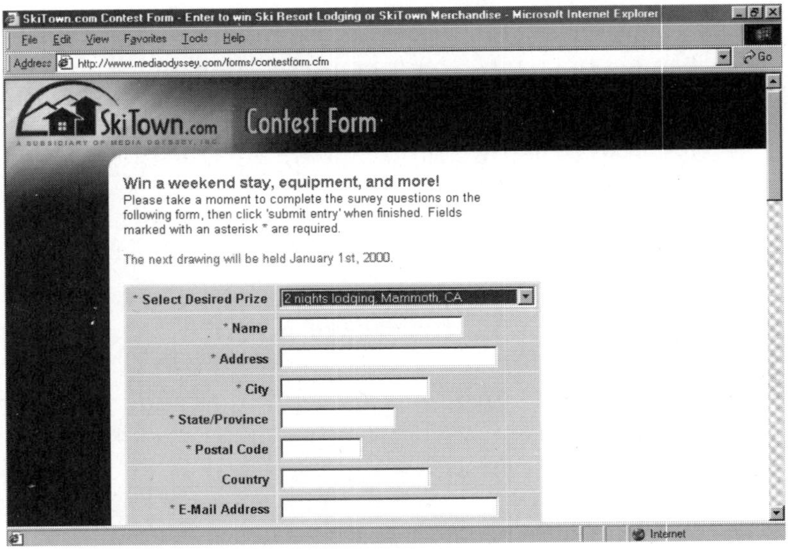

**Figure 17.6.** Contests are a great way to bring back repeat traffic.

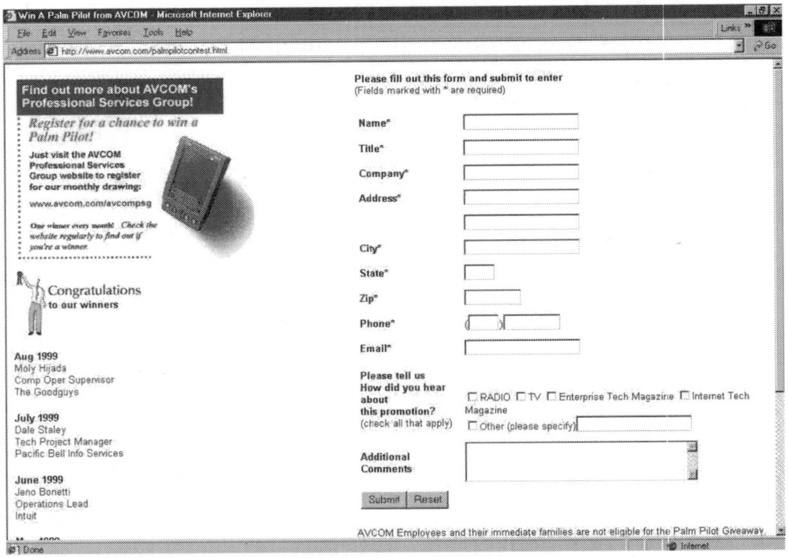

**Figure 17.7.** AVCOM offers its visitor a chance to win a Palm Pilot. Monthly draws can generate a lot of repeat traffic.

You can turn a contest into a competition. If your Web site relates to cooking or baking, ask entrants to submit their best recipe using your food product. People will visit your site to see the winning recipes, and you may get some ideas for future marketing efforts. Other competitions may include things like best photo with product X, best short story about product X, best drawing of product X, and so on. This creates better brand awareness and reinforces sales of your product. The closer the contest relates to your product, the better. Instead of offering just one prize, offer a number of smaller prizes as well. This makes the odds look better and people feel they have a better chance of winning.

Before you go ahead with holding any kind of contest, check out all of the legal issues. There may be restrictions that you don't know about (e.g., you may be required to purchase a legal permit to hold lotteries). You should also remember to ask the entrants the e-mail address at which they would like to be notified of the winner. This, again, grants you permission to e-mail them to tell them who the winner was, and also to inform them of the specials that you may have at your site that month.

## Using Employment Opportunities to Increase Visitors

People involved in a job search or interested in new job opportunities will revisit your site occasionally to see your list of available positions. See Figure 17.8 for a sample employment page.

## Create Useful Links from Your Site

Provide visitors with links to other sites similar to yours or a meta-index of links that would be of interest to your target market. Do not put outbound links on your home page. Place them down a level or two after the visitors have seen all the information you want them to see before you provide the links away from your site. Try exchanging links with others so you receive a link from their site to your site. As long as the links are of value to your visitors, people will come back to see if you have found any new and interesting sites for them to visit.

**Figure 17.8.** Lycos provides information on employment opportunities from their Web site.

You might consider asking if they would be interested in being notified when you make update your list of links, or just updates to your site in general. By offering this, if they choose to do so, you have the opportunity to send people an e-mail message and remind them about your site while presenting them with new information about what might be going on with your site. Remember to use your signature file containing your URL. This way the viewers can link through to your Web site directly from the e-mail.

## Investing in Online Chat Sessions

Chat rooms are very popular (Figure 17.9) and, to some, even addictive. If you have a chat forum on your site, make sure that the topic relates to your business and that participants are likely to be your

**Figure 17.9.** Yack.com is a very popular place for people of all ages to locate sites with interactive events, including online chat sessions.

target market. To encourage repeat visitors you could change the topic from day to day or week to week. You could also have celebrity appearances in your chat sessions. These sessions should be regularly scheduled, and the upcoming events should be posted on your site so that your visitors will know what is going on when, and will not miss the session if it is of importance to them. They could be on Sunday from 3 to 5 p.m., or on Tuesday from 7 to 9 p.m. Also remember to have the information in your signature file and do some postings through your appropriate mail lists and newsgroups to promote the event.

You should try to post the topics of the discussions at least a week in advance so that your visitors will remember to come for the entire session if they are interested in the topic. You would be surprised how many people would schedule time so that they could chat with someone special or knowledgeable in an area that interests them. You might also think of asking your visitors if they would be interested in being notified of the upcoming chat sessions or celebrities who may be visiting your site to chat. This again gives you the opportunity to e-mail people, at their request, and present them with information that will entice them to visit your site again. You can also ask your community who they'd like to see as a guest or what topics they would like to see discussed.

## Providing a Tip of the Day to Encourage Repeat Visits

Have a section that offers cool tips that relate to your business, your products/services, or your target market as in Figure 17.10. These tips can be one sentence to one paragraph long. If visitors find your advice helpful, they will return repeatedly to see what interesting piece of information you have displayed that day. Ask your visitors if they would be interested in receiving the tip via e-mail or notification when the tip has been updated so they could then visit your Web site.

## Ensuring Your Site Gets Bookmarked

Encourage visitors to add you to their bookmark list. Somewhere on your site display the call to action "Bookmark me now!" (see Figure 17.11). A call to action is often effective. Make sure the title of the page that has the "Bookmark me now!" clearly identifies your site and its contents in an enticing way, because the title is what will appear in the bookmark file as a description. Whenever I see "Bookmark this site now!" I always consider it. Sometimes I do, sometimes I don't, but I always consider it. Often, when the call to action is not presented, I don't think about it, and don't bookmark it. Then days later when I want to go back there, I wish I had remembered to bookmark.

## World Interaction with Bulletin Boards

It can be very satisfying to see people join in from all over the world just to interact with each other about a topic that relates to your Web

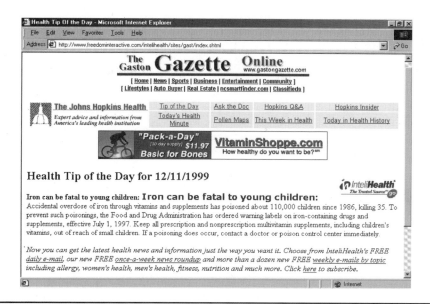

**Figure 17.10.** Health Tip of the Day. Tips of the day can encourage repeat visitors.

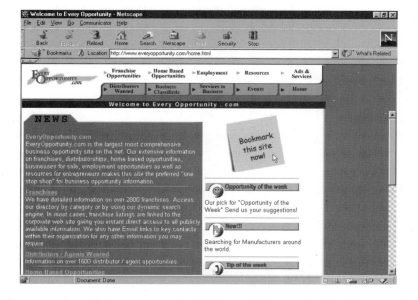

**Figure 17.11.** When you see a "Bookmark this site now!" call to action, nine times out of ten you will at least consider it.

site, as shown in Figure 17.12. Beware, you will have to keep an eye on the messages and may even have to play referee occasionally.

## Inviting Visitors to Contribute with Surveys

Performing surveys is a way to increase the traffic to your site. For people to want to fill out the survey and see the results, the survey topic must be interesting. To encourage input, the survey results might only be available to participants. Your survey could be on a topic concerning current events or something pertaining to your industry. The more controversial or debatable the topic of the survey, the more people will visit to contribute or see the results. If you want to draw a very targeted audience, pick a topic that would be interesting to that market alone.

**Figure 17.12.** The Speaker Café is a great bulletin board where people can request information about professional speakers for conferences and trade. shows.

In performing these surveys you are building repeat traffic and you are gathering valuable information on your market. If you hold an interesting survey every week or every month, then you will be sure to retain a loyal audience of repeat visitors. If your surveys are newsworthy, then you can send out press releases to publicize the results and gain publicity for your site.

Your surveys should be short and to the point. Let people know why you are asking visitors to do the survey and when the deadline is. Make your questions clear and concise. The responses should be Yes/No or multiple choice. When reporting the results, don't just put them on your Web page. Post the results to newsgroups and mailing lists that would be interested. Don't forget to add your sig.file. If you are holding weekly or monthly surveys, let people know via your sig.file what the next survey topic will be and that there is more information on your Web site.

Again, you should ask people if they'd like to be notified of survey results, either via e-mail or by prior notification as to when the results will be posted on the site so they will be able to visit your site and find out. You might also ask if they'd like to be notified when you are conducting a new survey.

An example of an online survey would be the StudyWEB (*http://www.studyweb.com*) online survey. They use this to find out how many people are actually using StudyWEB (Figure 17.13) and to receive suggestions for their Web site. This provides good feedback for StudyWEB, but also shows the Web site's users that they care about their visitors.

## Encourage Repeat Visits with Your "Site of the Day"

Having your own "Site of the Day" or "Site of the Week" listing, as in Figure 17.14, will mean a lot of work, searching the Internet for a cool site to add, or looking through all the submissions. However, if your picks are interesting to your audience, you may find that avid Internet users come back every day to see what great new site is listed. Remember that this must be updated on schedule; displaying a week-old Site of the Day will reflect poorly on your site and your company. For more information see Chapter 11 about hosting your own award site.

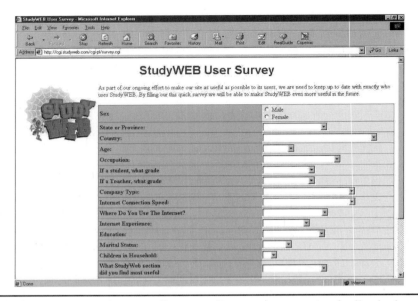

**Figure 17.13.** StudyWEB offers an online survey to receive feedback about their site. This helps them to improve their site for its visitors.

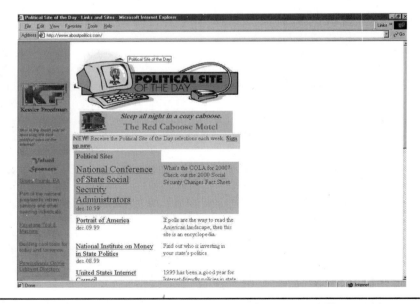

**Figure 17.14.** The Political Site of the Day focuses on different politics-related Web sites and offers an e-mail notification service to inform its visitors of the new site of the day.

## Keep Them Happy with Cartoons

Displaying relevant cartoons keeps your site dynamic and fun. You do not necessarily have to create all of the content and features yourself. If you update this weekly, ask if visitors would like to be notified via e-mail when you update your Web site. A good example of a site that uses cartoons is the M-Bug site (*http://www.cartoon2000.com/net.html*), which continuously provides humor to its viewers (see Figure 17.15).

## Sending Postcards Around the Internet

Visitors can create original postcards that can be e-mailed to their family and friends (see Figure 17.16). The postcards should be able to be identified as coming from your site—have your logo and URL

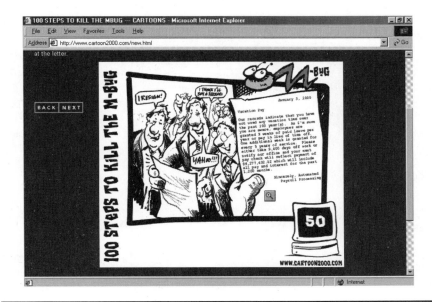

**Figure 17.15.** The M-Bug offers amusing cartoons to its viewers and has a e-mail list that informs their visitors when they put a new cartoon on their site.

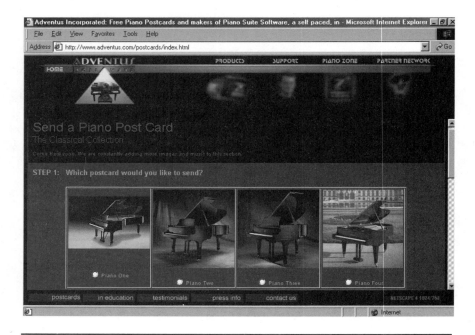

**Figure 17.16.** Adventus allows you to send online postcards to friends.

displayed somewhere on them. I can't begin to count the number of beautiful cards I have received via e-mail from my 12-, 11-, and 9-year-old, each with a beautiful verse and complete with audio and video. The cards have come via the Blue Mountain Card site, and, yes, I have noticed that my recent offline card purchases have happened to be from the same company.

## Benefiting from Humor with Jokes and Trivia

"Laughter is the best medicine" and could prove to be a popular feature of your Web page, as in Figure 17.17. People enjoy trivia, or a "thought of the day," and there are many sources for you to draw from. Be sure and update regularly. Again this gives you the opportunity to ask if your visitors would like to be notified when you update your Web site.

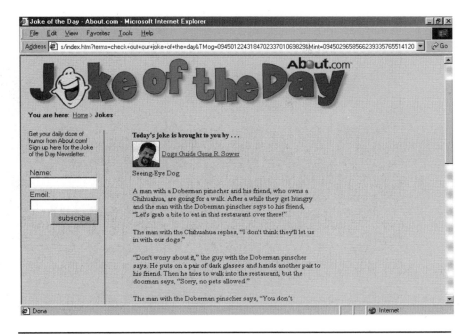

**Figure 17.17.** About.com has a joke of the day that you can view online or sign up to receive in your e-mail box in the form of a newsletter.

## Who Doesn't Love Games?

More and more sites are featuring fun activities and games on their sites. (A sample game site is shown in Figure 17.18.) Just about anything goes here. You can host anything from a Star Wars trivia contest to having guests play an interactive game with other visitors.

## Keep Customers in Touch with Update Reminders

Ask visitors to your site if they'd like to be notified when there are updates or content changes to your pages. This is similar to a mailing list except you only write to the "list" when changes have been made. This is effective when you have a newsletter or a frequently visited calendar of events on your site.

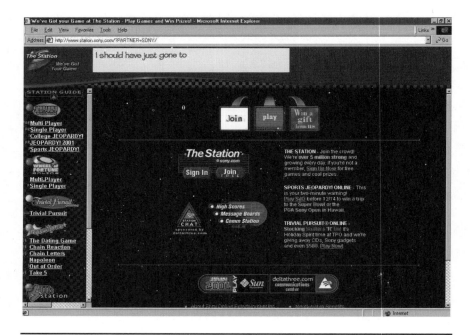

**Figure 17.18.** Sony Online has many games for their users to enjoy.

## Special Events Reminder Services

People can sign up to be reminded of something via e-mail on specified dates (see Figure 17.19). This feature was originally thought of by a florist to remind people about important dates. You can remind people about any number of things relating to your business. If you own a site that sells fishing and hunting gear, you could get people to sign up to be reminded when certain fishing or hunting seasons start. You should try to develop a reminder service that relates to something that you sell from your site. In your reminder you can include suggestions about what fishing fly works best at this time of the year

Reminder services are becoming very popular with e-commerce sites. Their services are very much appreciated by busy people who are not good with remembering dates. This has saved me on more than one occasion and made it very easy to purchase from the site

**Figure 17.19.** Graphic Products has an e-mail reminder system you can sign up to receive an e-mail when you are low on supplies.

that provided the reminder. I have five nieces and nephews across the country. I have registered their birthdays with a site that also asked for some details about the reminder. Things like what the date is, the relationship that I have with the person, their age, things they enjoy, and how far ahead of time that I want to be notified. Like clockwork, 10 days prior to Kyle's birthday I got this e-mail:Susan, your nephew Kyle's birthday is in 10 days. He will be 12 years old. Kyle likes Gameboy video games. We happen to have several that may be appropriate as a gift for Kyle. Click here for more details.

I am then able to choose the gift that I want to purchase, the paper I wanted it wrapped with, and the text that I want on the card that will be attached to the gift. Then I simply provide the address I want it sent to and give them my credit card number, and they send it off. Everyone is happy, especially me.

## Adding Image with Advice Columns

Some Web sites are incorporating advice columns, as in Figure 17.20. People will return again and again to read the e-mails asking for advice and to see the responses that are given. This also helps perpetuate an image of your company as an expert in your given field.

## Internet Resources

**More Hits for Your WWW Site**
*http://www.adze.com/zine/morehits.html*
Instruction on how to get people to keep coming back to your site.

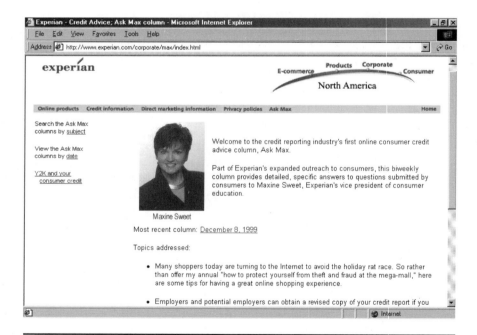

**Figure 17.20.** A column that gives consumer credit advice.

### Web Developers Virtual Library
*http://www.stars.com*
A comprehensive illustrated encyclopedia of Web technology, the WDVL is for Web masters and Internet developers. It's a well-organized gold mine of tutorials, demos, and links to great resources.

### 10 Secrets of the Web Masters
*http://www.i-strategies.com/10secret.html*
A guide to Web design and strategy to get visitors and make them return.

### Guide to Web Style
*http://www.sun.com/styleguide*
Sun Microsystems' cookbook for better Web site design to encourage repeat visitors.

## Design Tips

### Five Most Serious Web Design Errors
*http://www.hp.com/Ebusiness/webdesign.html*
Web designer tips to avoid fatal flaws that could cause your site to fail.

### Yale Style Manual—Table of Contents
*http://info.med.yale.edu/caim/manual/contents.html*
A good example of a detailed Web design manual to keep visitors coming back.

### Web Architect
*http://argus-inc.com/design/webarch.html*
Archive of Web Review site design features to help you get the perfect layout.

### Web Page Design—Introduction
*http://www.wpdfd.com*
Web design from the perspective of typography and graphics to keep visitors happy; no HTML.

### Pulling the Plug-Ins

*http://www.cio.com/archive/webbusiness/060198_main_content.html*
Web plug-ins are finally on the outs with Web designers. So how should you cram all that interactivity in your Web pages without alienating your visitors? Go here and find out.

### Conservatism of Web Users

*http://www.useit.com/alertbox/980322.html*
Statistics show that Web users are adopting new Web technologies at slower rates, affecting how you should design your site.

### Features—How To—Elements of Web Design

*http://www.builder.com/Graphics/Design*
CNET's elements of good Web design to help in your Web page design.

# 18

# Maximizing Media Relations

**Y**our online media strategy can be extremely effective in building traffic to your site. Press release distribution can be done easily. Build the right list of e-mail addresses or make use of one of the online press distribution services. Most reporters and writers have e-mail addresses. Some do not like to receive e-mailed press releases; others prefer the e-mail versions. When e-mail press releases are sent out, reporters will reply by e-mail; they will expect your response within 24 hours. Develop a media kit that you can e-mail out to editors. In this chapter we cover:

- Developing your online media strategy

- Public relations vs. advertising

- Online public relations vs. traditional public relations

- Effective press releases

- Press release and distribution services online

- How to distribute press releases online

- Providing an area for media on your site

- How to find reporters online

- How reporters want to receive your information

- Encouraging republication of your article with a direct link to your site or article

- Providing press kits online

- Electronic newsletters

- Resources

## Managing Effective Public Relations

Media relations are very important to your marketing efforts. The best results are achieved when you integrate both online and offline publicity campaigns. Press release distribution can be accomplished easily if you have an established list of reporters and editors, or if you make use of a press distribution service.

Maintaining effective public relations will deliver a number of benefits to your company. Your company and products can be given exposure through press releases, and a positive image for your company will be portrayed. Your relationship with current customers will be reinforced, and new relationships will be formed.

## Benefits of Publicity vs. Advertising

Media coverage, or publicity, has a major advantage over paid advertisements. Articles written by a reporter carry more weight with the public than ads do because the media and reporters are seen as unbiased third parties. Articles printed in media publications are given more credibility by the public than paid advertisements. Another advantage of distributing press releases is that it is more cost effective than advertising. You have to pay for advertising space on a Web site or time on the radio, but the costs of writing and distributing press releases are minimal.

One of the disadvantages of press releases compared to advertising is that you don't have control over what is published. If the editor decides to cast your company in a negative light, then there is nothing you can do to stop him or her. If the writer of the piece does not like your company, for whatever reason, this may come across in the article. Basically, after your press release is distributed you have no control over what will be written about your company.

It is important to note that when generating publicity, you may lose control over the timing of your release as well. For example, you may want an article released the day before your big sale, but the editor may relegate it to a date the following week. There is nothing you can do about this. It is not a good idea to rely exclusively on publicity for important or newsworthy events, because if the release is not reviewed and considered newsworthy, you may be stuck with no promotion at all.

## What Is a Press Release?

Before you begin your media campaign you should know what press releases are and how to write them. Press releases are designed to inform reporters of events concerning your company that the public may consider newsworthy. Press releases can get your company free public attention. A press release is a standard form of communication with the media. Press releases must contain newsworthy information. Companies that continually send worthless information in a blatant attempt to get their name in the press will not establish a good relationship with the media.

### Writing a Press Release

Your press release should follow a standard format, which is described in the following paragraphs.

**Notice of Release**

The first thing the reader sees should be

*FOR IMMEDIATE RELEASE*

unless you have sent the information in advance of the time you would like it published. In that case state it as follows:

*FOR RELEASE: Wednesday, April 14, 2000 (using the date you want it released.)*

Remember that no matter what date you put here, the publication can release the information before or after the specified date. If the news is really big, it is not likely that the publication will hold it until the date you have specified.

**Header**

The header should be in the upper-left corner. It should contain all of the contact information for one or two key people. These contacts should be able to answer any questions regarding the press release. If reporters cannot get in touch with someone to answer their questions, they may print incorrect information or even drop the article all together.

*Connex Network Incorporated*
*Suite 301*
*800 Windmill Road*
*Dartmouth, Nova Scotia*
*Canada B3B 1L1*
*Tel 902-468-2578 Fax 902-468-2233*
*Contact: Susan Sweeney*

**Headline**

Your headline should summarize your message and make the reader want to continue reading.

### City and Date

Name the city you are reporting from and the date you wrote the press release.

### The Body

Your first sentence within the body of the press release should sum up your headline and immediately inform the reader why this is newsworthy. With the number of press releases reporters receive, if you don't grab their attention immediately they won't read your release. Begin by listing all of the most relevant information first, leaving the supporting information last.

Ask yourself the five Ws (who, what, where, when, and why) and answer them up front. Write the press release just as if you were writing a newspaper article for publication. Include some quotes from key individuals in your company and any other relevant outside sources that are credible. If there are any statistics that support your main message, include them as well. Your last paragraph should be a short company description.

### The Close

If your release is two pages long, center the word "-more-" at the bottom of the first page. To end your release, there are three ways of standard notation to do this: center the symbol "#," the word "end," or the number "-30-" at the end of your message. A sample press release is shown in Figure 18.1.

## Advantages of Interactive Press Releases

Online press releases take the same standard format as offline press releases, but the online press release can be interactive, with links to a variety of interesting information that supports your message. Reporters can easily find out other facts by following your links. Additional items included in your interactive press releases are:

**Figure 18.1.** A press release on about.com referring to iPRINT.com. This press release contains a hyperlink to iPRINT.com's home page.

- A link to the e-mail address of the media contact person in your organization

- A link to the company Web page

- Links to articles and related issues both on the corporate Web site and on other sites

- Links to graphics and pictures for illustration. If your story relates to a product, have a link to a graphic that can be used. The reporter or individual can simply right-click, "Save picture as...," and incorporate the images in the story

- Links to key corporate players, their biographies, their photos, and possibly some quotes. Journalists usually include quotes in their stories

- A link to a FAQ section where you can have frequently asked questions and a few that you wish were frequently asked.

Figures 18.2 through 18.6 are examples of online press releases.

## Sending Press Releases on Your Own vs. Using a Distribution Service

When distributing press releases on your own, you save the money it would cost to have a service do it. You can also be more targeted in your efforts than a service would. Some services' lists may be outdated or incomplete. Their lists of reporters and editors may not be comprehensive and may not have been updated. On the other hand, some services may get your press release taken more seriously. A reporter who recognizes the name of the service may be more receptive

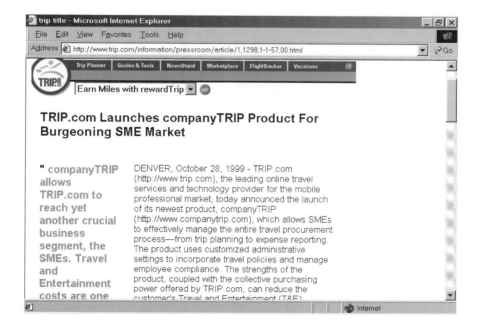

**Figure 18.2.** This press release contains textual URLs within the release that can easily be used if the document is printed for later reference.

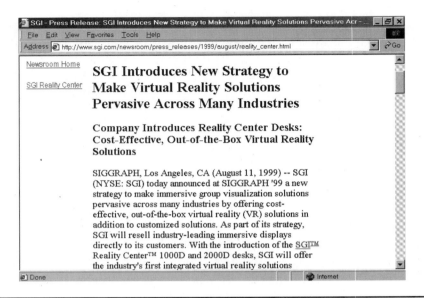

**Figure 18.3.** A press release that contains a hyperlink to more information on the product being discussed.

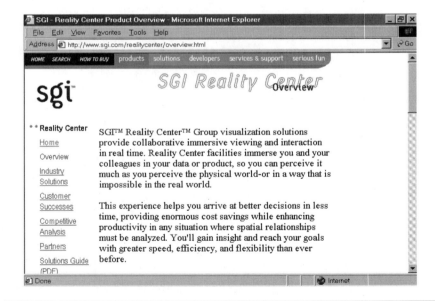

**Figure 18.4.** If users follow the hyperlink in Figure 18.3, they are directed to this page.

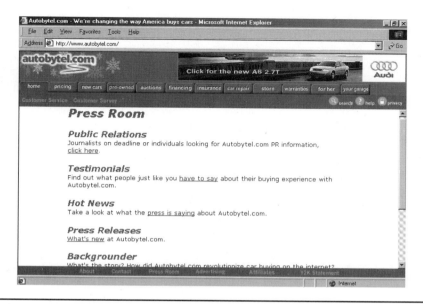

**Figure 18.5.** AutoBytel's Press Room includes press releases, testimonials, hot news, company background information, corporate bios, contact information, and a fact sheet.

than if it were to come from an unknown company. Using a service is bound to save you a lot of time.

If you decide to send your press releases on your own, you will have to build a list of journalists. When reading publications, look for the names of reporters and find out their contact information. If you don't know who to send a press release to at any publication, you can always call and ask for the name of the appropriate editor. Subscribe to a personalized news service to receive articles about your industry. This is a great way to find the names of journalists who might be interested in what you have to say.

There are a number of online resources to assist you in building your press distribution list, such as the one shown in Figure 18.7. Mediafinder (*http://www.mediafinder.com*) is a Web site that may be useful. It provides access to a database of thousands of media outlets including magazines, journals, newspapers, newsletters, and catalogs. Press Access (*http://www.pressaccess.com*) has a large database of journalists and industry analysts (Figure 18.8). Their press access

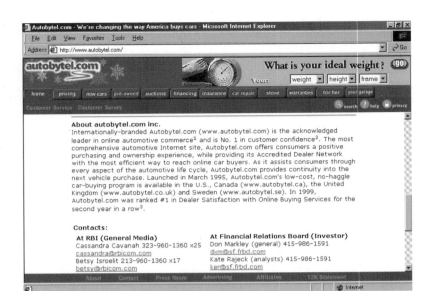

**Figure 18.6.** Each of AutoBytel's press releases contains company and contact information.

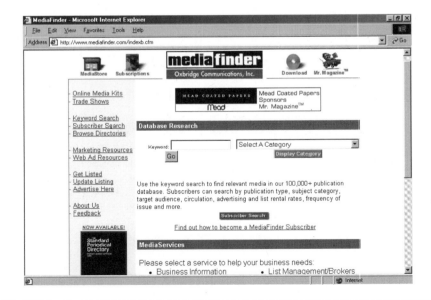

**Figure 18.7.** Use MediaFinder to locate appropriate magazines, journals, newspapers, newsletters, and catalogs.

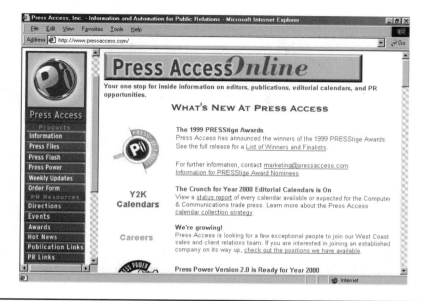

**Figure 18.8.** Press Access Online provides information on editorial calendars, editors, and their preferences.

editorial database is available online, 24 hours a day, and contains in-depth information on journalists, publications, calendars, and so on. MediaMap (*http://www.mediamap.com*) is another public relations resource and has detailed profiles on more than 20,000 media contacts, including their phone numbers, fax numbers, e-mail addresses, and work preferences (Figure 18.9). They also have editorial calendars that tell you who will be writing a scheduled story, what the topic of the story is, and when it will be written.

There are a number of press release distribution services online (Figure 18.10 and 18.11). You will find a number of them in the Internet Resources at the end of this chapter.

## Golden Tips for Press Release Distribution

When distributing your press releases, don't send them to the news desk unaddressed. Know which editor handles the type of news in

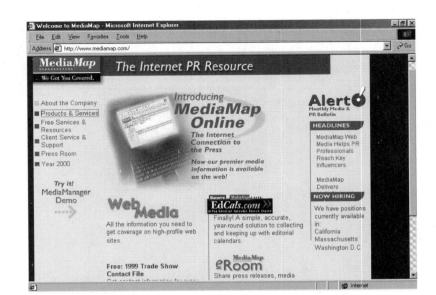

**Figure 18.9.** MediaMap is a software and media information company.

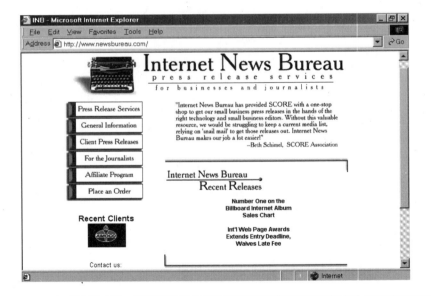

**Figure 18.10.** An e-mail press release service company, including the distribution and writing of e-mail press releases.

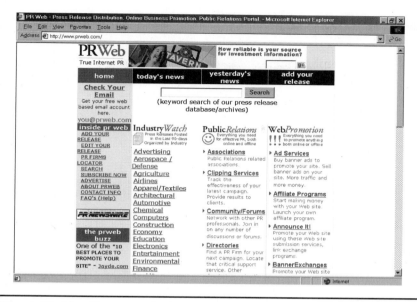

**Figure 18.11.** You can submit your press release to PRWeb.

your release and address the press release to that person. Don't send the press release to more than one editor in any organization unless there is more than one angle to the information in the press release. Call ahead, if possible, to discuss and solicit the editor's interest in your press release before sending it. Also, follow up with a phone call a few days later to ensure it was received and to answer any questions. Be sure to review editorial calendars of publications in your industry to see if there are upcoming articles where your story may make a contribution.

## Press Release Timing and Deadlines

One of the most important things to remember when sending a press release or advisory is the deadline. Know how far in advance you should send your information for each of the different media. Here are some time guidelines for your press release distribution.

### Monthly Magazines

For monthly magazines you should submit your press releases at least two to three months before the issue you want it to appear in. Magazines are planned far in advance, because it often takes a number of weeks to have the magazine printed and in subscribers' mailboxes.

### Daily Newspapers

It is a good idea to have your press release arrive on the editor's desk at least several weeks in advance. If it concerns a special holiday, you should send it even earlier.

### TV and Radio

When submitting press releases to TV and radio, remember that you may be asked to appear on a show as a guest. Be prepared for this before you submit the release. TV and radio move very quickly; A story that has been given to the news director in the morning may appear on that evening's news.

## Formatting Your E-mail Press Release

Your press releases can be e-mailed. Some reporters prefer e-mailed releases; others say they prefer mailed or faxed releases. Check the reporter's preference before you send your press release. If you send e-mailed press releases, make sure that your e-mails are formatted properly. Refer to Chapter 7 for guidelines on how to create effective e-mail messages.

Keep your e-mailed press releases to one or two pages with short paragraphs. It is best to include the press release inserted in the e-mail. Do not send your press release as an attachment. You don't know which platform or word processing program the reporter is using. You might be using Microsoft Word 2000 on a PC, but the reporter could be using an incompatible program on a Mac and will not be able to open the file. There may also be problems downloading, which may prevent your release from being read. The person on the receiving end of your e-mail may be using an old computer with a slow dialup connection, meaning what may take you 2 minutes to transfer might take the recipient 20 minutes to download. In addition, you may be using a PC platform but the reporter may be using a MacOS-based computer. Someone who spends 20 minutes downloading your e-mail only to find out it's useless won't be impressed—great start to getting the journalist to do a positive story on you!

Make sure the subject line of your e-mail is compelling. E-mailed releases can easily be deleted, unopened, by journalists, and quite often they are, because journalists receive large volumes of these daily. Make sure your e-mail is clear and concise. Get to the point with the first sentence. If you don't grab the reader's attention at the beginning of the release, the recipient may not keep reading to find out what your news is.

It's very important to be able to send press release information in digital format. The journalist, with a quick copy and paste, will then have the "first draft" of the story (Figure 18.12). You have made it very easy for the journalist, who can then edit the draft and have a story very quickly. Everybody loves to save time, and a lot of these journalists are under tight deadlines.

## What Is Considered Newsworthy

Your press release has to contain newsworthy information for it to be published. One of the main concerns for public relations representatives is figuring out what is considered newsworthy and what isn't. You have to have a catch, and, if possible, it should appeal to some sort of emotion. Here is a list of newsworthy items:

- A merger or partnership between your company and another

- A free service or resource offered by your company to the general public

- A survey or forum discussing an already hot news topic that is being held by your company

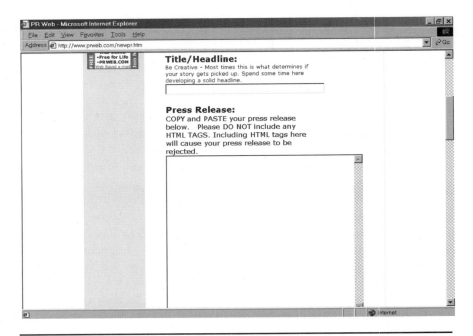

**Figure 18.12.** You'll save a lot of time if you can copy and paste your press release.

- The appearance of a celebrity at a company event or upcoming online promotions

- Your participation in a trade show

- The findings of a report your company has conducted

- A breakthrough in technology resulting in a significant new consumer product

- The development of new strategic alliances or partnerships

- A charitable contribution by your company

- A milestone anniversary that your company is celebrating

- An award presented by your company

## What Isn't Considered Newsworthy

Some things that aren't news to the general public may be news to targeted trade magazines and journals. Use your own judgment when trying to determine if your press release is news or just an excuse to get your company's name in the press. If your release focuses on any of the following, it is probably not newsworthy enough to publish.

The launch of a new Web site has not been news for a number of years now. Unless the site is based on a breakthrough in Internet technology or serves the public interest in an innovative way, you won't get a mention in the news. Nor is a new feature or change to your Web site newsworthy information. Even if your site has undergone a major overhaul, this is not news to the general public.

Launching a new product is not newsworthy unless the product represents a significant breakthrough in some area. The upgrade of an old product simply won't cut it.

## Preparing Your Press Kits/Media Kits

Your press kit is an essential item at press conferences and interviews. This kit can also be sent to reporters when they request more information about a press release you have sent to them. Your press kit should start with a folder displaying your company logo and basic contact information. The folder should have pockets inside so that different sheets of information can be inserted. The following items should be included in your press kit:

- A press release outlining the newsworthy event

- A company history

- Brochures

- Other articles written about your company

- Pictures

- Background information on key players

- FAQs and answers to anticipated questions

- Quotes from key individuals

- Contact information

- Business card

## Develop an Online Media Center for Public Relations

If publicity is a significant part of your public relations strategy you should consider developing an online Media Center as part of your site (see Figures 18.13 and 18.14). The Media Center should be easily accessible from your navigation bar. It would include all the components needed by a journalist when doing a story on your company.

**Figure 18.13.** Microsoft Media Center's Press Pass makes information readily available to the press.

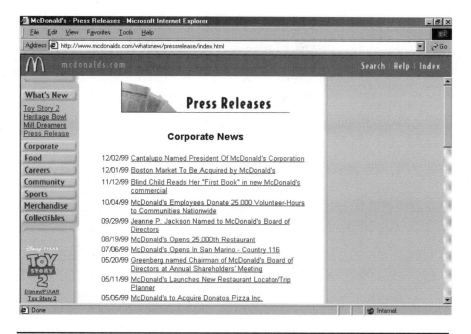

**Figure 18.14.** McDonald's provides an archive of their press releases online.

Journalists should be able to find pictures to include in the story and all the information necessary to do their due diligence. Journalists should be able to send a question to the appropriate media contact within the organization with one click. The Media Center should include:

- A chronology of press releases distributed by the company

- The company's history and background information

- An electronic brochure

- Links to other articles written about your company

- Links to pictures of a related product or products. Perhaps have a gallery where journalists can choose the pictures they want to include in their story with a right mouse click and "Save image as."

- Background information on key company personnel, along with their pics, bios, and quotes.

- A link to your company's media contact and contact information

- FAQs and answers to anticipated questions

By having a Media Center on your site you are sending a clear message to the journalist. You are saying, "You're very important to me! I want to provide you with everything you need to quickly and easily complete your story on our company." With the Media Center you are providing all the information, in a format journalists can use, to enable them to do the story no matter what time they choose to do it.

## Internet Resources

### Press Releases

#### Press Release Tips for PR People
*http://marketing.tenagra.com/releases.html*
Talks about what one expects to receive and how you should write releases.

#### Executive Summary: Understanding News
*http://www.x-summary.com/tips/980526.phtml*
Improve the reception of your press releases by knowing what is news and what isn't.

#### PR Tips
*http://www.profilepr.co.uk/prforum/PRTIPS/PRTIPS6.HTM*
A British agency reviews the pros and cons of e-mail press releases.

#### Care & Feeding of the Press
*http://www.netpress.org/careandfeeding.html*

Journalist's manifesto for how PR people should work with the media.

### Don't Drop the PR Ball
*http://www.searchz.com/wmo/dontdroppr.shtml*
A brief example of how a PR pro blew it with a reporter.

### Xpress Press—Email Press Release Information
*http://www.xpresspress.com/PRnotes.html*
Information on how to write and format a press release to be distributed by e-mail.

### A Template for a Killer Press Release
*http://www.netrageousresults.com/pr/prtemplate.html*
Example format for a successful press release to get yours noticed.

## Where to Submit Your Press Releases

### E-mail Press Release Service Comparison
*http://www.urlwire.com/email-releases.html*
A decent comparison between different e-mail press release services. Caution: The author owns the first one listed.

### Partyline
*http://www.partylinepublishing.com*
The standard media placement newsletter for the public relations trade.

### PR Newswire Home Page
*http://www.prnewswire.com*
A leading source for worldwide corporate media, business, the financial community, and the individual investor.

### Internet News Bureau Press Release Service
*http://www.newsbureau.com*
For a fee you can distribute your press release to thousands of online media outlets here. Also links to a number of good PR resources.

### WebWire
*http://www.webwire.com/*
An Internet press release resource.

## Promote Mailing Lists and Newsletters

### Tell Liszt about Lists
*http://www.liszt.com/submit.html*
Register your mailing list with a major online database to get yourself noticed.

### NewJour Welcome Page
*http://gort.ucsd.edu/newjour/NewJourWel.html*
Home for many Internet newsletters.

### The List Exchange
*http://www.listex.com*
Directory of mailing lists and resources for those who run them.

## Paid Help

### Internet Media Fax
*http://www.imediafax.com*
Custom online news distribution service that creates targeted media lists "on the fly."

### Internet Wire
*http://www.internetwire.com* (Figure 18.15)
The Internet Wire offers online press release distribution via e-mail.

### Xpress Press News Release Distribution Service
*http://www.xpresspress.com*
Press releases delivered electronically by e-mail to 4000 journalists and media members in the United States and internationally.

## Tips for Printed Press Releases

### 13 Tips for Sending Effective Press Releases
*http://www.poewar.com/articles/releases.htm*
Tips to get the best results with press releases.

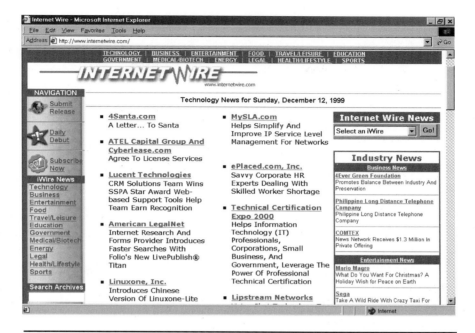

**Figure 18.15.** InternetWire is an online press release distribution company.

# 19

## Online Publications

More than 60% of Internet users frequently read online publications. Identify appropriate marketing opportunities by searching for and reading e-zines that are relevant to your business. In this chapter we will cover:

- What are electronic magazines?

- Finding online sites to advertise or arrange links

- How to find appropriate e-zines for marketing purposes

- Submitting articles to appropriate e-zines

- Advertising in appropriate e-zines

- E-zine resources online

**E-zines**
Electronic
magazines

### Appealing to Magazine Subscribers on the Net

A recent NPD Online Research survey shows that six out of ten Web users frequently read online publications, or **e-zines.** This is one of the reasons they are among the most popular marketing tools on the Internet. Five years ago there were a few hundred e-zines in publication. Now there are thousands of e-zines dedicated to a wide variety of topics such as travel, business opportunities, food, child care—you name it. For any topic you are interested in, there are quite likely several e-zines dedicated to it.

## What Exactly Are E-zines?

E-zines, or electronic magazines, are the online version of magazines. They contain information regarding a certain topic in the form of magazine articles and features. Some e-zines are Web site based and others are e-mail based.

Many offline magazines provide a version online as well (Figure 19.1). *Time, People,* and *Sports Illustrated* are all accessible via the Internet. Some of these provide the full version of their traditional magazine. Others are selective about the articles they provide, and still others provide last month's edition.

## Web-Based E-zines

There are Web-based e-zines that have only an online presence (Figure 19.2). These e-zines are accessed through their Web sites by browsing from page to page. They have the look and feel of a traditional magazine. They include lots of glossy pictures and advertisements. Usually there is no charge to view the Web based e-zines, but some do charge a subscription fee. These Web-based e-zines tend to be as graphically pleasing as offline magazines.

## E-mail E-zines

E-mail e-zines are not nearly as pretty as the Web-based e-zines. They tend to be more content oriented and, as such, tend to be more of a target marketing mechanism. E-mail e-zines tend to be several pages

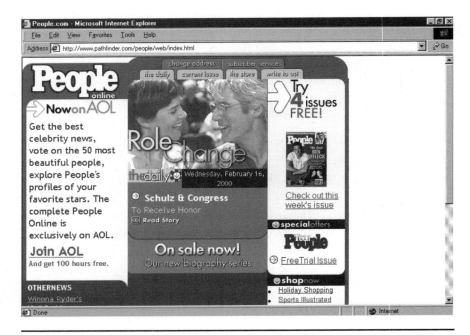

**Figure 19.1.** P*eople Magazine* is an example of an offline magazine that also has an online version.

in length with several articles and often have classified advertising. Circulation of these e-zines is often in the thousands. Most of these e-zines run weekly or biweekly editions.

Individuals interested in receiving these e-zines subscribe and the e-zine is delivered straight into their e-mail boxes. Those individuals who are interested in the subject have taken the time to subscribe and ask to receive the information directly in their e-mail box. Once you have found an e-zine that caters to your target market, the e-zine may be a very valuable marketing vehicle.

Every subscriber to an e-mail based e-zine has access to the Internet. These people regularly receive and send e-mail, and quite likely surf the Net. If you advertise in this type of medium and place your Internet address in the ad, your prospective customer is not more than a couple of clicks away from your site.

People subscribe because they are interested. Even if they don't read it immediately when it is received, they usually read it eventu-

**Figure 19.2.** VW Vortex is an example of a web-based e-zine.

ally. Otherwise, they would not have subscribed. Subscribers will see your URL and product advertisements. For this reason, e-mail e-zines are a great marketing tool.

## Using E-zines as Marketing Tools

Online publications are superior marketing tools for a number of reasons. They can be used in a number of different ways to increase the traffic to your Web site. You can:

- Advertise directly

- Be a sponsor

- Submit articles

- Send press releases

- Start your own

## Finding Appropriate E-zines for Your Marketing Effort

There are many locations online to find lists and links to both Web-based and e-mail e-zines. A number of these resources are listed in the Internet Resources at the end of this chapter.

The most important element of choosing an e-zine is to choose one that reaches your target market. The reason e-zine ads are effective is that there is a high correlation between the target customer and the magazine's subscribers. If you advertise in an e-zine simply because it has the largest subscriber rate, you will probably be disappointed unless your products or services have mass market appeal.

You should review a number of the e-zine-listing sites, such as the one shown in Figure 19.3. Some of these sites have search capabilities on appropriate keywords. Others have their e-zines listed by category. Once you have a list of e-zines you feel fit well with your marketing objectives, you should subscribe and begin receiving and reviewing these e-zines.

## The Multiple Advantages of E-Zine Advertising

One of the major advantages of e-zine advertising is the life span of your ads. E-zines that are delivered to e-mail addresses will be read by the recipient and sometimes saved for future reference. Many e-zines archive their issues with the ads intact. Advertisers have received responses to ads that are several months old!

Another advantage of e-zine advertising is that e-zines are often shared with friends and associates. Your ad may be passed around a number of times after it first enters the mailbox of the subscriber. You are being charged for the ad based on the number of e-mail subscribers. Therefore, the extra viewers of your ad will be at no cost to you.

One of the most tangible advantages of e-zine advertising is the relatively low cost. E-zines need to fill all of their available space. If an

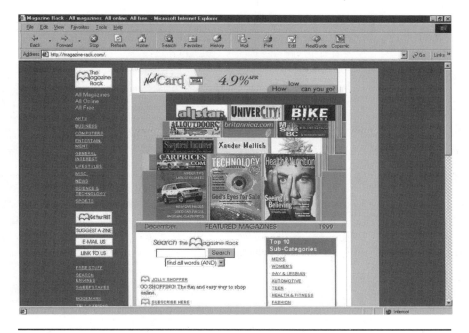

**Figure 19.3.**   The Magazine Rack *(http://magazine-rack.com)* provides a searchable directory of online magazines, newspapers, journals, and e-zines.

e-zine advertising section has empty spaces, they are often willing to negotiate. Some will even barter with you, advertising space at a discounted price in exchange for their e-zine promotion on your Web site.

E-zines provide a very targeted advertising medium. People subscribe to various e-zines because they have a genuine interest in the topics covered. This provides a major advantage over other advertising mediums. E-zine ads have been shown to have very high response rates due to their targeted nature.

## Guidelines for Your Advertising

Once you have found e-zines that reach your target market, you should consider a number of other factors before you make your final decision on placing your ad.

- Check the ads displayed in the e-zine for repetition. If advertisers have not advertised more than once, then they probably did not see very positive results.

- Respond to some of the ads and ask the advertisers what their experiences were with advertising in that particular e-zine. Be sure to tell them who you are and why you are contacting them. If you are up front, they will probably be receptive to your inquiry.

- Talk to the e-zine publisher and ask questions (e.g., how many subscribers there are). Ask what other advertisers have had to say about their results. Find out what types of ads they accept and if there are any restrictions. Maybe the e-zine has a set of advertising policies that you can receive via E-mail.

- Find out if your ad can have a hypertext link to your Web site. If the e-zine allows hypertext links, make sure you link to an appropriate page, one that is a continuation of the advertisement or a page that provides details on the item you were advertising. Provide a link to the order form from this page to assist the transaction.

- In some cases the e-zine will have an editorial calendar available to assist you with the timing of your ad. The editorial calendar will tell you what articles will be included in upcoming issues. If an upcoming issue will have an article relating to your type of products or services, you may choose to advertise in that issue. You might contact the editor regarding a product review or submit an article relevant to the issue topics.

- Make sure that the advertising rates are reasonable based on the number of subscribers, and ask yourself if you can afford it. If you are not in a position to pay for the advertising now, ask if there are any other arrangements that could be made. For example, the publisher may accept a link on your Web site in exchange for the ad.

- You should develop your ads with your target customer in mind. They should attract your best prospects. Wherever possible you should link to your site or provide an e-mail link to the appropriate individual within your organization.

- You should develop a mechanism to track advertising responses. You could use different e-mail accounts for different ads to determine which ads are bringing you the responses. You can also use different URLs to point the viewer to different pages within your site. If you have a good traffic-analysis package you will be able to track the increase in visitors as a result of your ad.

- Make sure you are versed in the publication's advertising deadlines and ad format preferences.

## Other Marketing Opportunities with E-zines

Besides advertising, a number of other marketing opportunities can be explored with e-zines (Figure 19.4). Once you have found the e-zines that cater to your target market, these e-zines may be appropriate recipients for your press releases. Refer to Chapter 18 for recommendations on press release development and distribution. The editors may also accept articles of interest to their readership. You might be able to incorporate information on your products and services in an interesting article that would fit the editor's guidelines.

## Starting Your Own E-Zine

You can start you own e-zine. Don't make this decision without lots of thought. There are lots of resources online regarding e-zine development and administration. If you do start your own e-zine, you should:

- Promote it to your target market through newsgroups, mail lists, your Web site, and your e-mail signature file. If you do promote your e-zine in newsgroups and mail lists, be sure it is appropriate to advertise your e-zine in a given newsgroup or mail list before you post. You do not want to be accused of

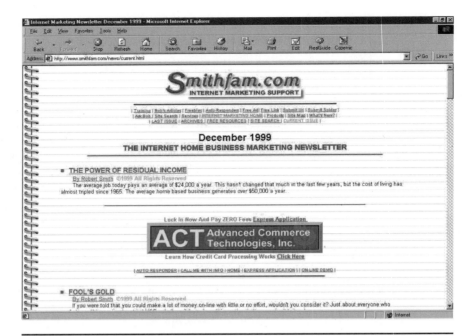

**Figure 19.4.** Smithfam.com *(http://www.smithfam.com/news/current.html)* provides an Internet marketing newsletter that is aimed at people who want to make money on the Internet.

spamming. However, promote your e-zine shamelessly on your site (let people subscribe to the e-zine on your site) and in your signature file.

- Provide an opportunity for subscribers to let others know. In your online e-zine, have a form that allows subscribers to e-mail a copy of the e-zine to their friends and colleagues. Use a call to action statement such as, "Do you know someone who might be interested in this e-zine? Click here to send them a copy." This is a great way to pick up additional subscribers because some of the nonsubscribers who read your e-zine might then become subscribers if your content is interesting to them.

- Make it easy for people to subscribe to your e-zine. Provide clear subscription instructions in each e-mail version of your e-zine and on the online version of your e-zine. Have a form handy on your site to collect e-mail addresses from people who wish to subscribe.

- Don't provide your list of subscribers to anyone. This will protect your subscribers' privacy and keep your list spam-free. Thus, when you mail your e-zine, use the BCC feature or use a specialized e-mail program that hides all the recipients' addresses so the entire list is not compromised. People will not be happy if they start receiving spam as the result of your e-zine.

- Provide great content. This goes without saying. If you have content that people want to read, they will remain subscribers. As the word about your e-zine spreads, you will have a large community of people who fit your target market reading it.

## Internet Resources

### The Magazine Rack
*http://magazine-rack.com*
Provides a searchable directory of online magazines, newspapers, journals and e-zines.

### Factsheet Five
*http://www.factsheet5.com*
A site dedicated to e-zines. How to's, reviews, FAQs, and a list of e-zines on the Internet. This is a selection of favorite Web sites.

### The Etext Archives
*http://www.etext.org/Zines*
Complete with a search engine, this site offers places to find all of your online publication resources.

### Electronic Newsstand
*http://www.enews.com*

Founded in 1993, this was one of the first content-based sites on the Internet. Since then, the site has grown to become the largest and most diverse magazine-related resource anywhere on the Web.

### MediaFinder
*http://www.mediafinder.com/magazines/mag0020.cfm*
A national directory of magazines with details on target audience, publisher, contact, telephone numbers, Web addresses, e-mail addresses, editorial descriptions, issue frequency, and subscription price. In a lot of cases there is an information request form attached should you want further details. Great resource!

### WebPlaces
*http://www.webplaces.com/e-zines.htm*
A meta-index of e-zines sorted by category.

### Ecola Newsstand
*http://www.ecola.com*
Ecola's Newsstand has over 6800 magazines, newspapers, and publications. There are over 100 categories of magazines to choose from.

### E-zine Search
*http://www.homeincome.com/search-it/ezine*
Billed as the world's ultimate e-magazine database. Searchable by category.

### InfoJump
*http://www.infojump.com*
Browse a huge directory of e-zines by category.

### LinkPad-Electronic Magazines
*http://www.referthem.com/pad/ezines.htm*
A list of Electronic Magazines and directories.

# 20

# Web Rings As a Promotion Tool

Web rings provide a different way to organize sites. They are a free service offered to the Internet Community. Web rings arrange sites with similar content by linking them together in a circle, or a ring. Each link in the ring is directed to a CGI script on the Web ring's server that sends the viewer on to the next site in the ring. There are literally thousands of rings with subjects such as communications, games, art, real estate, and so on. If there isn't a ring suitable for your site, you can create your own. The types of visitors you will receive from participating in the Web ring will be potential customers who are responsive to the content of your site and curious about your products or services. In this chapter we cover:

- What are Web rings and how do they work?

- Promotion possibilities with Web rings

- How do I participate and what will it cost?

- Where to find Web rings that work for your company

- Web ring resources on the Net

## An Effective Alternative to Search Engines and Directories

Web rings are a fast-growing service on the Internet, providing one of the easiest ways for visitors to navigate the Internet. In each of its tens of thousands of topic-specific rings, member Web sites have linked their sites together, thus permitting more targeted visitors to reach the joined sites quickly and easily.

People are becoming increasingly dissatisfied with search engines and directories as tools to identify specific topic-related sites. Searches on a specific keyword have yielded results that often include totally unrelated sites. For instance, if you were planning a vacation to Mexico and you wanted to search for resorts in Mexico, the search engine results would likely include sites somewhat related but not exactly what you were looking for. The results would include book titles at Amazon.com related to Mexico travel, personal pages with other people's experience traveling in Mexico complete with pictures from their family vacation, travel agencies, and tour company sites. The Web ring provides an alternative to these tools.

Site owners typically trade links with other Web sites to help advertise each other's sites. The Web ring was initially developed to enlarge the scope of link trading. A Web ring joins together many sites with a common topic.

Two of the major Web ring sites are:

- WebRing at *http://www.webring.org*

- LoopLink at *http://www.looplink.com*

## What Are Web Rings?

A Web ring is made up of a number of topic-specific sites that are grouped together, as shown in Figure 20.1. There are Titanic Web rings, Beanie Baby Web rings, prenatal care Web rings, BMW Web rings, and remote sensing Web rings in the list of over 80,000 Web rings that exist today. At *webring.org*, Web rings fit into several major categories:

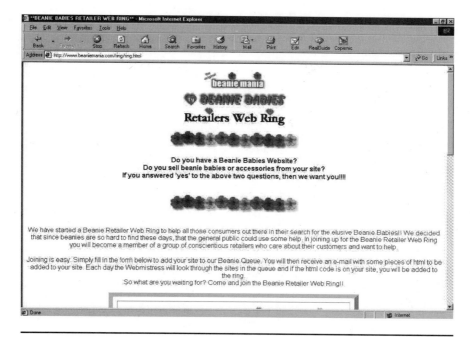

**Figure 20.1.** The Beanie Retailer Web ring displays the common Web ring graphic at the bottom of the page. The navigation tool allows you to travel easily throughout the ring.

- Arts and Humanities

- Computers

- Business and Economy

- Internet

- Health

- Recreation and Sports

- Entertainment

- Society and Culture

- Miscellaneous

At looplink.com they also have many categories:

- Arts and Entertainment

- Business

- Computers

- Health

- Home and Leisure

- Information Sources

- Internet

- Online Shopping

- Science and Technology

- Society and Culture

- Sports

- Travel

- Multimedia

Each of these major categories has a number of subcategories, and each of the subcategories has a number of individual rings.

Rings can contain any number of sites. There must be at least five before the ring will be listed in the directories. Generally, the rings will contain somewhere between 20 and 200 sites. Some rings are smaller, and some rings are substantially higher, with close to a thousand sites included.

Each ring was started and is maintained by an individual Web site owner. Through navigation links found most often at the bottom of member pages, visitors can travel to all or any of the sites in a ring.

They can move through a ring in either direction, going to the next or previous site, or listing the next five sites in the ring. Visitors can also jump to a random site in the ring or survey all the sites that make up the ring.

An extraordinary system, Web rings are entirely open and free of charge to both visitors and members. As more and more people discover Web rings, we will see phenomenal growth in this as a preferred method to surf the net. Today Web rings are experiencing growth rates in excess of 10% monthly. Member sites total over 1,300,000, and Web rings total over 80,000.

## How Do Web Rings Work?

To surf a ring, all you have to do is use the links at the bottom of the page in the Web ring block. At the bottom of a Web ring participant's pages, you will find the Web ring navigation aid. A common Web ring graphic will include links to the "Next" site in the ring, the "Previous" site in the ring, or a "Random" site in the ring. You also have the option, in many cases, to see a list of the "Next 5" sites in the ring or to view the entire "Index" of the ring's sites. Once you begin surfing a ring, there is no clear beginning or ending, just a circle of related material. The Web ring program compensates for sites that are unreachable because they no longer exist or have server problems. You will always be able to navigate the loop.

When using a search engine you are provided with a list of resulting sites, only some of which are appropriate. You visit the sites listed and then, depending on which browser you are using, you may use your "Back" button to return to the results page to make another selection. With a Web ring this backing out is unnecessary. Once you're finished reviewing a site in the ring you proceed to the next site that is of interest or simply surf through the connected sites one by one.

## How to Participate in Web Rings

The first thing to do is find Web rings that are appropriate for your product or service, those that cater to your target market. You can review the directories at the WebRing site *http://www.webring.org* and also at the LoopLink site *http://www.looplink.com.*

Once you have found an appropriate Web ring you contact the owner to ask permission to join. See Figure 20.2 for an example of this. The owner will review your site to determine your "fit" with the theme. Once you are accepted, the owner will provide you with the required code and accompanying graphics, which you will insert on your page. The ring owner provides all the required material, you slip it into your HTML file, and that's that.

Once the code is on your site, webring.org or looplink.com monitors the traffic and collects the statistics for your site as they do for all Web ring sites. This is very beneficial to you because you can see how much traffic you are getting through the Web ring.

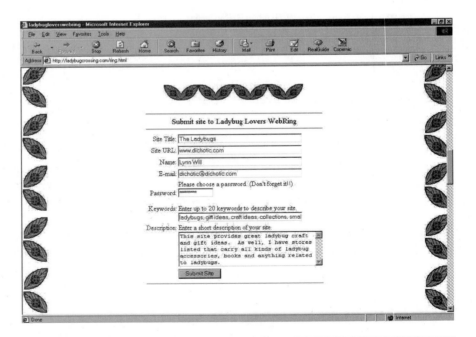

**Figure 20.2.** This inclusion request was taken from The Lady Bug Lovers Web ring to show how easy it is to join a Web ring.

Any Web site owner who feels no existing ring is suitable can apply to create a new ring. If the application is approved, *webring.org* or *looplink.com* will provide all the necessary code and instructions. New Web rings are listed in the directory once they contain at least five sites.

## Web Ring Participation Costs

The cost to participate in these Web rings is absolutely nil. No application fees, no charge for the approval, no charge for the code to be inserted on your pages, no charge for the increased traffic a Web ring brings.

## The Benefits of Web Rings

There are many benefits to both the users of Web rings and the participating Web sites. Benefits to the user include:

- Web rings provide a great navigation tool when looking for more information on a specific topic.

- Web rings are easy to use. They provide one of the most efficient ways to find specific content on the Internet.

- Web rings avoid the duplication found in search engines, where a site may appear several times in one search. Each site is linked only once in each Web ring.

- Web rings speed up search time.

- Web rings eliminate sifting through mounds of search engine results for appropriate sites.

Benefits to participating Web sites include

- Web ring participation increases the number of targeted visitors to your Web site.

- The organizers of the Web rings make it easy to monitor how successful your ring is. Traffic reports and "top" rings statistics are made available to participants.

- Web rings drive traffic to your site.

## Business Reluctance to Participate in Web Rings

One of the biggest hurdles Web rings face in being adopted by the business sector is that when you join a ring, you are linking to the competition, as shown in Figure 20.3. It is likely that this mentality explains why Web rings have been so popular for personal sites and special-interest groups, but have failed to catch on in today's business community. But, again, small businesses and retail-oriented sites have

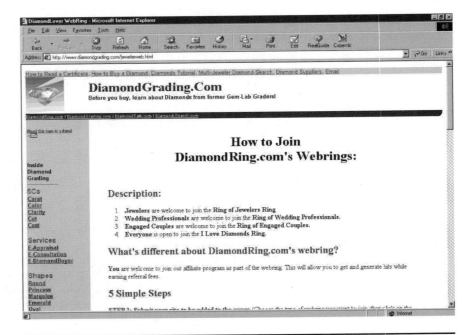

**Figure 20.3.** The Ring of Jewelers Web ring is an example of a ring that contains many competing businesses.

not shied away from rings. For example, rings and banner programs are hot marketing strategies for stores that sell collectibles. This is particularly true for hard-to-find collectibles. Take the Beanie Babies phenomenon: *Not* being on a Beanie Baby Web ring or participating in Beanie-specific banner programs could be a crucial mistake for vendors. After all, if a customer hits a site and it doesn't have a specific Beanie Baby, the quest isn't over—it's on to the next site. What better way to get there than via a ring? Your site might just be the next one.

Lately we have seen a growth in commercial application of Web rings. There are a few reasons for this:

- A number of articles have appeared in Internet marketing magazines related to the high volume of traffic through these Web rings. Businesses have sometimes found that the bulk of the traffic to their site is coming through the Web ring.

- Other articles talked about the benefits of being conveniently located near your competition bringing more traffic for everyone. Several likened it to what happens in the real world in the fast food industry. When a McDonald's opens, you quickly see a Burger King, Wendy's, Pizza Hut, Kentucky Fried Chicken, and Taco Bell all open up close by. This means more business for everyone.

## Other Marketing Opportunities Provided by Web Rings

When you have found a Web ring that attracts your target market you can participate and enjoy the increase in visitors to your site. Figure 20.4 is an example of this type of Web ring. Web rings provide an array of other opportunities as well.

You can search through the list of participants in a Web ring to arrange reciprocal links. You can also search a Web ring for banner advertising purposes. You can either exchange banners or purchase advertising on these sites. You can find sites that may be appropriate for cooperative advertising purposes. You can exchange coupons with another site you are linked to, which works especially well when you sell noncompeting products to the same target market.

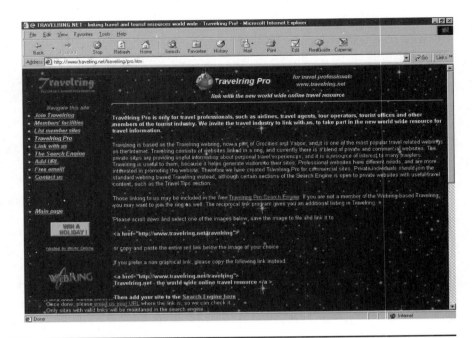

**Figure 20.4.**   The Travelring Pro is an example of a professional Web ring. This one is exclusively for members of the tourist industry.

## Internet Resources

### Web Ring—The Shape of Things to Come
*http://www.webring.org*
Web rings are one of the fastest and most exciting ways to navigate the World Wide Web. In each of its tens of thousands of rings, member Web sites have banded together to form their sites into linked circles. Their purpose is to allow more visitors to reach them quickly and easily.

### LoopLink—The Traffic Building Site
*http://www.looplink.com*
Sites of a particular subject together in a loop. A visitor to any loop site can easily move forward or backward through the loop and visit other loop sites within that subject area. This drives targeted quali-

fied traffic to all the loop sites. Surfers don't want to deal with mounds of irrelevant search engine results. They want to visit sites on topics they love. It's so simple, and everybody's a winner.

### RingSurf
*http://www.ringsurf.com*
RingSurf is a completely free service that lets user quickly, easily, and reliably navigate thousands of related Web sites organized by areas of interest. Joining a Web ring is great way to increase traffic to your site.

# 21

# Effective Offline Promotion

There are many benefits to cross-promoting your Web site using traditional media and print materials. Your Web site can answer a lot of questions and provide more information than you can print in a magazine or newspaper ad. Your site can be kept up-to-date with the latest information available. People can request additional information or order online. In this chapter we cover:

- Tips for offline promotion of your Web site

- Offline promotion opportunities

## Offline Promotion Objectives

Since visitors can be directed from offline promotion to request additional information or order online, you should promote your URL on every piece of promotional material you produce! The more exposure your URL receives, the more likely it is that people will remember it when they go online.

Be creative with your offline promotion campaign. Brainstorm with innovative thinkers to come up with a number of good places to promote your URL; for example, try displaying your URL in your TV and radio commercials, magazine and newspaper ads, and billboards. The more places your URL appears, the more it will get noticed. Some businesses even incorporate their URL into their building and vehicle signage. Answer your telephone "YourCompany Name.com, Good Morning." This is quite effective in letting people know that you want them to visit your Web site and providing them with your URL at the same time. Next time they have a question or want to place an order, they may go directly to the Web site.

Displaying your URL in traditional media encourages people to visit your site for more information about your company. Another benefit is that people can usually order from your Web site. Naturally, your site should be up-to-date, with all of the latest information on products, prices, and sales promotions. If a six-month-old advertisement is seen in a magazine, as long as the URL is displayed in the ad, readers can go to your site and get current information. Your Web site is your most effective advertisement, but it is an advertisement that people have to know about before they can view it.

## URL Exposure Through Corporate Literature and Material

It is important that your corporate image be consistent in your online and offline promotional campaigns. Businesses should use the same colors, style, fonts, logo, and tag lines on all of their marketing materials. As a rule of thumb, try to place your URL on everything you put your logo on—which means just about every piece of corporate literature. Make sure to include your URL on the following:

- Letterhead

- Business cards

- Corporate brochures

- Envelopes

- Checks

- Fax coversheets

- Report covers

- Flyers

- Advertisements

- Direct mail pieces

- Newsletters

- Press releases

- Media kits

## URL Exposure Through Promotional Items

If your company uses promotional items as giveaways at trade shows and events, it is a good idea to incorporate your Web site marketing with these items. Figures 21.1 and 21.2 are some examples of the different promotional products that you can order on the Internet for your business. Promotional items that are used in and around computer workstations are ideal because your URL is visible when people are in a position to actually visit your site. Some examples are:

- Mouse pads

- Diskette holders

- Screen cleaning kits

- Software

- Screen savers

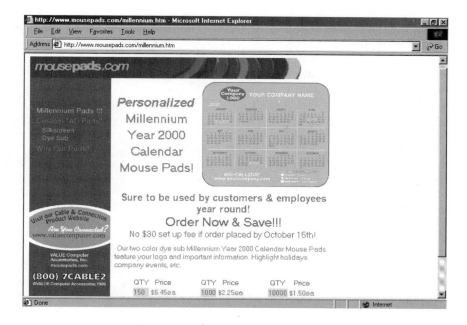

**Figure 21.1.**   Mousepads.com is a site where you can order personalized mouse pads.

- Pens and pencils

- Scratch pads

- Coffee mugs

- Coasters

- Letter openers

- Stress balls

- Calendars

- Sticky notes

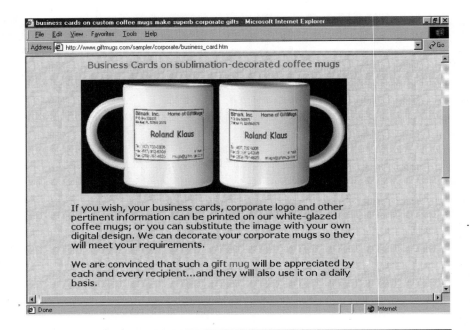

**Figure 21.2.** Put your business card on a coffee mug.

## URL Exposure Through Clothing

Articles of clothing are another great promotional item. When people wear an article of clothing with your URL on it, they become a walking billboard for your site. If you have a corporate uniform, your URL could be displayed. Figure 21.3 shows just a few of the items that you can put your URL on. Put your URL and a catchy phrase or tag line on items such as:

- Golf shirts

- T-shirts

- Sweatshirts

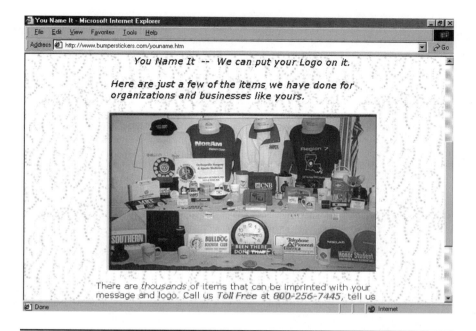

**Figure 21.3.** There are hundreds of promotional items that you can put your URL on.

- Hats

- Aprons

- Jackets

## URL Exposure on Novelty Items

Novelty items can be an effective place to print your URL. If your target market is a younger audience, then put your URL on items that will appeal to them, such as:

- Frisbees

- Balls

- Beach towels

- Sunglasses

- Key chains

- Magnets

- Chocolate bars

- Bumper stickers

## Promotion with a Touch of Creativity

Be creative and come up with catchy slogans that have a connection with the promotional item. For example,

- **Clocks:** "Take some time to visit our Web site at…"

- **Rulers:** "For a measurable difference visit us at…"

- **Coffee mugs:** "Take a break and visit our Web site at…"

- **Tape measures:** "Visit our Web site at *http://www. YourURL.com* and see how our site measures up."

- **Magnifying glasses:** "You don't need one of these to see that our site is the best. Come visit us online at…"

- **Watches:** "Isn't it about time you visited us at…"

- **Bookmarks:** "Take a break from reading and visit our Web site at…"

## URL Exposure on Your Products

If possible, put your URL on your products themselves. This is an innovative idea that Joe Boxer has implemented. They stitch their URL into the waistband of their underwear.

## Internet Resources

### Promotional Webstickers
*http://www.websticker.com/products.htm*
Simple ideas to effectively promote your Web site offline.

### Bizine
*http://www.bizine.com/profit.htm*
Increase your profits by coordinating online and traditional offline marketing. An article by Bob LeDuc.

### Free Pint
*http://www.freepint.co.uk/issues/040399.htm*
"12 Offline Ways of Promoting Your URL" by Nikki Pilkington

### HCS
*http://www.hcsweb.net/OfflinePromotion.htm*
This includes a checklist of possible places you can include your Web site address.

### Digital-Women.com
*http://www.digital-women.com/unique.htm*
This includes unique ideas for online and offline promotion.

### WebCMO
*http://www.webcmo.com/report/opss1/offline.htm*
A survey report on offline promoting.

### PC Mojo
*http://pcmojo.com/pcmojo/offline.htm*
Information on why you need to promote your site off the internet.

### Advertising Concepts
*http://www.bumperstickers.com/ad.htm*
Why Use Promotional Products? This site gives you good promotional ideas and what these promotional products will do for you.

### Mohawk Advertising
*http://www.logomall.com*
Mohawk advertising sells hundreds of promotional items online for your business. (See Figure 21.4)

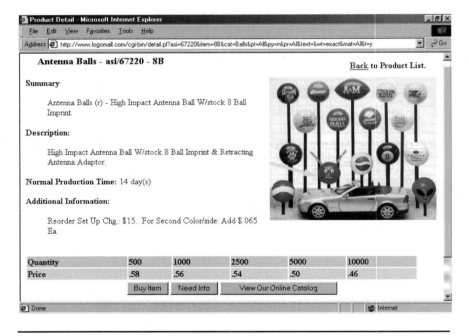

**Figure 21.4.** Mohawk Marketing Corporation sure has some different promotional ideas.

# 22

# Web Traffic Analysis

Today technology not only allows us to generate interactive Web sites for our viewers, it also allows us to learn about our viewers as well. Many Web sites are now using Web traffic analysis software that enables them analyze not only what page of the Web site their visitors came to first, but also where they came from, how long they were there, and what they did while they stayed. In this chapter you will learn:

- What you Web server's log files can tell you

- How analyzing log files with Web traffic analysis software can benefit your Web site

- How to develop a profile of your visitors

- How to optimize your Web site to accommodate your visitors

- How to get the most for your marketing dollar

- How to generate leads for your business

- How analysis software can help you to manage your online advertising business

- How you can get Web traffic analysis software for your Web site

- Popular brands of Web traffic analysis software

## Do You Know Who Is Visiting Your Web Site?

Retailers have always spent endless hours trying to analyze the shoppers who visit their stores. They are constantly trying to collect data about their markets so that they can decide what the best forms of advertising are for their target market, what consumers really want in order to make wiser buying decisions, what services are important to them, what product features their target market is looking for, and so on. The same thing is happening today on the Internet. Companies are constantly collecting data on their target market—their needs, wants, preferences, and desires. Most people are unaware that they are even doing this.

Web traffic analysis software is helping companies to focus on their target market like never before. It is helping them to understand the traffic on their Web site, and is enabling them to make the necessary changes that are critical to receive the results that they desire from their Web site. "But how do they do it?" you ask.

## Using Log Files to Your Advantage

All Web servers log a list of all the requests for individual files that people have requested from a Web site. These files will include the HTML files and their embedded graphic images and any other associated files that get transmitted through the server. These files can be analyzed by Web traffic-analysis tools to generate the following data:

- The number of visitors to your home page

- Where the visitors came from in terms of their IP addresses

- How many times each page on your Web site was requested

- What time, day of the week, and season people access your site

- Which browser your visitor is using

- Which keywords or phrases your visitors are using to find your site using a search engine

- Which advertisements are viewed the most on your Web site

- Detailed information on visitors and demographics

This may not sound like very important information; however, there are some very amazing things you can do with this data. Like any good experiment you must collect the data first, complete the experiment, and then make the recommendations.

## Analyzing Log Files with Web Traffic Analysis Software

By analyzing the data from your log files, you can generate results that could significantly increase the popularity and success of your Web site. By tracking the visitors on your Web site in terms of where they spend their time, how they came to your site, and if they do what you want them to do, you can fine-tune your Web site to fit the specific needs of your target market.

### Developing a Profile of Your Visitors

By analyzing the log files you can find out a lot about your audience. You can see how the majority of your audience came to your site and what they like to do while they are there—what they do meaning whether they request information or not, if they download products, or if they are interested in free giveaways. You can use this information to find out if your site needs to be changed to accommodate the needs of your visitors. For example, if you find that a lot of your visitors are spending a lot of time on your What's New page, maybe it would be in your best interest to start a monthly mail list to inform your audience of the happenings of your Web site.

The log files can tell you when your audience is entering your site. For example, if the log files indicate that your traffic is mostly at night, you could predict that most people visit your site from home. Since most homes do not have high-speed access, you may want to check your graphic sizes to make sure that it is not taking too long for your site to load. If your analysis tells you that not many people visit your site on Saturday, you may want to select this day as your maintenance day. You don't want to make changes to your site on days when you receive high traffic because it is very displeasing if your visitors receive HTTP 404 errors because your site is temporarily down.

You can also see your visitor's IP address, which the software will translate into the geographical location of your visitor, some of the software is even capable of narrowing the data down to the city (see Figure 22.1 and 22.2). From a marketing perspective this can benefit you in planning your marketing efforts in other media. If you are planning a television campaign for your business, you may want to start in a city that frequently visits your site, thus increasing the chance of a successful campaign.

It is very common for Web traffic-analysis software to indicate which browser your visitors are using when visiting your Web site

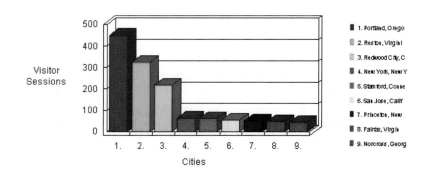

**Figure 22.1.** WebTrends can tell you what cities are bringing you the most online traffic.

| Most Active Cities | | ? |
|---|---|---|
| | **City, State** | **Visitor Sessions** |
| 1 | Portland, Oregon, United States | 449 |
| 2 | Reston, Virginia, United States | 325 |
| 3 | Redwood City, California, United States | 218 |
| 4 | New York, New York, United States | 62 |
| 5 | Stamford, Connecticut, United States | 60 |
| 6 | San Jose, California, United States | 55 |
| 7 | Princeton, New Jersey, United States | 49 |
| 8 | Fairfax, Virginia, United States | 48 |
| 9 | Norcross, Georgia, United States | 44 |
| 10 | Washington, D.C., United States | 39 |
| 11 | New Berlin, Wisconsin, United States | 33 |
| 12 | Mountain View, California, United States | 32 |
| 13 | Houston, Texas, United States | 31 |
| 14 | Cambridge, Massachusetts, United States | 30 |
| 15 | San Diego, California, United States | 30 |
| 16 | Chicago, Illinois, United States | 29 |
| 17 | San Francisco, California, United States | 28 |
| 18 | Dallas, Texas, United States | 26 |
| 19 | Palo Alto, California, United States | 24 |
| 20 | Santa Clara, California, United States | 23 |
| **Total For the Cities Above** | | **1,635** |

**Figure 22.2.** The same data presented in a table.

(see Figure 22.3). Although you want to have a Web site that is designed to be compatible with older and newer browsers, this data can be used to your advantage. Older browsers that cannot read Java scripting properly and that do not have the proper plug-ins for a Flash introduction may still be in use by your viewers. However, if a higher ratio of your viewers are using the latest browsers, you could incorporate more of the latest technology into your site. Remember that you should always offer a "skip flash" option of your site and the latest Java plug-ins for people with older browsers.

## Which Pages are Popular, and Which Pages Are Not

When you look at the log files and see where your audience is spending most of their time on your site, you can also tell where they are not. You can then take this information to determine what the popular pages on your site incorporate that the less-popular ones do not. Perhaps the popular pages are similar to the less popular, but are visited by a specific source (i.e., search engines, newsgroups). Maybe

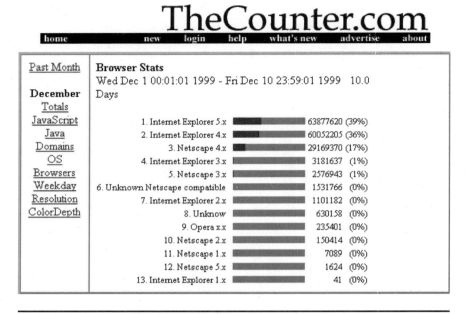

**Figure 22.3.** TheCounter.com offers a free service that can analyze many aspects of Web traffic, including what browsers people used to view your site.

there is a content problem on the less-popular pages, or maybe they take longer to load than the other pages, and visitors do not want to wait for them to load. Whatever the case may be, you can take this information and attempt to fix those problems that would keep visitors from spending time on all the pages of your site.

### Find Out How Each Visitor Found Your Site

By finding out how each visitor came to your site, you can boost your traffic tremendously (see Figure 22.4). You can take this information to help you with the allocation of your online advertising budget. For example, if most of your traffic is coming from the Excite search engine (*http://www.excite.com*), you could consider purchasing a banner advertisement on that page. The same theory goes if your traffic is coming from a newsgroup, meta-indexes, and so on.

**Figure 22.4.**   HitBox Enterprise allows you to view what search engines people are using to find your site.

If you have a number of doorway pages (for more information on doorway pages see Chapter 4) it would be good to know which ones are drawing the most attention. If the statistics reveal that four out of ten doorway pages are sending most of the traffic to your site, you should analyze the other six doorways to see if you can make them more effective. Maybe the keyword prominence is too low and they are not as effective as you thought when you designed them. If so, you should tweak these pages, then resubmit them to their corresponding search engines.

You can also find out where your visitors go when they leave your Web site. You want your viewers to stay at your site as long as possible. If you notice that the majority of your viewers are not traveling through your entire site and are not viewing important information that you want them to see, you may want to manipulate the layout of your Web site to decrease the "flight effect." If you notice that your top exit page is your home page, you may want to try a whole new approach because people seem to be turned off from searching through your site from the beginning.

Single-access pages are pages on your Web site that are accessed through a link, or search engine, and then are immediately exited. If a high percentage of your Web site traffic is a result of these pages, it is very important that you convey a strong message while you have the visitor's attention. If you have pages like this you should reevaluate what is on those pages and try to come up with content that will entice your visitor to search through the rest of your site.

Some of the more advanced software can tell you which keywords and phrases that your visitors used to find your site using a search engine. This is extremely valuable information because you can use these keywords to increase your popularity in the search engines. By knowing the most popular keywords your visitors are using to visit your site, you can make sure you use them in your Meta tags, Alt tags, and page titles, and in the text of your page for higher placement in the search engines. Also, by seeing which search engines are being used more by your visitors, you may choose to purchase a banner ad or keywords for that engine to achieve maximum visibility to your visitors.

Another benefit of observing who is watching your site is that you can see when spiders and crawlers from search engines have crawled to your page. This means that you will most likely have your site indexed on their corresponding search engine. This is good to know, because it not only reassures you that you are going to be indexed, but also because by knowing this you do not resubmit your site to the search engine and risk spamming. As explained previously in Chapter 4, if you are caught spamming some of the search engines, you will banned from their index.

### Identifying Your Target Market

After you have collected data from your log files and used the Web traffic analysis software to determine which demographics are actually visiting your site, you then must determine whether this is the demographic that you want to target. If it is not, you must then determine how you are going to reach your target market. For example, you may find that you should change your online advertising campaign. Or perhaps you should reevaluate your Internet marketing strategy, taking into consideration the new data that you have collected.

## Find Out What Forms of Online Promotion Work for Your Site

When you first launch your Web site you are going to aggressively implement your Internet marketing strategy by experimenting with all of the different forms of online marketing. However, when you analyze who is actually visiting your site and you find out where the majority of your traffic is coming from, you can then determine where to focus the majority of your marketing efforts. You may find that a link on a Web site is resulting in a high amount of traffic to your site; therefore, you may want to consider purchasing a banner advertisement on that site. The same goes for all of the other forms of Internet marketing. If after a short period of time your analysis software tells you that you are receiving low traffic (if any) from a banner ad that you had purchased, you may want to pull it off of that site and designate your investment to another site on the Internet. This is a good way to make sure you get the most for your investments in online marketing.

## Managing Your Online Business

If you are involved in selling online advertising on your site, Web traffic analysis software can save you a lot of work. When you place your client's banner advertisement on your site, the analysis software can not only track how many people have viewed that specific banner, but also how many people have clicked through. This makes billing your clients very easy, for all you have to do is read the reports generated by your software. If your clients pay per click-through, you simply look up the figure, and charge them the appropriate fee. The same goes for paying based on CPM.

## How Do You Get Web Traffic Analysis Software for Your Site?

If you would like to purchase Web traffic analysis software you can do so, but for it to work it has to be installed on the server where you host your Web site. If you host your own Web site you will definitely have to purchase your own software; however, if you are paying an ISP to host your Web site, they should already be able to provide some sort of analysis software. Most people don't take advantage of the tremendous marketing opportunities available by analyzing their traffic; therefore, they do not ask their ISP about the software. It should be available, for you are paying for their services. If it is not, simply ask them to purchase the Web traffic analysis software of your choice, for they would much rather have you as a client then say no. In some cases they may charge you an additional fee for this service.

## Popular Web Traffic Analysis Software

If you do decide to purchase your own Web traffic analysis software, there are many different brands, which do many different things. The following is a list of the more popular brands of Web traffic analysis software.

### Web Crumbs
*http://www.thinweb.com/products/webcrumbs/*
WebCrumbs, (Figure 22.5) brought to us by ThinWeb.com, is a Web site analysis tool that provides real-time performance analysis reports by using Dynamic Navigation Technology (DNT). You will be able to monitor usage patterns, judge your Web site's overall effectiveness and customize you Web page to best fit your target audience. WebCrumbs allows you to analyze your visitors' patterns, where they came from and what they do while visiting your Web site. You can track banner ads that are pointed toward your Web site to calculate the best investment for your online marketing budget. WebCrumbs easily plugs into Web servers, which cuts down on the large cost of purchasing additional technical products to run the software. The easy-to-use graphical administrator allows you to simply point and click, which makes WebCrumbs easy to use.

**Figure 22.5.** WebCrumbs from thinWEB is an excellent Web site traffic analyzing tool.

## WebTrends Enterprise Suite
*http://www.webtrends.com/*
The WebTrends Enterprise Suite is one of the most comprehensive Web site analysis software packages available. It provides you with reports on everything from the number of views your banner ads receive on another Web page to which keyword was used when a visitor found your site using a search engine. You can easily target specific hits and user sessions that include file types and names, entry pages, time and day, user addresses, or any other medium that may have pointed a visitor to your page. WebTrends develops detailed advertising reports, which tell you how often banners on your Web site are viewed and how often people click through. This assists you in selling and billing space to your clients. This is an all-in-one piece of Web traffic analysis software that does more than answer the question of who is actually visiting your site.

### ARIA Enterprise
*http://www.andromedia.com*

One of the higher-end Web traffic analysis tools, ARIA can help you to develop comprehensive Internet marketing reports, including daily, weekly, and monthly traffic trend reports, demographic and geographic reports, and top visitor domain reports. Definitely capable of handling sites with larger amounts of traffic, ARIA has the power to report visitors' behavior in real time on multiserver sites that receive tens of millions of page views per day. ARIA Enterprise is a piece of e-intelligence that can help you optimize your marketing strategy. Know your customers' needs, and keep them coming back for more.

### net.Analysis by net.Genesis
*http://netgen.com*

net.Genesis offers one of the best log analyzing systems. One of the first and one of the best for medium to large sites. Great for intranet access and analysis by non-tech-savvy users. Good integration with IBM Net.Commerce.

### NetTracker eBusiness Edition
*www.sane.com/products/NetTracker/ebiz.html*

NetTracker uses an Oracle database engine, which is great for most companies because they don't need a database administrator to use it. The Business Edition can handle really large log files with the speed and agility of an Oracle8 database. This Business Edition also lets you access your data for additional analysis using standard reporting tools such as Crystal Reports and products from Cognos, Information Builders, and more. This product contains 79 standardized summaries, plus you can create and save your own. NetTracker generates usage reports for multiple Web sites, proxy servers, firewalls, and FTP sites.


## Internet Resources

### Free Web Traffic-Analysis Services

### TheCounter.com
*http://www.thecounter.com*

The counter provides free tracking services to its members. By placing a small image on your Web site they will tell you information such as when your visitors came, from where and by using what browser. If you are just experimenting with Web traffic analysis you can't go wrong with The Counter.com

### The Hitometer
*http://www.hitometer.com*
The free Hitometer service offers an extensive choice of counters, and reporting of URL statistics, such as how many visitors visit your site per day, month, and year. You can receive your reports online, or have them sent to your e-mail.

### eXTReMe Tracker
*http://www.extreme-dm.com/tracking/*
The eXTReMe Tracker is a free service that offers comprehensive real-time reporting with no limit on the amount of traffic that you receive on your Web site. It is capable of tracking your visitors' geographic location, their domain, e-mail address, the browser that they are using, and much more. The eXTReMe Tracker is a very comprehensive service that is completely free.

### HitBox
*http://www.get.hitbox.com*
HitBox is designed for ad-supported, personal, or e-commerce sites. Capable of developing user profiles, tracking which sites refer your visitors to your site, and how much traffic you receive on a daily, monthly, and annual basis. HitBox can also track how your visitors navigate around your Web site, which can help you in customizing your Web site to your viewers needs.

### SuperStats.com
*http://www.superstats.com*
SuperStats.com is a free service that allows you to retrieve real-time statistics for your Web site 24 hours a day, 7 days a week. Find out who's visiting your site, how they found it, and when they were there.

### Pagecount
*http://www.pagecount.com*
They provide you with a free graphical page counter that shows how many times your page has been viewed. Their statistics show how

many people viewed your page, a breakdown of page views by date, day, and time, and a list of where the requests for your page originated. This sounds fantastic, and the only catch is that you must display one of their banner ads on every page of your site that contains the counter.

### AccessWatch
*www.accesswatch.com*
AccessWatch is open source shareware. AccessWatch generates browser statistics, referrer, page views, and other Web site traffic statistics.

## Web Traffic-Analysis Education

### Demystify Your Log Files
*http://www.builder.com/Servers/LogFile/index.html*
This article written by Olufemi Anthony explains in detail how your log files produce traffic-analysis data. Although this article was written in 1998, it goes over different terminology and gives descriptive examples that can help you to understand what exactly goes on in your Web servers log files.

### There's Gold in Them There Log Files
*http://www.wdvl.com/Internet/Management/index.html*
This article written by Charlie Morris touches on the different things that you can interpret from log files when analyzed by Web traffic-analysis software. It touches on different features that are available with different software.

### Web Traffic Analysis Software Comparison
*http://www.iw.com/extra/logchart.html*
This is a chart that breaks down the different features that are available with the different types of software. It compares the different features from low to high end software and also gives the cost of purchasing the software to assist you in your decision making when preparing to purchase your own software.

# 23

# Webcasting

Webcasting is defined by Netlingo *(http://www.netlingo.com)* as "using the Internet, and the World Wide Web in particular, to broadcast information. Unlike typical surfing, which relies on a pull method of transferring Web pages, Webcasting uses push technologies."

According to a study conducted by Arbitron New Media and Northstar Interactive, 70% of the Webcast audience clicks for content information, and while listening/viewing streaming media, nearly 60% click through for advertising information. Their study also states that approximately half of the Webcast audience buy online advertised products and 44% click online ads. The majority of Webcast users tune in from home (63%), followed by users at work (47%). In this chapter, the topics covered include:

- Streaming versus nonstreaming media (also known as rich media)

- Advertising with rich media

- Barriers to acceptance of Webcasting

- Uses of Webcasting

- Prominent Webcasters

## Streaming vs. Nonstreaming Media

Before we explain the marketing implications of Webcasting or rich media, it is important to explain some of the terms and what is required by the end user to view them. Webcasting consists primarily of video and audio. Whatis.com defines rich media as follows:

> *Rich media is an Internet advertising term for a Web page ad that uses advanced technology such as streaming video, downloaded applets (programs) that interact instantly with the user, and ads that change when the user's mouse passes over it. For example:*
>
> *An ad for a Hollywood movie that includes a streaming video sample of a scene from the movie*
>
> *A mouse cursor that changes to an image on a particular Web site if the user requests it*
>
> *A standard size banner ad that includes an inquiry form about ISDN installation, capturing the user's filled in personal information, and telling the user they will be contacted by a company representative—all simply by interacting with an ad on an online publisher's Web page.*

We will talk about streaming and nonstreaming content, with most emphasis placed on streaming because it has the highest promotional potential. What is the difference between streaming and nonstreaming? To put it simply, streaming is presented as it arrives. RealAudio files are an example of streaming media. Meanwhile, nonstreaming requires you to download the entire clip/file before you can listen/view it. AVI, MP3, and MOV file formats are nonstreaming file formats.

- **Video:** This category would include both streaming (Real Audio, G2, and Windows Media Player formats) and nonstreaming video formats (such as AVI and MOV files). Streaming video is often sent from pre-prepared files but is usually distributed as a live broadcast feed. Examples of this include news clips, movie clips, and online movie presentations.

- **Audio:** Audio includes streaming and nonstreaming formats. Real Networks is by far the current king with their RealAudio. Another major leading provider of streaming audio is Macromedia with their Shockwave.

Obviously, streaming video file formats contain an audio element to them as well. After all, a movie clip is much more interesting when there is sound associated with it. Other popular Webcasting or push technologies formats include:

- **ASF (Advanced Streaming Format).** Designed to store synchronized multimedia data and deliver the data over a large variety of networks and protocols.

- **CDF (Channel Definition Format).** Permits Web developers to push information to users through the use of channels.

Push technologies involve sending information to your target market across the Internet. Internet users install software on their system that receives content from the Webcaster. For example, they might receive the latest sports scores, the current weather conditions in 20 cities around the world, or current headlines. The information is "pushed" to the client's system. This is different from "pull" marketing, in which the clients specifically request content from a Web site by loading it into their browser.

Technically speaking, e-mail is one of the earliest forms of push technology. Internet marketers send e-mail messages to individuals in their target market without permission to do so from each of the recipients. However, we all know that this is spam. Savvy Internet marketers can still use e-mail to push their message to potential clients, but they must have the potential clients' permission beforehand.

Webcasters can utilize push technologies much as Internet marketers do with e-mail marketing campaigns. Real Networks *(http:// www.real.com)* has been involved in the Webcasting field for several years. Their RealPlayer software is a prime example of how to utilize push technology. The basic version of the player can be downloaded for free from the Real Networks Web site. Observing Figure 23.1, you can see how active channels have been incorporated into the RealPlayer application. Clicking on one of the active channels in the "Channels" menu automatically connects the user to a streaming audio/video presentation from the site of one of Real Networks' partners. In this way, Real Networks helps its partners (ESPN, Fox, ZDNet, etc.) brand themselves through the RealPlayer Webcasting software, and Real Networks likely receives a healthy sum of money in exchange for this advertising.

**Figure 23.1.** RealPlayer receives Internet channels. You can subscribe to new channels or view the channel information of Real Network's partners.

The RealPlayer software permits you to subscribe to other channels as well. Thus, Real Networks gives users a free application but the company profits from RealPlayer by selling advertising space. Real Networks is the perfect example of how Webcasting can be used to quickly achieve brand recognition and earn additional revenue.

Aside from Real Networks, these other companies also provide software to allow for the distribution of channels:

- Microsoft Active Channels software: *(http://www.microsoft.com)*

- Netscape Communicator's Netcaster: *(http://www.netscape.com)*

- PointCast EntryPoint software: *(http://www.entrypoint.com)*

## Advertising with Rich Media

Rich media can be used by companies by purchasing a "commercial" that precedes an online presentation or audio event, or they can be developed and used by the company on their own Web site to provide greater sense of interactivity, which will result in more repeat traffic. For an example of this, go to Broadcast.com *(http://www.broadcast.com)*. Broadcast.com provides current streaming audio and video footage of almost any event you could imagine. For instance, you can listen to the commentary of an entire NHL hockey game. However, just before the game gets underway, you will be greeted by a 25-second audio advertisement. Why is this good advertising?

- Rich media averages higher recall.

- Rich media advertising leaves a deeper impression on customers than a static banner ad.

- Higher customer recall of rich media makes it easier to brand a company name or product.

- Rich media has higher click-through rates.

- Rich media is more "likeable."

### Higher Recall

@Home *(http://www.home.com)* and Intel *(http://www.intel.com)* recently conducted a rich media study consisting of 30,000 survey responses. In their study, rich media (broadband) advertising averaged 34% higher recall than standard narrowband advertising. This means people are more likely to remember your company's streaming media presentation than a static banner ad.

### Better Branding

It goes without saying that better customer recall leads to better branding. Creating brand awareness with banner ads is difficult because banner ads are not very interactive. The combination of sight and sound possible with rich media advertising makes it much more effective than a static image or looping animated GIF.

### More Click-Throughs

A banner ad incorporating Java or Flash media will have more than twice the number of click-throughs than a static banner ad. Static banner ads average less than one click-through per hundred impressions. If you have a banner ad that actively engages the customer, you can achieve higher click-through rates and generate more sales leads.

### More Likeable

@Home and Intel concluded that a nonstreaming interactive banner ad offers a 20% potential increase in likeability. People will be more likely to interact with a banner ad that has a game of some sort built into it as opposed to a static image. Therefore, an interactive banner ad has the potential to attract a lot of people who are not usually inclined to click on banner ads of any sort. Likewise, a 30-second spot in a streaming multimedia presentation (i.e., watching the Superbowl online) is going to be more acceptable to a user than a pop-up banner ad. The bottom line is that if people like you, they will probably buy from you. Both streaming and nonstreaming broadband media advertising increase your chances of making a positive impression on the customer.

### More Reasons to Use Rich Media Advertising

Given the high recall rates, the cost per branding impression (i.e., the number of times a customer must view the ad before becoming familiar with your brand) decreases. This increases your ROI (Return On Investment) because you do not have to invest as much in rich media advertising to get your message across as you would with traditional advertising. For instance, to brand your company's name or product using television advertising would require a substantial financial investment. People change the channel during commercial breaks, so it is harder to reach television viewers.

However, someone who intentionally subscribes to an Internet channel, is viewing and listening to information that person is interested in. Plus, it is more of an effort to switch channels on the Net than it is to do so watching television. Therefore, the user's tendency to remain tuned in is higher. Also, the Internet is a worldwide network. Television, magazines, and other traditional marketing vehicles are more regionalized. Therefore, a rich media advertisement streaming across the Internet has the potential to reach a much larger audience.

## The Barriers of Webcasting (Rich Media) Acceptance

With every new medium, there are bound to be barriers to its public acceptance. Webcasting, both streaming and nonstreaming, is no different. There are six primary obstacles that Webcasting must overcome before it becomes a publicly acceptable advertising medium.

## Cost

The possibilities are there, but so are the costs, and you must be aware of this. Developing streaming media and nonstreaming media can be quite expensive. Moreover, if you're looking to advertise on a site that applies video and audio content, you must be made aware that most of the sites that apply this technology are high-budget, high-volume, and high-bandwidth sites, and will likely ask for quite a fee to advertise.

You must also consider the potential return on investment. We pointed out earlier that rich media advertising has a higher recall rate than standard Web advertising. Also, rich media is more cost effective and efficient for branding purposes. Therefore, the initial expense of producing a rich media advertisement may be quickly recovered by the interest and sales the ad will generate.

## Rich Media Advertising Is Not Accepted by All Sites

Although a lot of sites do not have the resources to offer Webcast advertising opportunities, a lot of major sites do. Content sites such as Launch.com and RollingStone.com place ads in front of some of the videos you can view on their site. These streaming media sites offer tremendous exposure opportunities for companies that advertise with them.

There are also sites such as MP3.com *(http://www.mp3.com)* that offer free Webcast advertising (Figure 23.2). On MP3.com, unsigned music artists can post MP3 versions of their songs for the world to hear. MP3.com is a high-traffic site as a result of the community of artists they have created, and the artists themselves benefit from the increased exposure. Given the number of Webcast companies and major companies getting involved with Webcasting, companies that do not utilize it may be left behind.

## Bandwidth Constraints

Both streaming and nonstreaming media require that users have high connection speeds in order to experience a Webcast as it is intended.

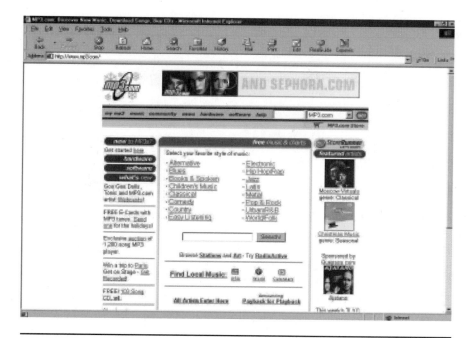

**Figure 23.2.** MP3.com offers artists a chance to post their music on the site. Listeners can then download both streaming and nonstreaming versions of any member artist's songs.

To view streaming content you will need a plug-in or player of some sort. Popular applications used to view/hear streaming content are:

- Windows Media Player

- Quicktime

- RealPlayer

- Macromedia Shockwave Player

It is important to note that the higher the connection speed, the more convenient the use of streaming content will be. If you're still using a 14.4 modem you're simply not going to get the performance needed to make it worthwhile. This presents an obstacle to people with slower Internet connection rates. Also, some people simply do not wish to download and install the plug-ins necessary to play rich media files. You will not be able to target your Webcasting advertising campaign towards these users.

### Irritates User

Does Webcasting annoy users? Sure it does. But this will only be the case for people with low bandwidth or less-robust machines. Also, some people despise advertising in any form, so you probably won't win over any of these individuals either.

However, @Home and Intel discovered from their rich media study that 75% of their users either "enjoyed" or "did not mind" rich media advertising on the @Home site. Could @Home boast the same level of advertising acceptance for a television ad? It's very unlikely they could.

### Too Complicated

The software to create rich media content exists and, with a little initiative, can be learned by anyone. You first have to determine if your target market is likely to be a user of rich media. Here are some software applications you should inspect if you have an interest in creating your own rich media/Webcasting files:

*Streaming Media Creation/Encoding Software*

- RealSlideshow Plus *(http://www.real.com)*. This product allows you to create your own streaming media slide show.

- Emblaze *(http://www.emblaze.com)*. Designed to enable delivery of rich media over any IP network, over any platform, and under any bandwidth.

- Liquid Audio *(http://www.liquidaudio.com)*. Offers solutions for encoding your music and serving it in a streaming media format.

- Stream Anywhere (http://www.sonicfoundry.com). The all-in-one solution for preparing audio and video multimedia for distribution over the Web.

- Quick Time 4 *(http://www.apple.com/quicktime)*. Create/edit streaming and nonstreaming video and audio files.

*NonStreaming Media Creation/Encoding Software*

- Macromedia Director 7 Shockwave Internet Studio and Flash *(http://www.macromedia.com)*. Generate powerful presentations and content for your Web site.

- AudioCatalyst 2.1 and Xing MPEG software *(http://www. xingtech.com)*. Create MP3 and MPEG files from source files.

- Real JukeBox *(http://www.real.com)*. Create MP3 files from CDs.

It is obvious that the software to create rich media exists, and most of it is not too difficult to learn. It just requires a little bit of initiative and patience.

## The Technology Changes Too Often

Webcasting is a relatively new medium. Of course, new standards are being introduced every few months. The key here is to watch what technologies the major Internet sites are using. If you see some of the major players in the Internet starting to use a particular Webcasting technology, you should investigate it. Generally, the learning curve for new technologies is not very steep because they are based on previous technologies.

# Uses of Webcasting

Despite the existence of a few barriers to using Webcasting as a promotional vehicle, you should investigate it if you think your target market may include early adapters to technology. Some important uses of providing rich media content to the general public include:

- Live continuous broadcasts of radio stations and networks

- Broadcasts of cable networks and television stations

- Coverage of sporting events (both streaming and nonstreaming footage)

- Live music including concerts and club performances (both streaming and nonstreaming footage)

- On-demand shows, corporate events, CDs, audiobooks, video titles, and so on

As bandwidth increases and more people have access to higher-end technology, Webcasting will become a regular part of our lives and be more accepted as an advertising medium. The transition to Webcasting has already begun, as is evidenced by the large number of prominent players already entrenched in the field.

## Prominent Webcasters

Yack.com *(http://www.yack.com)* is an excellent resource to locate sites with streaming audio and video content (Figure 23.3). It divides the information into easy-to-follow categories such as sports, music, and news. It also provides the time and location of the respective events. Because the public enjoys using streaming media for a variety of purposes, the advertiser will benefit from enhanced branding campaigns and increased recognition, ultimately leading to higher sales.

Recently Broadcast.com *(http://www.broadcast.com)* and Yahoo! *(http://www.yahoo.com)* merged (Figure 23.4). Yahoo!'s Broadcast has Webcast over 36,000 live events including the last Super Bowl, the NHL regular season and Stanley Cup Playoffs, and even the online premiere of Casablanca. Visit *http://advertising.broadcast.com/ad_demos/index.html* to learn more about their advertising opportunities. They offer gateway ads, channel and event sponsorships, mul-

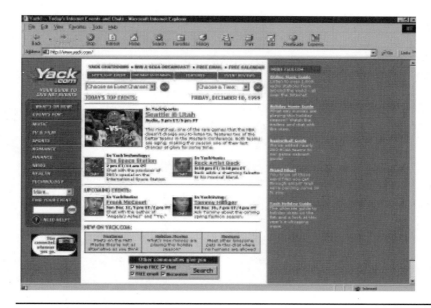

**Figure 23.3.** Yack.com offers streaming audio and video content.

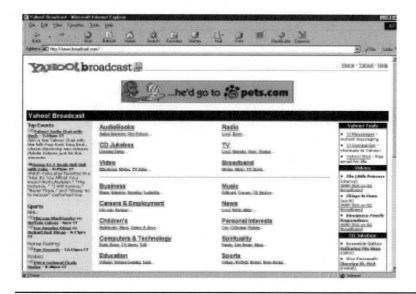

**Figure 23.4.** Recently acquired by Yahoo!, Broadcast.com is perhaps the largest and best-known provider of streaming media events.

timedia ads, and traditional banner ads. More appropriate to this chapter is the ability to purchase slots and insert Internet-only commercials within Yahoo!'s programming.

The image in Figure 23.5 was taken from a streaming video demonstration on *http://www.broadcast.com*. You can think of it in terms of watching a commercial on TV in some respects. When the user clicks on Webcast of Court TV, Real Player loads as well as a pop up window for Volvo. Before the show begins Real Player presents a commercial, much like one you would watch on your television.

As you can imagine, you're going to pay a premium to have an ad of this caliber placed on a site, and it may not be within the budget of a small to medium-size business; however, we do not want to leave any options uncovered.

Similar to the preceding example, EntertainmentBlvd.com's *(http://www.entertainmentblvd.com)* vidnet places video commercials before allowing you to view a video (Figure 23.6). When selecting to

**Figure 23.5.**   Volvo's streaming media advertisement on Broadcast.com.

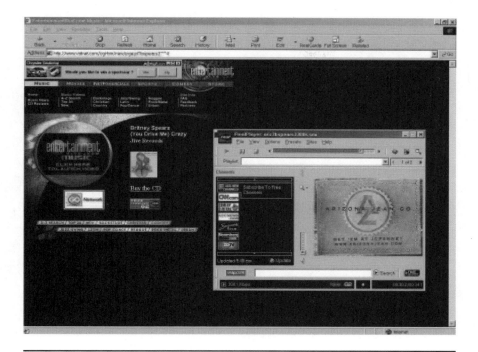

**Figure 23.6.** EntertainmentBlvd.com shows us how cross branding can be done with streaming media.

view Britney Spear's "Crazy" video, a streaming video commercial for Arizona Jeans was prominently displayed first.

Staying within the EntertainmentBlvd.com network, you can go to another section of their site called NetFomercial.com (Figure 23.7). The purpose of this site is to sell products using streaming video infomercials, much like the ones you watch on TV.

DiscJockey.com (Figure 23.8) is another popular site that offers a host of interactive advertising opportunities for multiple demographic segments. Of importance to this chapter is the ability to purchase audio advertisements. Before you hear your selected station, an audio advertisement is played. You can contact them through their Web site *(http://www.discjockey.com)* for more information.

A major use of streaming audio comes in the form of Internet-only radio stations and traditional radio stations who broadcast their signal online. For the radio stations it's an ideal opportunity to in-

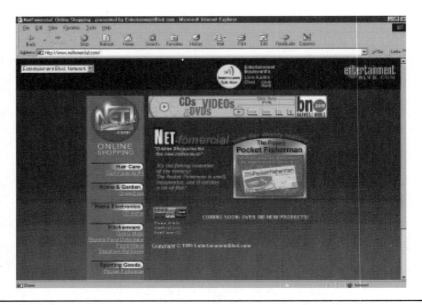

**Figure 23.7.** If you are interested in streaming media advertising, NetFomercial.com is the place to visit.

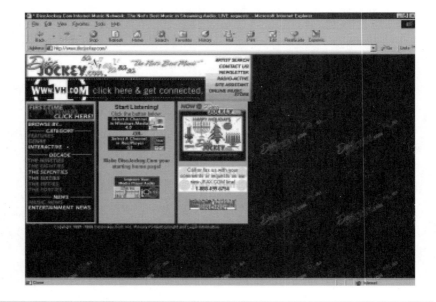

**Figure 23.8.** Advertise on Web radio stations courtesy of DiscJockey.com.

crease market share and increase the number of loyal listeners. Web-Radio.com *(http://www.web-radio.com)* has a large directory of over 2700 radio stations broadcasting over the Internet (Figure 23.9). InternetNews.com *(http://www.internetnews.com)* reported in September 1999 that one of every four radio stations with a Web site is Webcasting. At that time, they projected that over 3000 radio stations would be Webcasting by the beginning of the year 2000.

The benefits here are twofold. A radio station will benefit from the broader exposure (worldwide as opposed to regional); however, these online radio stations provide an excellent opportunity for others to advertise online. Since online radio listeners broaden the potential audience for a radio station, the station could charge advertisers higher rates. This source of revenue is unquestionably attractive, which is why radio stations are scrambling to establish themselves in the Webcasting world.

HotelView's *(http://www.hotelview.com)* Web site is an interactive video library of hotels (Figure 23.10). Perhaps you own a bed and breakfast near a waterfront location. You can use a streaming or

**Figure 23.9.** Almost 3000 radio stations now stream their programming across the Internet. The existence of Web-Radio.com is evidence of the growth in this field.

**Figure 23.10.**    HotelView.com helps hotels and bed and breakfast businesses promote themselves online with streaming media.

nonstreaming video clip to display this scenery, much like when you receive a video tape from a travel agency demonstrating the beauty of a potential vacation destination.

AltaVista *(http://www.altavista.com)* has recently redesigned their site (Figure 23.11) to claim title as the number one search engine on the Web and has applied much more emphasis on Webcasts. Why did they do this? The popularity of audio and video on the Web is exploding, they needed to include this information. Then, too, their competitors are doing it.

Webcasting is a technological phenomenon that offers Internet companies and traditional companies marketing on the Internet a new way to reach their customers. Many Internet giants have already seized the Webcasting reins and now deliver rich media content and advertising to the world. Perhaps you would be wise to do the investigate Webcasting and do the same.

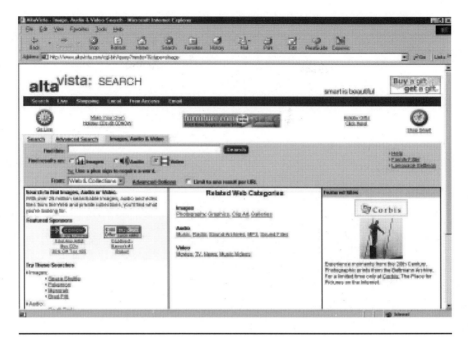

**Figure 23.11.** You can search for streaming audio and video on AltaVista.

## Internet Resources

**OII—Webcasting Standards**
*http://www2.echo.lu/oii/en/webcast.html#RDF*
Explanation of Webcasting standards.

**Broadcast.com**
*http://www.broadcast.com*
Broadcasting over 36,000 live events, Broadcast.com is a streaming media industry giant. They were recently purchased by Yahoo!

**Castanet**
*http://www.marimba.com/doc/general/current/introducing/introducing.html*
Marimba's Castanet is a system for distributing, installing, and updating software and content over intranets and the Internet.

### ChannelSEEK
*http://channelseek.com*
ChannelSEEK is a comprehensive Webcast and streaming media guide for the Web. Even streaming MP3 audio from multiple sites. Watch hundreds of movies and listen to music with your computer.

### ChannelSeven.com
*http://www.channelseven.com*
A large resource for Internet development, marketing, and advertising executives. This site contains information on rich media advertising.

### Dick Becker's LIVE Radio Stations
*http://www.geocities.com/ResearchTriangle/1803/*
Radio and TV stations broadcasting live on the Net via RealAudio, RealVideo, NetShow, Windows Media Player, Streamworks, and AudioActive.

### Digital Librarian: Audio, Video, Rich Media
*http://www.servtech.com/~mvail/audio.html*
A librarian's choice of the best audio and sound resources on the internet. Updated weekly. Meta-index.

### International Webcasting Association
*http://www.webcasters.org*
The IWA serves as the meeting place for companies active or interested in the delivery of multimedia (audio and video) services to consumers or business customers via the Net and other networks.

### OnTheAir.com
*http://www.ontheair.com*
A reference site listing the best sites that provide links to live radio and television from across the United States and around the world. Over 1000 stations available live on your computer.

### Real Networks
*http://www.real.com*
Innovators in the field of streaming media, Real Networks has several popular Webcasting software applications including RealPlayer, RealJukebox, and RealSlideshow.

### Scour
*http://www.scour.net*
Find audio, video, images, and animation at this guide to online multimedia. Search the index for multimedia files or navigate through their category directory.

### Streaming Media World
*http://www.streamingmediaworld.com*
Streaming Media World offers media player reviews, news, tools, tutorials, discussion forums, and cool links devoted to streaming video, audio, MP3, multimedia, and GIF animation.

### The Media CHANNEL
*http://www.mediachannel.com*
A guide to video on the Internet.

### Web-Radio
*http://www.web-radio.com*
A comprehensive directory of radio stations (broadcasting) on The Web.

### Webreference.com
*http://www.webreference.com/multimedia/video.html*
A directory of multimedia tools including Windows Media Player, Real, Emblaze, and Macromedia.

### VideoDome.Com Networks Inc.
*http://www.videodome.com*
Offers a variety of Internet OnDemand video solutions to meet your online video needs.

### VideoSeeker
*http://www.videoseeker.com*
The leading Internet video service offers a wealth of streaming video clips and a complete online video guide. Check out exclusive Must See video from NBC, including comedy from *SNL, The Tonight Show,* and *Late Night with Conan O'Brien,* as well as the latest music videos, celebrity interviews, movie trailers, MSNBC news, live Webcasts, and more.

**VirtualTuner.com**
*http://www.virtualtuner.com*
Directory of live and on-demand radio links for the Internet.

**Yack!**
*http://www.yack.com*
A guide to online events. With co-branding and personalized event services, Yack is the main portal for searching and finding all Internet events. Yack.com list of Webcasts.

# 24

## Grand Opening Tips for Your Web Site Virtual Launch

Just as you would have a book or software launch, you can have a Web site launch. In preparation for the Web site launch you must develop an appropriate launch strategy. In this chapter we cover:

- Development of your Web site launch strategy

- Web site announcement mailing lists

- Direct e-mail postcards to your customers or prospective clients

### Launching and Announcing Your Web Site

A new Web site or your new location in **cyberspace** can be launched in many of the same ways as you would launch a new physical store location. This may involve both online and offline activities. Just as you would prepare a book launch strategy or a new software product launch strategy, you can develop an appropriate launch strategy for your new Web

**Cyber-
space**
Virtual
location
where Web
sites live

site. Sometimes a launch strategy may be more work than the benefit that will be gained. On the other hand, if you are opening the next Amazon it is imperative.

## Your Web Site Virtual Launch

Let's take a look at a traditional retail store grand opening. For the grand opening, which usually lasts for an evening or a day, there will be invitations to the media, press releases distributed, invited guests, opening ceremonies, advertising, and possibly gift giveaways.

A Web site virtual location launch occurs in cyberspace, and the "grand opening" can last for a day, a week, or a month. Many of the activities you include in your traditional grand opening can also be included in your Internet grand opening. The effectiveness of your launch can be increased with the following tips.

- Media attention can be generated through the distribution of press releases online and offline. (See Chapter 18 for press release distribution information.)

- Guests can be invited to your online opening through postings in newsgroups, newsletters, "What's New" sites, banner advertising, direct e-mail, and signature files, as well as offline direct mail and advertising.

- Opening ceremonies can be just as exciting online as offline. They can last for a month rather than a day. The opening must be designed to be of interest to the target market.

- You can feature special guests in chat areas for your grand opening or several special guests over the duration. Again, relate your guests and the topic to be discussed to the needs/ wants of your target market.

- You can have contests that require visitors to visit various parts of your site to compete for prizes. Perhaps they have to complete a multiple-choice quiz the answers to which are found throughout your site. This way you encourage your guests to visit all those pages you want them to. You can also ask if they would like to be notified via e-mail of the winner. This gives you an opportunity to send them e-mail with their permission.

- You can have audio and video greetings from your site.

- You can have press releases regarding your opening available for download by the media. Make your press release interactive (see Chapter 18 for details on how to do this).

- There are many other innovative "grand opening" attention-grabbers that can be brainstormed with appropriate marketing and public relations individuals.

- Special free gifts can be provided to the first 20 or 50 visitors to your site. You can also provide prizes to the first 100 to link to your site.

- Do some offline advertising for your new URL (see Chapter 21 for innovative offline opportunities), or take advantage of online advertising via Announcement sites.

Whatever you decide to do, make it memorable, make it appropriate for your target market, and provide reasons for them to return.

## Internet Resources

**Netscape What's New**
*http://netscape.com/home/whats-new.html*
This site selectively publishes information on new sites. To warrant a mention your site must somehow be unique...perhaps using the latest Netscape technologies.

**Best-Web-Sites Announcement List**
You can join this mailing list by sending the message "sub BESTWEB your name" to *listserv@vm3090.ege.edu.tr.*

### Site Launch
*http://www.sitelaunch.net*
Site Launch offers guides, tools, and information for Web masters. Takes you through everything you need to get more visitors.

### Nerd World What's New
*http://www.nerdworld.com/whatsnew.html*
The newest links added to Nerd World and a place to show off your site. Not just for nerds.

### LaunchBot
*http://www.launchbot.com*
A listing of what's new on the home page front. Instructions here on how to get your site listed with them.

# About the Author

## Susan Sweeney, C.A.

Renowned industry expert and consultant, Susan Sweeney C.A., tailors lively keynote speeches, full and half day seminars and workshops for companies, industries, and associations interested in improving their Internet presence and increasing their Web site traffic and sales. Susan is the founder and President of **Connex Network Inc.** an international Internet marketing and consulting firm. Susan holds both her Chartered Accountant and Certified General Accountant designations. She is an experienced Internet Marketing professional with a background in computers, marketing, and the Internet. Susan is the author of several books on Internet Marketing as well as numerous articles concerning Marketing on the Internet, Export Marketing, and The Internet and Business. She is a member of the Canadian Association of Professional Speakers, the National Speakers Association, and the International Federation for Professional Speakers. Susan is also the Treasurer and an executive on the Board of Directors of the Information Technology Industry Association of Nova Scotia, as well as a member of the Board of Directors for the Canadian Association of Professional Speakers.

Connex Network is a marketing firm, providing Internet and international marketing consulting and training services to industry and government. Their clients range in size from single person start-up operations to multi-million dollar international firms. Their primary services include Internet Marketing Workshops, Internet Marketing Strategies, Web Site Report Cards, Internet Marketing Consulting, Market Research and Competitive Analysis. During their workshops and training sessions they ensure their clients have a complete understanding of the principles involved with developing a strong online presence. The team of Internet marketing analysts at Connex is highly trained in the area of Internet marketing and all stay up to date with the latest technological advancements and industry trends in the online marketing world. Every person on the team has extensive practical hands-on experience and the necessary skills to use proven tips, tools, and techniques to generate high volumes of traffic to your site.

As a result of technological change and global competitiveness the need for a strong Internet presence is essential. Susan instructs individuals with her enthusiastic personality combined with her vast hands-on international marketing experience, which keeps her listeners informed, and captivated. Let Susan help you increase your traffic and make your business prosper!

Susan Sweeney, C.A.
Connex Network Inc.
Suite 300, 800 Windmill Road
Dartmouth, Nova Scotia, Canada B3B 1L1
Phone: 902-468-2578  Fax: 902-468-2233
*www.connexnetwork.com*
*susan@connexnetwork.com*

# Appendix A

# Terminology

**404 B File Not Found** This message is returned from a Web server when a requested document cannot be found.

**Animated GIF** Special image editing applications can meld several GIF images into a single image, much like slides in a slide show. Each of the images is displayed briefly in turn to create the illusion of motion (similar to cartoon flipbooks).

**ASCII Text File (American Standard Code for Information Interchange)** The worldwide standard format for text files in computers and on the Internet. The code represents all the uppercase and lowercase letters, numbers, punctuation, etc. There are 128 standard ASCII codes, in which a 7-digit binary number, 0000000 through 1111111, represents each character.

**Autoresponder** A program that automatically responds to incoming e-mail. It is like an electronic fax-back system for e-mail.

**Backbone** Large transmission lines that carry data being transferred from smaller lines. These lines or paths connect local or regional networks together for long-distance communication. The connection points are known as network nodes or telecommunication data switching exchanges (DSEs).

**Banner Ad** A graphical advertisement on a Web site that links to a particular promotion when the user clicks on it. Banner ads are used to increase product awareness and company and brand identity, and can be a source of revenue (advertising revenue) to the site that hosts the banner ad.

**BBS (Bulletin Board System)** A computer that can be reached by computer modem dialing (or by Telnet) for the purpose of sharing or exchanging messages or other files. Some BBSs are devoted to specific interests; others offer a more general service. The definitive BBS List says that there are over 40,000 BBSs worldwide.

**BCC (Blind Carbon Copy)** Including e-mail addresses in the BCC field of an e-mail message will hide all the addresses aside from each recipient's address.

**Benchmark** A point of reference by which something can be measured or compared. In surveying, a "bench mark" (two words) is a post or other permanent mark used as the basis for measuring the elevation of other topographical points.

**Branding** Creating public awareness of a company, product, or service so that the company, product, or service is quickly and immediately identified and associated.

**Browser** The software used to view the various kinds of Internet resources or sites.

**Bulk e-mail** A group of identical messages e-mailed to a large number of addresses at once. This is a technique commonly employed by spammers, and it results in many very unpersonalized e-mail messages.

**Cache** A place to store something more or less temporarily. Web pages you request are stored in your browser's cache (pronounced "cash") directory on your hard disk. When you return to a page you've recently looked at, the browser can get most of the information from the cache rather than the original server. A cache saves you time and the network the burden of some additional traffic. You can usually vary the size of your cache, depending on your particular browser.

**CGI (Common Gateway Interface)** Guidelines that define how a Web server communicates with another piece of software on the same machine, and how the other piece of software, the CGI program, talks to the Web server. Any piece of software can be a CGI program if it handles input and output according to the CGI standard.

**CGI-bin** This is the most common name for the directory on a Web server that holds a CGI program. Most programs located in the

CGI-bin directory are text files, scripts that are executed by binaries located elsewhere on the same machine.

**Chat** Real-time conversation between one or more individuals across a network. IRC and ICQ are common forums for such discussions often held in topic-driven "chat rooms."

**Clickstreams** The paths a user takes as he or she navigates a Web page or cyberspace in general. Advertisers and online media providers have developed software that can track users' clickstreams.

**Click-Through** A hit generated from a banner advertisement when a user clicks on the banner ad.

**Click-Through Rate** This is the percentage of banner ad views that result in a user clicking on the ad (a click-through).

**Cookie** On the Internet, a cookie refers to a piece of information sent by a Web server to a Web browser. The browser software is expected to save the cookie and send the information back to the server whenever an additional request is made. Cookies may contain information such as user preferences, registration or login information, online shopping cart info, etc.

**Cost Per Click** The rate charged to an advertiser each time a user clicks on their banner ad. This is one method site owners can use to collect advertising revenue from banner ads.

**Crawlers** Crawlers quietly comb through Web sites and index the information they find.

**CPM (Cost Per Thousand)** Banner ad rates are typically measured in cost per thousand page views—shorthand for the cost of delivering a marketing message to 1000 people.

**CPTM (Cost Per Thousand Targeted)** This implies that the audience you have targeted is of a particular demographic. (See "Demographics")

**Cybermall** A collection of online storefronts better known as an Internet shopping mall.

**Cybernaut** A person who uses the Internet.

**Cyberspace** Used to describe all areas of information resources available through computer networks and the Internet. William Gibson originated the term in his novel *Neuromancer.*

**Data Mining** Obtaining specific information from a data warehouse by running queries. Marketers can determine how many people in a database file fit a certain demographic and then market to that particular group of individuals.

**Data Warehouse** A place for storing, retrieving, and managing large amounts of any type of data. Data warehouse software often allows you to conduct fast searches as well as advanced filtering. Planners and researchers can use this database freely without worrying about slowing down day-to-day operations of the production database.

**Database Marketing** Actively maintaining and updating a database of clients and potential clients (data warehousing), mining the data for specific demographic information (data mining), and focusing your advertising campaign on the target market. For instance, once you determine the people in your database who fit a particular demographic, you can then send a targeted e-mail marketing message to these people.

**Demographics** Specific data about the size and characteristics of a population or audience that can be used for marketing purposes.

**Domain Name** The unique name that identifies an Internet site. A domain name always has two or more parts, separated by dots. The part on the left is the most specific, and the part on the right is the most general. A given machine may have more than one domain name, but a given domain name points to only one machine. For example, the domain names *connexnetwork.com* and *yahoo.com* can both refer to the same machine.

**Download** The transferring of data from one computer to another across the Internet.

**DTD (Document Type Declaration)** Specifies the organization that issued the language specification and the exact version of the specification. This information is typically found at the beginning of an HTML document or other programming documents. In XML, a DTD specifies the meaning of every tag and tag attribute contained within a set of XML pages.

**E-Commerce** The process of buying and selling of goods and services on the Internet.

**E-Mail (Electronic Mail)** Mail messages, usually text, sent from one person to another via computer. Messages can also be sent automatically to a large number of addresses on a mailing list.

**Effective Frequency** The optimum regularity with which you execute an e-mail marketing campaign.

**Emoticons** Symbols made from punctuation marks and letters that look like facial expressions. Commonly used in e-mail and in Internet chat rooms to convey expressions and additional meaning to written text.

**Exposure** How broadly known your company or your product is from the Internet.

**Extranet** A new buzzword that refers to an intranet that is partially accessible to authorized outsiders. Whereas an intranet resides behind a firewall and is accessible only to people who are members of the same company or organization, an extranet provides various levels of accessibility to outsiders. You can access an extranet only if you have a valid user name and password, and your identity determines which parts of the extranet you can view.

**E-Zine, Ezine (Electronic Magazine)** Used to describe an electronic magazine, including those of print magazines such as *National Geographic* and *Newsweek* that have electronic editions. Thus, an e-zine database includes both electronic-only magazines and electronic-edition magazines.

**FAQ (Frequently Asked Questions)** The most common questions on a particular subject or problem area. There are hundreds of FAQ files on subjects as diverse as car repair and franchise advice.

**Firewall** A set of related programs located at a network gateway server to protect the resources of a private network from users of other networks.

**Flame, Flaming** Flaming usually involves the use of harsh language directed toward a group or individual for sending unwanted messages (marketing) on a newsgroup or mailing list.

**Forums** Another name for a newsgroup in which people are formed together in a group to chat and discuss.

**FTP (File Transfer Protocol)** The common method of moving files between two computers through the Internet medium. FTP is a method for logging onto another computer or Internet site for the purpose of retrieving and/or sending files.

**Hit** A single request from a Web browser for a single item from a Web server; thus, for a Web browser to display a page that contains three graphics, four "hits" would occur at the server: one for the HTML page, and one for each of the three graphics. Hits are often used as a rough measure of visits on a server.

**Home Page, Homepage** The main Web page for a business, organization, person—or simply the main page of a collection of Web pages.

**Host** Any computer on a network that can hold files available to other computers on the network. It is quite common to have one host machine provide several services to other machines, such as WWW and Usenet.

**HTML (HyperText Markup Language), HTM** The coding language used to create documents for use on the World Wide Web. These documents have a file extension of HTML or HTM. HTML code looks a lot like old-fashioned typesetting code, where you surround a block of text with codes that indicate how it should appear. HTML or HTM files are meant to be viewed using a World Wide Web client program, such as Netscape or Internet Explorer.

**HTTP (HyperText Transport Protocol)** The most important protocol used in the World Wide Web for moving hypertext files across the Internet. Requires an HTTP client program on one end, and an HTTP server program on the other.

**Hypertext** Clickable text that links to another document; that is, words or phrases in one document that can be clicked on by a reader, causing another document to be retrieved and displayed.

**Image Map** A single graphic that has multiple hot links to different pages or resources.

**Impression** Sometimes used as a synonym for view, as in ad view. Online publishers offer, and their customers buy advertising measured in terms of ad views or impressions.

**Interstitial Ad** Meaning in between, an advertisement that appears in a separate browser window while you wait for a Web page to load. Interstitials are more likely to contain large graphics, streaming presentations, and applets than conventional banner ads, and some studies have found that more users click on interstitials than on banner ads. Some users, however, have complained that interstitials slow access to destination pages.

**Intranet** A private network inside a company or organization that uses the same kinds of software found on the public Internet, but that is only for internal use and cannot be viewed outside the network.

**ISDN (Integrated Services Digital Network)** A faster way to move more data over existing regular phone lines. Rapidly becoming available around the world, it is priced comparably to standard analog phone circuits. It can provide speeds of roughly 128,000 bits per second over the regular phone lines.

**ISP (Internet Service Provider)** A provider that allows access to the Internet. Usually there is a cost to the consumer, although there are still some free community networks.

**Java** A programming language that is specifically designed for writing programs. It can be safely downloaded to your computer through the Internet and immediately run without fear of viruses or other harm to your computer. Using small Java programs, called applets, Web pages can include functions such as animations, calculators, and other fancy tricks that cannot be done by normal HTML.

**LAN (Local Area Network)** A network limited to the local area, usually the same building or floor of a company.

**List Server Software** An application installed on a publicly accessible server that manages messages sent to and from a mailing list. This software is required if you intend to administer your own publicly accessible mailing list.

**Login** The account name used to gain access to a computer system, not a password. Also can mean the act of entering onto a computer system.

**Lurking** Reading Usenet newsgroups, consumer online service forums, or Internet mailing lists without posting anything. A lurker is a person who observes what everyone else is doing within that group.

**Mailbots, Bots** Software programs that automatically respond to all incoming e-mail. A mailbot, or autoresponder, replies to them by sending the author a file or message.

**Mailing List Manager** A software program that collects and distributes e-mail messages to a mailing list (see "List server software").

**Mailing List, Mail List** A system that allows people to send e-mail to one address, whereupon their message is copied and sent to all other subscribers to the list. This method allows people with different kinds of e-mail to participate in discussions together.

**Meta-Index** A listing of Internet resources pertaining to a specific subject category, intended as a resource to those who have an interest in specific topic. A meta-index is simply a collection of URLs for related Internet resources, all arranged on a Web page by their titles.

**Net** The shorthand version for Internet.

**Netiquette** Internet etiquette.

**Netizen** From the term "citizen," referring to a citizen of the Internet, or someone who uses networked resources.

**Netpreneur** An online entrepreneur.

**Netscape** Web browser and the name of a company. The Netscape browser was based on the Mosaic program developed at the National Center for Supercomputing Applications (NCSA).

**Newbie** A newcomer to the Internet

**Newsgroups** Name given to discussion groups on Usenet.

**Opt-In Mail List** People are given the choice to take part in a system that allows people to send e-mail to one address, whereupon their message is copied and sent to all other subscribers to the list. This method allows people with different kinds of e-mail to participate in discussions together.

**Page View** The number of times a page is viewed.

**Password** A code used to gain access to a locked system known only to one person or a specific group of individuals. Good passwords contain letters and nonletters and are not simple combinations such as *john12*.

**Portal** A new term, generally synonymous with gateway, for a World Wide Web site that is or proposes to be a major starting site for users when they get connected to the Web or that users tend to visit as an anchor site.

**Posting, Post** A message entered into a network communications system, such as a newsgroup submission.

**Privacy Policy** A policy for protecting the privacy of individually identifiable information. When an organization is engaged in online activities or electronic commerce, it has the responsibility to implement and post a privacy policy.

**Registration** You submit personal information to become part of a mailing list or newsgroup, in order to receive other information in return.

**ROI (Return On Investment)** The amount of profit you obtain from your original investment.

**Secure Server** A network-accessible (i.e., the Internet) computer that uses SSL (Secure Socket Layers) for encryption to allow for private online transactions. The encryption protects an online shopper's credit card and personal information from being compromised while conducting an e-commerce transaction.

**Search Engine** The most popular way to find resources on the Internet. There are numerous search engines, each with its own unique style and capabilities.

**Server** A computer that stores information and makes these files available to other users on a network or the Internet.

**Signature** A block of information used at the end of every message or online document sent by that user.

**Site** A unique location on the Internet to post your information and get noticed.

**Snail Mail** A slang term for the regular postal service

**Spam, Spamming** An inappropriate attempt to use a mailing list, Usenet, or other networked communications facility as if it were a broadcast medium by sending the same message to a large number of people who didn't ask for it.

**Spider** An automated program that indexes documents, titles, and/or a portion of each document acquired by traversing the Web.

**SQL (Structured Query Language)** A specialized programming language for sending queries to databases.

**Store Front** A set location on the Web that stores and displays a collection of information about you and your business.

**Streaming Media** The simultaneous transfer and display of the sound and images on the World Wide Web.

**Subject** The subject line in an e-mail message stating the topic of the mail.

**Subscribe** Submitting information to an e-zine or mail list in order to receive information.

**Superstitial** Nonbanner rich media ads that can be any size on the screen and can be authored in most any creative format. Preloaded using a patent-pending "polite" delivery system that eliminates the latency problems often experienced with streaming online advertising solutions, superstitials only play on a user-initiated break in surfing, such as a mouse click.

**Telnet** A program that allows people to log on to other computers or bulletin board systems on the Internet and run software remotely from their location.

**Thread** A sequence of responses to an initial message posting. This enables you to follow or join an individual discussion in a newsgroup from among the many that may be there.

**Unsolicited E-Mail** E-mail ads sent to people without their consent.

**Upload** The transfer of a file from your computer to a server online.

**URL (Uniform Resource Locator)** The standard way to give an address of any resource on the Internet that is part of the World Wide Web (WWW). The most common way to use a URL is to enter into a WWW browser program, such as Internet Explorer, Netscape, or Lynx, and type it in the location bar.

**Usenet** A discussion-groups system. Comments are passed among hundreds of thousands of machines, with over 10,000 discussion areas, called newsgroups.

**User session** A person with a unique address who enters or reenters a Web site each day (or some other specified period). A user session is sometimes determined by counting only those users who haven't reentered the site within the past 20 minutes or a similar period. User session figures are sometimes used to indicate the number of visitors per day.

**VaporLink** A link within a site on the Internet is supposed to lead to more information (hypertext). A vaporlink is one that has become nonexistent and does not lead anywhere, a dead link.

**Virtual Community** A community of people sharing common interests, ideas, and feelings over the Internet or other collaborative networks.

**Virus, Viruses** A program (or programs) that, when executed, contaminates a user's hard drive, often with unwanted results (erases files, sends unauthorized e-mail from your machine, contaminates other documents, etc.).

**Visitor** Person who has accessed or visited your site.

**Web** The shorthand version of World Wide Web.

**WWW (World Wide Web)** The whole constellation of resources that can be accessed using Gopher, FTP, HTTP, Telnet, Usenet, WAIS, and some other tools. Also referred to as the universe of hypertext servers (HTTP servers), which are the servers that allow graphics, text, sound files, etc., to be mixed together.

# Appendix B

# Newsgroups

The following list of newsgroup categories is provided compliments of Lewis S. Eisen, Law and Technology Consultant, Ottawa, Ontario, Canada: *http://home.magmacom.com/~leisen/mlnh/mlnhtables.html.*

Each of these newsgroup categories has a number of subcategories. Each sub-category will have a number of sub-subcategories.

## A

| | |
|---|---|
| a2000. | Amsterdam 2000, Nederland (ISP) |
| ab. | Alberta, Canada |
| abingdon. | Abingdon, Oxon, UK |
| abq. | Albuquerque, New Mexico, USA |
| acadia. | Acadia University, Nova Scotia, Canada |
| acs. | University of Calgary computer science, Alberta, Canada |
| acs. | Ohio State University, USA |
| adass. | Astronomical Data & Archiving Systems & Software |
| ahn. | Athens-Clarke County, Georgia, USA |
| ak. | Alaska, USA |
| akr. | Akron, Ohio, USA |
| alabama. | Alabama, USA |
| alc. | Newsgroups discussing alcohol |
| algebra. | Discussions about algebra |
| algonet. | Algonet, Sverige (ISP) |

| | |
|---|---|
| alt. | Usenet alternative newsgroups |
| aol. | America Online, ISP |
| apana. | Australian Public Access Network Association |
| apc. | Association for Progressive Communications |
| apk. | APK Net, Ohio, USA (ISP) |
| ar. | Grupos de Argentina |
| arc. | NASA Ames Research Center, California, USA |
| argh. | ARGH network, Deutschland |
| arkane. | Arkane Systems, UK |
| aston. | Aston University, Birmingham, England |
| asu. | Arizona State University |
| at. | Oesterreich (Austria) |
| athena. | M.I.T., Cambridge, Massachusetts, USA |
| atl. | Atlanta, Georgia, USA |
| aus. | Australian and Australasian newsgroups |
| austin. | Austin, Texas, USA |
| auth. | Aristotle University of Thessaloniki, Greece |
| autodesk. | Autodesk Inc. corporate newsgroups |
| av. | Antelope Valley, California, USA |
| az. | Arizona, USA |

**B**

| | |
|---|---|
| ba. | San Francisco bay area, California, USA |
| backbone. | Prima e.V., Dortmund, Deutschland (ISP) |
| balt. | Baltimore, Maryland, USA |
| baynet. | Bayerische Bürgernetze, Deutschland |
| bburg. | Blacksburg, Virginia, USA |
| bc. | British Columbia, Canada |
| bcs. | Boston Computer Society, Massachusetts, USA |
| be. | Belgique/Belgïe/Belgien (Belgium) |
| bend. | Bend, Oregon, USA |
| bermuda. | Bermuda |
| best. | Best Internet Communications, California, USA |
| bhm. | Birmingham, Alabama, USA |
| bionet. | Biology Network |
| birmingham. | Birmingham, England |
| bison. | Manitoba, Canada |
| bit. | Originating from BITNET (IBM mainframe) |
| biz. | Usenet business newsgroups |
| blgtn. | Bloomington, Indiana, USA |

| | |
|---|---|
| bln. | Berlin, Germany |
| bnr. | Bell-Northern Research |
| bocaraton. | Boca Raton, Florida, USA |
| bochum. | Bochum, Deutschland |
| boston. | Boston, Massachusetts, USA |
| boulder. | Boulder, Colorado, USA |
| br. | Brasil |
| brasil. | Brasil |
| bremen. | Bremen, Deutschland |
| bremnet. | Bremen und Umgebung, Deutschland |
| brocku. | Brock University, Ontario, Canada |
| byu. | Brigham Young University, Utah, USA |

## C

| | |
|---|---|
| ca. | California, USA |
| cabot. | Cabot College, St. John's, Newfoundland, Canada |
| cais. | Capital Area, USA (ISP) |
| calgary. | Calgary, Alberta, Canada |
| calstate. | California State University, USA |
| caltech. | California Institute of Technology, USA |
| cam. | Cambridge area, England |
| can. | Canada |
| canb. | Canberra, Australia |
| capdist. | Albany (Capital District), New York, USA |
| carleton. | Carleton University, Ottawa, Ontario, Canada |
| cd-online. | CD-Online, Nederland (ISP) |
| central. | Internet Company of New Zealand (ISP) |
| centralor. | Central Oregon, USA |
| cern. | Cern, Geneva, Switzerland |
| ch. | Switzerland |
| chi. | Chicago, Illinois, USA |
| chile. | Chile |
| chinese. | China and Chinese-language newsgroups |
| christnet. | Christian Network |
| cid. | Cid, Berlin, Deutschland (ISP) |
| cis. | Cyberhalk Internet Services, USA |
| cisnet. | University of Malta, Computer Information Service, Malta |
| cityscp. | Cityscape Internet Services, UK (ISP) |
| cityweb. | Cityweb Network GmbH, Deutschland |
| cl. | CL-Netz (German-language newsgroups) |

| | |
|---|---|
| claranet. | Claranet, UK (ISP) |
| clari. | Clarinet News Service (commercial) |
| cle. | Cleveland, Ohio, USA |
| clinet. | Clinet, Finland (ISP) |
| cmc. | Chambers Multimedia Connection, Eugene, Oregon, USA (ISP) |
| cmh. | Columbus, Ohio, USA |
| cmu. | Carnegie Mellon University, USA |
| cna. | Chinese-language newsgroups |
| co. | Colorado, USA |
| comp. | Usenet computer newsgroups |
| compuserve. | CompuServe (ISP) |
| computer42. | Computer42, Deutschland (ISP) |
| concordia. | Concordia University, Québec, Canada |
| conn. | Connecticut, USA |
| cor. | Corvallis, Oregon, USA |
| cornell. | Cornell University |
| courts. | U.S. court decisions |
| cov. | City of Coventry, West Midlands, UK |
| covuni. | Coventry University, West Midlands, UK |
| cs. | University of British Columbia computer science, Canada |
| csn. | Colorado SuperNet, USA |
| cth. | Chalmers University of Technology, Göteborg, Sverige |
| cu. | University of Colorado, USA |
| cville. | Charlottesville, Virginia, and region, USA |
| cym. | Wales and Welsh newsgroups |
| cz. | Czech Republic newsgroups |

**D**

| | |
|---|---|
| dal. | Dalhousie University, Halifax, Nova Scotia, Canada |
| dc. | Washington, DC, USA |
| ddn. | Defense Data Network, USA |
| dds. | Dutch Freenet language groups |
| de. | International German-language newsgroups |
| delaware. | Delaware, USA |
| demon. | Newsgroups from the Demon network, UK |
| denver. | Denver, Colorado, USA |
| det. | Detroit, Michigan, USA |
| dfw. | DallasBFt. Worth, Texas, USA |
| dk. | Danmark (Denmark) |
| dod. | Department of Defense, USA |

| dortmund. | Dortmund, Deutschland |
| dsm. | Des Moines, Iowa, USA |
| dti. | Dream Train Internet Inc., Japan (ISP) |
| duke. | Duke University |
| dut. | Delft Institute of Technology, Nederland |

**E**

| easynet. | Easynet, UK (ISP) |
| ed. | Edinburgh, Scotland |
| edm. | Edmonton, Alberta, Canada |
| eduni. | Edinburgh University, Edinburgh, Scotland |
| ee. | Eesti (Estonia) |
| efn. | Eugene Free Computer Network, Eugene, Oregon, USA |
| es. | Grupos de España |
| esp. | Grupos en español |
| eug. | Eugene/Springfield, Oregon, USA |
| eunet. | European Networks |
| example. | Bogus hierarchy reserved for standards documents |
| execpc. | ExecPC Internet, New Berlin, Wisconsin, USA (ISP) |
| eye. | Eye WEEKLY Newspaper, Toronto, Ontario, Canada |

**F**

| ffo. | Frankfurt (Oder), Deutschland |
| fido. | Originating from Fidonet |
| fido7. | Russian-language Fidonet |
| finet. | Finland and Finnish-language alternative newsgroups |
| fj. | Japan and Japanese-language newsgroups |
| fl. | Florida, USA flora. FLORA Community Web, Ottawa, Ontario, Canada |
| fnal. | Fermi National Accelerator Laboratory, Illinois, USA |
| fnet. | Originating from Fnet (France) |
| fnord. | Fnord Discordian Network |
| fr. | International French-language newsgroups |
| francom. | Groupes de discussion en français |
| franken. | Franken, Deutschland |
| fras. | Freie Amiga Software (German Amiga binaries) |
| free. | Entirely unregulated newsgroups |
| freenet. | Groups originating from freenets |
| ftech. | Frontier Internet Services, UK (ISP) |
| furr. | Furrynet, USA |

**G**

| | |
|---|---|
| ga. | Georgia, USA |
| gay. | Gay and Lesbian newsgroups |
| gbg. | Göteborg, Sverige |
| geometry. | Discussions about geometry |
| ger. | GerNet, Deutschland (ISP) |
| git. | Georgia Institute of Technology, USA |
| gnu. | GNU operating system |
| gov. | Government information newsgroups |
| govonca. | Government of Ontario, Canada |
| greenend. | The Green End Organization, Cambridge, UK |
| grk. | Greece and Greek-language newsgroups |
| gruene. | Partei Die Grünen/Bündnis 90, Deutschland |
| gu. | University of Göteborg, Sverige |
| gwu. | George Washington University, Washington, DC, USA |

**H**

| | |
|---|---|
| hacktic. | Dutch/English hackers' newsgroups, Nederland |
| halcyon. | Halcyon Corporate newsgroups |
| hamburg. | Hamburg, Deutschland |
| hamilton. | Hamilton, Ontario, Canada |
| han. | Hangul-language newsgroups (Korean) |
| hannet. | Hannover, Deutschland |
| hannover. | Hannover, Deutschland |
| harvard. | Harvard University, Massachusetts, USA |
| hawaii-online. | Hawaii-Online (ISP) |
| hawaii. | Hawaii, USA |
| hebron. | Hebron, Israel |
| helsinki. | Helsinki, Finland |
| hepnet. | High-Energy Physics Network |
| hfx. | Halifax, Nova Scotia, Canada |
| hiv. | HIV-related issues |
| hk. | Hong Kong |
| hna. | Hunter Network Association, Australia (ISP) |
| hookup. | Hookup, Canada (ISP) |
| houston. | Houston, Texas, USA |
| hr. | Croatian newsgroups |
| hrnet. | Human Rights network |
| hsv. | Huntsville, Alabama, USA |

| | |
|---|---|
| hum. | Humber College, Etobicoke, Ontario, Canada |
| humanities. | Usenet discussions about Humanities |
| hun. | Magyarorszag (Hungarian newsgroups) |
| hy. | University of Helsinki, Finland |

### I

| | |
|---|---|
| ia. | Iowa, USA |
| iaf. | Internet Access Foundation, Nederland |
| ibm. | IBM-based newsgroups |
| ibmnet. | IBM Global Network |
| ic. | ICONSULT, Deutschland (ISP) |
| iconz. | Internet Company of New Zealand (ISP) |
| idirect. | I-Direct (ISP) |
| ie. | Ireland |
| ihug. | The Internet Group, New Zealand (ISP) |
| iij. | IIJ (ISP) |
| iijnet. | IIJ (ISP) |
| in. | Indiana, USA |
| infko. | Universitaet Koblenz, Deutschland |
| info. | Internet technical information |
| inforamp. | Inforamp, Canada (ISP) |
| intel. | Intel Corporation |
| interlog. | Interlog, Canada (ISP) |
| is. | Iceland and Icelandic newsgroups |
| israel. | Israel |
| it. | Italia |
| ithaca. | Ithaca, New York, USA |
| iu. | Indiana University, Indiana, USA |
| iupui. | Indiana University-Purdue University at Indianapolis, USA |
| ivm. | IVM GmbH, Deutschland (ISP) |

### J

| | |
|---|---|
| japan. | Japan and Japanese-language newsgroups |
| jaring. | Jaring network, Malaysia (ISP) |
| jerusalem. | Jerusalem / Y'rushalayim / al-Quds, Israel |
| jhu. | Johns Hopkins University, Baltimore MD, USA |
| jogu. | Johannes-Gutenberg-Universitaet Mainz, Deutschland |
| jusos. | JungsozialistInnen, Deutschland |

**K**

| | |
|---|---|
| k12. | International educational network |
| ka. | Karlsruhe, Deutschland |
| kanto. | Japanese-language newsgroups |
| kassel. | Region Kassel, Deutschland |
| kc. | Kansas City, Kansas/Missouri, USA |
| kennesaw. | Kennesaw State University, Georgia, USA |
| kiel. | Kiel, Deutschland |
| kingston. | Kingston, Ontario, Canada |
| knf. | Kommunikationsnetz Franken e.V., Deutschland |
| knox. | Knoxville and surrounding area, Tennessee, USA |
| koblenz. | Koblenz, Deutschland |
| ks. | Kansas, USA |
| ksu. | Kansas State University, USA |
| kth. | Royal Institute of Technology, Stockholm, Sverige |
| kun. | Katholieke Universiteit Nijmegen, Nederland |
| kw. | Kitchener-Waterloo, Ontario, Canada |
| ky. | Kentucky, USA |

**L**

| | |
|---|---|
| la. | Los Angeles, California, USA |
| laurentian. | Laurentian University, Sudbury, Ontario, Canada |
| leeds. | Leeds, England |
| li. | Long Island, New York, USA |
| life. | LifeNet Christian Network |
| lon. | London, England |
| lou. | Louisiana, USA |
| lspace. | Discussions about Terry Pratchett |
| lu. | Luxembourg newsgroups |
| luebeck. | Luebeck, Deutschland |
| lv. | Latvian newsgroups |

**M**

| | |
|---|---|
| malta. | Malta and Maltese newsgroups |
| man. | Manitoba, Canada |
| manawatu. | Manawatu district, New Zealand |
| maus. | Originating from MausNet (Deutschland) |
| mc. | Mississippi College, Clinton, Mississippi USA |
| mcgill. | McGill University, Montreal, Quebec, Canada |

| | |
|---|---|
| mcmaster. | McMaster University, Hamilton, Ontario, Canada |
| md. | Maryland, USA |
| me. | Maine, USA |
| medlux. | Russian-language medical newsgroups |
| melb. | Melbourne, Australia |
| melbpc. | Melbourne PC User Group, Australia |
| memphis. | Memphis, Tennessee, USA |
| mensa. | Discussions among members of Mensa |
| metocean. | Metocean, Japan (ISP) |
| metu. | Middle East Technical University, Ankara, Turkiye |
| mex. | Mexican newsgroups |
| mi. | Michigan, USA |
| miami. | Miami, Florida, USA |
| microsoft. | Microsoft newsgroups |
| midlands. | English midlands, UK |
| milw. | Milwaukee, Wisconsin, USA |
| misc. | Usenet miscellaneous newsgroups |
| mistral. | Brighton, England |
| mit. | Massachusetts Institute of Technology |
| mn. | Minnesota, USA |
| mo. | Missouri, USA |
| mod. | Moderated newsgroups |
| ms. | Mississippi, USA |
| mtl. | Montréal, Québec, Canada |
| mu. | Marquette University, Milwaukee, Wisconsin, USA |
| muc. | München, Deutschland |
| muenster. | Muenster, Deutschland |
| mun. | Memorial University, Newfoundland, Canada |
| mv. | MV Communications, Inc. (ISP) |
| mx. | México |

**N**

| | |
|---|---|
| nagasaki-u. | University of Nagasaki, Japan |
| nanaimo. | Nanaimo, British Columbia, Canada |
| nas. | NASA Numerical Aerospace Simulation Facility, USA |
| nasa. | National Aeronautics and Space Administration, USA |
| nashville. | Nashville, Tennessee, USA |
| nb. | New Brunswick, Canada |
| nbg. | Nuernberg, Deutschland |

| | |
|---|---|
| nc. | North Carolina, USA |
| ncar. | National Centre for Atmospheric Research, Colorado, USA |
| ncf. | National Capital Freenet, Ottawa, Ontario, Canada |
| ncle. | Newcastle (and Hunter Valley), Australia |
| ncsc. | North Carolina SuperComputing, USA |
| nctu. | National Chiao-Ting University, Taiwan |
| nd. | North Dakota, USA |
| ne. | New England area, USA |
| nebr. | Nebraska, USA net. Usenet II (usenet2.org) |
| netscape. | Netscape, Mountain View, California, USA |
| netz. | Originated by Netz e.V.,Deutschland |
| nevada. | Nevada, USA |
| neworleans. | New Orleans, Louisiana, USA |
| news. | Usenet news |
| newsguy. | Newsguy News Service |
| nf. | Newfoundland, Canada |
| nh. | New Hampshire, USA |
| ni. | Northern Ireland |
| niagara. | Niagara Peninsula, Canada/USA |
| nj. | New Jersey, USA |
| nl. | Nederland |
| nlnet. | Nlnet (ISP) |
| nm. | New Mexico, USA |
| no. | Norge (Norway) |
| nord. | Norddeutschland |
| nordunet. | Nordic National Research Network |
| north. | Weser-Ems Region, Deutschland |
| northwest. | Northwest region of England, UK |
| nrw. | NordrheinBWestfalen, Deutschland |
| ns. | Nova Scotia, Canada |
| ntua. | National Technical University of Athens, Greece |
| nu. | Newcastle University, Australia |
| nv. | Nevada, USA |
| nwt. | Northwest Territories, Canada |
| nwu. | Northwestern University, Illinois, USA |
| ny. | New York State, USA |
| nyc. | New York City, New York, USA |
| nyu. | New York University, USA |
| nz. | New Zealand |

## O

| | |
|---|---|
| oau. | Orlando, Florida, USA |
| oc. | Orange County, California, USA |
| oecher. | Aachen, Deutschland |
| oerebro. | Örebro, Närke, Sverige |
| ogi. | Oregon Graduate Institute, USA |
| oh. | Ohio, USA |
| ok. | Oklahoma, USA |
| okinawa. | Okinawan newsgroups |
| oldenburg. | Oldenburg, Deutschland |
| olnet. | Oldenburg und Umgebung, Deutschland |
| on. | Offenes Netz Luebeck, Deutschland |
| online. | Telenor Online, Oslo, Norge (ISP) |
| ont. | Ontario, Canada |
| or. | Oregon, USA |
| osu. | Ohio State University, USA |
| ott. | Ottawa, Ontario, Canada |
| owl. | Ostwestfalen-Lippe, Deutschland |
| own. | One World Net |
| ox. | Oxford University, UK |

## P

| | |
|---|---|
| pa. | Pennsylvania, USA |
| pb. | Der Fahrgastverband PRO BAHN, Deutschland |
| pdaxs. | Portland Metronet, Oregon, USA |
| pdx. | Portland, Oregon, USA |
| pei. | Prince Edward Island, Canada |
| peru. | Groupos del Peru |
| pgh. | Pittsburgh, Pennsylvania, USA |
| phil-priv. | The Philippines and Filipino newsgroups |
| phl. | Philadelphia, Pennsylvania, USA |
| phoenix. | Phoenix, Arizona, USA |
| phx. | Phoenix, Arizona, USA |
| pi. | Planet Internet, Nederland (ISP) |
| pinnacle. | Pinnacle, UK (ISP) |
| pipex. | Pipex (ISP) |
| pitt. | University of Pittsburgh, Pennsylvania, USA |
| pl. | Polska (Polish-language newsgroups) |
| planet. | PlaNet FreeNZ co-operative, New Zealand |

| | |
|---|---|
| pnw. | Pacific North-West (USA/Canada) |
| prima. | Prima e.V., Dortmund, Deutschland (ISP) |
| princeton. | Princeton area, New Jersey, USA |
| prodigy. | Prodigy (ISP) |
| ps. | People of Scandinavia (ISP) |
| psi. | PSINet (ISP) |
| psu. | Pennsylvania State University, USA |
| pt. | Portugal and Portuguese newsgroups |
| pu. | Princeton University, New Jersey, USA |
| purdue. | Purdue University |

**Q**

| | |
|---|---|
| qc. | Quebec, Canada |
| queens. | Queens University, Kingston, Ontario, Canada |

**R**

| | |
|---|---|
| rabbit. | Rabbit Network (ISP) |
| rain. | RAINnet (ISP) |
| realtynet. | Real estate network |
| rec. | Usenet recreational newsgroups |
| redhat. | Red Hat Software, North Carolina, USA |
| region. | Mittlehessen, Deutschland |
| relcom. | Relcom, Commonwealth of Independent States (ISP) (Cyrillic) |
| rg. | Rio Grande Valley, New Mexico/Texas, USA |
| rhein. | Rhein area (Cologne and Bonn), Germany |
| ri. | Rhode Island, USA |
| rmii. | Rocky Mountain Internet (ISP) |
| roanoke. | Roanoke, Virginia, USA |
| ru. | Rutgers University, New Jersey, USA |
| ruhr. | Ruhrgebiet, Deutschland |
| rv. | Rogue Valley, Oregon, USA |
| rwth. | Rheinisch-Westfälische Technische Hochschule, Deutschland |
| rye. | Ryerson University, Toronto, Ontario, Canada |

**S**

| | |
|---|---|
| saar. | Saarbruecken, Deutschland |
| sac. | Sacramento, California, USA |
| sackheads. | Sysadmins with too much time on their hands |
| sacramento. | Sacramento, California, USA |
| sae. | World Council of Hellenes Abroad, Greek language |

| | |
|---|---|
| salford. | University of Salford, UK |
| sanet. | SAnet (South Africa) |
| sat. | San Antonio, Texas, USA |
| sba. | Santa Barbara, California, USA |
| sbay. | South Bay region, San Francisco, California, USA |
| schl. | Newsgroup echo of KidLink mailing lists |
| schule. | German-language school newsgroups |
| sci. | Usenet science newsgroups |
| scot. | Scotland and Scottish newsgroups |
| scruz. | Santa Cruz, California, USA |
| sd. | South Dakota, USA |
| sdnet. | San Diego, California, USA |
| sdsu. | San Diego State University, California, USA |
| se. | Sverige (Sweden) |
| sea. | Seattle, Washington, USA |
| seattle. | Seattle, Washington, USA |
| sfnet. | SuomiBFinland, Finland and Finnish-language newsgroups |
| sfu. | Simon Fraser University, British Columbia, Canada |
| sg. | Singapore |
| sgi. | Silicon Graphics, Inc. |
| shamash. | Jewish newsgroups |
| si. | Slovenian newsgroups |
| simcoe. | Simcoe County, Ontario, Canada |
| sj. | Saint John's, Newfoundland, Canada |
| sk. | Saskatchewan, Canada |
| sk. | Slovakian newsgroups |
| slac. | Stanford Linear Accelerator Center, USA |
| slo. | San Luis Obispo, California, USA |
| slonet. | SLONET (ISP) |
| snafu. | Snafu, Deutschland (ISP) |
| soc. | Usenet social issues newsgroups |
| socs. | McGill University School of Computer Science, Quebec, Canada |
| sol. | sol.net Network Services, Milwaukee, Wisconsin, USA |
| solent. | Solent, UK (ISP) |
| solinet. | Gewerkschaftliche Themen (German trade unions) |
| sonoma. | Sonoma County, California, USA |
| south-wales. | Southern Wales and Welsh newsgroups, UK |
| spk. | Spokane, Washington, USA |
| spokane. | Spokane, Washington, USA |

| | |
|---|---|
| srg. | Swiss Broadcasting Corporation |
| srjc. | Santa Rosa Junior College, California, USA |
| stgt. | Stuttgart, Deutschland |
| stl. | St. Louis, Missouri, USA |
| stmarys. | St. Mary's University, Nova Scotia, Canada |
| su. | Stanford University |
| sudbury. | Sudbury, Ontario, Canada |
| sunet. | Swedish University Network, Sverige |
| surfnet. | Dutch university newsgroups, Nederland |
| swipnet. | Swipnet Tele/2, Sverige (ISP) |
| swnet. | Sverige (Sweden) |
| syd. | Sydney, New South Wales, Australia |

**T**

| | |
|---|---|
| t-online. | T-Online, Deutschland (ISP) |
| tacoma. | Tacoma, Washington, USA |
| talk. | Usenet talk newsgroups |
| tamu. | Texas A & M University, USA |
| taos. | Taos, New Mexico, USA |
| tba. | Tampa Bay, Florida, USA |
| tct. | Discussions about Therianthropy |
| tdw. | Tidewater, Virginia, USA |
| tele. | Tele Danmark Internet (ISP) |
| terranova. | Terra Nova Visuals, Finland |
| thur. | Thuringia, Deutschland |
| tin. | TIN, Italia (ISP) |
| tip. | The Internet Plaza, Nederland (ISP) |
| tipnet. | Telia, Sverige (ISP) |
| tn. | Tennessee, USA |
| tnn. | The Network News (Japanese) |
| tor. | Toronto, Ontario, Canada |
| torfree. | Toronto Freenet, Ontario, Canada |
| toulouse. | Toulouse, France |
| tp. | Toppoint, Kiel, Deutschland |
| tr. | Turkiye and Turkish-language groups |
| trentu. | Trent University, Ontario, Canada |
| triangle. | Research Triangle Park, North Carolina, USA |
| trumpet. | Discussions of Trumpet programs |
| tulsa. | Tulsa, Oklahoma, USA |

| | |
|---|---|
| tvontario. | TVOntario, Ontario, Canada |
| tw. | Taiwan |
| tx. | Texas, USA |

**U**

| | |
|---|---|
| u3b. | Discussions on AT&T 3B systems |
| ualberta. | University of Alberta, Canada |
| uark. | University of Arkansas, USA |
| ubc. | University of British Columbia, Canada |
| uc. | University of California, USA |
| ucalgary. | University of Calgary, Alberta, Canada |
| ucam. | University of Cambridge, UK |
| ucb. | University of California at Berkeley, USA |
| ucd. | University of California, Davis, USA |
| ucsb. | University of California at Santa Barbara, USA |
| ucsc. | University of California at Santa Cruz, USA |
| udes. | Université de Sherbrooke, Québec, Canada |
| uf. | University of Florida, USA |
| ufra. | Unterfranken, Deutschland |
| uiowa. | University of Iowa, USA |
| uiuc. | University of Illinois, UrbanaBChampaign, USA |
| uk. | United Kingdom |
| ukc. | University of Kent at Canterbury, UK |
| ukr. | Ukraine and Ukranian-language newsgroups |
| uky. | University of Kentucky, USA |
| ulaval. | Université Laval, Québec, Canada |
| um. | University of Maryland, USA |
| umiami. | University of Miami, Florida, USA |
| umich. | University of Michigan, USA |
| umn. | University of Minnesota, USA |
| umoncton. | University of Moncton, New Brunswick, Canada |
| umontreal. | Université de Montréal, Québec, Canada |
| unb. | University of New Brunswick, Canada |
| unc. | University of North Carolina at Chapel Hill, USA |
| unisa. | University of South Australia, Adelaide, Australia. |
| uo. | University of Oregon, USA |
| uoc. | University of Canterbury, Christchurch, New Zealand |
| upenn. | University of Pennsylvania, USA |
| uqam. | Université de Québec à Montréal, Canada |

| | |
|---|---|
| us. | United States |
| usask. | University of Saskatchewan, Canada |
| usf. | University of South Florida, USA |
| usu. | Utah State University, USA |
| usyd. | University of Sydney, New South Wales, Australia |
| ut. | University of Toronto, Ontario, Canada |
| utah. | Utah, USA |
| utcs. | University of Texas, Computer Science, USA |
| utk. | University of Tennessee, Knoxville, USA |
| utexas. | University of Texas, USA |
| uunet. | Originating from UUNet (UNIX) |
| uva. | University of Virgina, USA |
| uvic. | University of Victoria, British Columbia, Canada |
| uw. | University of Waterloo, Ontario, Canada |
| uwa. | University of Washington, USA |
| uwarwick. | University of Warwick, UK |
| uwash. | University of Washington, USA |
| uwindsor. | University of Windsor, Ontario, Canada |
| uwisc. | University of Wisconsin, Madison, USA |
| uwm. | University of Wisconsin, Milwaukee, USA |
| uwo. | University of Western Ontario, London, Canada |

**V**

| | |
|---|---|
| va. | Virginia, USA |
| van. | Vancouver, British Columbia, Canada |
| vatech. | Virginia Polytechnic Institute and State University, USA |
| vechta. | Universitaet Vechta, Niedersachsen, Deutschland |
| vegas. | Las Vegas, Nevada, USA |
| vic. | Victoria, British Columbia, Canada |
| vmsnet. | Originating from Digital VAX network |
| vol. | Telecom Italia Video On Line (ISP) |
| vpro. | VPRO TV-station newsgroups, Nederland |
| vt. | Vermont, USA |
| vu. | Vanderbilt University |

**W**

| | |
|---|---|
| wa. | Western Australia |
| wales. | Wales |
| wash. | Washington, USA |
| west-virginia. | West Virginia, USA |

| | |
|---|---|
| westf. | Westfalen, Deutschland |
| wi. | Wisconsin, USA |
| wimsey. | Wimsey, British Columia, Canada (ISP) |
| witten. | Witten, Deutschland |
| wlu. | Wilfred Laurier University, Waterloo, Ontario, Canada |
| wny. | Western New York, USA |
| worldnet. | AT&T Worldnet |
| worldonline. | World Online, Nederland (ISP) |
| wpi. | Worcester Polytechnic Institute, Massachusetts, USA |
| wpg. | Winnipeg, Manitoba, Canada |
| wxs. | World Access/Planet Internet, Nederland (ISP) |
| wyo. | Wyoming, USA |

**X**

| | |
|---|---|
| xs4all. | Xs4all, Nederland (ISP) |

**Y**

| | |
|---|---|
| yakima. | Yakima, Washington, USA |
| yale. | Yale University, Connecticut, USA |
| yk. | Yellowknife, Northwest Territories, Canada |
| yfn. | Youngstown, Ohio Free-Net, USA |
| yolo. | Yolo County, California, USA |
| york. | York University, Ontario, Canada |
| ysu. | Youngstown State University, Ohio, USA |

**Z**

| | |
|---|---|
| z-netz. | Originating from Z-Netz (German newsgroups) |
| za. | South Africa and Afrikaans newsgroups |
| zipnews. | Zippo's News Services (commercial) |

*© 1999 Lewis S. Eisen. Reproduction in whole or in part is permitted so long as original author is duly credited.*

# Appendix C

# Search Engines

## The Most Popular Search Engines

The algorithms the major search engines use to determine your site's ranking and the information reference to index your site change quite often, so what may hold true today may not hold true tomorrow. I recommend visiting the respective search engines before you submit and reviewing any material available in regard to site submissions. Many search engines have information on their submission pages, on help pages, and sometimes on a submission tips page. You can also check out various sites on the Internet that offer submission tips and tricks for the major search engines, some of which are included within Chapters 3 and 4 of this book. Two of my favorites are Search Engine Watch *(http://www.searchenginewatch.com)* and Search Engine World *(http://www.searchengineworld.com)*.

### AltaVista
**Site Address:** *http://www.altavista.com/*
**Submission Address:** *http://www.altavista.com/cgi-bin/query?pg =addurl* or click on "Add a URL" from AltaVista's home page.

AltaVista went live in December 1995. In August 1999, CMGI, Inc. acquired 83% of AltaVista's outstanding stock from Compaq. As well, Shopping.com and Zip2 became wholly owned subsidiaries. AltaVista consists of multiple platforms: AltaVista Search, AltaVista Live, AltaVista's Shopping.com, and AltaVista Local Portal Services.

**Pages (millions):** 250
**Meta tag support:** Yes
**Index body text:** Yes
**Frames support:** Yes
**Image maps:** Yes
**Alt text:** Yes
**Link popularity affects position:** Yes
**Keywords in title important:** Yes
**Higher rankings for reviewed sites:** No
**Case sensitive:** Yes
**Title:** Page title; if none, "No Title"
**Description:** Meta tag or first text on page
**Time to index submissions:** 24-48 hours
**Type:** Spider, Scooter
**Tips:** AltaVista likes keywords that are located near the top of your page, so use descriptive keywords where possible. Keywords used in the title of your page also seems to influence page rankings.

### Excite

**Site Address:** *http://www.excite.com/*
**Submission Address:** *http://www.excite.com/info/add_url* or click on "Add URL" from Excite's home page.
Has been around since 1995. Excite bought out WebCrawler in 1996. These acquisitions are still independently operated.
**Pages (millions):** 150
**Meta tag support:** Yes
**Index body text:** Yes
**Frames support:** No
**Image maps:** No
**Alt text:** No
**Link popularity affects position:** Yes
**Keywords in title important:** Yes
**Higher rankings for reviewed sites:** No
**Case sensitive:** No

**Title:** Page title; if none, "Untitled"
**Description:** The few most dominant sentences on your page
**Time to index submissions:** 2-3 weeks
**Type:** Spider, Architext
**Tips:** Make the first 100 characters of your page as descriptive as possible. Excite will try to make the description from the text at the start of your page, but will keep going until it is satisfied that it has enough descriptive sentences. Your sentences must be complete for Excite to use them in forming your description. This does not necessarily mean that uncompleted sentences at the beginning of your page will not be used. Excite would just rather use complete sentences.

### Go/Infoseek

**Site Address:** *http://infoseek.go.com/*
**Submission Address:** *http://www.go.com/AddUrl?pg=SubmitUrl.html* or click on "Add URL" from Infoseek's home page.
InfoSeek has been online since 1995. It is a very well-known search engine. InfoSeek also manages a directory separate from its search engine. Sites are listed categorically, and some are even reviewed and recommended by InfoSeek.
**Pages (millions):** 75
**Meta tag support:** Yes
**Index body text:** Yes
**Frames support:** No
**Image maps:** Yes
**Alt text:** Yes
**Link popularity affects position:** Yes
**Keywords in title important:** Yes
**Higher rankings for reviewed sites:** Yes
**Case sensitive:** Yes
**Title:** Page title; if none lists the first line on page
**Description:** The meta tag; if none, first 200 characters in body of page
**Time to index submissions:** 1-7 days
**Type:** Spider, Sidewinder
**Tips:** Use the Alt attribute because Infoseek will include these in your description. This is especially helpful for sites that are mainly graphical in content. Never use keywords that do not relate to the content of your site. Infoseek punishes those who do with lower rankings.

**Google**
Site Address: *http://www.google.com/*
Submission Address: *http://www.google.com/addurl.html* or click on "Add your URL" from Google's About page.
Google was founded in 1998 by Larry Page and Sergey Brin and has quickly become a very popular search tool on the Web.
Pages (millions): 70B100
Meta tag support: No
Index body text: Yes
Frames support: Yes
Image maps: No
Alt text: No
Link popularity affects position: Yes
Keywords in title important: Yes
Higher rankings for reviewed sites: No
Case sensitive: No
Title: Page title; if none, URL
Description: First text found on page, including hypertext links
Type: Spider, Googlebot
Tips: Keywords in your domain name and link popularity will really help you out with Google. To increase your link popularity, get other sites to link to you, and consider reciprocal links to other sites.

**HotBot**
Site Address: *http://www.hotbot.com/*
Submission Address: *http://hotbot.lycos.com/addurl.asp* or click on "Add URL" from HotBot's home page.
HotBot was launched in 1996. HotBot uses Inktomi's search engine technology.
Pages (millions): 110
Meta tag support: Yes
Index body text: Yes
Frames support: No
Image maps: No
Alt text: No
Link popularity affects position: Yes, HotBot uses DirectHit.
Keywords in title important: Yes
Higher rankings for reviewed sites: No
Case sensitive: Mixed
Title: Page title; if none, lists URL

**Description:** Meta tag; if none, uses approximately the first 240 to 250 characters in the body of your page
**Time to index submissions:** 48 hours
**Type:** Uses Inktomi's Spider
**Tips:** If you do a search and feel your site is not positioned correctly in the search results, then you can let the people at HotBot know about it. Send all the relevant information to *bugs@hotbot.com.*

**Lycos**
**Site Address:** *http://www.lycos.com/*
**Submission Address:** *http://www.lycos.com/addasite.html* or by clicking on "Add Your Site to Lycos" from their home page.
Lycos went online in 1994. Lycos is a well-recognized spider.
**Pages (millions):** 50
**Meta tag support:** No
**Index body text:** Yes
**Frames support:** Limited support
**Image maps:** No
**Alt text:** Yes
**Link popularity affects position:** No
**Keywords in title important:** Yes
**Higher rankings for reviewed sites:** No
**Case sensitive:** No
**Title:** Page title; if none, URL
**Description:** A snippet of the page that has been determined to represent it
**Time to index submissions:** 2 weeks
**Type:** T-Rex
**Tips:** Don't have an image map at the beginning of your page because Lycos will be unable to interpret it.

**NorthernLight**
**Site Address:** *http://www.northernlight.com/*
**Submission Address:** *http://www.northernlight.com/docs/regurl_help.html* or click on "Register URL" from NorthernLight's home page.
NorthernLight started in September of 1995. Their Web results are combined with information from premium material, giving you access to books, magazines, databases, and newswires.
**Pages (millions):** 189

**Meta tag support:** No
**Index body text:** Yes
**Frames support:** Yes
**Image maps:** Yes
**Alt text:** No
**Link popularity affects position:** No
**Keywords in title important:** Yes
**Higher rankings for reviewed sites:** No
**Case sensitive:** Modified sensitivity
**Title:** Page title
**Description:** Approximately the first 25 words of the page body
**Time to index submissions:** 2 weeks
**Type:** Spider, Gulliver
**Tips:** Submit only *one* of your pages to NorthernLight; let their spider find the remaining pages on your site.

**WebCrawler**
**Site Address:** *http://www.webcrawler.com/*
**Submission Address:** *http://www.webcrawler.com/info/add_url/* or click on "Add your URL" from their home page.
WebCrawler has been around since 1994 and has since been purchased twice. It is now owned by Excite, but is still operated independently.
**Pages (millions):** 2
**Meta tag support:** Yes
**Index body text:** Yes
**Frames support:** No
**Image maps:** Yes
**Alt text:** No
**Link popularity affects position:** Yes
**Keywords in title important:** Yes
**Higher rankings for reviewed sites:** Yes
**Case sensitive:** No
**Title:** Page title; if none, lists URL
**Description:** Meta tag; if none, looks at first textual information body of page
**Time to index submissions:** 2-3 weeks
**Type:** Uses Excite's Spider
**Tips:** Use of keywords in your page titles, descriptions meta tag, keywords meta tag, and in content near the top of your page all influence your ranking with WebCrawler.

### Yahoo!

**Site Address:** *http://www.yahoo.com/*

**Submission Address:** To submit to Yahoo! you must visit their site, find an appropriate category that relates to your page, and then click on "Suggest a Site."

Established in 1994, Yahoo! is a well-recognized directory. It is the largest of its kind and is the most popular with Internet users. Yahoo! is a directory, but it does not read pages on the net like the other search engines discussed here. To have your site added to Yahoo!, you must fill out a submit form on the site. You must register your site in a category and your site is checked by employees to verify that it matches the category you have chosen. If your site is commercial in any way, you must register it in a subcategory of Business and Economy.

**Pages (millions):** 1.2+

**Time to index submissions:** 6-8 weeks

**Tips:** Yahoo! gives higher rankings to sites that are reviewed. When submitting pages submit your base URL, (e.g., *http://www.yourdomain.com/* ), because this stands a greater chance of being indexed by Yahoo!. Take your time to find the most appropriate subcategories for your site and be sure to fill out their submission form completely and accurately. Yahoo! is very picky about who they add to their directory.

## Other Search Engines and Directories

### 555-1212.com

**Site Address:** *http://www.555-1212.com*

**Submission Address:** *http://www.infospace.com/info.go555/ submit.htm*

In addition to area code lookup, you can shop online, find businesses near you, get your friends' telephone numbers and e-mail addresses, browse classified ads, and much more.

### AOL.com Search

**Site Address:** *http://search.aol.com/*

**Submission Address:** *http://search.aol.com/add.adp*

This is AOL's search engine. It once ran off of the Excite engine but now uses the DMOZ.org directory. Submit to DMOZ.org, and AOL Netfind will also list your site.

### Ask Jeeves!
**Site Address:** *http://www.askjeeves.com*
**Submission Address:** *N/A*
Ask Jeeves accepts fully worded questions and crawls through search directories, engines, and meta-directories until an answer is found. You cannot submit a site directly to Ask Jeeves.

### BigStuff.com
**Site Address:** *http://www.bigstuff.com/*
**Submission Address:** *http://www.bigstuff.com/add.htm*

### The Biz
**Site Address:** *http://www.thebiz.co.uk*
**Submission Address:** *http://www.thebiz.co.uk/default.asp?page= submit&listby=all*
The Business Information Zone has been developed for users seeking UK-relevant business information, products, and services on the Internet, whether users are in the United Kingdom or overseas.

### BizWeb
**Site Address:** *http://www.bizweb.com*
**Submission Address:** *http://www.bizweb.com/InfoForm/*
BizWeb is a Web business guide to 43,165 companies listed in 194 categories.

### Cyber411
**Site Address:** *http://www.cyber411.com*
**Submission Address:** *N/A*
Cyber411 obtains its search results from multiple search engines. You cannot submit a site to it directly.

### Direct Hit
**Site Address:** *http://www.directhit.com*
**Submission Address:** *http://www.directhit.com/util/addurl.html*
Direct Hit is a relatively new search engine that bases its search criteria on page popularity.

### DMOZ Open Directory Project
**Site Address:** *http://www.dmoz.org*
**Submission Address:** *http://www.dmoz.org/add.html*

DMOZ is a directory in which actual humans review your site's content to determine whether or not it meets their standards. Many major search engines including AOL Netfind and AltaVista incorporate the DMOZ directory listings into their own search results.

### Dogpile
**Site Address:** *http://www.dogpile.com*
**Submission Address:** *N/A*
Dogpile obtains its search results from multiple search engines. You cannot submit a site to it directly.

### FAST Search
**Site Address:** *http://www.alltheweb.com*
**Submission Address:** *http://www.alltheweb.com/addurl.html*
FAST Search currently indexes more than 200 million Web documents with the eventual goal of indexing 1 billion.

### GoTo.com
**Site Address:** *http://www.goto.com*
**Submission Address:** *http://www.goto.com/d/about/advertisers/*
GoTo is the one of the fastest, easiest, most relevant search engines on the Web, as well as the small advertiser's best friend. You select the search terms that are relevant to your site. Then you determine how much you are willing to pay on a per-click basis for each of those search terms. The higher your "bid," the higher in the search results your site appears. It's targeted, cost-per-click advertising and you set the cost per click.

### iAtlas
**Site Address:** *http://www.iatlas.com*
**Submission Address:** *http://www.iatlas.com/ash/registry/*
A business-related search engine

### Internet Promotions MegaList
**Site Address:** *http://www.2020tech.com*
**Submission Address:** *http://www.2020tech.com/submit.html*
20/20 Technologies is a one-stop Internet advertising solution. Their services include Web page design, Internet research, and Internet promotions. The submission URL lists dozens of useful search engine submission resources.

### ICQ iT!
Site Address: *http://www.icqit.com*
Submission Address: *http://search.icq.com/default.asp?act.addurl=addurl*
Submit your site to one of the largest chat networks on the Internet.

### Keyword.com
Site Address: *http://www.keyword.com*
Submission Address: Visit the site and enter a keyword.
This is a free service that allows you to "reserve" a keyword and have searches for a keyword directed immediately to your site. Only one keyword can be reserved per site. Your Internet keyword will remain active as long it is entered a minimum of six times every 60 days.

### Linkcentre Directory
Site Address: *http://linkcentre.com*
Submission Address: *http://linkcentre.com/addurl.html*
Search the Linkcentre Directory or add your Web page immediately for greater exposure on the Internet.

### LinkMaster
Site Address: *http://www.linkmaster.com*
Submission Address: *http://www.linkmaster.com/register.html*

### LookSmart
Site Address: *http://www.looksmart.com*
Submission Address: *http://www.looksmart.com/aboutus/partners/subsite2.html*
LookSmart is a large, selective Internet search directory. Many engines, including MSN Search, currently use it to determine their own search results.

### Manufacturers Information Net
Site Address: *http://mfginfo.com*
Submission Address: *http://mfginfo.com/htm/infoform.htm*
This site provides a complete source of information for industry and those services related to manufacturing. Use the search engine to locate information on manufacturers, suppliers, profes-

sional services, and many more resources on and off this Web site.

### MasterSite
**Site Address:** *http://mastersite.com*
**Submission Address:** *http://mastersite.com/addurl.htm*

### McKinley's Internet Directory
**Site Address:** *http://www.mckinley.com*
**Submission Address:** *http://magellan.excite.com/info/add_url/*
Magellan's technology offers a unique way to search the Web: by concept. Like most search engines, this one is programmed to look for documents containing the exact words you entered into the query box, but Magellan goes further and looks for ideas closely linked to the words in your query. This feature broadens your search.

### Metacrawler
**Site Address:** *http://www.metacrawler.com*
**Submission Address:** *N/A*
Metacrawler obtains its search results from multiple search engines. You cannot submit a site to it directly.

### MSN Search
**Site Address:** *http://search.msn.com*
**Submission Address:** *http://search.msn.com/addurl.asp*
This is Microsoft's entry into the search engine fray. You can submit one URL per day to their engine.

### NationalDirectory
**Site Address:** *http://www.nationaldirectory.com*
**Submission Address:** *http://www.nationaldirectory.com/addurl.html*
Claims to be the "least spammed" search directory on the World Wide Web.

### Nerd World
**Site Address:** *http://www.nerdworld.com*
**Submission Address:** *http://www.nerdworld.com/nwadd.html*
Nerd World's most prominent feature is their search engine and subject index.

### Netscape Search
Site Address: *http://search.netscape.com*
Submission Address: *http://home.netscape.com/netcenter/smallbusiness/onlineessentials/addsite.html*
Netscape, maker of one of the world's best-known browsers, also has its own search/portal site.

### SavvySearch
Site Address: *http://www.savvysearch.com*
Submission Address: *N/A*
SavvySearch obtains its search results from multiple search engines. You cannot submit a site to it directly.

### SiteExplorer
Site Address: *http://www.sitexplorer.com*
Submission Address: *http://www.sitexplorer.com/add.html*
Another search engine to add your site to.

### Small Business
Site Address: *http://www.bizoffice.com*
Submission Address: *http://www.bizoffice.com/submit.html*
Small and home-based business links. Hundreds of links to quality sites.

### Snap
Site Address: *http://www.snap.com*
Submission Address: *http://www.snap.com/LMOID/resource/0,566,-1077,00.html?st.sn.ld.0.1077*
A human-compiled directory that also supplements its results with Inktomi's database.

### Trade Wave Galaxy
Site Address: *http://www.einet.net/galaxy.html*
Submission Address: *http://www.einet.net/cgi-bin/annotate?/galaxy*
Galaxy is known as the professional's guide to a world of information.

# Appendix D

# Internet Marketing Resources

Internet Resources for each topic covered in the book are located at the end of each chapter. Here, additionally, we have included a number of great Internet marketing resource sites.

### A1 WWW Promotion Sites
*http://www.a1co.com*
Excellent resource for locating hundreds of directories, indexes, and catalogs that will list your site for free. Also has a handy tool for locating large e-zine sites.

### Al Czarnecki Communications
*http://www.web.net/alcom*
A communications site with tips and resources to help you build important relationships, public relations, social marketing, and fund raising.

### Adbility.com: Adbility's Web Publishers' Advertising Guide
*http://www.adbility.com/WPAG/*
Adbility's Web Publishers' Advertising Guide contains hundreds of listings, with directory pages categorized into subsections and subpages related to Web site promotion.

### Advertising Age's Business Marketing Online
*http://www.netb2b.com/*
Offers business-to-business marketers educational information on creating and running a Web site including case studies and how-to articles.

### Ad Resource: Internet Advertising and Web Site Promotion Resources
*http://adres.internet.com/*
Ad Resource features information on Internet advertising and Web site promotion that helps individuals understand the World Wide Web and e-mail advertising, and attract visitors to their site.

### BizGold
*http://www.bizgold.com/*
Resources for home-based businesses, small businesses, and entrepreneurs to help succeed on the Internet in making money and establishing an online presence.

### ChannelSeven.com
*http://www.channelseven.com/*
Internet advertising and marketing campaign news. A great resource for builders, advertisers, and marketers of Internet businesses.

### ClickZ Network
*http://www.clickz.com/*
All kinds of articles related to advertising and business.

### CNET.com B Web Building
*http://www.builder.com/*
Just about everything you need to know surrounding Web site design and construction.

### Connex Network Incorporated
*http://www.connexnetwork.com*
Connex Network provides consulting services to companies interested in marketing on the Internet. Their Web Site Report Card reviews your site against 50 criteria and provides feedback to assist you in improving your site from a marketing perspective. Their Internet marketing strategies are prepared specifically for your company

with your objectives, your products and services, and your target customers in mind. Connex also delivers general and company-specific Internet Marketing Workshops. Connex Network Incorporated is owned by the author of this book.

### CyberAtlas
*http://cyberatlas.internet.com/*
Internet statistics and market research for Web marketers.

### CyberPulse
*http://www.cyberpulse.com*
Bob and Varda Novick know their stuff when it comes to online marketing. Excellent resource area covering mailing lists, newsgroups, advertising, promotion, etc. Don't let the plain graphics fool you.

### Deadlock Dispatch
*http://www.deadlock.com/promote*
If you're really serious about your promotion campaign, there's a whole new world of in-depth articles and really clever online marketing strategies one mouse-click away.

### Directory of Ezines
*http://www.lifestylespub.com/cgi-bin/ezines.cgi?10166*
Lifestyles is the presenter of The Directory of Ezines, a well-researched, up-to-date list of internet newsletters that accept classified advertising. Each listing within The Directory of Ezines tells you everything you need to know about advertising in a specific newsletter.

### eBoz! Your Guide to Creating Successful Websites
*http://www.eboz.com/*
A resource for information pertaining to Internet marketing and direct marketing.

### DrNunley.com
*http://drnunley.com/*
Tips on marketing, advertising, on-line marketing, and the Internet.

### E Weekly
*http://www.eweekly.com*
An online newsletter that contains articles on small business and

Internet commerce and marketing. Back issues are also available. There are a number of connections to projects of the sponsor, Cyber Media.

### Gator's Bite
*http://www.gators-byte.com*
A weekly column dedicated to helping your potential customers find your site and keep coming back! You can join the Gator's mailing list that sends you the weekly information. Check out past articles as well.

### InfoJump B The Magazine & Newspaper Article Search Engine
*http://www.infojump.com/*
Over 4000 online publications and over 5 million articles from on-line magazines, newspapers, journals, newsletters, and e-zines. If you plan to publish an e-mail newsletter, be sure to get it listed here.

### Information City: Web Tools and Internet Software
*http://www.freereports.net/*
Help for the new or experienced Web master. Variety of free tools and resources, resell products, and information on search engines.

### InfoScavenger
*http://www.infoscavenger.com/engine.htm*
This site provides an annotated hotlist of resources to help you get your Web page to appear at the top of the list when someone uses AltaVista, InfoSeek, or other engines to find you. This Web site has a nice, specific mission.

### Internet Business Webliography
*http://www.lib.lsu.edu/bus/marketin.html#Internet*
Links to information related to the Internet, business on the Internet, and marketing online. This site also contains many links to other sites containing marketing related information.

### Internet Marketing Center
*http://www.marketingtips.com/main.html*
All kinds of tips, strategies, and secrets for Internet marketing, online advertising, and Web site promotion. There is also a newsletter you can sign up for.

### Internet World: The Voice of E-Business and Internet Technology
*http://www.internetworld.com/*
Magazine containing Internet news, marketing, management, infrastructure, ISP marketing, and e-commerce development.

### Marketing SuperSite
*http://www.ntu.edu.sg/library/int-mktg.htm* and *http://www.ntu.edu.sg/library/ecomm.htm*
This resource list from the National Technology University in Singapore is almost too big. Contains links to a massive number of articles and Web sites concerned with promotion, marketing, and commerce on the Internet.

### Meta Tag Builder
*http://www.MetaTagBuilder.com*
This free area (provided by NetPromote) helps site owners create Meta tags in the correct format simply by inputting Web site information and clicking a button.

### NetPromote
*http://www.NetPromote.com*
This site provides a free Web promotion service for companies and individuals. NetPromote also offers consulting services that guarantee top-20 placement on the major search engines, plus unlimited resubmissions to the best search engines for life, for free.

### Promotion 101
*http://www.Promotion101.com*
This division of NetPromote provides a free online tutorial to help Web site owners learn how to better their placement on search engines and increase traffic to their sites. Includes the Ultimate Top 20 Search Engine Placement Guide. Also articles on optimizing Web pages.

### Search Engine Showdown
*http://www.notess.com/search/*
Detailed analysis of Internet Search Engines, their features, databases, and strategies.

### SelfPromotion.com

*http://selfpromotion.com*
Automatically add your URL for free to over 100 of the biggest and most important indexes and search engines! Apply for hundreds of awards and improve your ranking in the search engines.

### Sitelaunch

http://www.sitelaunch.net/
Sitelaunch is a good source of free tools, guides, and resources to help you with your Web site.

### Site Promotion Resources

*http://www.pageresource.com/promorec/index.html*
Resources for Web site promotion.

### Smithfam's Internet Marketing Resources

*http://www.smithfam.com/*
All kinds of tips, tricks, ideas, concepts, and strategies that successful marketers are using to create wealth online.

### StatMarket

*http://www.statmarket.com/*
Real-time source of Internet statistics and user trends including Internet demographics, market statistics and market trends.

### Submit It!

*http://www.submit-it.com*
You can use Submit It! to register your URL with hundreds of search engines and directories.

### The Internet Monitor

*http://www.internet-monitor.com/*
Tips, articles, and seminars on proven marketing strategies for trade publishers.

### The Tenagra Corporation B Internet Marketing Resources

*http://marketing.tenagra.com/imr.html*
Links and information about Internet marketing.

### VeryHot.com

*http://www.veryhot.com*
Links to many great Internet marketing tools.

### Virtual Promote

*http://www.virtualpromote.com/home.html*
A great source of information and tools to get your site noticed.

### Web Resources

*http://www.webresource.net*
Lots of good information on HTML and creating and maintaining a Web site.

### Website Promotion Tools

*http://www.newapps.com/appstopics/Win_95_Web_Site_Promotion_Tools.html*
A large list of programs of interest to Web masters to help in Web site promotion.

### WebStep 100

*http://www.mmgco.com/top100.html*
John Audette of Multimedia Marketing Group put together this list of the top 100 directories, indexes, and catalogs. The links are all annotated, and you can get to each site's registration page from the link on WebStep.

### Webmaster Resources

*http://www.webmaster-resources.com*
A handy and useful site for helping you design your own Web site. Good advice, lots of links, and plenty of useful information about Web hosting companies, awards, tracking programs, mailing list servers, Web site promotion, and sponsorships.

### The WebMaster's Notebook

*http://www.cio.com/WebMaster/wm_notebook_front.html*
This comprehensive site contains information of value to anyone that runs, or wants to, a WWW site: tools and links, technology notes, online Web seminars, Web reports, and the WebMaster Magazine.

### Webmasters' Guild

*http://www.webmaster.org/*

Not-for-profit, professional organization for Web masters—to disseminate information and discuss issues of concern to Web masters: network configuration, interface and graphical design, software development, business strategy, writing, marketing, and project management.

### Webmaster Magazine

*http://www.web-master.com*

An electronic magazine that examines the use of the Web by and within business. Topics include how companies are using the Web to improve operations, reduce expenses, and connect to their customers.

### Webmaster Reference Library

*http://webreference.com*

Hundreds of carefully selected and annotated Web sites and articles of interest to Web masters.

### WebPromote Weekly

*http://www.webpromote.com/*

The WebPromote Resource Center provides information, tools and products for marketers to be more effective on the Web. Featuring WebPromote Weekly, FreeSubmit, and the META Tag Builder.

### WebWorkers Top 10 Web Business Directories

*http://www.webworker.com*

Resources for creating and promoting an online business. Outstanding Web business opportunities and Web business services that enable the prospective entrepreneur to be successful.

### Wilson Internet Services

*http://www.wilsonweb.com/webmarket*

This site links to marketing information (more than 225 online articles primarily directed toward marketing small businesses on the Web). Topics include how to design a Web site, how to market on the Web, and marketing theory.

# Appendix E

# Implementation and Maintenance Schedule

To accomplish the best results from your Internet marketing strategy, you should develop an Implementation and Maintenance Schedule.

## Schedule

Every Implementation and Maintenance Schedule will be different since every company's Internet marketing strategy will be different. See Table E.1 for a sample schedule. We have provided brief explanations in the following paragraphs to help further clarify the items included in this sample.

## Search Engine Submissions

You should take your list of directory and search engine submissions and divide it into four groups. Weekly, you should take one group, go to each of the directories and search engines in that group, and search for your company by name and also by several keywords. If you appear in the first 10 to 20 search rankings and are happy with the description, you don't have to do anything with that search engine or directory.

| Name | Weekly | Biweekly | Monthly | Bimonthly | Quarterly | Yearly |
|---|---|---|---|---|---|---|
| Domain Name | | | | | | ✓ |
| Search engine submissions | ✓ | | | | | |
| Press release | | | | ✓ | | |
| Banner advertising | | | ✓ | | | |
| Update/rename titles | | | ✓ | | | |
| Cool sites | | | ✓ | | | |
| Check competitors | | | | | ✓ | |
| Cybermalls | | | | | ✓ | |
| Newsletter | | | ✓ | | | |
| Newsgroups | ✓ | | | | | |
| Mailing list postings | | ✓ | | | | |
| Guest book | ✓ | | | | | |
| Signature files | | | ✓ | | | |
| Mailing lists | | | ✓ | | | |
| Links | | ✓ | | | | |
| What's new | ✓ | | | | | |
| Calendar of events | ✓ | | | | | |
| Employment opportunities | ✓ | | | | | |
| Offline promotion | | | | | ✓ | |
| Tune-up | | | | | ✓ | |
| Web browser testing | | | ✓ | | | |

**Figure E.1.**  Implementation and Maintenance Schedule.

However, if you do not appear or are not satisfied with the description, you should resubmit all your pages to that directory or search engine. The search engines and directories purge their databases from time to time to ensure all entries are current. The next week take the next group and go through the same process. This way you check every directory and search engine at least monthly to ensure you are still there and easily accessible.

### Press Releases

Press releases should be scheduled at least bimonthly. If you have a major announcement, the press releases may be more frequent.

### Banner Advertising

Check banner advertising locations of your ads. Determine the effectiveness of these ads and look for new sites for more exposure. Check prices and traffic flow of these new sites to determine how relevant they may be in increasing the traffic to your site. Adjust your banner advertising strategy accordingly.

### Title Pages

Update and retitle your pages monthly unless you add a new section that requires more frequent updates (for example, Tip of the Week). Retitling your pages and updating your site is useful for two main reasons. First, spiders, crawlers, and bots are continuously visiting sites to see if there have been changes (they update their information accordingly). Second, many of your site visitors use software that lets them know when their bookmarked sites have been updated. They will only revisit your site when they know there have been changes.

### Cool Sites

Submit to Cool Sites, Site of the Day, or Top 5%. To better your chances of becoming one, you should check on how often to apply, usually monthly.

## Check of Competitors

You should regularly review your competitors' sites.

## Cybermalls

Cybermalls continually change, as does everything, so do a quick check to find new malls or changes to the ones that interest you.

## Newsletter

A newsletter should be scheduled monthly so you are getting your name and information in front of clients and potential clients on a regular basis.

## Newsgroups

Newsgroups that you participate in should be visited every couple of days, and you should try to post messages. The more often you post, particularly providing answers to queries or assistance, the more recognized and valued you are (and is your expertise). Make sure you have the sig. file attached for maximum marketing effect.

## Mailing Lists

New mailing lists appear daily. Review (and update if appropriate) those that you participate in on a monthly basis.

## Guest Book

Your guest book should be checked and monitored so you can see who is visiting and what they have to say. Weekly you should copy the new contact list to the appropriate databases (e-mail lists, newsletter, etc.).

## Signature Files

Keep your sig. files current. Review and change them on a regular basis with new information or achievements.

## Links

The more reciprocal links you can get, the better off you are. You should constantly be looking for additional, appropriate sites from which to be linked. As a minimum, you should schedule time bi-weekly to actively seek appropriate link sites.

## What's New

Your What's New page should be updated regularly, weekly if possible.

## Calendar of Events

If you choose to have a calendar of events on your site, ensure that it is kept current, at least updated weekly.

## Employment Opportunities

This section should also be monitored and updated weekly, deleting positions that have been filled and adding new positions as they become available.

## Offline Promotion

Make sure that your offline marketing materials and your online materials are consistent (message, logos, corporate colors, etc.). Also ensure that, where appropriate, you include your URL in your offline promotion materials. This should be checked at least quarterly.

## Tune-Ups

Tune-ups should be done quarterly unless changes are made to the site. One location to check is Web Site Garage at *http://www.websitegarage.com*. Here you can check spelling, browser compatibility, HTML design, link popularity, loading time, and much more.

## Web Browser Testing

Test your site with the major Web browsers. This should be done whenever there is a new release of Netscape or Internet Explorer. You should check monthly to determine if there have been new releases.

# Index

## Reader Feedback Sheet

Your comments and suggestions are very important in shaping future publications. Please email us at *moreinfo@maxpress.com* or photocopy this page, jot down your thoughts, and fax it to (850) 934-9981 or mail it to:

**Maximum Press**

Attn: Jim Hoskins

605 Silverthorn Road

Gulf Breeze, FL 32561

_____

_____

_____

_____

_____

_____

_____

_____

_____

_____

_____

_____

_____

_____

_____

_____

_____

_____

_____

_____

_____

*101 Ways to Promote
Your Web Site
Second Edition*
by Susan Sweeney, C.A.
552 pages
$29.95
ISBN: 1-885068-45-X

*Marketing
With E-Mail
Second Edition*
by Shannon Kinnard
352 pages
$29.95
ISBN: 1-885068-51-4

*Business-to-Business
Internet Marketing,
Third Edition*
by Barry Silverstein
528 pages
$29.95
ISBN: 1-885068-50-6

*Marketing on
the Internet,
Fifth Edition*
by Jan Zimmerman
480 pages
$34.95
ISBN: 1-885068-49-2

*Internet Marketing
for Information
Technology
Companies*
by Barry Silverstein
464 pages
$39.95
ISBN: 1-885068-46-8

*Internet Marketing
for Your Tourism
Business*
by Susan Sweeney, C.A.
592 pages
$39.95
ISBN: 1-885068-47-6

*Building Intranets
with Lotus Notes &
Domino, 5.0,
Third Edition*
by Steve Krantz
320 pages
$39.95
ISBN: 1-885068-41-7

*Internet Marketing for
Less Than $500/Year
by Marciaa Yudkin*
$29.95
ISBN: 1-885068-52-2

To purchase a Maximum Press book, visit your local bookstore
or call 1-800-989-6733 (US) or 1-850-934-4583 (International)
online ordering available at *www.maxpress.com*

*Exploring IBM
RS/6000 Computers,
Tenth Edition*
by Jim Hoskins
and Doug Davies
440 pages
$39.95
ISBN: 1-885068-42-5

*Exploring IBM
AS/400 Computers,
Tenth Edition*
by Jim Hoskins and
Roger Dimmick
576 pages
$39.95
ISBN: 1-885068-43-3

*Exploring IBM
S/390 Computers,
Sixth Edition*
by Jim Hoskins
and George Coleman
472 pages
$39.95
ISBN: 1-885068-30-1

*Exploring IBM
Network Stations*
by Eddie Ho,
Dana Lloyd, and
Stephanos Heracleous
223 pages
$39.95
ISBN: 1-885068-32-8

*Exploring IBM
Personal
Computers,
Eleventh Edition*
by Jim Hoskins
and Bill Wilson
384 pages
$39.95
ISBN: 1-885068-39-5

*Exploring IBM
Technology, Products
& Services,
Third Edition*
edited by Jim Hoskins
240 pages
$54.95
ISBN: 1-885068-44-1

To purchase a Maximum Press book, visit your local bookstore
or call 1-800-989-6733 (US/Canada) or 1-850-934-4583 (International)
online ordering available at *www.maxpress.com*